BRIAN LEVISON has a lifelong interest in
for several years. His books include *Amazi*
and *Classical Music's Strangest Concerts & Cl*
anecdotes co-written with Frances Farrer).
has published three collections of poetry. His poems have appeared in
The Cricketer and his work has been broadcast on BBC Radio 4 and
BBC1. Several texts have been set to music, including the oratorio
Exodus, first performed in 2002.

───────────

'An amazing compilation of every facet of cricket imaginable – bright and
breezy reading. Both a high quality 20/20 – a huge variety of entertainment
coming from the most unlikely sources! – and a timeless Test because it is
the sort of book you can dip in and out of and still not lose the thread!
A triumph of devotion to the game!'
Rachael Heyhoe Flint

'There is a treat around every corner... this will stay on the
bedside table for some time... It is a splendid reminder that we have
the best game in the world, and the best writers too.'
Richard H. Thomas, *All Out Cricket*

'Ranges far and wide through the literature of the game...
almost certainly the only book in history to combine the best bits of
Gus Fraser and Charles Dickens. Something for everyone then.'
Andy Bull, 'The Spin', *Guardian*

'Perfect material to help ease you through the cricket breaks
on a glorious summer's day... or to alleviate boredom spent sheltering
from the belting rain under the pavilion.'
Holly Gillett, *Sports Gazette*

ALL IN A DAY'S CRICKET

An anthology of
outstanding cricket writing

COMPILED BY

BRIAN LEVISON

CONSTABLE

Constable & Robinson Ltd
55–56 Russell Square
London WC1B 4HP
www.constablerobinson.com

First published in the UK by Constable,
an imprint of Constable & Robinson Ltd, 2012

This paperback edition published in the UK by Constable, 2014

A copy of the British Library Cataloguing in Publication
Data is available from the British Library

ISBN 978-1-47211-719-9 (paperback)
ISBN 978-1-78033-906-1 (ebook)

Design & typography by Andrew Barron
Printed and bound by CPI Group (UK) Ltd, Croydon, CR0 4YY

1 3 5 7 9 10 8 6 4 2

To my grandfather Samuel Lazarus,
who took me to Lord's to see Compton and Edrich,
and to my grandson Jordan Urban,
whom sixty years later I took to see KP.

...The fielders draw long shadows
Through an evening clear and high.
Too soon into the pavilion
Players, umpires and I:
May there be cricket always
In the Long Room in the sky.

Brian Levison, 'Timeless Test'

Contents

Foreword XVII
Introduction XIX

1

'A THOROUGHLY ANGLO-SAXON INSTITUTION'
The Evolution of Cricket (J. N. Crawford) 2
A Girdle Round the Earth (F. S. Ashley-Cooper) 4
How It Started (P. C. G. Labouchere, T. A. J. Provis and
Peter S. Hargreaves) 8
Cricket and the Pyramids (Anonymous) 10
The Dawn of Cricket (H. T. Waghorn) 12
A Cricketer's Notebook (Charles Box) 15
My Consulate in Samoa (W. B. Churchward) 17

2

START OF PLAY
Bangers and Bats (Marcus Trescothick) 24
Cricket Memories (R. L. Hodgson) 26
Wide (Michael Simkins) 27
A Cricketer at the Breakfast Table (Alan Gibson) 29
Cricketing Reminiscences and Personal Recollections
(W. G. Grace with Arthur Porritt) 32
Opening the Innings (Rachael Heyhoe Flint) 34
It's a Great Day for Being a Boy (David Walker) 37

3

LET'S PLAY HERE
Cricket Fields and Cricketers (Neville Cardus) 42
Recollections of Lord's and the Marylebone Cricket Club
(William Slatter) 50
'Rocky' and 'Local Rules' (Tony Hutton, Mick Bourne
and Brian Senior) 51

The Oval (Dudley Carew) 52
Cricket on the Ice (E. V. Lucas) 54
Cricket in the Backblocks (Colin Imray) 58
Diary of a Cricket Lover (Vernon Coleman) 62

4

THE TOOLS OF THE TRADE
April (R. C. Robertson-Glasgow) 66
Bat and Ball (W. J. Lewis) 67
Felix on the Bat (Nicholas Felix) 68
Cricket in Denmark (P. C. G. Labouchere, T. A. J. Provis
and Peter S. Hargreaves) 71
A Jammy Bastard (Marcus Trescothick) 76
Progress of Cricket (John Nyren with Charles Cowden Clarke) 77
Weights and Measures (R. C. Robertson-Glasgow) 80
Kent and London (Hugh Barty-King) 82

5

GETTING THERE
Forty Seasons of First-Class Cricket (R. G. Barlow) 86
Seventy-One Not Out (William Caffyn) 87
Slaves of the Lamp (Alan Gibson) 89
Early Reminiscences (G. H. R. Mountifield) 90
Village Cricket (Gerald Howat) 91
Disgraceful Scenes at Lord's (Robert Lynd) 94
The 'How' and the 'Why' We Crossed the Atlantic
(R. A. Fitzgerald) 96
Alfred Shaw, Cricketer: His Career and Reminiscences
(Alfred Shaw) 99

6

PITCH AND TOSS
Lord's on the Big Day (Jim Fairbrother) 104
Trent Bridge Ground-Keeper (Richard Daft) 108
Recollections of Lord's and the Marylebone Cricket Club
(William Slatter) 109

The Gatekeeper (R. C. Robertson-Glasgow) 112
A Cricketer on Cricket (W. J. Ford) 114
Winning the Toss (R. E. S. Wyatt) 115
Bumpers, Boseys and Brickbats (Jack Pollard) 116
The Toss at the 2011 World Cup Final (Vic Marks) 117

7

DRINKS BREAK
The Light and the Dark (C. L. R. James) 120
The Experimental Matches (William Dennison) 121
Cricket at the Universities (S. J. Southerton) 123
Lord Harris in India (A. A. Lilley) 124
Cricketers (Samuel Reynolds Hole) 125

8

THE PROFESSIONAL LIFE
County Round: April–May (Dickie Dodds) 128
Haircut (Phil Tufnell) 131
One Hundred for Eddie (Marcus Trescothick) 135
Batting Orders (Mike Brearley) 136
Random Reflections (Frank Chester) 138
Fox on the Run (Graeme Fowler) 139
And After (C. B. Fry) 141
A Cricket Pro's Lot (Fred Root) 143
Cricket with the Lid Off (A. W. Carr) 145

9

KEEPING COUNT
The Men in White Coats (Teresa McLean) 148
Knowing the Score (Keith Booth) 149
Scores Real and Imaginary (W. E. W. Collins) 152
A Yorkshire Cockney (Alan Gibson) 155
Recollections of Lord's and the Marylebone Cricket Club
(William Slatter) 156
A Summer Saturday (Harold C. Woods) 157

10

It's Not Cricket

W. G. – Too Clever to Cheat? (Sir Derek Birley) 164

Bumpers, Boseys and Brickbats (Jack Pollard) 167

Radcliffe – Spilling Blood for Victory (Harry Pearson) 171

Alfred Shaw, Cricketer: His Career and Reminiscences (Alfred Shaw) 175

The Mohali 'Fix' (Shaharyar M. Khan) 178

My Tour Diaries (Angus Fraser) 182

The English Game of Cricket (Charles Box) 182

Cricket in the Fiji Islands (Philip A. Snow) 184

11

Heroes

Everybody's Hero (Sir Ian Botham) 188

Ranjitsinhji's 154 Not Out (A. A. Lilley) 195

The Wicket at Melbourne (Frank Tyson) 197

The Cricketers of My Time (John Nyren) 202

A Hobbs Innings (Dudley Carew) 204

Fights for the Ashes 1882–86 (George Giffen) 207

Caste: Up from Serfdom (Ramachandra Guha) 211

The Three Pears (A. A. Thomson) 214

Plan of Pavilion Seating on the Worcester Ground (MCC) 219

12

'One of Life's Best Experiences'

My Tour Diaries (Angus Fraser) 222

Lord's (Rachael Heyhoe Flint) 223

The Sentiment of the Ball (A. E. Crawley) 226

Goodbye to the Razor-edge (Frank Tyson) 228

A Personal Perspective (Christopher Martin-Jenkins) 228

A Day at the Home of Cricket (Toby Pullan) 230

The Book of the Ball (A. E. Crawley) 232

Club Cricket and Umpires (Richard Daft) 235

The Memories of Dean Hole (Samuel Reynolds Hole) 236

Sports and Pastimes (William Howitt) 237

13

ON TOUR

Heyhoe! (Rachael Heyhoe Flint) 242

Fox on the Run (Graeme Fowler) 242

Cricketing Reminiscences and Personal Recollections
(W. G. Grace with Arthur Porritt) 245

Line and Length (Frances Edmonds) 251

My Tour Diaries (Angus Fraser) 254

14

'SO OVER TO THE CRICKET AT...'

So Over to the Cricket at . . . (John Arlott) 258

Radio: A New Career (Alan McGilvray) 261

Quiet Studio (Michael Simkins) 267

Insect Bites and Missing Luggage (Adam Mountford) 270

The Middle Men (Alan McGilvray) 275

15

LUNCH INTERVAL

Cricket Scores 1730–1773 (H. T. Waghorn) 280

The Pick of the Bunch (A. W. Carr) 280

Diary of a Cricket Lover (Vernon Coleman) 281

Cricket in the Fiji Islands (Philip A. Snow) 283

Julius Caesar (William Caffyn) 286

The Lazy Tour of Two Idle Apprentices
(Wilkie Collins and Charles Dickens) 288

Careful Arrangements (Lord Harris) 290

16

'THE MEN IN WHITE COATS'

The Men in White Coats (Teresa McLean) 294

Cricket Extras (Dickie Dodds) 295

Smiles (Frank Chester) 298

Cricketers (Samuel Reynolds Hole) 306

The Golden Era (C. B. Fry) 308

The Duties of an Umpire (William Sapte) 309
The Men in White Coats (Harold C. Woods) 310
Umpiring Curiosities (An Old Cricketer) 314

17

MORE HEROES
Players Past and Present (F. S. Ashley-Cooper) 318
Rags to Riches (Mike Brearley and Dudley Doust) 321
County Cricket Introduces Me to Some Famous Players
(A. A. Lilley) 328
Patient Merit (C. L. R. James) 330
The Demon Bowler (R. L. Hodgson) 333
Kings of Cricket (Richard Daft) 336
Difficult Targets: W. R. Hammond (R. C. Robertson-Glasgow) 339
A Cricket Pro's Lot (Fred Root) 341

18

WHAT TO DO WHILE WATCHING CRICKET
Dawn of The Blob (Harry Pearson) 346
Diary of a Cricket Lover (Vernon Coleman) 351
How I Built my Wisden Collection (Derek Barnard) 353
Eliza Watches Cricket (R. L. Hodgson) 355
Name Dropping (Frank Keating) 357

19

TEA INTERVAL
A Two-Days' Innings (A. A. Lilley) 364
Tennyson's Captaincy at Leeds (Robert Lynd) 365
Seventy-One Not Out (William Caffyn) 366
The Diary of Thomas Turner (Thomas Turner) 367
Cricket Memories (Edward Rutter) 368
Two Cricket Grounds (E. V. Lucas) 369
Hints to Young Players (William Sapte) 370
Hints to Old Players (William Sapte) 371

20

EXTRAS

A Cricket Match in 2000 A.D. (W. J. Ford) 374
The First Netting-Boundary Game (Andrew Ward) 379
The Street Called Fleet (C. B. Fry) 382
Against the Current (C. L. R. James) 384
Indian Cricket through the Ages (Boria Majumdar) 386
How to Get Out (W. E. W. Collins) 391
Personalities (Col. Philip Trevor) 395
The Village Heath (Alec Waugh) 397

21

'THE LONG ROOM IN THE SKY'

Introduction to the Wisden Book of Obituaries (Benny Green, ed.) 406
The Death of G. H. Hardy (C. P. Snow) 409
Silence of the Heart (David Frith) 411
Cricket in the Fiji Islands (Philip A. Snow) 415
Fatalities on the Cricket Field (An Old Cricketer) 416

22

THE LAST OVER

'Last Over, Gentlemen' (Lord Harris) 420
Hastings (Dudley Carew) 422
Introduction to Kings of Cricket (Andrew Lang) 424
The Lure of Cricket (E. V. Lucas) 425

Acknowledgements 430
Index 436

Foreword

ONE LEARNS WITH experience, unfortunately, that the greatest of men have feet of clay. It is a shame, because we like our heroes, our icons, our role models.

Large sections of the modern media rely on celebrities to appeal to a mass market, and there is probably a childish gene in most of us that craves fame and the privileges it brings. Those who achieve celebrity by whatever means, however – some through ambition and hard work, others by polishing divinely bestowed talent, a few by natural physical beauty and a willingness to exploit it, a few more through sheer notoriety – soon learn that to be famous is a mixed blessing.

It requires a responsibility which proves too much for some. For an unfortunate few it brings loss of privacy, and in politics and sport in particular even the worthiest of the mighty tend to fall sooner or later. So we do well sometimes to remember and dwell upon not the infamous, but the unfamous; not the well documented, but the often unconsidered. 'Some mute inglorious Milton here may rest, some Cromwell guiltless of his country's blood.'

This is a refreshing collection of writings on cricket not because it neglects to praise some of the famous men and women of the game – it does – but because it concentrates more on what some of the earlier anthologists referred to, in deference to the most assiduous of early cricket researchers, F. S. Ashley-Cooper, as the highways and byways.

Most of us know something about Alastair Cook or Sachin Tendulkar or Don Bradman but I dare say that no one will be aware until he or she delves into the pages that follow that Frederik Ferslev is truly one of the unsung heroes of cricket, a Dane who worked with extraordinary determination during the Second World War to find a means of making new bats to keep the game going under German occupation in a country that has never been especially associated with bats and balls.

We could not play or watch cricket without 'quilt binders and pod shavers', groundsmen and rollers, umpires and scorers, stumps and bails, pads and gloves, captains and coins, boundaries and (well, in my day at least) bars. Where better to mix warmly with opponents, discuss the Test team, revel in a successful day or forget a bad one?

Even the great had bad ones. I was surprised to read W. G. Grace, the Great Cricketer, admitting that in 1859, albeit at the age of only eleven, he played eleven innings for the West Gloucestershire Club that produced twelve runs. Less so that Rachael Heyhoe Flint (now the Baroness) made 'about 380 not out' in the garden against her elder brother and his friends, or to be reminded that Alfred Shaw took 13 for 11 against 22 of Wellington on the 1877 tour of New Zealand.

There is humour in the ensuing pages: Raymond Robertson-Glasgow on Somerset's gateman; Alan Gibson on the travelling that overshadowed the joys of reporting county cricket; or Mike Brearley on why Bob Barber summoned him on to the field with a fresh pair of gloves. There is drama – Frank Tyson describing his greatest day, Angus Fraser recalling Lara's 375 out of 593 – and poignancy: Graeme Fowler reflecting on the professional's need on tour to 'catch your emotions, bottle them and throw away the bottle'.

About the only pleasure missing is poetry, which is noble of an editor who has won prizes for his own work in this field. But good writing was his sine qua non, and there is plenty of that. Dudley Carew, to give but two examples from the same piece: 'Hobbs played his innings as an actor plays a part in a play he has written himself'; and 'Sandham . . . works in cool monotones, never attempting the heroic, but seeing that everything he does is in perfect taste.'

Cricket, as Sam Johnson might have averred, has all that life affords. Almost every aspect is touched upon in this delightful collection. It is the product of wide reading, deep interest and a versatile mind.

Christopher Martin-Jenkins

Introduction

IN A WAY, a cricket match at whatever level is a minor miracle given the many things that have to come together for it to take place.

This book takes a different approach from many other cricket anthologies. While it is a selection of high-quality writing, it also has an underlying theme: all the activities that take place in order for a day's play simply to happen. This provides scope for writing not often found in anthologies, about spectators, umpires, groundsmen, scorers, players (famous and unknown), travel arrangements (home and overseas from club to international level), venues, equipment, the life of cricketers off the field as well as on, some of the less savoury aspects of the game, and how the love of cricket so often has its roots in childhood. And, of course, there is the excitement of the cricket itself, its great games and its greatest players.

Contributors range from the best-known names, such as John Arlott, Neville Cardus, C. L. R. James and E. V. Lucas, to contemporary figures like Marcus Trescothick, writing about his introduction to cricket at the age of three; Angus Fraser, thrilled to meet Nelson Mandela; Phil Tufnell, shanghaied by Mike Gatting; Rachael Heyhoe Flint, on being the first woman to step on to the Lord's ground as a player; Harry Pearson, Graeme Fowler, David Frith and many more. From a century and more ago come the words of John Nyren, C. B. Fry, F. S. Ashley-Cooper, Alfred Shaw, Nicholas Felix, James Pycroft, H. T. Waghorn, Richard Daft and W. G. Grace.

Entertaining writers who may have fallen a little from public notice are also included, such as Alan Gibson, Dudley Carew, Vernon Coleman, Alec Waugh and Robert Lynd. You might not expect to find the old Essex cricketer Dickie Dodds in these pages but he has much of interest to say about the life of the county circuit professional cricketer who never quite makes it to the top level. And there are vignettes, some unexpectedly moving, such as Mrs W. G. Grace weeping at the Oxford–Cambridge match.

It seemed right to start with the basics – what is cricket? According to J. N. Crawford, it is 'A Thoroughly Anglo-Saxon Institution', though claims by the Egyptians, Scandinavians and others are not ignored. 'Start of Play' shows that for W. G. Grace, Marcus Trescothick, Rachael Heyhoe Flint and others the passion for cricket strikes early and is enduring. Finding a playing area, from Lord's to a clearing in the Malaysian jungle, is a matter of urgency ('Let's Play Here'); as is acquiring bats, ball and stumps, and the proper outfit ('The Tools of the Trade'). 'Getting There' deals with the sometimes difficult business for both spectators and players of travel; 'On Tour' gives us a taste of another side of this experience. Meanwhile the groundsman has been hard at work, and 'Pitch and Toss' covers the two factors which perhaps most affect a game's outcome.

Those who have never been good enough to play for a living imagine that it must be the ideal occupation. 'The Professional Life' shows something of what it's like behind the scenes for the players, as does 'The Men in White Coats' for the umpires, 'Keeping Count' for the scorers, and 'It's Not Cricket' for aspects of the game that challenge the boundary between fair and unfair play.

But it is the cricket itself and the outstanding players and their achievements around which the game centres. 'Heroes' and 'More Heroes' feature the greats of the long and recent past involved in some of their most famous exploits, sometimes in their own words (Giffen, Botham, Tyson), sometimes in the words of those who played alongside them (Dick Lilley on W. G. Grace and Ranjitsinhji; Fred Root on Larwood; John Nyren on Noah Mann), and sometimes in the words of a beguiled but knowledgeable reporter (C. L. R. James on the overlooked West Indian wicketkeeper Piggott; Dudley Carew on Hobbs; R. L. Hodgson on Spofforth; R. C. Robertson-Glasgow on Wally Hammond; Dudley Doust on Derek Randall).

There is a facet of cricket which is perhaps best caught by the phrase Angus Fraser used to describe meeting Nelson Mandela: 'One of Life's Best Experiences'. That an adult such as Fraser or Tyson can articulate the feeling is not surprising, but, as Toby Pullan shows, a fifteen-year-old can do so too.

'What to Do While Watching Cricket' is for those occasions when the mind wanders during the day's play. Drinks, Lunch and Tea intervals have been thoughtfully catered for with shorter pieces. If you are not at the ground, a radio will keep you in touch with the action ('So Over to the Cricket at . . .'). 'Extras' are excerpts that did not fit neatly into any of the above categories but which were too good to leave out.

The distinguished mathematician G. H. Hardy is reported to have said on his death-bed, 'If I knew that I was going to die today, I think I should still want to hear the cricket scores.' There are probably many cricket-lovers who would say the same. 'The Long Room in the Sky' and 'The Last Over' both deal in their own way with close of play.

Selections range from the mid-eighteenth century right up to the present day. I have tried to represent names familiar from other anthologies with less well-known pieces. I hope there are writers here who will be discovered and enjoyed for the first time. The omission of fiction and poetry is deliberate.

I would particularly like to thank Jill Haas, Andrew Ward, Matthew Levison and Derek Barnard for giving very generously of their time, help and advice. I would also like to thank Neil Robinson, Librarian at Lord's, Jo Miller, Librarian at The Kia Oval Library, the ever-helpful staff at the Bodleian Library for their assistance, and Dan Balado-Lopez.

Brian Levison, Oxford

1

'A THOROUGHLY ANGLO-SAXON INSTITUTION'

The Evolution of Cricket

J. N. CRAWFORD

J. N. (Jack) Crawford (Surrey and England) first played for England in 1906 aged only nineteen. From *The Practical Cricketer*, published just three years later.

EVER SINCE WE as a nation became distinctly English we have played cricket, if not exactly in the form we know to-day. The precise origin of the game is lost in antiquity, and the fact that the sport has stood the test of the intervening centuries is a very tangible proof of its usefulness and favour. As a patriotic Britisher, I take little account of the traces which assign the genesis of cricket to Rome, Greece, and even Persia. Those peoples of the long-ago doubtless had some sort of ball game, and it is likely enough that ball games in general had a more or less common beginning. Cricket, in the strict sense, I believe to be a thoroughly Anglo-Saxon institution.

There are several references to the game being played in mediaeval times. Chaucer has an allusion to it, though even the charm of his masterpiece cannot induce me to wade through 'The Canterbury Tales' to locate the place. An ingenious writer in the *Gentleman's Magazine* for March 6th, 1788, construed an entry in the household account of Edward I as representing a cricket allowance for his son, Prince Edward, from the use, among the games detailed, of the word *creag*, presumably a variant of the Saxon *cricce*, a wooden club, of which the modern term Cricket is deemed to be a derivative. The implements at this time appear to have been of a very primitive character, with a two-stump wicket bearing some resemblance to a dwarf goal-post.

In the Bodleian Library, at Oxford, there is, as Joseph Strutt notes in his 'Sports and Pastimes', an MS., dated 1344, 'which represents the figure of a monk in the act of bowling a ball to another, who elevates a straight bat to strike it; behind the bowler are several figures waiting to stop or catch the ball, their attitudes grotesquely eager for a "chance". The game is called "club-ball", but the score is made by hitting and running as in cricket.'

So things went on until in the eighteenth century we see the game definitely evolving towards the form it now takes. Apparently it throve most in the Home Counties, and in 1744 Kent beat All England. The game was spreading apace by this time, and it became quite fashionable for gentlemen, noblemen, and even Royalty to play for large wagers, so much so that in 1748 a test case was brought, but the Court of King's Bench decided that the practice was not illegal.

In 1750 the famous Hambledon Club, which included professionals, was formed, the first regular institution of the kind on record. Last season a celebration match was played at the old Hants village. Hambledon played All England annually, and nearly always won. In the match played in 1777, when Aylward, the Hambledon player, scored 167, probably a record innings then, three stumps were used for the first time.

The Hambledon Club gradually declined, and in 1789 the world-famous Marylebone Cricket Club was formed, the ground-man, Thos. Lord, securing a lease from the Duke of Dorset in the district from which the club takes its name. When the lease expired the club moved, after a short interval, to its present quarters at St. John's Wood, still named Lord's, after its superintendent. By the time the nineteenth century dawned the game was played by a number of counties, clubs, improvised teams, and schools, besides being seen on village greens all over the country. Single-wicket matches also had a considerable vogue.

In 1827 Lillywhite, the famous Sussex bowler of that day, caused a sensation by introducing overhand (really round-arm) bowling, which staggered the opposing teams, and met with a protest as being unfair, all bowling having hitherto been 'the graceful underhand of the old school'. A good many county matches were played, although a regular championship was not constituted till a good many years later. The Surrey County Club was founded in 1845, and, having been granted a favourable lease of Kennington Oval by the Duchy of Cornwall, soon obtained a position of eminence in the cricket world.

In 1866 W. G. Grace burst upon the scene, and created a remarkable impression from the first. The development of the modern system has been too complex for a hard-and-fast date to be assigned; it is the outgrowth of accumulated improvements rather than of sudden transformation. In a wide sense, however, it may be dated from 'W. G.'s' appearance. The top hat on the cricket field and side wagers have receded from view, overhand bowling proper becomes established (although 'W. G.' worked havoc with the round-arm variety), we become accustomed to billiard-table wickets, delicate strokes like the late cut are more cultivated, the arrangement of the field is revised, including the disappearance of long-stop, the county championship is a fixed institution, countless clubs, composed of all ages and all classes, spring up all over the country, and teams tour every part of the globe where English-speaking communities abide, even carrying the bat and stumps into alien lands.

A Girdle Round the Earth

F. S. ASHLEY-COOPER

F. S. Ashley-Cooper was a cricket historian and statistician.
From *Cricket Highways and Byways* (1927).

DETAILS OF THE beginnings of cricket in France are lost in the mists of antiquity, for it can be said, as of many other countries, that the game was played there before details were published. Yet we know that as early as 1777 Boydell issued an engraving showing a match in progress at Belle Isle, and that within the next decade it was only the outbreak of the French Revolution which prevented the Surrey team, on the suggestion of the Duke of Dorset, then our Ambassador in Paris, going over to show the game in the Bois de Boulogne. The eleven, in fact, had journeyed as far as Dover – Yalden, the wicket-keeper, had been chosen captain – when, most unexpectedly, it was met by the Duke, who was flying before the coming storm. Soon after the Napoleonic wars the game took firm root in the country, owing largely to the presence of lace-workers from Nottingham, and before the middle of the last century clubs existed, if they did not actually flourish, at Dieppe, Calais, Boulogne, Bordeaux, St. Servan, Paris, St. Omer, and other places. Tom Creevey, writing in his *Journal* under date 'Cambrai, July 16, 1818', tells how, 'To-day I rode to see a cricket match between the officers near the town, and presently the Duke of Wellington rode there likewise, accompanied by Mrs. Hervey and Miss Caton . . . He asked me to dine with him that day, but I was engaged to the officers who were playing the match.' As early as 1833 St. Omer met Boulogne three times, the former team including Mr. Wettenhall, senior, aged sixty-two, four of his sons and a grandson. Messrs. Woodbridge and Charles Beauclerk, both well known at Lord's, were supporters of the St. Omer Cricket Club, whose ground was described as 'an open plain, a fine sward, on a free-stone bottom, which makes it peculiarly elastic'. It was, therefore, evidently superior to that at Boulogne, which was stated to be 'a meadow, which was cropped last year'. In 1840 home-and-home matches were played between Calais and the River Cricket Club, of Dover, 'after being three years on the *tapis*', and five years later a good cricket ground was formed at the residence of Mr. N. Johnstone, at Lescure, Bordeaux. At the last-mentioned place the game flourished so well that during the first season about forty members, a third of whom were French, were enrolled. An impetus to the game across the Channel was given by occasional visits of teams from Nottingham, and respecting one of these events – in 1846 – the late Dean Hole wrote:

> That England has no rival
> Well know the trembling pack,
> Whom Charley Brown by Calais town
> Bowl'd out behind his back,

the said Brown possessing the genius of being able to deliver the ball at a good pace round his back with astonishing precision.

Since those far-distant days several well-known clubs, including M.C.C. and Butterflies, have played in France, and such events have almost invariably been productive of curious comments from the locals, whose views were, to say the least, generally original. Thus, when the M.C.C. were in Paris in 1867, a Frenchman remarked to 'Bob' FitzGerald: 'It is a truly magnificent game, but I cannot understand why you do not engage a servant to field for you instead of having so much running about to do yourself.' And in a report of the play it was recorded: 'The bowler, grasping the ball in the right hand, watches for the favourable moment when the attention of the batsman is distracted, and then launches it at him with incredible force; the batsman, however, is on the alert; he strikes it to an enormous height, and immediately runs.' This quaint view of things recalls the fact that, whilst the Emperor (Napoleon III), Empress and Prince Imperial were watching a match between Bickley Park and Beckenham, long-on brought off a difficult and spectacular catch. A minute or so later a gentleman-in-waiting, hat in hand, approached the successful fieldsman with a message from the Emperor, thanking him very much for his performance, and asking him to do it again. On another occasion the Emperor asked whether a certain West Kent match was being played for money, and Frederick Edlmann answered in his most dignified manner,

'No, sire; for honour.' At least once, however, the same Napoleon proved a good friend to cricketers. He had visited the Paris Cricket Club, and had the game explained to him, and this circumstance saved the club, for a few days afterwards an old Oxford man, while making a run, tripped, fell and broke his arm. The matter was at once reported to the police, and the club was about to be suppressed as dangerous, when an appeal to the Emperor prevented so dire a calamity.

Reference to the Paris Cricket Club recalls that, in 1865, there was published a handbook of twenty-four pages entitled, *La Clef Du Cricket; ou Courte Explication De La Marche et Des Principales Règles De Ce Jeu. Par An Old Stump, M.P.C.C.* It dealt with cricket generally, and gave the twenty rules of the Paris Cricket Club.

The Club was formed in July 1863, and among its early Presidents were the Duke of Edinburgh and the Duc d'Aumale. In 1865 it presented to the Prince Imperial an outfit consisting of two bats, two sets of stumps (silver mounted, with ebony bails), two balls, pads, gloves and spiked boots; also a treatise on the game. The articles were enclosed in a handsome and massive mahogany case lined with green velvet, and on the lid of which was an engraved silver plate bearing the inscription, 'A son Altesse Impériale, Monseigneur le Prince Impérial.' The gift called forth the following acknowledgement to M. Drouyn de l'Huys, the Club's President:

Tuileries, June 1, 1865.

Sir,—The foundation of a cricket club cannot fail to promote the development of the public health, if the practice of the game should become as general as I desire, and as your efforts give reason to hope. I heartily applaud this institution, and accept with pleasure the implements of the game which you have had the kindness to offer to the Prince Imperial. You are well aware, Sir, of my sentiments of high esteem and goodwill for yourself.

Eugénie.

At the same time the Prince forwarded two thousand francs to the Club as a mark of the interest he took in its welfare, and in the following year, when he became a member, promised to subscribe one hundred francs annually.

The Emperor, when he visited the ground in 1865, confessed, 'Je n'y comprends rien du tout.' The Empress rejoined in English: 'I understand a great deal, and I hope that next year the little Prince will have learnt this interesting game.' Despite his ignorance of the finer points of cricket, His Majesty proved a good friend to the Club, and before the commencement of the season of 1867 granted it an important concession by giving it permission, through the Prefect of the Seine, to enclose and level its ground in the Bois de Boulogne.

The unconscious humour of which the French mind has proved so prolific was never more in evidence than in a 'Guide', in which, by means of a conversation, an attempt was made to explain the intricacies of the game:

'Let us, then, observe the cricket game, my dear Gaston.'

'But, my dear Henri, the cricket game I do not understand.'

'Eh, bien, here is the tram; let us seat ourselves, and as we go I explain. There are eleven men on each side, two umpires, two wickets, a ball, and some guards, since the ball is very hard. A player stands at the wickets, and, behold, one hurls down at him the ball, the no-ball, the wide ball, the leg-break, the googly, the head-break, the rapid, the very slow. C'est terrible! Mon Dieu, you will admire! The batter, who has a flat club, makes the strokes – the on-drive, the off-drive, the back-cut, the upper-cut, the leg-pull and the left hook, strokes of a skill incroyable. The crowd cries "Brava!" like M. le Professeur Hall at the Opera. But, alas! The batter misses the ball; the wicket is knocked down. One cries "How out?" and the umpire nods the head. Thereupon the batter retires, and they place upon the board his score and the letters l b w. Sometimes the umpire cries "Over!" and all walk over to the other side for the sake of exercise. The game, Gaston, is of great simplicity. And – I almost forget – wearied by the continual striking of the ball, the batters, too, for the purpose of recuperation, run swiftly up and down between the wickets.'

'It seems very dangerous, Henri.'

'True! For me, I would rather exercise myself with diabolo or dominoes.'

How It Started

P. C. G. LABOUCHERE, T. A. J. PROVIS AND
PETER S. HARGREAVES

After failing to find the origins of cricket in Romania, Holland and Germany,
the authors follow a line of inquiry further north.
From *The Story of Continental Cricket* (1969), with a foreword by Colin Cowdrey.

THE GAME OF cricket is played by the local inhabitants in only a very few places in Europe proper: in Holland and Denmark (the main centres), Malta and Corfu – and the thought of Corfu led us naturally to Greece and to Homer. Homer had little to say about ball games, mentioning them only once, in the story of Odysseus meeting with the princess, Nausikaa. Nausikaa played them herself, and we read of how she threw the ball at one of her maidens, and of how, missing the girl, the ball disappeared into the whirling waters from where it could not be recovered – 'wild return', 'overthrow', 'faulty backing up' and 'lost ball', all in one incident! Nausikaa's father, King Alkinoos, held a Games in honour of Odysseus, and for use at this meeting a ball was made 'of purple' by one Polybos. The colour was nearly right for a cricket ball. It is possible that these ball games were part of religious ceremonies peculiar to this island, and if it was in truth Corfu, then the taking up of the game of cricket by the inhabitants of that island might be explained as the forces of an ancient tradition in their history working on them to create a racial predisposition for ball games. But Homer has told us that Nausikaa's island was 'at the edge of the world', and Corfu could only be said to be this if Greece was the blind poet's entire world.

All the trails seemed cold, with the exception of the old Finnish game 'kurra'. We filed this game, played by 'the Seven Brothers', for future reference, and decided to make a fresh start, this time approaching our subject through the etymology of the word 'cricket'. The Concise Oxford Dictionary gave us: 'Cricket: etym. dub.; OF has *criquet*, a game, (also) a stick to aim at.' It might be thought that there was little here to work on, but our determination not to accept any authority without critical examination came to our aid, and this definition immediately supplied us with a lead.

'OF has *criquet*'. How could this interesting word have found its way into the French language? – for it did suggest a gallicization of a word borrowed from some other tongue. The Reverend James Pycroft, in his classic work, *The Cricket Field*, had relied to some extent on an etymological approach in his paragraphs of speculation on the name of the game. He had traced it back to an earlier game called 'creag', and to a derivation from the Saxon word 'cricce'. Pycroft was on the right track, obviously, but did he go far enough north? We continued onwards past North Germany to Scandinavia to find what we submit here to be another likely – perhaps more likely – root in the Danish 'krøget', a dialect word derived from the Old Norse 'kraekr' which itself was an *ablaut* of Old Norse 'krókr'. Every Scandinavian authority has agreed that 'krókr' was the original root word from which the English 'crook' – as used by a shepherd – was descended. This was by no means out of place, for it has been propounded that cricket was a game first played by shepherds using the crook as a bat, and this theory is not without its supporters. The crook would indeed be an admirable instrument for playing balls bowled along the ground.

The English words 'croquet' and 'crochet' are also derived from the French, and there can be little doubt that both these and 'criquet' are derived from the same root. Following the theory of its derivation from the Nordic languages, it is possible that the root word of 'criquet' was taken to France by the Vikings and is in fact Norman French in origin: its meaning having been perverted to some degree. From France it could have travelled to England, like many another notable, with William the Bastard. If, indeed, the true root word, the Old Norse 'krókr', had not already been introduced by the marauding bands of Vikings who first ravaged, and became then absorbed by, the British people long before the time of William and his 'Frenchified' Northmen.

In matters of such ancient date which come to us through centuries of misuse and corruption, we can deal only in probabilities, and we now found it probable that the name of the game was of Scandinavian origin.

Cricket and the Pyramids

ANONYMOUS

From the anthology *The Light Side of Cricket* (1898), edited by E. B. V. Christian.

❧

'MY PREDECESSORS IN the study of Egyptology,' said the Professor, 'have wasted much energy and misdirected much ingenuity in attempts to discover why the Pyramids, those wonders of the world, were erected. With imperfect knowledge this was inevitable. But for us, in this twenty-first century, the riddle is answered, the oracle speaks plainly, the sphinx is no longer dumb. The truth is this: *the Pyramids were erected to commemorate the exploits of great cricketers*. It would be presumptuous, even with our fuller knowledge, to say that the first great age of cricket was the Egyptian; there may yet be found some record of cricket of a still earlier date. But at least we may say that one of the first brilliant epochs in the history of the game occurred under the third and fourth Egyptian dynasties. Darkness was again to fall upon the earth; the great game, with its gay refinement, its infinite lessons for mankind, its mirth, its joyousness, was to be forgotten; but here at least it flourished. It flourished; and not only as the game of the people, but as the sport of kings. The Memphite monarchs, we know from the records so strangely preserved, were adepts at the great game, and the greatest of all was Khufu, the Cheops of Herodotus, the greatest bat Egypt produced. Now it was Khufu who erected the great Pyramid. Why?

'Why was the Pyramid of Ghizeh erected? To commemorate the greatest score then known, the finest achievement of even that great sportsman Khufu! We know from his cartouche that he was a great bowler, for a duck and an egg appear there, evidently a suggestion of the fate of his opponents. But as a batsman he was even greater, and his score of 482 was long the record. Now the height of the Pyramid was originally 482 feet. This is more than a coincidence; this is evidence. In the admiration excited by the great score of Khufu the people insisted on commemorating the achievement by erecting this great monument. It is probable that it is erected on the very site of the exploit – probably the match was played on a matting wicket under the very centre of the Pyramid. It was of this innings, which must have lasted many hours, that Leigh Hunt was thinking when in his fine sonnet on The Nile he spoke of the 'eternal stands' of the Egyptians. It was here, when stumps were drawn for the day, and the crowd had streamed down to the river and the boats, that the ground man noticed (as Leigh Hunt finely puts it) that

> "Then comes a mightier silence, stern and strong,
> As of a world left empty of its throng
> And the void weighs on us."

We may, each of us, notice this at night on any of the great cricket grounds now. . . .

'It is strange,' continued the Professor, 'that this, the true explanation of the cause and method of building the Pyramids, was so long ignored. That great man, that mixture of ignorance and inspiration, Napoleon, knew the truth intuitively. "Soldiers," he cried, when his troops were beneath the shadow of the great monument, "*twenty centuries look down upon you.*" This was scarcely a figure of speech. The monument of Khufu's twenty centuries towered above them. One relic of the game as played in Egypt lingers with us still. We all know the Pavilion Cat; happy the batsman who sees that harbinger of good fortune, the black, pavilion cat, as he goes towards the wicket! And in Egypt I need not remind you the cat – because of its association with the game – was honoured as divine. . . .'

The Dawn of Cricket

H. T. WAGHORN

H. T. Waghorn was a cricket historian and statistician.
The Dawn of Cricket was published in 1906.

❧

TO TRACE CRICKET to its commencement seems almost an impossible task, for in spite of much research, it is still unknown when it was first introduced or played. It is generally agreed that England was its birthplace. Kent in early times stood pre-eminent in cricket. Surrey, Sussex and Hampshire followed.

It was between the years 1770 and 1780, that a great and decisive improvement took place, and that cricket first began to assume that skilful and scientific character which it now possesses. The following references to the game have been unearthed, and arranged chronologically.

[...] According to the following extract the county of Surrey appears to have been an early home of the game. I find in 'The History of Guildford', 1801, is a passage which reads as follows: 'Anno 40, Eliz. 1598. John Derrick, gent., one of the Queen's Majestie's coroners of the county of Surrey, aged fifty-nine, saith this land before mentioned left to John Parvish, inn holder, deceased, that he knew if for 50 yeares or more. It lay waste, and was used and occupied by the inhabitants of Guildford to saw timber in, and for sawpits, and for makings of frames of timber for the said inhabitants. When he was a scholler in the Free School of Guildford, he and several of his fellows did run and play there at crickett and other plaies (games). And also that the same was used for the bating of bears in the said towne, until the said John Parvish did enclose the said parcell of land.'

The word cricket appears in the following work, being about the first time mentioned in any dictionary.

'A Worlde of Wordes, or most copious and exact dictionarie in Italian and English, collected by J. Florio'. Printed in London, 1598.

'Sgrillare, to make a noise as a cricket, to play cricket-a-wicket, and be merry.'

In a dictionary of French and English by Randle Cotgrave, 1611, which seems to be the first dictionary giving the word cricket, the following appears: 'Crosse, f. a crosier, or Bishop's staffe; also a cricket staff; or the crooked staffe;

wherewith boys play at cricket. Crosser – to play at cricket.'

1635–40. In the 'Life of Thomas Wilson', Minister of Maidstone, published anonymously in 1672, p. 40, the following is mentioned: 'Maidstone was formerly a very profane town, inasmuch that I have seen morrice-dancing, cudgle-playing, stool-ball, crickets, and many other sports openly and publicly indulged in on the Lord's Day.'

The above must have been written some 30 or 40 years before his life was published, as the said Thomas Wilson was born in 1601, and died at or about the age of 52.

He had not been many years at Otham (1635) before the book, commonly called the 'Book of Sports on the Lord's Day', was presented to him, with a command that he should publish it the next Sunday in his church, which he objected to.

1637. 'Voyages and Travels of the Ambassadors', by John Davies, 1662, p. 297. 'They play there also a certain game which the Persians call Kuitskaukan, which is a kind of mall or cricket.'

1653. 'The Works of Rabelais' translated by Sir Thomas Urchard (Urquhardt) vol. I. chap. xxii, p. 61: The games of Gargantua. There he played cricket. This being one of the games mentioned. (The ancient way of spelling the word in French is Croyser, the modern Croyzer, which may mean as above for Crosser).

1676. 'The Diary of Henry Teonge', 1825, p. 150, (Aleppo Turkey). 'On May 6, 1676, this morning early (as the custom is all the summer long) at least forty of the English, with his worship the Consull, rode out of the city about four miles to the Greene Platt, a fine valley by the river syde, to recreate themselves, where a princely tent was pitched; and we had several pastimes and sports, as duck-hunting, fishing, shooting, hand-ball, krickett, scrofilo; and then a noble dinner brought thither, with greate plenty of all sorts of wines, and lemonade, and at six we returned home in good order, but soundly tired and weary.'

[. . .] The earliest mention of the game of cricket, which I am able to trace in any newspaper are the following notices: 'The Post Boy', March 28 to 30, 1700. 'These are to inform Gentlemen, or others, who delight in Cricket-playing. That a match at Cricket, of 10 Gentlemen on each side, will be Play'd on Clapham-Common near Fox-Hall, on Easter-Monday next; for £10 a Head each Game, (five being design'd) and £20 the Odd one.' 'The

Postman', April 3–5, 1705: 'This is to give notice to any person whatsoever, that they do not presume to play at foot-ball, or cricket, or any other sport or pastime whatsoever, on Walworth Common, without lease of the Lords of that Manor, or their Bayliff, Henry Morris, as they will answer the same when they are sued at Law for so doing.'

[. . .] The earliest cricket in America appears to be, New York, May 6, 1751. 'Last Monday, a match of cricket was played on our Common, for a considerable wager, by eleven Londoners against eleven New Yorkers. The game was played according to the London method, and those who got most notches in two hands to be the winners. The New Yorkers went in and got 81; then the Londoners went in and got but 43; then the New Yorkers went in again and got 86; and the Londoners finished the game with only getting 37 more, leaving the New Yorkers victorious by 87 notches.'

The first account of cricket in India is the following extract from 'The Madras Courier', February 23, 1792: 'The Calcutta Club have challenged the gentlemen of Barrackpore, and Dum-Dum. They were to meet for a trial of their skill in the manly exercise of cricket, in the Second Week of February, on the Esplanade, Fort William, Calcutta.'

'The above contest was to be happily followed by a plentiful dinner, when both parties might try their ability in another way.'

The first recorded cricket in the Arctic Regions:-

'March 23, 1823. – The weather was so pleasant, and the temperature in the Sun so comfortable to the feelings when a shelter could be found from the wind, that we set up various games for the people, such as cricket, foot-ball and quoits, which several of them played for many hours during the day.'

❧

A Cricketer's Notebook

CHARLES BOX

From the preface of *A Cricketer's Notebook* (1881).

∾

O F LATE OUR much-beloved old game of cricket has grown wonderfully in the public estimation in all lands where the English language is spoken.

When I was a boy, some seventy years ago, its greatest matches were rarely noticed in the newspapers of the day. When they did appear a few lines only were given to them, whereas now their celebrations occupy almost whole columns in all the leading daily news, and they are described with as much precision as the grand reviews of our troops, and a field-day of cricket excites as much attraction as a field-day of military manoeuvres. As a science, its rules and laws are now as well established as those of the game of chess, and the former requires as much exercise of the body as the latter does of the mind.

It is somewhat extraordinary that our volatile friends on the Continent take no notice of them, and that their sons know so little of the game; indeed, both the French and German youth have no games whatever that make any approach to it in wholesome exercise of the limbs and body, and the muscles of its limbs. In all my ramblings abroad in many lands I never saw any games whatever with bat and ball. Not even with trap-bat could I learn they were conversant. Beyond the soldiering of one and the gymnastics of the other I never could learn that they had any manual exercise whatever.

Only where the English language is spoken by Englishmen is its name celebrated; but our American brethren have no notion or aptitude of it. Yet our Australian brothers are the smartest and finest cricketers in the world, and we and they make no concern of the thousands of miles between us to enjoy the pleasure and hard work of a challenge.

'What great effects from trivial causes spring.' It is easy to be discerned how much the practice of this game has contributed to the formation of the manly character of Englishmen. I remember being on the grounds of the Chatham Lines when the Emperor Nicholas, one of the former Emperors of Russia, with Colonel Paisley and some soldier boys (drummers and others), witnessed a game of cricket, which he had never seen before, but had a great desire to see, from what he heard of it as a national game. Taking up the ball, which had fallen near him, he handled it and felt it and weighed it, and then said to the colonel, 'I don't wonder at the courage of you English, when you teach your children to play with cannon balls.'

The former Sultan of the Turks once saw some English officers playing the game. After it was over, 'Wonderful, wonderful,' said he, 'what exertion the game requires; but why don't you make your servants do all this?'

I am told the game was once witnessed by some Chinese, who seemed to admire it greatly. After a few weeks the same party was invited to see a cricket match by some Chinese, who in the interval they were told had learnt it. It is well known what great imitators are the Chinese, and not much surprise was occasioned by it. The ground in the neighbourhood of Shanghai was chosen, bats, ball, and stumps were provided, but not all were disposed of to the players for preparation. Some of the English residents were much interested. They came, they said, to see how many runs they would make, for they had never seen a Chinaman run in their lives. When the game began all the fielders were gathered together in a lump, and the gabble was deafening. The bowler gave his first bowl. When the ball was thrown a long string was attached to it, the end of which was secured to the bowler's thumb. Of course the ball could only traverse the length of the string, thereby avoiding the necessity of any long fielder, and only two runs in all the play were accomplished. The English laugh became unlimited, but the poor Chinese looked much abashed and foolish, for they evidently expected to be praised for their ingenuity in saving bodily exertion.

❧

My Consulate in Samoa

W. B. CHURCHWARD

W. B. Churchward was British consul in Samoa from 1881 to 1884.
He wrote the account of his time there in 1887.

❧

FOR THE FIRST two years of my stay in Samoa, neither I nor any of the
few British residents could ever persuade one single Samoan to join in
our cricket, although their congeners, the Tongan residents in the group, were
always ready for a game.

In Tonga the game was adopted so strongly, to the neglect of all domestic
pursuits, that a law had to be passed to prevent their playing for more than
one day a week. All at once the village of Apia Samoa was seized with a most
frantic desire to fathom the mysteries of the game, and to become proficient
in its practice; owing, it appeared, to some discussion the Samoan inhabitants
had had with some Tongans who had twitted them on the subject of their
ignorance of so grand an amusement.

A deputation attended on the Judge, a Britisher, and myself, requesting
us to instruct them in the strict 'Fa'a Peritania' – British manner – of playing
cricket, for that was the version they wanted to learn, and not the 'Fa'a Tonga'
– Tongan – one. They explained that as it was a British sport, we as British
were likely to know more about it than the Tongans, and they thought that we
could teach them in such a way that they might be able to beat these boasting
men. We accordingly took them in hand, and soon succeeded in instilling the
initial idea into their heads.

For a time all went on very smoothly, but the quiet and serious English
style did not suit them long. One by one, innovations of their own and Tongan
manufacture crept into the game, until soon nothing remained of cricket, *pur
et simple*, but the practice of one man bowling a ball to another man trying to
hit it. All the rest of the proceedings were purely of their own manufacture.
However, this Samoan cricket found great favour all round, giving as it did
in its improved form the excuse, always welcome, and never rejected, for
feasting and parade, so dear to all Samoans. Soon all the neighbouring towns
were playing, and cricket at last becoming quite an epidemic, it not only took
possession of the island of its origin, Upolu, but crossing the straits on both

sides, spread all over Tutuila and Savaii, until the whole group was infected with it. Age, sex and dignity alike fell under its influence, until at last there was not a village in which it was not vigorously practised to such a degree as to seriously interfere with domestic affairs.

The Germans were loud in their condemnation of cricket, seeing in it, quite irrespective of probable reduced supply of native produce for them to deal in, an inclination to favour things British, which it always was their studied practice to condemn and underrate, to the glorification of their own importance; and although they could not effect a cure in the provinces, they did succeed in putting such restrictions on the game in the municipality of Apia, that in the most popular play-places it was rendered impossible to carry it on. It was restricted on account of its danger, one ball having gone near to a woman in the course of over a year's play. I don't mean for one moment to say that these lunatics did not carry their frenzy to a somewhat hurtful extreme, but I am sure that the only damage done was to themselves; for I maintain that if they had never thought of cricket they would not have made an ounce more copra than they did. I also know that a very large amount of money must have passed into the hands of the store-keepers for cricket material and dresses, a different style of which they had new for nearly every match. These being the facts, the reason for so much Teutonic opposition must be sought elsewhere.

The processions on match-days are fearful and wonderful to behold. Headed by their Faamasinos, or judges, as they term their umpires, to the dulcet strains of the penny whistle and drum, banners flaunting gaily on the breeze, dressed up in the latest novelty specially designed for the purpose – most likely gone tick for at their pet store – bewreathed and begarlanded to an outrageous extent, the players in single file march through the town in swaggering military order. Each one is armed with his bat, shouldering it as though 'twere a war-club, and, at the word of command from their officers, goes through an entire special manual exercise whilst *en route* to the field. These officers are generally dressed in full naval uniform, with swords and cocked-hats complete, and are continuously running up and down the ranks, keeping their men in place and showing them off to the fullest extent in their power.

Following them close up will be the non-effective brigade, consisting of the women and children belonging to the doughty cricketers, also in gala dress, and carrying with them large quantities of eatables and drinkables for the refreshment of their relations about to do battle for the credit of the village they belong to.

It was the invariable practice of the Apia men on turning out for a match to halt in front of my Consulate, and drawn up in line receive word of command, 'Salute the British Consul!' whereupon the whole line would perform a studied exercise with their bats and arms, equivalent in signification, I suppose, to the 'present', whilst the band, with the colours in front of them, performed a duet for my benefit. They would then form up again in single file, and move off to their game.

This again roused the jealous suspicions of the Germans; for this compliment was never extended to anyone else but the Municipal Magistrate – who was a Britisher – and the one to whom they chiefly owed whatever they knew about cricket.

Their antics in the field beggar description. Each different club would have a distinct method of expressing its joy at the dismissal of an adversary from the wickets; some of them, of a most elaborate nature, must have taken much careful drilling in private to ensure such perfect performance in public.

The conventional number of eleven is thoroughly put on one side. It is nothing unusual to see thirty or forty opposed to one another, and I have known them to play as many as two hundred odd a side. The fact is, that these matches are of one town against another, in which all insist upon taking a hand. These huge meetings, as may be readily imagined, last a week or more, junketing going on the whole time, and generally wind up with a big feast.

Once, during a time of trouble, cricket assumed a political importance, by the aid of which the natives hoped to tide over a dangerous time until their expected relief arrived in the shape of British annexation, to put them out of their misery. They had officially written to England offering their country, and then, to avoid all further complications or roughly exacted explanations, they determined to start a cricket match of such stupendous proportions that it would last until they got an answer from home; during which time they considered that, being engaged in playing, they had a valid excuse for not taking notice of any business that might unpleasantly crop up. In fact, the entire Government was playing cricket, and could not be disturbed.

The game began, but I don't know whether it was ever finished or not. Anyhow, I don't think it had any particular effect upon the usual run of politics;

but I do know that their letter to England never was answered. Shortly after this incident the Germans were very much down upon the natives, finding fault with everything they did, and continually informing them that their insignificant little group was insulting the great German Empire; and they eventually forbade the King, under dire penalties, to play the game called 'cricket' at his seat of government.

Another instance of cricket entering within the sphere of politics occurred somewhere about the middle of 1885. It was at the time that the rebel King was at Leulumoega, talking rather loudly about war upon Malietoa, who, out of regard for his promises to the foreign Powers not to begin war, was very loth to take extreme measures; and, in consequence, had incurred the displeasure of some of the principal chiefs, amongst whom were many Apia men.

About this time Apia was due to play a cricket match at Iva, a district in the neighbouring island of Savaii; and with this proclaimed intention, to the number of about two hundred, they embarked in their boats one fine morning and set off. No one had the smallest idea but that it was the peaceful expedition it was stated to be, and having been a well-known arrangement previous to political matters assuming an ugly look, no suspicion whatever was engendered.

Nothing more dangerous than cricket-bats and balls were seen going on board; but I am afraid that if the mats had been lifted, it would have been found that for every bat there was an accompanying Snider or Winchester rifle, and that balls of not quite so harmless a nature formed the principal part of the ballast.

It turned out afterwards that secret messengers had been sent out some days before to the Iva people and others, informing them of the scheme, which was – without the King's knowledge, under the pretence of playing cricket – to assemble as great a number as possible, make a sudden descent upon the rebel stronghold, and put an end to the disturbance at one stroke.

It was hoped, and, indeed, to the last moment seemed probable, that neither the enemy nor the King would think that there was anything more deadly in the wind than the accustomed innocent cricket, and week or so of feasting.

Everything prospered well for the scheme. Whilst the juniors, to keep up appearances and to lull suspicions, were steadily playing, the old warriors were arranging all details for the raid. Everything was complete; but, as is usual in all things Samoan, no secret can be long kept, and the very night that the purpose was to have been put into action, a messenger from the King arrived forbidding it.

Within the last six months of my stay in Samoa, the cricket rage weakened very considerably in Apia and its vicinity, owing to a new craze seizing upon all, both young and old alike.

On the arrival of Woodyear's Electric Circus, the entire population went mad for it.

2

START OF PLAY

Bangers and Bats

MARCUS TRESCOTHICK

Marcus Trescothick made his debut for Somerset in 1993 and played seventy-six
Tests for England between 2000 and 2006. From *Coming Back to Me* (2008).

◆

YOU'VE HEARD OF people who eat, drink, sleep and dream cricket. For a
large part of my life, that was me.

My earliest memories are not of teddy-bears, bows and arrows, mud pies
or ray-guns, but of bats and balls, and mainly bats. I can't recall when I first
picked one up, but I have retained a fuzzy memory of what happened when
I did. It felt great, and even better when I hit a ball with it. That feeling has
never left me.

I was born into a cricket-mad family. With my dad Martyn – a stalwart,
top-order batsman and brilliant slip fielder for Keynsham Cricket Club,
in between Bristol and Bath, good enough to play second team cricket for
Somerset and be offered a contract which he turned down – and my mum
Linda, already well into her eventual 35 years of making the club teas, it was
hardly surprising that I should have an interest in the game.

But an article in the local paper, recording the birth of Marcus Edward
Trescothick at 9.15 a.m. on 25 December 1975, weighing a 'healthy' 9lb 4oz, said
it all. Under the headline 'On The Team For 1991?', it read:

The couple, who live at Glenwood Drive, Oldland Common, already
have a three-year-old daughter Anna, aged three.

Said Martyn: 'I was secretly hoping for a boy, and he will have every
encouragement to become a cricketer when he grows up.'

While that first paragraph was apparently put together by someone who had
necked a glass too many of the Christmas spirit, the second one was spot on.

Mum tells me I had a little plastic bat thrust into my hands at 11 months
old, only a couple of weeks after I started walking, and, from that moment, I
went round hitting everything I could find. If there weren't any balls to whack
I'd have a go at those square wooden alphabet bricks, an early indication of my
preference for sport over academic life. When I was about two, a family friend

called Roger Loader cut a small bat down to a blade of around six inches and gave it to me as a present. It had a bit more go in it than the plastic one and, by all accounts, I was absolutely lethal with it. When mum and I returned after dropping off Anna at school, we'd get back in the house and I'd plead 'bowl to me, mum, bowl to me'. In the kitchen, in the living room, in the garden, wherever she happened to be, I'd hand the ball to her, she'd bowl it, I'd hit it, fetch it, carry it back to her and say again: 'bowl to me, bowl to me'. I never got tired of this. How she didn't I'll never know. No wonder, whenever they heard me coming, our pet cats, Cricket and Biscuit, would run for their nine lives. Anna thought I was just plain daft.

When I was four, dad went on a cricket tour to Sussex and came back with my first very own new bat, a Gray-Nicholls Powerspot which I still have at home to this day, and it was carnage. In the living room there were three sets of wall lights, each with two lamps under their own shades. By the time I had finished, of the six lamps and shades only one remained intact. I'd had all the rest. And one day, I managed to put a bouncy rubber ball straight through one of the French doors, clean as a whistle. Mum and dad never seemed to mind too much. In fact I was more likely to get told off for not hitting the ball hard enough than for the latest breakage.

From as young as I can remember, if I wasn't tugging at mum's skirts pleading with her to 'bowl to me' or outside in the garden with dad, playing cricket, and by now, football as well, I was glued to the television whenever the cricket was on, so much so that mum would often find me standing in front of it, bat in hand, repeating the shots I'd just seen. She is convinced that is how I became a left-handed batsman even though I am naturally right-handed. In those days, the late 70s and early 80s, the England side was dominated by right-handed batters like Graham Gooch, Geoff Boycott, Chris Tavare, Peter Willey and Ian Botham. David Gower was about the only one who batted the other way round. So, in mirroring the right-handers I was actually adopting a left-hander's stance and practising the shots left-handed. The shots played by Gooch and Beefy obviously appealed to me more than the ones played by Boycott and Tavare.

Inevitably there were scrapes. I've still got a y-shaped scar on my left hand from when I tripped on the doorstep bringing in the milk and I very nearly became living proof of the warning passed down by parents to kids from the beginning of time: 'It's all good fun until somebody loses an eye'. I had my luckiest escape thus far when I tried to climb up the washing machine, planted both Wellington-booted feet through the open door, slipped sideways, and the door hinge made a deep cut along my eyebrow.

By the age of six, whenever people asked me what I was going to do when I grew up, I didn't just say 'play cricket', I said 'play cricket, of course'.

Cricket Memories

R. L. HODGSON

R. L. Hodgson wrote under the nom-de-plume 'A Country Vicar'.
Cricket Memories was published in 1930.

❧

MY EARLIEST RECOLLECTIONS of cricket are of myself – a very small boy, dressed in a plaid frock and white socks – trembling before the terrific bowling of my nurse. J. M. Gregory, the Australian bowler of 1921, with his long run and alarming leap into the air, did not frighten the professional batsmen of England more than my beloved Ann terrified me. She bowled underhand, in the style which used to be designated as 'sneaks', or 'grubs'; but the ball – a small, hard one, made of India-rubber – had a horrible trick of rising unexpectedly from the surface of my father's lawn and striking me a devastating blow on my bare legs. The cook's bowling I despised; it was very slow and entirely guileless. But that of my nurse dominated me for, at least, one whole season.

❧

Wide

MICHAEL SIMKINS

Michael Simkins is an actor and writer. He is watching the first Test against
West Indies in 1966 at Old Trafford. From *Fatty Batter* (2007).

❧

RIGHT TURN AND I'm in the inner sanctum, the rear parlour, the
epicentre of my universe. Dad is sitting at the table with his dog-eared
copy of William L. Shirer's *The Rise and Fall of the Third Reich* on the table in
front of him, the only book he ever reads. Except it lies unopened.

'Dad—'

'Shhhhh. I'm watching the cricket.'

I've heard about cricket. Dad often watches it during his brief lunch-break
when it's on telly in the summer. Someone bowls a ball to someone else who
hits it with a bat, after which everyone stands round pontificating. A cross
between rounders and *Does the Team Think?*.

Dad has liked cricket ever since he was a little boy. His own childhood
hero was a famous batsman called Jack Hobbs, whom his own dad used to
take him to see at the Kennington Oval when he was a kid. One of Dad's
favourite stories is how he once got Jack Hobbs's autograph, and how to this
day he regrets his decision a few years later to swap it for a balsa-wood glider.
I think he made the right decision. Personally I'd rather have the test card on.
At least you get some jolly oompah music.

With no sign of Mum or dinner, I break off a triangle with my teeth and
settle down in the chair by the TV set, allowing Tobler's exotic medley of milk
chocolate, crushed almonds and honey to churn gently in my mouth.

And then I see him.

At first it's almost impossible to make him out. He looks like nothing
more than a large white bed sheet moving in the dark interior of the pavilion
behind the serried rows of slumbering middle-aged men outside.

But there he is again. Moving with purpose and at some speed in the
dim interior, just a snatched glimpse of a large gelatinous object between a
bloke in a panama hat and another with horn-rimmed spectacles. A flash of
sunlight reflecting off freshly Windolened glass as doors are thrown open,

and he lumbers out of the darkness of the pavilion and down the steps.

He barrels down, two at a time, his huge stomach wobbling up and down each tread like a giant blancmange, the flesh straining against the flimsy buttons of his cricket shirt. He seems an amalgamation of every fat kid who has ever sat in the corner of a school changing room having gym shoes thrown at him by his classmates.

People this shape and size don't appear on professional sport. They appear on programmes like *Tonight* and *South Today*, where they describe to a smirking interviewer how they've got into the *Guinness Book of Records* by breaking the world record for the number of boiled eggs eaten at a single sitting.

But he reaches the middle of the pitch, leans stiffly down to flick away a blade of grass from the crease, holds his bat carefully in front of the wicket and looks up at the umpire before gesturing with two fingers. In the distance the bowler, a huge black man with a dazzling smile, steps forward as if about to start a slow rumba, and next thing he's hurtling forward, his body charging across the turf as if shot from a cannon.

Another triangle slips into my mouth. I've not even bothered to unwrap it properly, and a large sliver of silver foil churns around, looking for one of my many fillings on which to unleash its deadly cargo. There can only be one winner here. Any minute now the bloke out there on the pitch is going to have a cricket ball wedged halfway down his throat, there's going to be blood and the spitting out of teeth, and men in gym shoes running on with bottles of TCP and bandages. I want to avert my gaze, but I can't. It's like watching a road accident. You know it's disrespectful to look but somehow you're mesmerised. I squint through splayed fingers. A whirl of the arms and the ball swinging through the air.

He rocks back, swivels on a huge ham bone of a right leg, rolls his wrists and, just as the ball is going to bury itself in his skull, his bat makes contact and the ball sails high, high into the sky and finally lands over the boundary, in among a load of spectators who scatter like pigeons to avoid being hit. A middle-aged bloke in a checked cardigan holds it briefly aloft in the stands in a gesture of triumph.

And as he waves the ball high above his head, the piece of silver foil, borne effortlessly on a ribbon of saliva, finds my deepest nerve ending in a bottom left premolar and deposits its sharp electrical charge.

By the time Colin Milburn has disappeared back into the pavilion, I've learnt my first cricketing statistic. England's new batting hero can hit ninety-four runs in less time than it takes a kid of ten to eat a Toblerone followed by a plate of fish in parsley sauce. I may be only ten, but I can spot a role model when I see one. He's not only fantastic at sport, but is obviously no stranger to a tub of Quality Street.

∿

A Cricketer at the Breakfast Table

ALAN GIBSON

Alan Gibson was a journalist and broadcaster.
From *Growing Up With Cricket* (1985).

∿

PLAYING CRICKET BY yourself is not much fun. Besides, it kicked up too much of a din in the hall. I soon devised a better system, with the assistance of my lead soldiers, of which I had a large and varied collection. I played with them on the bedroom floor, using one hand for batting and the other for bowling. I soon learnt to keep a rough score, and father, seeing that I was working at it, bought me a scorebook. I must have filled dozens of those shilling scorebooks. When Essex were doing badly, I would replay the match in the bedroom, pausing only to shout downstairs to mother 'O'Connor's got his hundred', or similar glad tidings. I wish I had kept some of those scorebooks, but all those records of mighty Essex victories in the early 1930s are lost. Nor did I confine myself to county cricket. I was an assiduous reader of the *Gem* and *Magnet*, and created matches between St Jim's and Greyfriars, the two schools (I suppose I must explain to the modern generation) that featured in those publications. I was always inclined to be a St Jim's man myself, but Greyfriars took some beating, and one of the most famous pairs ever to open an innings on that bedroom floor were Harry Wharton and Bob Cherry. Farmer Road School also played matches there, and I stooped to include myself in the eleven. I did not overdo things by scoring centuries. It was my habit to bat at, say, number seven, and make a careful, match-winning twenty-five or so. It was a nice blue carpet with a good pile. The gas fire was at one end, the cabin trunk at the other, and this was how I always thought of the ends, whoever was playing. Some of the fieldsmen necessarily had to be placed under the bed, which involved much bending and stretching on my part at the end of each over. I can remember now the sense of it, the smell of it. One small boy crawling around with his soldiers on the floor: and all the magic of Lord's and Greyfriars. I can see Larwood as he came on from the cabin trunk end – Essex fifteen to win and a couple of wickets left – in all the majesty of a Zulu warrior.

For though I have called these toys my 'soldiers', they were an assortment, by no means all military. There were cowboys, Indians, and even civilians, relics of a Hornby railway. One of these, a plump middle-aged gentleman with a bowler hat, represented Hobbs, when he happened to be playing, and I think never anyone else. That was how we thought of Hobbs then: senior, apart, not to be impersonated. You knew he would be travelling first class. The Zulu warrior was always the fast bowler. If he was not being Larwood, he was Nichols or Farnes or Hurree Jamset Ram Singh. My supply of 'soldiers' was not sufficient to allow every cricketer to have only one incarnation. When I played myself, I went to the wicket as a sailor. There gradually developed a division between the soldiers (red coats) and the others. My side was 'the others', so they usually won. But the soldiers possessed a marvellous slow left-arm bowler. He had originally been the player of the big drum in the Coldstream Guards band (a splendid Christmas present from one of the wealthier members of father's congregation). He had lost his drum and his head, and there was a hole in his chest where the drum had been attached, but I had a great affection for him. In the winter, when I turned my attention to football, he played inside-left much in the manner of Alex James, lying cunningly behind the rest of the forwards, the midfield link.

I do not think I ever really lost the delight of my lead soldiers' cricket. It was just that as I grew older I became rather ashamed of playing with them and would wait till my parents were out: once they came back early, and found me on the blue carpet with the whole gallery set out, and I felt a bit silly, especially as I was giving a running commentary. ('Now it's Hurree Singh again to Tom Merry . . .'). So I progressed from carpet cricket to table cricket. There have been many varieties of this. In one form or another, it is probably as old as the game itself. There is a pleasant account of one variation in Eric Parker's book, *Playing Fields*, published in 1922. The book was in some ways Eton's answer to *Tom Brown's Schooldays*. I found it rather dull, and have never been tempted to read it again, but I must say in its defence that Bernard Darwin liked it. On a rainy day, two young Etonians were playing table cricket.

You wrote down the names of two elevens on two sheets of paper and then dotted a pencil with your eyes shut on another piece of paper, which was marked with 'fourers', 'sixers', 'caught', 'bowled' and so on.

'That's another six to W.G. By Jove, he is hitting. That's seven out of the ground now. That makes him 202.'

'Bet he'll soon be bowled, then.'

'Bet he isn't.'

'There you are, then. Bowled Spofforth. Told you so.'

'Well, he's made two hundred, anyhow. Spofforth's average must be simply rotten.'

'Ass! He's only just gone on.'

'Why didn't you put him on before, then? Just shows.'

But this was a primitive form of the table game, though widely played. If you had enough patience, you could allow nearly every possibility to be taken into account. Robertson-Glasgow once found a couple of youngsters who had a square marked 'PM', which stood for 'pulled muscle'. It is, however, too chancy to give a realistic representation of cricket on a scoresheet, and the temptations to dishonesty, by the merest winking of an eye as you stab at the sheet, are more than most schoolboys can withstand. A better variation is to choose a page of a book opened at random and take the letters on the page one by one, each representing a ball and its outcome. This rules out cheating but limits variety since there are only twenty-six letters in the alphabet. It was in this form of the game that Robertson-Glasgow himself, who had chosen a team of composers against a team of authors, suddenly found that one of his principal batsmen, Beethoven, had been run out. He at once envisaged the scene: 'Ah, deaf, poor chap. Never heard the call.'

❧

Cricketing Reminiscences and Personal Recollections

W. G. GRACE WITH ARTHUR PORRITT

W.G. was about six years old in 1854. These Reminiscences were published in 1899.

❧

IF I WAS NOT born a cricketer, I was born in the atmosphere of cricket. My father, who was a keen sportsman, was full of enthusiasm for the game, while my mother took even more interest in all that concerned cricket and cricketers. When I was not much taller than a wicket I used to wonder what were the hard cuts, leg hits, and long drives, about which my father and brothers were constantly talking. As far back as I can remember cricket was a common theme of conversation at home, and there was great excitement in the house when some big match was coming off in the neighbourhood.

[. . .] My earliest recollections of any cricket match are connected with a visit which William Clarke's All England team paid to Bristol in 1854. Clarke's combination used to travel about the country, playing matches against eighteen or twenty-two players of different districts. In this way a great deal was done to stimulate interest in cricket, as a visit from the All England team was a red-letter day wherever they went. My father organised this match, and captained the local twenty-two. The game took place in a field behind the Full Moon Hotel, Stokes Croft, Bristol, and I remember driving in to see the ground which my father's gardener and several other men were preparing. It was originally a ridge and furrow field, and had been specially re-laid in the previous autumn. The pitch was first rate, but the rest of the ground was rough and uneven. I was with my mother, who sat in her pony-carriage all day. I don't remember much about the cricket, but I recollect that some of the England team played in top hats. My mother was very enthusiastic, and watched every ball. She preserved cuttings of the newspaper reports of this and most other matches, and took great care of the score books. I have several of her scrap-books, with the cuttings pasted in, and very useful I find them, because in those days 'Wisden's Annual' was not in existence, and no proper record was kept. I see from the score-book that my eldest brother, Henry, and my Uncle Pocock played besides my father. The All England brought down a first-class team, consisting of A. Claik; Bickley, who was a grand bowler; S. Parr; Caffyn, the great Surrey man; George Parr, the famous Nottingham cricketer; Julius Caesar, of Surrey fame, and one of the very best all round cricketers of his day; George Anderson, the genial Yorkshireman, one of the finest hitters of his time; Box, the celebrated wicket-keeper; J. B. Marshall, who was a great supporter of cricket; Edgar Willsher, of Kent; and W. Clarke, the slow underhand bowler – most of whose names are still famous in the annals of cricket. It is doubtful whether nine men out of the eleven could have been excelled and as was only to be expected, the West Gloucestershire twenty-two were beaten – by 149 runs.

[. . .] I learned the rudiments of cricket when quite a child. As small boys we played about the garden in a rough and ready way, and used to make the nurses bowl to us. In 1850 my father had moved from Downend House to the 'Chestnuts', which was a great improvement, because it had two orchards, and the grounds were larger. My father laid out a cricket pitch in one of the orchards, which E. M., who was already a keen cricketer, improved by his own efforts. My father, my brother Henry, and my Uncle Pocock practised at every spare moment, and we youngsters fielded for them from the time we could run about. Then they would give us a few balls, so I soon learned how to handle a bat. Uncle Pocock took special pains with me, and helped me a great deal, by insisting on my playing with an upright bat, even as a child. I soon got so fond of the game that I took every opportunity of playing, and when I couldn't play proper cricket, I used to chalk a wicket on a wall and get a stable-boy and one or two youngsters from the village to join me. So I got some sort of practice – sometimes with a broom-handle instead of a bat. We played all the year round, and at all hours of the day. I consider that a great deal of my quickness of eye is due to the fact that the boys with whom I played bowled a very large proportion of fast underhand 'daisy cutters', which used to jump about in a most erratic way, and needed a lot of watching. I also played fives, a game which is good practice for the eye during the winter months.

When I was at boarding-school cricket was encouraged by the masters, and I used to play as often as possible. Then I began playing for the West Gloucestershire Club, in which my father was the leading spirit. Of course, I used to go in last, and if I got a run or two I thought I was very lucky. As early as 1857 I played three or four innings for the West Gloucestershire Club. I was then only a boy of nine, and I couldn't be expected to do very much against the elevens we played, which were composed of grown-up men. As I grew older I played oftener, and in 1859 had eleven innings, which realised twelve runs. The year 1860 marks an epoch in my cricket career. On the 19th and 20th of July (I was then in my twelfth year), I was selected to play for West Gloucestershire against Clifton, which was a keen rival of my father's club, and one of the crack teams in our neighbourhood, as it is to-day. I mention that particular match, because it was the occasion of the first score I remember making. I went in eighth (my brother E. M., who at this time was in rare form, had already made 150, and my Uncle Pocock 44) and added 35 before stumps were drawn. My father and mother were delighted, and both were very proud next day when I carried my score on to 51. I do not think my greatest efforts have ever given me more pleasure than that first big innings.

～❧

Opening the Innings

RACHAEL HEYHOE FLINT

Rachael Heyhoe-Flint (Baroness Heyhoe Flint) captained the England women's cricket team from 1966 to 1978. From *Heyhoe!* (1978).

～❧

SUMMER MEANT CRICKET, and I have fond memories of packing up a picnic lunch or tea and setting off with Father in the car. From a very early age I took along my own scorebook and pencil, and it was rumoured that I could score a cricket match competently before I could even string a sentence together in a school book.

I was only eleven when I went along to watch Father playing cricket for the Technical College on a day when they were one man short. Amazingly, I soon found myself marked down to bat at number eleven for the college and had to go out to the crease to stave off defeat. The pads reached my waist and the bat felt like a tree trunk, but the men were kind enough to bowl me a few slowish half-volleys, and to everyone's surprise I managed to score two or three undefeated runs and save the game.

Back at school, I was chiefly restricted to the orthodox girls' games – hockey and netball in the winter, tennis and rounders in the summer. But things began to change when Lancashire-born Mary Greenhalgh, a representative cricket and hockey player, arrived to take charge of our PE department. In the summer of 1954, she took a somewhat rebellious school party to the Edgbaston Test ground to watch the Midland women's team play the touring New Zealanders. This was euphoria for me. Not only were we missing school lessons to watch cricket, but it was women's cricket, played at a very high standard.

As I studied the game that day at Edgbaston, I made up my mind that this was the life for me. Afterwards, we were allowed to go and meet the New Zealanders, and the autographs I avidly collected are still in my possession today. But I came away with more than signatures. I came away with an image of an exciting, challenging life, travelling the world playing cricket, meeting people. It seemed everything I wanted out of life, and I think it was there and then that I determined I must play cricket for England women – though, if the truth were known, I wasn't even sure whether England had a women's cricket team!

Looking back now at the team photograph of the 1954 Wolverhampton Girls' School cricket XI, it is interesting to find that I am one of three girls who in fact went on to play for England – an extraordinary achievement for a single school. The other two were Jackie Elledge and Ann Jago (known to us all as Sago), great friends of mine long after we had all left schooldays behind.

If this was in fact the time when I decided my future, I certainly lacked nothing in the way of support and encouragement. My parents were, I believe, genuinely pleased at the sporting direction I had chosen, and my father would often spend hours bowling at me in the garden.

Our house seemed to be adopted as the sporting Mecca by the entire adolescent population of the road, but even when alone, I was never lost for something to do. I devised my own method of solitary practice, suspending a cricket ball on string from an overhanging plank attached to a low gutter, and patiently drove the ball backwards and forwards until my arms ached and the gutter nearly fell off.

Brother Nicholas and his friends at first tried to exclude me from their back-lawn cricket matches. For some time, I was delegated as preserver of the flower beds. In other words, they deigned to let me field, but refused me the chance to either bat or bowl.

After serving my apprenticeship in the covers, however, they relented and allowed me an innings, presumably with the conviction that it wouldn't last long anyway. I shocked them all by batting undefeated for three days and accumulating a score of about 380 not out. By the end of it, they were so frustrated – I think pride came into it, too – that they declared the opening of the football season and switched games, despite the fact that it was only mid-June.

Being four years older, Nicholas was able to bully little sister quite successfully. But he did, at least, teach me a great deal about courage.

I had to put up with such harrowing indignities as having the vacuum cleaner held over my head so that my plaits were sucked up to the machine. I had to join in crazy 'dares', which included jumping off a twelve-foot-high balcony on to a mattress on our lawn – only when our parents were out, of course.

Nicholas also involved me in his cycle speedway team, which he called the Penn Rockets, and he taught me how to ride a motor-bike. At least, he showed me how to operate clutch, gears and throttle and launched me off over the fields near our home. What he had omitted to explain was how to work the brakes!

Eventually, I became accepted by his mates, almost as one of the gang, although they insisted on nicknaming me Lizzie after that obnoxious Violet Elizabeth Bott in the 'Just William' books who was always threatening to 'scweam and scweam until I'm sick'. To them, I had several uses, not the least important of which involved being sent round to neighbours' houses to retrieve lost cricket balls and footballs, exerting all my feminine charm!

The family on one side of us grew tired of our games and would often refuse to return the ball. But that was almost a relief compared with the house on the other side, where the people were friendly enough but their fearsome vicious bulldog would threaten permanent damage to anyone who set foot on his territory. Duelling with that dog certainly sharpened up my reflexes – as it would have done for anyone whose job it was to bend down and find cricket balls under the rhododendrons with a snarling, snapping creature bearing down on one's seat at a rate of knots.

The garden games involved a simple system of scoring runs, including six if you cleared a fence or hit the house wall on the full or twelve if you cleared the roof. If you broke a window, however, you were out! Not only that, but you also abandoned your part in the game to race into town by bicycle and collect the necessary replacement pane of glass before my parents could discover any damage. I think our local glazier must have been familiar with every window pane in our house, and several surrounding houses, by the time we had grown up.

It's a Great Day for Being a Boy

DAVID WALKER

David Walker is a freelance writer. From *It's Not Lord's: A West Yorkshire Cricket Anthology* (2011), which he edited and published.

❧

ONE SEPTEMBER SUNDAY in 2004, Almondbury Casuals CC, a very friendly cricket club, visited Upperthong. The match was not about a result or performances, though there were some. All that really mattered were the upper reaches of the Holme Valley, bathed in warm Indian Summer sunshine, and playing cricket. It has to be said that balmy weather and Upperthong do not often go together, exposed as it is to vicious storms that sweep down from Holme Moss.

Two youngsters played for Upperthong that day, one on the pitch with his dad and the other in the car park. It got me thinking of all the young lads over the years who have knocked about at cricket. Strange games reminiscent of those informal pastimes played before rules were invented and written down.

Such impromptu occasions are part of the preparation for formal cricket. They are also important lessons in the art of growing up. Take the average domestic backyard or school playground. It is here where juniors sharpen their competitive edge against marauding older brothers and pale fifth formers with nicotine-stained fingers.

At school, a minimal set of kit is essential and old and knackered is preferable. Don't take that dark brown heirloom, signed by Len Hutton, discovered after days of rummaging in the attic, or you will never see it again. Balls must be bald. Stumps are dangerous and on no account must they be used; wall and chalk is quite sufficient. The track will vary from rough and stony to hard uneven clay and there must be no fear of body contact as several hundred matches are played simultaneously, side by side. Bad light and rain-stopped-play are rare. Indeed a wet ball can be an advantage as it leaves a distinctly visible trace on chalk and clean bowled cannot be disputed. LBWs are, however, extremely contentious in this style of cricket, as they can be in the more orthodox forms. It's a battleground, where a talent for survival is swiftly rewarded. Being able to play with a plank for a bat and a ball that barely bounces is clearly valuable, but think of the benefits accruing from attempting to retrieve a square cut from an irate '5 Remove' psychopath whose knuckles scrape along the floor.

In the back garden, the object of the game is not to lose the ball. It's all about defence and occupying the crease, much to the frustration of older brothers. They in turn respond by changing the rules to suit them.

'Owzat?'

'Not out, you dollop.'

'How come, it 'it off stump.'

'It never, look here there's a mark on't door frame.'

'We said door frame were going to be off stump.'

'Did we 'eck.'

Another nine-year-old stamps his feet and walks back to his mark next to the clothes post. Apart from batting for days, his main weapon is the donkey drop, lobbed as high as his bedroom window, pitching as a half-volley some thirty seconds later, just outside the line of off stump. But he must choose his time carefully. He must wait for the moment when older brother's eyes wander and glaze, that instant when concentration has moved internally to Maxine Hargreaves, her with the big charlies down at number seven. What did he see in her?

Got 'im. The ball sails away to long-off, into Mr Grumps' potato patch, where it will stay until autumn, that bit of the year when the harvest gives birth to hundreds of chewed moth-eaten tennis balls.

'Six an' out, you're out.' The nine-year-old does an impression of an aeroplane in an acrobatics display. Older brother stands bemused, wondering whether he's been had. This is chess, where tactics and planning, capitalising on strengths, minimising weaknesses, patience, a strong nerve and sheer native wit are cultivated. And, when there are no more balls, David and Goliath will go and find another game to play.

That September Sunday in 2004, two boys played for Upperthong. One played on the pitch with his dad; a bowler of promise, a first-ball duck and a steep learning curve. The other, fully present and correct in whites, helmet, pads and gloves, played in the car park between two sets of full-sized metal stumps that came up to his shoulder. A left-hander, he played alone during the Casuals' innings, straight driving, blocking, square cutting and taking quick singles. Every so often he would pause, and turn and look at the action out in the middle. After a minute or so he would turn away and get back down to the business at hand.

And the match result?

Upperthong more than 250 for 6 off 35 overs

Casuals 190 all out in 34 overs

❧

3

LET'S PLAY HERE

Cricket Fields and Cricketers

NEVILLE CARDUS

Sir Neville Cardus was the author of many books about music and cricket.
From *Days in the Sun* (1948).

THERE IS SURELY some interaction between a cricket team and the ground it mainly lives on – does not the play of the side assume tone and colour from the scene? Yorkshire cricket has the aspect of Bramall Lane and Leeds – dour, and telling of stern competitive life with smoke and real industry about. Can you imagine the shrewd Lancashire game quite at home under a June sky at the Saffrons? Does not there come through the cricket of Sussex the brown and sunny flavour of Eastbourne and Hove when the time of day is noon and the earth seems humming with heat? The plain homeliness of the Midlands is expressed by Leicestershire cricket: it has no airs and graces, no excessive refinements. See an innings by Cole, of Leicestershire, and you ought not to be long guessing from the smack of rotund nature about it that he has passed the main portion of his days in the sun on a field with rustic benches running intimately round. No, it is not mere fancy to say: 'Show me a cricket team in action and I'll tell you where is its native heath.'

Take Lord's, for example. The country spirit, the circumscribed life denoted by country, is not for Lord's. For your good cricketer the ends of the earth have come to a resting-point at Lord's, and wherever he may be at the fall of a summer's day his face should turn religiously towards Lord's. Lord's is the Cosmopolis of cricket. And which county do you find playing the bulk of its games at Lord's? Why, naturally enough, the team that, less than them all, gives us the definite county flavour. Middlesex has ever been as cosmopolitan as Lord's itself – a side gathered from the earth's corners, West Indians, Australians, even Yorkshiremen! A man from Huddersfield sat in the crowd at Lord's a season or two ago, and as he watched Middlesex beating his own county he was stirred to a protective derision – a derision which he cultivated as balm for the wound that defeat at cricket must always bring to Yorkshiremen. 'Middlesex?' he asked of the throng around him. 'Wheer's Middlesex? Is it in Lundon?' His barb was well directed; London obliterates the county boundaries, and neither at Lord's nor at the Oval do you feel the clannishness that stings you in the atmosphere of Old Trafford or Bramall Lane. To be eloquent of authentic county demands a certain narrowness, a contentment with those things of the earth, and that part of the earth, which Providence has placed immediately at one's doorstep. County means nature – and at Lord's cultivation borne on the winds of the world has rather expelled nature. Watch Hearne move fastidiously towards a century; watch Bruce or Crutchley batting, and you are looking on cricket played in the drawing-room of civilized men and women. And at those times when Bosanquet bowled at Lord's there came into the game the touch of exquisite decadence that marks a true Cosmopolis. Frankly, I have never yet been able to fix Hendren into my notion of Lord's; he is quite indecently provincial in his relish of a thumping boundary.

There is, of course, in the life of a cultivated cricketer little that is sweeter than a summer morning at Lord's, a morning when the sky is a blue awning blown out with soft wind, and the trees at the Nursery End make a delicate motion. 'The Nursery End at Lord's!' The phrase sets memory astir, for have we not read in days of old in those evening papers our boyish eyes scanned that 'Richardson went on at the Nursery End', that 'Ranjitsinhji glanced Noble to the rails at the Nursery End'? Because Max Beerbohm has never written an essay called 'Going to Lord's on a July Morning' we have proof he has never in his life walked down the St. John's Wood Road with a day of cricket in sunny weather before him. But perhaps it is not given to the man who lives only round the corner from Lord's and can visit it every day to feel its appeal as keenly as the man from the North, who not more than three or four times a year walks down the St. John's Wood Road. Let the morning be quiet and mellow and there seems in the air about the St. John's Wood Road, at least to one not too familiar with the place, a sense of the dead old days, causing a melancholy which no doubt one ought to be ashamed of. The mind is made by this something in the St. John's Wood air to play with fancies of Victorian greatness hanging about the spot; of a gleaming hansom cab at the entrance and a black-bearded man, looking mountainous in everyday clothes, getting out while folk standing round murmur '"W.G."!'; of simple-faced men in wide, uncreased trousers proceeding along the pavement – the names of them, likely enough, Lockwood, Lohmann, Richardson – all keen to 'get at the old 'un'. No lover of cricket as he wanders about Lord's can very well keep the thought of Grace from his mind, for though Grace was a Gloucestershire man surely he larded the green earth at Lord's till the very spirit of him may be said to have gone into the grass. You see, just as Lord's is too large in spirit to stand for any one county or for any one space of time in cricket's history, so did the amplitude of Grace transcend Gloucestershire and his little day. At Lord's, with a June morning spending its warmth, one feels a kind of resentment that there should ever have been a bourne put by nature on W.G.'s capacity to endure and play the game till he was utterly tired of it. Is not Lord's here for him now just as ever it was, and a summer day here also, one so fresh that it casts clean out of the understanding the thought of years that pass away? Why should it ever happen to a cricketer that a June morning comes on which the sun begins in the old comfortable way to climb the sky, and Lord's stands in the light, full of summer-time animation, and he no longer there to know of it?

Leave Lord's one day and to-morrow discover Bramall Lane and you enter another world. Frankly, the cricket field at Sheffield is a blasted heath, but, as Shakespeare knew, it is on blasted heaths that matters of grim moment come to pass. A Lancashire and Yorkshire match is not to be thought of at Lord's; here at Sheffield the scene tells a plain tale of the stiff energy of North Country life, and it provides the right setting for a battle between ancient hosts where the informing spirit is of a dour and combative blood feud. Squat chimneys outside the ground loom black, and even on a Bank Holiday the air contains a hint of furnaces and steel smelters. And to the man who likes his cricket moving dramatically on the right stage the Bramall Lane crowd is a work of art. It is a multitude which seemingly throws out a white heat and causes the game to boil over prodigiously. Who at Sheffield on Whit Monday in 1922 will ever forget the great crowd that watched Yorkshire struggling for a first innings' advantage over Lancashire the day long? It was a crowd unashamedly partisan. No room had the red-hot ranks for the equanimity that can look on an issue and say: 'May the best side win.' This vast gathering lived the violent afternoon through to one thought, to one thought alone: 'Down with Lancashire. Trample the Red Rose in the dust.' Here we had a partisan temper which sought to persuade events in Yorkshire's way. There was surely not a man on Bramall Lane's desolate plain that afternoon who would not have held up his hands to the sky till pain scourged him had he believed that such a martyrdom would keep the hurly-burly favourable to his county. Not magnanimous, you might well say; still, there is an aspect to partisanship as brittle as this which is not entirely to be despised. If the Sheffield crowd cannot attend to the amenities at the sight of an advance by the ancient foe, if it is driven in the hour of Yorkshire's adversity to a fury and apprehension that have no use for a magnanimous admiration of the skill of the conquerors, we may wish ourselves far away from such a crowd, and thank our stars cricket does not breed many like it, but we certainly cannot deny that here is 'character', here is rich red blood and abundant spirit.

I have heard folk from the South say of cricket at Sheffield that it simply is not cricket. Their preference has been for the game as it is played with trees and country graciousness around. But why put a limit to cricket's appeal; why deny her infinite variety? Lancashire and Yorkshire at Bramall Lane is not less cricket than any match in an old meadow at Little Slocombe on the laziest day in June. Cricket, indeed, has many facets; it can satisfy most of the human animal's interests and emotions, and, as we have seen, it is sensitive to most of our moods and our habitations. It can stir one, at Sheffield, into a very man of war; it can soothe one, at Tonbridge, to the sweetest peace. In turn, it can sound a clarion note that sets the combative spirits in the blood running agog like hey-go-mad, as Tristram Shandy would say; and in turn it can capture the summer's own music.

Kent cricket, as you may see from a mile's distance, was born of Canterbury and Tonbridge – an innings by Woolley is a pastoral. And those who have Miss Mitford's eyes for the summer game will find cricket at Worcester lovable. The pretty field there, true, is overshadowed by the town and its industry, but all the bricks and mortar of the place are huddled at one side cosily, and there is the cathedral to look at. The Worcester cricket ground is in the midst of meadow-land; the scent of grass is here all day and a wide space of sky above. Here a cricket-lover may seek out a corner of the field, lie down at full length and watch the game from a distance. (There is some enchantment about watching the movements of men in white through the sun's haze from a long way off.) And well does Worcestershire cricket suit countryside ease and humour. It is even a virtue in a place so full of green loveliness as this that Worcestershire often cannot play severely expert first-class cricket. The rough conflict of the championship manner would seem surely to mock Worcester's drowsy landscape. This is a cricket field apt for the country club game, and it is the happy country club cricket Worcestershire plays.

Looked at from strict first-class standards, Worcestershire's bowling these last few years has been rather a joke. Better far to look at it from the tolerant country club view. Let us talk of the Worcestershire bowlers not with the names they are known by in the list of first-class averages, but by names like Smith, Jones, Brown, and Robinson – all names of jolly good fellows for a country club match. Smith we all know; he possesses strong views on the leg-break, but somehow it never comes off 'in the middle'. Jones has a complete mastery over the principles of the googly – in the smoke-room when he is playing matches over again in reminiscent mood. Brown once got a wicket against the M.C.C., and of course there is always a chance that he will some day do it again. And Robinson boasts an ability to swerve with a new ball; he goes on at the outset of the innings, and will be ready again when the 200 is up! How they must enjoy their summers down at Worcester!

The world of Kent and Worcestershire cricket and the world of Yorkshire cricket might appear far apart, yet Lancashire manages to make the best of both. At Old Trafford the game has a hearty sportsmanship, yet this is an efficiently ordered ground, which never lets you forget that Manchester knows a thing or two about getting and spending. Old Trafford, like Lancashire cricket, is both utilitarian and human. Makepeace, who plays the game as a machine might play it, is at home at Old Trafford, but so was Johnny Briggs, a cricketer who was always smiling. Old Trafford possesses a nice name, and more of the open air gets into it than into Kennington Oval, for there still are fields outside Old Trafford, so that its beautiful stretch of turf does not cause you to ask, as the turf at the Oval does: 'How on earth did it get here?'

The Old Trafford crowd is fond of Lancashire cricket, but not so jealous of it that there will not be generous applause for a triumphant invading host. When Lancashire collapses the Old Trafford crowd will simply curse the county players heartily for a while and ease its heart that way. But at Leeds one afternoon, when Yorkshire collapsed against Notts, though the crowd took a rather lasting sorrow with it to tea, no word of complaint or distrust was uttered against Yorkshire cricket. There, in a word, is the difference between a Lancashire crowd's regard for its county XI and the Yorkshire crowd's. The one is based on the notion that after all cricket is only a game and hence need not ever be an occasion for a gnashing of teeth; the other sees in cricket – that is, in Yorkshire cricket – one of the finer passions of life, a possession of the clan not to be rudely handled. The Yorkshireman's intolerance of an enemy's prowess is simply the measure of the Yorkshireman's pride in his county's genius for cricket.

The Australians find the best light in the country at Old Trafford – no nonsense about waving trees there! And at Old Trafford the Australians have made history. The writer, for one, will always remember Armstrong sitting on the grass at Old Trafford, refusing to go on with the game until the crowd, which was in a bad temper, for a wonder, stopped barracking him. He will also never forget the innings Darling played at Old Trafford in the 1902 Test match – a small innings numerically, but how lion-hearted! It was a day of lowering clouds and Australia was in an awkward situation. Darling came in and played a death or glory innings, the fitful sun glinting on his bat. Not in great Test matches, though, has Old Trafford found its true heart, but when Hornby and Barlow were at the wicket and we all looked devotedly on as 'the run-stealers flickered to and fro'. Perhaps Old Trafford is less Lancashire than Manchester; there is not much in its prosperous shape – the pavilion is the image in stone and mortar of your successful Manchester man – that tells of the county's scrambling little mill towns where cobbled streets go up and down hill. None the less it is more like Lancashire county than Kennington Oval is like Surrey county. For if Lord's is cosmopolitan, the Oval is distinctly metropolitan. One of the ironies of the game, surely, is that Surrey, with its hills and downs, has in cricket come to be associated with Kennington and a setting of bleak tenements and confident announcements (on hoardings) about somebody's pale ale and dry gin. Little of breezy country air passes over the Oval. And so, because the Oval incessantly comes to mind when one thinks of Surrey cricket, one is driven to thinking of the Surrey team as made up wholly of the stuff of Cockaigne. Bobby Abel was the personification of Surrey cricket seen through the air of the Oval; the pert lift of the cap on his head, the slick dexterity of his play, with bat at an impudent angle – all these gave cricket a Cockney accent. Poor Tom Richardson, with his sun-tanned face and black hair, was, I can hardly think, rarely in his heart's home with the odours of modern Vauxhall about him. Why cannot Surrey find for occasions a pleasant field somewhere, say, near Cranleigh?

Nottinghamshire cricket has never been unfaithful to Trent Bridge. That perfect pitch at Trent Bridge went a long way towards the making of the

Nottinghamshire cricket tradition. For on a cushion of Trent Bridge marl, batsmanship was tempted to proceed comfortably along the lines of least resistance. The poor bowler was at a discount at Trent Bridge in fine weather; no long and keen challenge was sent from him to the batsman. 'Keep your wickets up, lads, and runs will come,' seems usually to have been the easy philosophy of Nottinghamshire cricketers – dwellers for a season's better part on Trent Bridge, a Lotos-land for batsman, a place where it was always afternoon and 360 for 2 wickets. That guileless turf at Nottingham accounted for Shrewsbury, whose every innings was the stately blank verse of batsmanship; accounted for Attewell, pitching the ball on a sixpenny piece's circumference till soothing monotony came over the onlooker; accounted for Scotton, the stonewaller: 'Block, block, block at the foot of thy wicket, O Scotton!' In its heyday Nottinghamshire cricket was fit for heaven and eternity. You could admire it like unflawed marble, but being human, you could not live with it for long. How powerfully the Trent Bridge pitch contributed to the cold Nottinghamshire cricket tradition of the past may best be understood if we look at the doings of the Nottinghamshire XI in 1907 – a wet summer. In that season Notts won the championship by cricket as brilliant as Kent cricket. The rain took from the Trent Bridge wicket its customary easefulness; no longer could a batsman dawdle on it all day while his score mounted almost without a thought from him, his innings growing in the warmth like a plant. No; he had now to get runs by art and quick wit against a spinning ball, and the Nottinghamshire XI responded beautifully to the stimulus of the new environment. To-day, one believes, the wicket at Trent Bridge is no longer as delicately nurtured on marl as it was in the old times: Nature in the grass is given a better chance of asserting herself. If this is the truth, we can hardly put it down to accident that nowadays Nottinghamshire cricket has perhaps a more lively habit of mind, a freer gait than ever it had; that A. W. Carr, wearing the mantle of A. O. Jones, is leading his batsmen from its ancient flat lands to slopes romantically uneven.

You can't get away from it – cricket does turn sensitively to the sun and the setting, moves to the passing of summer in England. True, they play cricket in Australia and South Africa; the game, in fact, has gone round the wide world. But not in the lands of dry light and parched brown earth is cricket the game we know and love here. Cricket as a combat and as a display of skill would be fascinating in the Sahara, no doubt; in England only does the soul of it unfold. You have never even wooed cricket, let alone won it, if you have looked on the game merely as a clever matter of bat and ball which, given a fine day and expert players, might be appreciated at any time of the year like football, which is as good to watch in December as in April or May. One, indeed, has heard folk ask for winter cricket, to be played in some glass-domed Olympia brilliant with electric light. The cricketer of soul knows better than this. He knows that whoever would appreciate cricket rightly must have a sense, as he sits in the sun (there can be no real cricket without sunshine), that he is simply attending to one part, and just one part, of the pageant of summer as it slowly goes along, and yet a part as true to summer as villages in the Cotswolds, stretches of gleaming meadow-land, and pools in the hills. Cricket in high summer is played with the mind of the born lover of it conscious the whole time that all this happy English life is around him – that cricket is but a corner in the teeming garden of the year. Pycroft in *The Cricket Field* writes of 'those sunny hours . . . "when the valleys laugh and sing"', and plainly the memories of them as he wrote his book were as memories of some sweet distillation of cricket itself. You see, at cricket there is a chance to bask in a comprehension of the summer-time setting and spirit; the game more often than not is a leisurely game. And so the watcher may be mindful, as the men in white come on to the field at the fresh of the morning, that the sun is beginning a lazy journey up the sky; that, while the game pauses in the hour for rest and lunch, the earth is smoking in the heat of noon; that at the fall of day, with its shadows and peaceful night – why, then the watcher of the game may also see the peach bloom come in evening skies. All things that matter are these to cricketers of heart and to our delectable game. Only on dull days and in dull places is cricket dull.

Recollections of Lord's and the Marylebone Cricket Club

WILLIAM SLATTER

William Slatter joined the Lord's ground staff in 1863 and rose to be head groundsman. His *Recollections* were published in 1914.

～❧

IN THE EARLY days of Lord's it was little more than an ordinary field, and when a match was played of any importance, it was surrounded and enclosed in by a circle of tents (which were used mostly for refreshments), and stalls for the selling of fruit, oysters, etc., and it is recorded that in or about 1825 a ball was hit into the crowd – it has been stated by Lord Hamilton – and it fixed itself on the point of a knife which happened to be in the hands of a woman who was about to open oysters; this must, of course, be taken 'cum grano salis'.

About the same time it is recorded that a gentleman who was a cripple was seated in a carriage on the south side of the ground, when a ball was hit towards him. He saw it descending, and in his fright of being hit, jumped up and got out of the way, and it has been stated that the ball fell in the carriage where he had been seated. Needless to say, he discharged the carriage and the coachman, and walked home the first time for years.

[...] The first pavilion was burned down, but how it caught fire no one could tell. When the excavations were dug out for the present pavilion, a stone was found embedded twelve feet in the clay. This had all the appearance of a thunderbolt, and I have (or should have) the stone in my possession now.

The fall of the ground from the edge of the grass 'north' to the edge of the grass 'south' was seven foot nine inches, but after the Hotel was erected in 1868 the lower portion of the ground was raised. The fall at the present time is about six foot eight inches. (The fall of the practice ground at the Wellington Road side from Wellington Place to St. John's Wood Road is over nine feet.)

Prior to about 1865, minor clubs rented a portion of the ground for matches and practice. The Westbourne Club had a pitch in front of the present luncheon room extension, somewhat nearer to the pavilion than where the Cross Arrow matches are played, and the St. John's Wood Club who made the Tavern their headquarters, had wickets running north and south in a line with the old racquet court.

[. . .] The mowing machine was first introduced at Lord's in 1868. Mr. Robert Grimston, who at that period was a very prominent person in the cricket world, had a great objection to its use, so that when he was in evidence, the machine had to be put in the cart shed.

'Rocky' and 'Local Rules'

TONY HUTTON, MICK BOURNE AND BRIAN SENIOR

From *Off the Beaten Track* (2006), the diary of three inveterate cricket-lovers who explore the whole of Yorkshire and beyond trying to find at least one game a day to watch.

❧

SUNDAY 15 JANUARY

BRIAN, MICK & TONY: Appletreewick v Malhamdale at the Appletreewick Oval. Amazingly, less than three weeks since our last cricket match of 2005 (the traditional Boxing Day game between North Leeds and the Northern Cricket Society) we found ourselves watching cricket (of a sort) at the Yorkshire Dales village of Appletreewick. Brian and Mick, together with Ian Cockerill of Lancaster who is a major source of information for us, had attended the previous year's game in January in a field across the road from the Buck Inn at Malham. They enjoyed a rare chance to see cricket being played in England in January so much that, prompted by information on Malhamdale's website saying this year's game would be on 15 January at Appletreewick, 1.30 pm, a party of five of us were in place well before the scheduled start.

We had just established that the game would be played in a large field opposite the New Inn when the Malhamdale team and supporters came marching down the middle of the road from the nearby Craven Arms. We followed them into the New Inn, where it soon became apparent that most of them had other priorities than cricket. As we patiently waited our turn at the crowded bar, the tone was set by the man in front of us ordering 14 pints of bitter. So we had a drink and some lunch, by which time it was almost 2.30 and getting both darker and colder. With some reluctance, the players took to the field about 2.45 with the number of overs reduced from 20 to 10 a side. The players were dressed in a variety of winter clothing, but at least the umpires wore white coats. However, one of them had a bottle of whisky in his pocket, the other a bottle of wine. These were not solely to keep the umpires warm, but were for the benefit of the players as well – one of the many local rules seeming to be that each bowler had a swig from a bottle before the start of each over. Other rules seemed to be no lbws, you could not be out first ball, and could not hit a boundary first ball – so a big hit had to be all run.

A major talking-point was the appearance of a man with county experience for Malhamdale. He was Paul ('Rocky') Ridgway who had been on the Lancashire staff and who we had seen opening the bowling for Lancashire 2nd XI. After an exciting last-ball finish, the two scorers, one of them armed with a hot water bottle, declared the result a tie on 81-5 each. However, our own perusal of the scorebook suggested that Malhamdale had won by three runs. Some months later we found an enjoyable report of the game on the Malhamdale website. Unfortunately, it contained one major error which stated the following: 'The crowd was amazingly swelled by a group of Lancashire cricket enthusiasts, who had traced this annual event on the Malhamdale website and came to spectate.' As four of us are residents of Yorkshire (although one was born in Lincolnshire), and only one from Lancashire, we took great exception to this – and we have now received an official apology.

The Oval

DUDLEY CAREW

Dudley Carew was a journalist and film critic.
From *England Over: A Cricket Book* (1927).

WHEN ONE WAS very young and hansoms jingled fascinatingly up Regent Street, there was only one cricket ground in the world – Lord's. Rumours came to boyish ears of another ground across the water, a fabulous ground surrounded by monstrous gasworks where Hayward could be seen building up classic centuries, but the place remained unreal and even nightmarish. A small boy's knowledge of London is vague. He knows his own roads and a few centres like Oxford Circus and Piccadilly Circus, and, if he is keen on cricket and has indulgent parents, the way the taxi goes to Lord's.

The broad sweep of St. John's Wood Road is friendly and familiar, and once inside the ground he knows with strict and professional regard for the exact site chosen for the wicket, the best place to sit. He gets to know the faces of the grey-flannelled match-card boys, and it thrills his sense of 'grown-upness' to buy a paper at the little shop by the tavern. He has the intense satisfaction of knowing his way about. But the Oval . . . somewhere in a wilderness called Vauxhall . . . . No; he would rather not go; and when uncles rattle money in their pockets and speak of Hayward and Hobbs he murmurs that Middlesex are playing at Lord's, and wouldn't uncle rather see Warner than Hobbs?

Even now I can never think of the Oval as a children's ground. I know that small boys flock there in their hundreds and cheer for 'our Jack' and 'old Percy', but for all that I feel they are out of place. The Oval has a sterner tradition than Lord's. There is no place for the airs and graces of the game there. 'If you come here,' its spirit seems to say, 'you will see good cricket, but you will not see it in comfort. You will probably have to stand or, at the very best, sit on hard, cold stone. You will have no view to distract and charm you, you will hear no lovely sounds of summer, but only the bells of passing trams.' In some moods that is exactly what one wants. One tires of people who use cricket as an excuse for lazing away an afternoon, and of women who knit or read cheap novels while great men are batting, and who yet profess to 'adore' the game. One does not meet such people at the Oval. Only men and women who have that real and strong love for cricket which must really seem perilously like madness to those who have not got it themselves.

Talk to some of the crowd there. You will find, perhaps as I have often found, an elderly man who will talk to you for so long as you care to listen of Abel and Richardson, Lohmann and Lockwood. While he is talking one has time to observe him carefully. One notices the square-toed, unpolished boots, the rucked waistcoat with the spot or two of grease on it, the clean, ill-fitting collar, and one wonders, if one has an inquisitive mind, what manner of life this man has led. What suffering has he been through, and what happiness? Who is his God, and what in life or in death does he most fear? One wonders what he has worked at, and whether his wife is alive, and whether he has children. One wants desperately to pierce to the reality behind the clothes and talk, and it is only after one has been listening to him for some time that one begins to realise that the reality may lie precisely in those words 'Abel', 'boundary', 'slow-bowler', he is perpetually uttering. We are always so insolently certain that the accidents which over-shadow the world such as death and suffering and love are of immense importance to everyone. We do not allow for the curious filter of the individual mind which can rob such words of all significance and distil from such apparently trivial occurrences as a cricket match, a night at a theatre, an unexpected five-pound note, essences of strength and purity. Looking at the particular old man to whom I spoke, the conviction grew on me that *this* was reality for him, this ground, this score-board and these slim, yellow stumps, and that he would carry out with him into the darkness, not the recollection of a woman's lips against his own or of the laboured, weakening breath of a child, but rather of Richardson walking back to begin his run or of Hobbs lifting his cap after completing his century.

All this has little to do with the Surrey and Cambridge match, but it has, I hope, something to do with the Oval and with the peculiar atmosphere of earnestness which impregnates the ground.

Cricket on the Ice

E. V. LUCAS

E. V. Lucas was a prolific writer and essayist on cricket.
From *Willow and Leather* (1898).

EARLY IN 1891, during the very hard frost that then gripped the country, cricket on the ice was played in various parts of Sussex – at Horsted Keynes, at Cuckfield, and at Sheffield Park. The Sheffield Park match is historic by reason of the inclusion of several county players.

The precise date of the Sheffield Park match was January 17th, and the two captains were Harry Phillips, the old Sussex wicket-keeper, and G. H. Lynn, a local cricketer well known in East Sussex. Phillips won the toss and decided to bat. There was a little chaff at this. 'You should put them in, Phil,' said one, 'the wicket's so wet.' 'Don't bat, Phil,' cried another, 'it's simply a mass of water!' But the little man laughed and had his way. Two other Sussex veterans – Walter Humphreys, the lob bowler, and Jesse Hide – were chosen to open the batting, and amid cheers they slithered to the wicket. Stubberfield, an old Sussex professional of an earlier period, umpired, majestic with a birch broom, and a bunch of red flannel round his right foot. The fieldsmen were distributed pretty much as they liked. Only three or four were on skates.

'Play, play, play!' cried Stubber (as he is familiarly called) at half-past twelve, and George Bean sent down the first ball. Bean was almost as much at home on the ice as on the grass, and bowled with his usual delivery; but W. Payne, at the other end, put in cautious lobs. Jesse Hide, who had swathed his boots in sacking, had the appearance of a gouty giant. The first ball was taken by Butt at the wicket; the next shot by, and was missed by long-stop. One run was scored. There should have been a couple, only Walter Humphreys was slipping about on his heels and shouting, 'No, no! I can't turn.' It was a pitifully truthful statement: on the ice a booted runner cannot turn. The third ball sent Humphreys' bat to square-leg; the fourth just eluded Butt's fingers, so that the reach over-balanced him and he ingloriously fell; and the fifth was cut to the boundary for two. Then Jesse Hide had another try. Everyone has heard his stentorian 'Go back!' on county grounds; on the ice he cried ten times louder. Only he did not there call 'Go back!' for it is useless, but 'Come on!' He made some good hits, including one for four, before he was run out. Walter Humphreys was run out too.

Charlwood and Clark took their places, and the former showed really capital style. Bean won two-thirds of a hat by bowling Clark and Bailey with successive balls. Clark had made four, and Bailey strode in intending at least to equal that score. He stood, bat in hand, on the treacherous crease, and waited for the ball. It came. There was a loud rattle, and all three stumps and the block of wood they were fixed in were seen scooting away in the direction of Tunbridge Wells. Bailey was out. A. Payne then joined Charlwood, and they collared the bowling entirely, and gave their opponents plenty of healthy exercise. One man in particular was made busy. There was a dogged perverseness about him that seemed to encourage the batsmen. While others of his colleagues were thankful if they could stop and return the ball on their feet, he seemed to be saddened if he kept upright. He was faithful to the notion that the best fielding is done on the back of the head. Perhaps he once saw Mr Royle field that way. Anyhow, he put his principles into practice, and must have done a mile at least on the back of his head during the game. In whatever part of the lake you might be you would be sure to hear a dull thud every few minutes, followed by a peal of laughter. It was his head. Other fieldsmen were not much less unlucky. Once, a very tempting catch was sent to mid-on. He forgot all about his skates and leaped high into the air to grab the ball, with his right hand high up. He failed to reach it, and then began to come down again. He came down flat.

When Charlwood had made 30 and A. Payne 33, they retired. Osborne, who followed, did not stay very long; and then Watson and the captain were together. Now, when Harry Phillips was on his feet, he batted excellently, showing, in fact, some of the form that so electrified the Australians in 1884; but – the pity of it! – he was hardly on his feet at all. It is no exaggeration to say that of the twenty minutes he was in he spent five on his stomach, five on his back, and three on his knees. Harry was one of the few players who wore skates, and though he could skuttle as well as anyone there, he could not pirouette. Cricket on ice demands pirouetting. Watson was only a little better. Yet, in spite of their falls and flounderings, Butt could not put down their wickets. One exciting series of overthrows ended in a tableau that everybody present must regret was not photographed. Phillips, on his hands and knees, two yards from the wickets, was tearing away at the yielding surface of the ice with his nails, trying in vain to get some purchase; he had flung his bat away long before. Butt, two yards behind the wickets, spread out as though he had been rolled, was also wriggling. Harry Phillips got in first.

When Watson's score was 9 and the captain's 5, and the total 109, exclusive of extras (which, after having run into four figures, had been disregarded by the scorers), for seven wickets, the bell rang for luncheon; and forty sportsmen ran up the hill to the Pavilion filled with as fine a hunger as ever fell to the lot of man.

In winter, with the thermometer registering ten degrees of frost, a cricket lunch is a more serious enterprise than the summer's hasty 'cold collation'. Hence it was half-past three before the teams were again in the 'field', and what little light there remained was needed for a photograph. So cricket was stopped for the day, and the match was never played out. The score of Phillips's side (irrespective of uncountable extras) read:

W. Humphreys, run out	5
J. Hide, run out	14
Charlwood, retired	30
Clark, b Bean	4
Bailey, b Bean	0
A. Payne, retired	33

Osborne, b Bean 9
H. Phillips (captain), not out . . 5
Watson, not out 9

TOTAL (for seven wickets) . . . 109

Major Markwick and H. Christ did not bat.

G. H. Lynn (captain), G. Bean, W. Payne, H. Butt, W. Quaife, W. G. Quaife, Skinner, Kellow, J. Gilbert, Maplesden, T. Christmas, H. Webber, and Hounsell.

The match, though cut short, had, however, progressed sufficiently far to enable the observer to note the following points of difference between the winter and the summer game:

In summer, the fieldsmen pick up a ball as it rolls; in winter, they wait till the ball stops, which may be a matter of minutes, and then describe an arc round it, and pick it up at the finish of the curve.

In summer, they throw it in as they run; in winter, they sit down first.

In summer, when a man is out the fieldsmen exchange catches; in winter they cut figures of eight or make an excursion down the pond.

In summer, the bowlers take a run before making their attack; in winter, they stand as still as possible, press their knees together, and thank Heaven if they can get rid of the ball without falling.

In summer, the umpires, wearing white coats, walk sedately to their places; in winter, wearing ulsters, they slide thither.

In summer, the umpires do not carry spirituous liquors in stone jars.

In summer, the cricketers leave their pipes in the Pavilion; in winter, they puff at them as they play.

In summer, the batsmen, in running, just touch the popping crease with the tip of their bats and hurry back again; in winter, they shoot a dozen yards past the bowling crease, beat the ice with their feet, wave their arms round their heads, plunge their bodies backwards and forwards, and then start for the other wicket.

In summer, a man sometimes is caught out.

It will be seen that cricket on the ice is more exciting than cricket on the turf.

Cricket in the Backblocks

COLIN IMRAY

This match took place in the 1920s in Malaysia, where Colin Imray
and his colleagues were working in the cigarette distribution business.
Cricket in the Backblocks was published in 1998.

~

WE LEARNT THAT an actual match threatened. It was to be on Saturday – it was now Tuesday – between Kota Bahru and The Gentlemen of the Ulu (Jungle). It was to be played near a place called Kuala Krai, about 20 or 30 miles from Kota Bahru, because this would be more suitable for the Ulus, who would be mainly rubber planters, prospectors and tin miners. It was clear that Aubrey had everything in hand. If I had time he would run me out before the big day, as he wanted to make sure that the ground was in order.

[…] Aubrey and I had our 'run out' to Kuala Krai. This entailed bouncing and grinding along a very rough jungle track in Aubrey's specially reinforced vehicle.

Eventually we came to a saucer-shaped hollow surrounded by virgin jungle that was being worked on by a posse of prisoners from the Kota Bahru gaol. Every now and then one of the guards would fire a shot from his rifle in order to scare off any wild animals that might be around. All kinds of creatures were said to live in these jungles.

Some of these prisoners were at work digging out tree stumps; others were disconsolately dragging a mat backwards and forwards along a flattish piece in the middle at the bottom of the saucer. This was to duty as the pitch, and Aubrey said it would be all right on the day.

It was now Friday, and the match was to be on the morrow. I felt a little dubious, but who was I to express an opinion? How did Aubrey manage to communicate with these remote Ulus, I wanted to know, as the telephone system, where it existed, was very rudimentary. 'Oh, that's quite easy,' said Aubrey, 'we do it by runner.'

Saturday morning dawned, and it was raining. At breakfast Gerald said, 'Oh God, poor Aubrey. I do hope it clears.' Eventually, the rain did stop, and when we repaired to Aubrey, there he was with all the gear and an umbrella, looking anxiously at the skies.

'Looks like a sticky wicket,' he said. 'Can't make up my mind what to do if I win the toss.' He had hired a van to convey the Kota Bahrus, and we were introduced to Aubrey's henchman, a European foreman of the Public Works Department who was also at that time warden of the local gaol.

Our team included a couple of Indians, two Chinese – one of them a big fat *towkay* – a Dutch sailor who had been left behind by his ship while in a drunken stupor, Aubrey's Goanese clerk to umpire at one end and a senior schoolgirl to do likewise at the other. There was another schoolgirl to do the scoring. At his wits' end to complete the XI, Aubrey had brought in a prison warder and a 'good' prisoner. The arrival of Gerald and myself had been a godsend. Another prisoner, categorized as 'semi-good', whom Aubrey had been coaching, would be the 12th man.

We left in convoy with Aubrey, Gerald and I, plus the gear in Aubrey's vehicle. We slithered and slid along the track and eventually arrived safe and sound at Krai.

The rain had kept off. The Ulus, less Mike Moran who was to captain the side, were all assembled – which says much for Aubrey's 'runner' system – and they were just as motley a lot as the rest of us. Few of them knew anything about cricket, and if they had known anything once, they'd forgotten it.

Aubrey was the only one on either side who was properly attired in whites, and there he was wearing his English club blazer and cap.

'Where's Moran?' asked Aubrey. Nobody seemed to know, and we had to start without him. Aubrey won the toss and decided to bat. 'Tricky decision to have to make,' he said.

He and I opened the innings and had already made quite a few runs on this very 'dodgy' wicket of Aubrey's, against bowling that – to say the least – lacked practice.

Then Moran arrived, late but unapologetic.

He started to bowl and the picture changed abruptly. On that unpredictable wicket his fast bowling was lethal. I was soon bowled neck and crop, and Aubrey received one in a tender place and had to be helped to the sidelines, where Halowe, who had arrived with Moran, was 'helping' the Chinese schoolgirl do the scoring.

Under Moran's ruthless attack we Kota Bahrus wilted and collapsed and the Ulus took new heart. Only a tail-end Indian in our line-up offered any further resistance. With bat flailing like a scythe, he somehow connected time and again and amassed 20 or so valuable runs, surviving two obvious run-outs when the schoolgirl umpire was looking the other way and conducting a sign-language conversation with her girl friend with the score sheet.

Aubrey wasn't the only casualty. Moran himself fell over in surprise and pummelled the ground as if in a fit after our lady umpire – put up to it by one of the close fielders – screamed in her high-pitched girlish voice 'Nar baall!' raising her right arm, as she had been instructed. But the demon bowler recovered from the indignity and wrought yet more havoc.

The *towkay* got one in the mouth, and after we'd had at least one more 'retired hurt' the last two Kota Bahrus refused to face the massacre, and we ended the innings with some 80 runs for 8 wickets.

In the meantime, the walking (or sitting) wounded had been joined by an Ulu who, fielding on the boundary, tripped over a tree stump, sat down heavily on some nasty spiked stuff, and was out of action.

Moran and a rubber planter who had once played for his school opened the Ulu batting, and I was deputed to bowl. The 'good' prisoner who, coached by Aubrey in the prison yard, had shown some aptitude, was to bowl at the other end. Aubrey, perforce, was still nursing his injury on the sideline.

Moran had clearly batted before. For a couple of overs, he played carefully, though nearly bowled by the 'good' prisoner from one that shot along the ground after hitting a bump. The 'good' prisoner's bowling action – be it noted – looked suspiciously like a throw.

Then Moran once again started to show his mettle. Leaping down the pitch to ball after ball, he let fly with straight and cover drives for four and six, deft flicks to fine leg, smashes to midwicket and deep square and just about all other points of the compass. We could do nothing with him.

Once, when he stood at the bowler's end and I waited for the ball to be thrown at me, Moran rubbed salt in the wound by asking me if I had any special reason for bowling to him without an extra cover. In fact, Gerald had reorganized the field in a moment of panic and left me naked, as it were.

There was one occasion when he might have been out. He skied one off my bowling and Gerald, fielding on the boundary at jungle-edge midwicket, judged it perfectly, but he was off-balance and his outstretched hands were not quite in the right place. The ball hit him on the shoulder and he too had to retire.

Then our keeper, the Dutch sailor, became difficult. Moran had stepped way out of the crease and missed the ball but our keeper failed to stump him. Here was a gift run-out, with Moran yards out of his crease, but the Dutchman just stood there and stared. Not to put too fine a point on it, he had no idea what to do as the ball was returned to him hard and low, and the lucky Moran was at least two yards from home.

Jim, the Foreman of Works, shouted, 'You stupid bastard.' With that the Dutchman cursed in his native tongue and kicked down the stumps. Aubrey was not amused.

However, we settled down to it again, but spent much time searching for the ball, dispatched into the jungle by Moran, who by now had his eye in and was having a field day.

Inevitably there came a time when we couldn't find the ball and reluctantly Aubrey produced his spare. When, shortly afterwards, that one was lost too, Aubrey saw his opportunity to save face. The opposition were two short of the modest target we had set without loss, but he pointed out that he'd started the match with two balls but both had been lost in the rough, and clearly the match could not be completed. It would have to end in a draw.

I remember that when we were searching for the second ball Moran said chattily, 'Look, paw marks: a tigress and her cub, and fresh too.'

There was in fact a certain altercation about who had really won – despite Aubrey's settling for a draw. The Ulus said that with Moran in full blast, the result was a foregone conclusion, but Aubrey insisted that the laws of cricket are the laws of cricket, and there the matter ended.

We were not quite finished, however.

As we were de-bussing at Kota Bahru, the Dutchman who had evidently been brooding, said to Jim the Foreman, 'You call me bastard, eh? Take that.' And without more ado he landed a punch that would have done credit to 'Gentleman' Jackson. Our Jim collapsed like a house of cards. Aubrey, whom I had expected to treat the matter as a grave breach of discipline, to say nothing of cricket etiquette, said, 'Perhaps we'd better leave and let them get on with it.'

&

Diary of a Cricket Lover

VERNON COLEMAN

Vernon Coleman is a former GP and author of over a hundred books.
This *Diary* appeared in 1984.

∾

SATURDAY 19TH MAY

MY PARENTS HAVE a holiday flat on the seafront at Budleigh Salterton, down in Devon, and I arrived here two days ago to work on a newspaper article that needed finishing quickly. With the typescript safely completed, Sue and I set off along the seafront for a gentle Saturday afternoon stroll. It is some time since I last came to Budleigh but it is still the most peaceful and relaxing of seaside villages. It is remarkable that such an exquisite resort should have succeeded in remaining so unspoilt. There are a good number of retired residents (the average age of the local voters must be nearer sixty than forty) and the only thing that breaks the silence is the tap tap tap of walking sticks and the rubberised shuffle of walking frames. There are no gaudy amusement arcades, and no noisy transistor radios. Budleigh (and indeed the same is true of the neighbouring town of Exmouth) has succeeded in remaining aloof from the commercial excesses of the 1980s. It stands like an elegant lady from the 1920s, untouched by progress; within sight of the future but firmly embedded in the past; surviving in, but not becoming part of, the final decades of the twentieth century. There are wooden beach huts, plenty of comfortable wooden benches and fishing boats galore pulled up on the shingle beach, their nets spread out to dry. There is no sign here of those two ubiquitous and destructive twentieth-century evils: plastic and electricity.

We were walking quietly along the sea front when suddenly the cliff on the landward side sloped down to ground level and there, some quarter of a mile out of the town, nestling on what looked like a reclaimed patch of estuary land, lay one of the most beautiful cricket grounds I have ever seen. The match, I found out, was a Devon League fixture between Budleigh Salterton 2nd XI and the Chudleigh 2nd XI, and although there were no spectators that I could see (there were, of course, a number of ladies busily occupied inside the pavilion doing things with plates and knives and, undoubtedly, mountains of Devon clotted cream, scones and strawberry jam), the teams were perfectly turned out. The batsmen had whiter shoes and pads than a good many professionals I have seen.

We walked slowly round the ground and watched a few overs. It was marvellous stuff, the very meat of English village cricket, enthusiastic and determined, but good-tempered and companionable. The second eleven players were trying harder than many professionals but doing so without ever forgetting the nature of the game. The fielders chased each ball as though their lives depended on it, but found time to congratulate the batsmen who had inspired their breathlessness.

It was a true example of English village cricket at its very best: teenagers, one boy and one girl, were doing the scoring; the groundsman's tractor, mower, heavy motorised roller and two smaller rollers were parked neatly near a storage shed; the green-and white-painted pavilion (with green flag with golden otter proudly flying from the roof) still smelled of fresh paint; and the silence was broken only by the sound of birds singing, and the cries of cricketers at play (a splendid change from blaring car horns, banging tins, and mindless chants from senseless and prejudiced spectators). To the left, there lay a still river, its surface opaque with algae, and behind the ground a small, muddy brook. And a couple of hundred yards in front there lay the western edges of the English Channel.

Those of us who love cricket and watch it on the big city grounds sometimes forget that this is where it all started, that this is what cricket is all about, that whatever they may do at Lords [*sic*] or at Trent Bridge, at Melbourne or at Barbados, it will never ever be as important as what happens on elegant village greens in the Budleigh Saltertons of England.

4

THE TOOLS OF THE TRADE

April

R. C. ROBERTSON-GLASGOW

After playing first-class cricket from 1920 to 1937, R. C. Robertson-Glasgow became a cricket correspondent and author. From *More Cricket Prints* (1948).

THIS IS THE time of year when the sentimental cricketer withdraws his bat tenderly from its winter bed and croons over it, as if it were a Stradivarius or a shoulder of mutton.

If he is doing the thing properly, he allows the immaculate blade to wave him back on the zephyrs of memory, and of exaggeration, to that 50 which he would have scored, had not his partner fallen to a slow full-pitcher. He may even lock the door, put on his favourite club-cap, and go through those strokes with which, but for his partner's futility, he would have won a famous victory. If he be a bowler, and nothing but, he will pass his fingers contentedly down the bat's edge and say: 'This one bisected the slips and flew, like a scalded cat, to the boundary; that one was the off-drive which found fine-leg so fast asleep.'

Such delights are not for me; for I have no bat. The best bats that I ever had have been other people's, returnable after use. It was always so. In earliest days at school I had a bat that was lovely to look upon; the grain was straight, not rudely broad nor miserably close; the blade was knotless, and I never oiled the splice. But it didn't work at all. It remained, like the sea-sirens, a beautiful and deadly ornament.

Years passed. I still bought a bat once in a while. I even lifted it, in response to the vendor's request that I should feel 'how well it comes up'; then I wrote my name on the back. I was using one such purchase in a match of some importance at Lord's when Tom Lowry, at short-leg, inquired: 'Tell me, do you buy your bats at Hamley's, or leave them in water overnight?'

Thenceforward I settled to borrowing. I studied the art inside-out. I came to know that batsmen who have made 0, especially l.b.w., do not lend with simplicity. I learnt that bats in oilskin are untouchable; that those in cloth cases may be won by judicious wooing; that those left standing in dim corners of the dressing-room are legal prey.

Then, one day in August, having brought off a successful touch of an expansive major of Artillery, I made what was, for me, a long score. The same thing happened in the second innings; and the owner offered me the bat; a generosity the more remarkable as he had just made 2 with his second-best. I am glad to remember that I kept my head. 'No, no,' I said, with profuse but fearful thanks; 'keep your bat. For, once it is my own, it will turn to an alloy of teak and tin.' He kept it.

So I shall not be withdrawing my bat tenderly from its winter bed. But already I am looking round for a cheerful lender.

Bat and Ball

W. J. LEWIS

From *The Language of Cricket* (1934), a lexicon of cricket terms.

BAT. The implement with which a batsman strikes the ball in the endeavour to make runs, and guards his wicket against the 'attack' of the bowler. The blade, pod, or striking part of a bat, about 22 in. in length and 4¼ in. in width, with a convex back and flattish face or striking surface, is shaped from a block of willow-wood. The handle, about 12½ in. in length, is spliced into the top end, between the shoulders of the blade, rounded, and bound round with twine. A handle is now usually made up of slips of cane glued together, with strips of whalebone and rubber inserted to lessen the sting caused by the impact of the ball on the blade of the bat. A *match bat* is one of superior quality for match-play, complying strictly with the Law specifying its dimensions. A *practice bat* is one suitable for use at practice. A *Harrow bat* is a smaller sized bat for a youth. Formerly, when the ball was bowled along the ground and was not pitched up to the batsman, the bat was a thick crooked stick or club, the blade being a curved pod, without projecting shoulders, turning outwards at the bottom. By the end of the eighteenth century, owing to the change in the style of bowling, the bat had come to resemble its present shape with a flattish straight blade, and with shoulders.

BALL. A solid ball composed of cork parings and fine twine wound tightly round a cube of cork and covered with leather, with which a bowler endeavours to dismiss a batsman, primarily by bowling down his wicket. A *match ball* is one of superior quality for match-play, of the size and weight specified in the Laws.

Felix on the Bat

NICHOLAS FELIX

Nicholas Felix (real surname Wanostrocht) was a famous nineteenth-century
cricketer. *Felix on the Bat* was published in 1845.

❧

As the greatest possible freedom of limb is necessary to the
accomplishment of a good Cricketer, so it is essential that we study a
little the dress. I propose, therefore, to devote this Chapter to the consideration
of those things, with which it is as well to be supplied, viz. bats, balls, stumps,
net, shoes, gloves, paddings, flannel vests, etc. etc.

Constitutions differ in most men. Climate and the ordinary customs
and exercises regulate the dress and costumes of most nations. In our sports,
each seems to have appropriated for itself the dress most suitable for the
required exercise. The huntsman, the sportsman, the Cricketer, and all who
engage in any of the athletic exercises where much activity is required, have
the appropriate uniforms, not without a due regard to comfort. The neglect
of these matters has often exposed the precipitate and hardy youth to the
dangerous consequences attending the great changes to which we are subject
in this unsettled climate. I may be excused, therefore, if I am a little particular
upon this head.

In the first place, I strongly recommend a cap made of chequered
woollen: it is light and cool to the head, absorbs perspiration, and (which is
not an insignificant fact) is not likely to blow off and hit the wicket. An under
flannel vest, or thin Jersey, I hold to be exceedingly useful in preventing the
too fast evaporation of the heat of the body. For the same reason, a cotton shirt
is better than a linen one; but the sleeves being large, many a man has lost
his wicket by the ball glancing off the folds; to say nothing of the annoying
decisions of careless umpires, and even of those who are ever watchful to do
their duty with the strictest regard to honesty. The best plan is to have a Jersey
not too tight a fit, with a shirt collar made to button on the top. A cotton
neck cloth may not look quite so dressy, but it is much better than a silk one,
because silk is a non-conductor of heat, and does not absorb perspiration. The
attention to this last-named fact is really worth your strictest regard. There
is all the difference between carelessness and prudence; and although, in my

recommendations of dress, I do not wish to be understood as giving directions for the proper cultivation of hot-house plants, yet without a due regard to the above considerations of health, your enjoyment in this exercise will be greatly curtailed, if not wholly suppressed.

The trousers should be made of flannel, well shrunk before it is made up, having six loops round the waistband, through which an Indian-rubber belt may pass, and help to do the duty of braces, which must be exploded whilst in the active exercise of hitting. Any socks or stockings are better than silk or cotton. Worsted is soft to the feet and less liable to chafe.

Take care to have the spikes of your shoes put in properly. The two under the bend of the foot should be nearer the top of the sole than is now the custom to put them, and the one in advance should be between and close under the division of the first and second toes. A grand secret of comfort is to have spikes put into shoes which you have worn for some time.

Always, whether at practice or whilst engaged in matches, wear paddings; for the uncertainty and the irregularity of the present system of throwing bowling is something dangerous; and one violent blow in the beginning of the season may incapacitate or discourage you for the rest of the year. False pride will actuate many to discard this means of preventing pain; but this pseudo fortitude will pay dearly for its obstinacy. The padding which I recommend as most becoming in its appearance, and most effective in its intentions, is to have longitudinal sockets, made (inside the leg of the trousers) of linen, half an inch apart, extending from two inches above the knee-pan down to the lower part of the trousers. Long slips of Indian rubber, half an inch thick, can always be inserted therein, and taken out as they go or come from the wash. And here let me strongly urge that your practice be conducted as much like match-playing as possible. Heedless hitting off careless bowling is worse than no practice at all; it is like shutting your eyes at Billiards, and hitting hard for the chances of the table. Lest I should not be rightly understood about the directions for the trousers, those of the right-handed hitter would require the sockets to be placed so as to defend the outside of the knee-pan of the left leg, the calf and outward ankle-bone, the inside of the knee-pan of the right leg, the shin-bone and the inner ankle. The trousers of the left-handed hitter would of course require the opposite to this.

Provide yourself with a box large enough to contain two bats, two or three balls, stumps and a complete change of dress. It should have a small till-box, to hold your watch and jewellery. And do not forget to have a phial of sweet oil at hand: of all the things that I have ever used, this has been the best. Some rub the bruise with vinegar and brandy; others use the first thing that comes to hand; but oil, oil is the 'sovereign'st thing on earth for an outward bruise'.

The way to ensure good practice is to hire professional bowlers, or club together and get a Catapulta, the nature and description of which I shall give in the latter part of this work. The way to secure much practice off either is to procure a large net, about twenty yards long, and six feet in height, strong enough to resist a powerful blow. It will save expense, time, and trouble. If you employ a professional bowler, it is encouraging to him to put some little trifle on the wicket (not too much, not too little), which, in addition to his pay, he is to have as often as he knocks it down. It is astonishing what good effect this little inducement will have with him as well as with yourself.

In taking leave of this part of my subject, I have only to say, that all these matters of equipment are to be obtained in the best possible style from Mr. Dark, of Lord's Cricket Ground, Marylebone; and of Mr. W. Caldecourt, Townsend Road, Marylebone, of whom also may be had the Catapulta, price 11*l*. 11*s* complete with the latest improvements.

Cricket in Denmark

P. C. G. LABOUCHERE, T. A. J. PROVIS AND
PETER S. HARGREAVES

From *The Story of Continental Cricket* (1969), with a foreword by Colin Cowdrey.

~&

JUST PRIOR TO the outbreak of war Danish cricket was in a comfortably flourishing position. The game was well-organized throughout the country: the standard of play was improving. Then came the German invasion, and the subsequent occupation of the country by German troops, in April, 1940. At the beginning, the Nazi Rosenberg doctrine of Nordic unity gave a semblance of mildness to the Occupation, but as the Danes showed less and less liking for the idea of collaboration, and acts of sabotage increased, so did the German rule strengthen its severity.

It would serve no purpose to enlarge upon the travel restrictions, curfew laws, the orders against assembly in groups, reprisals, arrests, and the remainder of the regulations designed to tame the occupied nation; but it is a remarkable fact that through it all cricket continued to be played in local tournaments and in friendly matches. Perhaps it was because cricket had always been regarded as a particularly English game, and the playing of it could be regarded as an act of semi-overt resistance. A great spirit of comradeship came into being during these war years, and today, a generation after the end of the war, many of the teams who played then are still together, playing friendly matches at an age when most have ceased their active interest in the game. In Jutland Axel Morild is the centre of the activities embodied in the Danish Forty Club, whilst in Copenhagen these move around the person of Carolo Ryhøj.

Yet with the best will in the world it is not possible to play cricket without the necessary equipment of bat and ball. All cricket gear had previously been imported from England, and this avenue was now effectively closed. Despite the greatest of care in the treatment of bats and balls the situation was close to catastrophe when an ordinary cricketer, Frederik Ferslev, took a hand in the game.

Ferslev was not a leader in the game, nor did he hold any official position, but his name deserves to be known and respected throughout the cricketing world. No cricketer anywhere can have exhibited such stubbornness and determination in the pursuit of his object – to keep the game alive in his country in the face of war, restrictions and difficulties of every kind. In the pursuit of his aim he must – in the eyes of the occupying power – have earned a sentence to the concentration camp – the equivalent for most of a death penalty – many times over. His photograph may be found in the records of the K.B. club as a member of the junior eleven of 1896 – a bright, intelligent-faced little boy with a firm jaw; he stands third from the left with his cap on the back of his head and a vaguely 'let-em-all-come' air about him.

Let him tell the story himself, as nearly as possible.

'My business, which was mainly based on imports from England, stopped completely when the country was invaded . . . and at the A.B. ground one day I was told that they were running short of bats. . . . I decided to try to fill the gap myself. . . . The biggest problem at the start was the finding of a suitable wood. Somehow I had got the idea that bats were made of silver poplar, and I visited many timber merchants, hunting for this wood. Only a few stocked poplar, however, and none of these knew whether what they had was silver poplar or not. They said – nobody ever asks us *that* question!

'The first bat I made was a laminate of two woods, the face being made of ⅜ in. ash and the back of pine to keep down the weight. I found out very quickly that ash is no good for cricket bats – the hardest drive moved the ball no more than twenty or thirty yards.

'My next bat was made of poplar, and although this wood was not good for the purpose the A.B. club asked for ten of them, and they were used throughout the 1943 season. The shape and size was exactly as the English bat, but the weight was not quite right, the bats being too heavy and the wood too soft. It was very difficult to bring a bat down below 2 lb. 6 oz. in weight. One of the Copenhagen sports equipment suppliers, F.I.B., got wind of what I was doing, and I made a further supply of the poplar bats which were distributed to other parts of the country through this firm.

'I had borrowed a number of old copies of *The Cricketer* to see if any of them contained information on bat-making, and here I had a stroke of luck. In an old copy from 1931, I found an article on the subject, and from this I learnt for the first time that bats are made of willow. More particularly from the wood of a tree known as *salix coerulea*, a cross between *salix alba* and *salix fragilis*. *Salix coerulea* was known as "the true cricket-bat willow", and grew, I read, particularly in Essex. Essex was a long way away in those days. I also learnt that the tree is felled at the age of eighteen years and split immediately into bat-lengths – clefts – which are then piled in the open air for a period of eighteen months, after which they are ready for use. The face of the bat has to be hardened by pressing, and the edges beaten or hammered to strengthen them.

'The problem now, which caused me many sleepless nights, was how to find the right wood, and how to press the face and edges of the bats when I had them made.

'First things first. Through a member of my family I was put in touch with Dr. agro. C. Syrach Larsen, who turned out to be the very man I needed. He knew everything there was to know about the willow trees of Denmark, and was able to tell me that the forester in the Gaunø-Lindersvold district had been visited *32 years previously* by a Scottish colleague who had recommended that he plant *salix coerulea* in a part of the woods which was peculiarly suited to it. On his return to Scotland he had sent seedlings to Denmark, and these were planted in the recommended spot, close to water. These were the only *salix coerulea* known to be in Denmark.

'I got in touch with the forester, Mr. Muus, who confirmed that he had about twenty *coerulea* standing in his district, and was willing to let me have two of them, but since they should properly be felled in January and it was now May, this would have meant my waiting eight months for the trees to be felled and a further 18 months for weathering. Over two years.

'I could not wait so long. A return to the article in *The Cricketer* told me that *salix alba* had been used for bats before the *coerulea* cross. This was, I thought, a fairly common type of willow in Denmark, but despite a search all over Copenhagen I found no timber merchant with a stock of it. I advertised in the newspapers and in the forestry paper, but with no result. I wrote to timber merchants on the island of Bornholm, far out in the Baltic, and one of them had had *alba* in stock until two weeks before my letter had arrived. It had been used to make herring boxes!

'Finally, when I was nearing desperation, I found a timber merchant on the island of Amager who was holding a stock of willow – of what kind he did not know. He could supply me with 2½ in. and 3 in. planks, just the thickness I needed.

'I had wood, but how was I to get a press made? This was an even greater problem than obtaining the wood, since every firm or workshop in Denmark, now in 1943, was under German control. I could never get a permit to have one made – it could only be done illegally. If anyone could be found to take the risk.

'But first of all, I had no idea how such a press should be constructed or how it should work. I got in touch with several machine-shops, and even with the Institute of Technology, but with no positive result. I lost many a night's sleep over this problem, but suddenly the answer came to me, and on rising I made a quick sketch of a machine which I thought might work. Then I hit on a good idea. I got in touch with Peter Petersen who had been one of the K.B. club's best batsmen around 1904. Peter was a civil engineer at the large Titan A/S engineering works and might be able to help me. I had found the right man! Peter Petersen not only helped me to make the working drawings for my machine, but somehow got permission from the Titan management for the press to be made at their Copenhagen factory.

[. . .] 'At the beginning of November, 1943, the press was ready, and I had the problem of mounting it solidly. According to my calculations it would exert a pressure of some ninety tons. I had had a test made with a spindle press exerting a pressure of ten tons, but this had only compressed the wood 1 mm. I got my press mounted, and as far as I could judge, had the right hardness. I fitted an old handle into the "V" and my first pressed willow blade was an accomplished fact.'

Mr. Ferslev now goes on to tell how his stocks of willow begin to run short, and how he manages to get two willow trees felled on the Copenhagen Common, and transported to the A.B. club ground where they are split and piled. The trees are over thirty years old, and since the wood is needed quickly, forced weathering and drying has to be used. Despite this the bats are found to be quite good in use. Now a new problem arises. . . .

'Old handles were running short, and cane for new handles was my next problem. None of the importers had any left, but finally, at the shop of a basket-maker I found some and was able to persuade the proprietor, Mr. Wengler, to reserve his entire stock for me. The handle of a cricket bat is made of from nine to sixteen pieces of cane, all of which have to be shaped, and it was no inconsiderable task which I had taken upon my shoulders to manufacture these. Over a thousand pieces of cane had to be shaped, bonded and turned – and all by hand. Thread for binding the handles was terribly difficult to obtain, and all I could find was two-strand hemp, which was not very suitable for the job. This was strictly rationed, and for weeks I queued up all over Copenhagen to get enough for my handles. I dyed the thread, but it became very fuzzy and had to be waxed. Beeswax was also rationed – even more strictly than thread – and again I went the rounds, this time of the Copenhagen shoemakers, who were most unwilling to part with even a small part of their hoarded stock.

'In May I was able to supply the F.I.B. people with my first consignment of bats of one hundred per cent Danish manufacture, and throughout May and June I was unbelievably busy, re-blading, re-handling, pegging and binding old bats.'

After the war Mr. Ferslev was asked if he had made a lot of money out of his monopoly in cricket bats during the war. To which he replied:

'I wouldn't call it a lucrative business, but I got a great deal of pleasure out of the actual work – I had never worked with my hands before – and I had the satisfaction of doing something towards keeping cricket alive during the years when we were out of touch with England.'

Before the end of the war Mr. Ferslev had also managed to get a press made for the manufacture of balls, and had made them good enough to stand up to a hammering of 400 runs, in August, 1944, without losing shape. In February, 1945, two *coerulea* were purchased from Mr. Muus, and transported by devious means, and at considerable cost, to Copenhagen, but in March, 1945, Mr. Ferslev became seriously ill, and to his great disappointment was unable personally to manufacture bats from 'the true cricket willow'. In May, 1945, the war ended.

A Jammy Bastard

MARCUS TRESCOTHICK

Marcus Trescothick made his debut for Somerset in 1993 and played seventy-six Tests for England between 2000 and 2006. From *Coming Back to Me* (2008).

❦

WHEN I TURNED up at pre-season training in 1993 I was ready in my own mind to take the next step, hoping that my chance would come soon and confident I would be big enough to take it.

And the kit. Oh Lord, the kit. If ever someone asked me to go on *Desert Island Discs*, if I managed to get past the title of the programme, as well as the complete works of Eminem to listen to there would be no question of my luxury item. It would be a spanking new kit catalogue stuffed page after beautiful page full of brand new kit. From a very young age my idea of paradise on earth on a rainy day was to pore over the pages of the latest catalogues revealing all the joys of this year's new kit; bats, pads, gloves, inners, boots, sweaters, shirts, boxes, arm-guards, thigh-pads; I adored them all, especially anything worn by Graeme Hick, whose batting I found inspirational to watch.

I was already obsessed by bats, to the extent that if anyone in the dressing-room wanted a couple of millimetres shaved off the bottom, or a new rubber grip put on the handle, I took it upon myself to do the job. And even if they didn't want me to, I'd do it anyway. Anything to do with bats and bat care, I was the expert, and that has never changed. Call me Doctor Blade. Even at this age I told Iain Fletcher that when I retired from playing I wanted to be a bat-maker and I still might, at that. Fletcher reckons my behaviour was something between dedicated and obsessive compulsive; which incidentally would explain a lot of other things like my sausage-only diet and later, when it was time to try and get myself fit for England, the fact that you would have to blindfold, cuff and gag me to get me away from the gym.

For now, when I turned up at Taunton as winter was giving way to spring that year and saw wave after wave of new kit coming in, all this brand new stuff to ponce around in was bliss. The idea that I was going to be given it for free, rather than have to pay, as I had done until this point – quite frankly I couldn't think of anything more wonderful on God's green earth.

❦

Progress of Cricket

JOHN NYREN WITH CHARLES COWDEN CLARKE

John Nyren (1764–1837) was a cricketer and writer; William Ward was a prominent cricketer of the same era. From *The Cricketers of My Time* (1833).

❧

MR WARD OBLIGINGLY furnished me with a small MS., written some years since by an old cricketer, containing a few hasty recollections and rough hints to players, thrown together without regard to method or order. From the mass, I have been able to select a few portions, thinking that they might possess some interest with those of my readers who take a pride in the game.

From the authority before me, it appears that about 150 years since, it was the custom, as at present, to pitch the wickets at the same distance asunder, viz., twenty-two yards. That the stumps (only one foot high, and two feet* wide) were surmounted with a bail. At that period, however, another peculiarity in the game was in practice, and which it is worthwhile to record. Between the stumps a hole was cut in the ground, large enough to contain the ball and the butt-end of the bat. In running a notch, the striker was required to put his bat into this hole, instead of the modern practice of touching over the popping-crease. The wicket-keeper, in putting out the striker when running, was obliged, when the ball was thrown in, to place it in this hole before the adversary could reach it with his bat. Many severe injuries of the hands were the consequence of this regulation; the present mode of touching the popping-crease was therefore substituted for it. At the same period the wickets were increased to twenty-two inches in height, and six inches in breadth, and instead of the old custom of placing the ball in the hole, the wicket-keeper was required to put the wicket down, having the ball in his hand.

The following account of a match played in the year 1744 has been selected by the writer above mentioned, in order to show the state of play at that time. It arose from a challenge given by Lord John Sackville on the part of the County of Kent to play all England; and it proved to be a well-contested match, as will appear from the manner in which the players kept the field. The hitting, however, could neither have been of a high character, nor indeed

---

*There must be a mistake in this account of the *width* of the wicket – J.N safe, as may be gathered from the figure of the bat at that time; which was similar to an old-fashioned dinner-knife – curved at the back, and sweeping in the form of a volute at the front and end. With such a bat, the system must have been all for hitting; it would be barely possible to block: and when the practice of bowling length-balls was introduced and which gave the bowler so great an advantage in the game, it became absolutely necessary to change the form of the bat, in order that the striker might be able to keep pace with the improvement. It was therefore made straight in the pod; in consequence of which, a total revolution, it may be said a reformation too, ensued in the style of play.

[. . .] Some years after this, the fashion of the bat having been changed to a straight form, the system of stopping, or blocking, was adopted; when John Small, Sen., of Petersfield, in Hampshire, became signalised as the most eminent batsman of his day, being a very safe player, and a remarkably fine hitter: and Edward Stevens, or, as he was commonly called, Lumpy, was esteemed the best bowler.

About the years 1769 and 1770, the Hambledon Club, having had a run of ill success was on the eve of being dissolved. It had been hitherto supported by the most respectable gentlemen in that part of the county. They determined, however, once more to try their fortune, and on the 23rd of September 1771, having played the County of Surrey, at Laleham Burway, they beat them by one run. Out of fifty-one matches played by the same club against England, &c., during the ensuing ten years, they gained twenty-nine of the number.

Several years since (I do not recall the precise date) a player, named White, of Ryegate, brought a bat to a match, which being the width of the stumps, effectually defended his wicket from the bowler: and, in consequence, a law was passed limiting the future width of the bat to 4¼ inches.* Another law also decreed that the ball should not weigh less than 5½ oz., or more than 5¾ oz.

On the 22nd of May 1775, a match was played in the Artillery Ground, between five of the Hambledon Club, and five of all England; when Small went in the last man for fourteen runs, and fetched them. Lumpy was bowler upon the occasion; and it having been remarked that his balls had three

*I have a perfect recollection of this occurrence; also, that subsequently, an iron frame, of the statute width, was constructed for, and kept by the Hambledon Club; through which any bat of suspected dimensions was passed, and allowed or rejected accordingly – J.N.

several times passed between Small's stumps, it was considered to be a hard thing upon the bowler that his straightest balls should be thus sacrificed; the number of the stumps was in consequence increased from two to three. Many amateurs were of opinion at the time, that the alteration would tend to shorten the game: and subsequently, the Hampshire gentlemen did me the honour of taking my opinion upon this point. I agreed with them that it was but doing justice to the bowler; but I differed upon the question that it would shorten the game; because the striker, knowing the danger of missing one straight ball with three instead of two stumps behind him, would materially redouble his care; while every loose, hard hitter would learn to stop, and play as safe a game as possible. The following record of a match, played shortly afterwards between the Hambledon Club and All England, at Sevenoaks, will prove whether my opinion were well or ill founded.

It was upon this occasion that Aylward fetched the extraordinary number of 167 runs from his own bat; – one of the greatest feats upon record in the annals of cricket; for, it must be borne in mind, that his success did not arise from any loose playing or incompetence on the part of his opponents – there would then have been no merit in the triumph; but he had to stand against the finest bowling of the day – that of Lumpy.

The reader will not fail likewise to remark the difference of amount in the score between the first and second innings on the England side; the men were either disheartened at the towering pre-eminence of the adverse party; or, which is more probable, the latter, like good generals, would not throw away a single chance; but although the odds were so greatly in their favour, they, instead of relaxing, or showing any indifference, fielded with still greater care than in the first innings; and, in consequence, their opponents did not score half their previous number of runs. This is the genuine spirit of emulation.

Weights and Measures

R. C. ROBERTSON-GLASGOW

After playing first-class cricket from 1920 to 1937, R. C. Robertson-Glasgow became a cricket correspondent and author. From *Cricket Prints* (1943).

❧

WHAT HAS HAPPENED to those measuring-gauges which were such a feature of the cricket in an earlier generation?

The Laws of Cricket have been revised nineteen times in the last fifty-six years, yet how many know that the bat shall not exceed 4¼ inches at its widest part, or be more than 3 feet 2 inches in length?

To what mathematical research do we owe the decision that the ball shall weigh not less than 5½ oz. and not more than 5¾ oz.? That it shall measure not less than 8¹³⁄₁₆ in. or more than 9 in. in circumference? The ¹³⁄₁₆ths is an extraordinary refinement; a most baffling fraction; one that would have warmed the heart of A. G. MacDonell's famous professor of ballistics. How many, too, are aware that by Law 51 the umpire may not bet? The bald tyranny of this statement has always astonished me. No Act of Parliament has ever dared to say as much.

There are certain illegalities, indeed, that rarely come our way. I have never been present when the ground has been 'beaten' during unauthorised hours. I have never seen the breaking of Law 26, when either of the batsmen, 'under pretence of running, or otherwise', has wilfully prevented the ball from being caught. It is the 'otherwise' that I wish to see. A nice case of Obstruction would come very welcome just now in this sombre world of ours.

Research in the writings of the notable Mr. Ward, in about 1833, shows how the matter of the bat was settled. 'Several years since,' he writes, 'a player named White, of Ryegate, brought a bat to a match which, being the width of the stumps, effectually defended his wicket from the bowler, and in consequence a law was passed limiting the future width of the bat to 4¼ inches.' I should like to have that bat of the ingenious Mr. White. He continues: 'Another law also decreed that the ball should not weigh less than 5½ oz. or more than 5¾ oz.' Now, that may be; but we are still not informed to what experiment or mathematical premise we owe these precise weights.

Nyren only says: 'I have a perfect recollection of this occurrence.' A somewhat pompous evasion. He also recalls that an iron frame, or gauge, of the statute width was constructed for, and kept by, the Hambledon Club, 'through which any bat of suspected dimensions was passed, and allowed or rejected accordingly'. That, too, is long lost. Which is a pity; as it should lie side by side with Mr. White's bat, as a perpetual memento of the fate of those who are just too clever.

Mr. Ward was not only a fine cricketer, but he was a thinker. In the course of advice to captains he says: 'If you bring forward a fast bowler as a change, contrive, if fortune so favours you, that he shall bowl his first ball when a cloud is passing over, because as this trifling circumstance frequently affects the sight of the striker, you may thereby stand a good chance of getting him out.' We can picture a fast bowler, under Mr. Ward's astute captaincy, itching to go on, and being calmed by his leader's words: 'No, not yet, wait for the cloud.' This, perhaps, is fair enough; less creditable, though, is the counsel: 'Endeavour, by every means in your power – such as, by changing the bowling, by little alterations in the field, or by any excuse you can invent – to delay the time, that the strikers may become cold and inactive.' I doubt if Mr. Ward's precepts will quite squeeze through the moral gauge!

I often think that it was not merely the poor pitches that caused the scoring to be so low in those days; for concentration by the batsmen must have been weak, when his head was filled with ledger-calculations on his own bets, those of his team, the opposing team, and various influential spectators. Small wonder that, while his brain flitted round finance, his stumps were flattened. Sometimes a match would be sold both ways, and history tells us of a single-wicket match in which both cricketers meant to lose, and that each waited grimly for the accidentally straight, and fatal, ball.

Kent and London

HUGH BARTY-KING

Hugh Barty-King is a historian and writer on a diverse range of subjects.
From *Quilt Winders and Pod Shavers* (1979).

◈

IT WAS IN THIS year of 1884 that John Wisden died, a bachelor. With no son to inherit the business, it was bought by his manager Henry Luff. Ten years later Wisden's were selling Luff & Week's Patent 'Marvel' Ball at 7s 6d 'made on an entirely new principle, less hard than most balls while their flight and playing qualities are perfection'. Henry Luff had decided to go in for manufacturing himself. In 1896 he told Henry Edgar, a Wanstead vet who came to Cranbourn Street to buy one of Duke's well-known seven and sixpenny 'best' cricket balls, that for many years he had supplied nothing but Duke's and Dark's but two years ago Duke's were bad and Dark's very bad. He realised something had to be done about that, so started making cricket balls on his own account. In 1894, Luff told Edgar, it was a question of competition between himself and Duke; the following year he thought Duke would be left behind altogether.

Naturally Luff the retailer, now also a rival manufacturer to Duke, would feel obliged to push his own cricket balls at the expense of all others. Duke expected this and could have no objection to it so long as the competition was conducted fairly. But one day in 1896 James Phillips the Test umpire told the Penshurst firm that anyone who now asked at Wisden's London showroom for a no 1 'best' Duke ball (wholesale price 72s a dozen and retailing at 7s 6d each) was sold the inferior and cheaper no 4 ball (wholesale price 54s a dozen and retailing at 4s 6d or 5s each), and charged 7s 6d. Duke made enquiries which not only confirmed this but indicated that Wisden were systematically representing to their Cranbourn Street customers and the world at large that Duke had gone to the bad and the quality of their cricket balls had fallen off; that in particular they were too hard for county cricket – hence the 'less hard than most balls' line in the description of the Luff & Week 'Marvel' ball.

Henry Edgar had gone to Cranbourn Street on instructions from Penshurst and was able to report that the ball which Henry Luff had personally sold him across the counter purporting to be a Duke no 1 Best and charged at 7s 6d was in fact the inferior no 4 for which he should have been charged 5s. So long as Duke's name was on the ball no gentleman demeaned himself to worry about 'tradesmen's' details such as whether it was a no 1 or a no 4; it was a Duke and Duke was best. No gentleman moreover would harbour the thought that the venerated Wisden would try and trick him. Luff played on this, but when in 1898 he was sued by the Penshurst firm in the High Court before the Lord Chief Justice he protested it was all a mistake. He had acted throughout under a misapprehension, he said – in spite of the fact that William Smith, his manager of twelve years, gave evidence that during the period that he was in Luff's employ it was a regular practice to offer the inferior ball as Duke's best and charge 7s 6d for it. Luff insisted he had always ordered 'Crown' balls from Penshurst and these he understood were their first quality balls.

In fact the cheapest of the four grades which he was selling as 'the best' was clearly marked 'no 4 Match' and bore no royal arms or Prince of Wales feather. The superior ball had these and was marked 'no 1 Best'. Duke's counsel said Wisden's action over three years had hit his clients hard and was 'driving them out of the market'. They only wanted their reputation cleared. It was not a question of money. Lord Russell thereupon entered judgement for the plaintiffs, Duke, on Wisden undertaking only to sell Duke cricket balls in future under their proper denomination.

5

GETTING THERE

Forty Seasons of First-Class Cricket

R. G. BARLOW

R. G. Barlow was a famously obdurate batsman and effective bowler for
England and Lancashire for several decades from the 1870s.
In this extract from *Forty Seasons of First-Class Cricket* (1908) he is travelling
on the *Peshawur* to Australia on the 1882/83 England tour.

❧

'WE WERE ABOUT 350 miles out of Colombo, and had not seen another
ship. It was Sunday night, about nine o'clock, and church service had
just concluded. I was looking over the side of our vessel, in company with
W. W. Read, Fred Morley, and others of our party, when I saw in the near
distance a full-rigged ship coming before a brisk breeze straight towards us.
I looked a moment, then exclaimed, "My word, she's coming too near to be
pleasant; there's going to be an accident, if they don't mind." I had scarcely
got the words out of my mouth when the prow of the vessel crashed into our
steamer, near the engine-room, tearing her plates and leaving an ugly gap large
enough to drive a coach and pair through. Then she sheered off and lay to.

'What my sensations were I cannot describe. Inwardly I bade everyone
at home good-bye. Ladies were fainting and praying, passengers and crew
rushed hurriedly about, while the captain called calmly for "the boats". I seized
and donned a life-belt; others did the same. The lifeboat and other small boats
were launched, and preparations were made to leave, as it was thought, the
sinking ship. But the ship was not sinking. By the mercy of Providence the
great rent in her side stopped about half a yard above the water-line. The sea,
too, was as calm as a mill-pond, and remained so during the four days that it
took us to put back to Colombo.

'We had 400 souls on board, the sea was infested with sharks, and one
shudders even now to think what would have happened had the blow gone
below the water-line, or had the collision occurred in a stormy sea. The ship
that collided with us was the "Glen Roy", about 1,500 tons burthen, and
we towed her back to Colombo. We were detained there nearly a week for
repairs. A vote was taken by the passengers as to whether we should wait for
the ship to be made seaworthy again, or go by another boat, and we decided
to wait.

'That collision practically finished poor Fred Morley. He had several ribs broken when the "Glen Roy" struck us, but the nature of his injuries was not known until we got to Melbourne. One day I found him crying like a child in his bedroom. When asked what was the reason he said, "I don't know what is the matter with me, but there is something seriously wrong somewhere." I spoke to Mr. Bligh, and he had Morley examined, with the result that the fracture of the ribs was discovered. We missed his bowling sadly during the tour. But the effect was much worse than that. The accident laid the seeds of a fatal illness. Morley did not live long after his return to England.'

The Colombo experience was not the only narrow escape Barlow had. 'On the 1881 trip, we had been out to supper across the river at Sydney, and being detained, just missed our boat. It was moving off when we reached the wharf. We were annoyed at our ill-luck. But that boat never reached its destination. It was split open in a collision and sent to the bottom, and several of those on board found a watery grave. I think Providence must have been watching over us on that occasion also.'

Seventy-One Not Out

WILLIAM CAFFYN

William Caffyn was a highly regarded cricketer of the mid-nineteenth century who took part in the first-ever cricket tour, in 1859 to North America. His autobiography *Seventy-One Not Out* appeared in 1900.

WHEN ONE CONSIDERS the difficulties of travelling from place to place in those days, it will readily be seen that the arranging of an attractive season's programme in the few leading centres of cricket was no easy matter. When one county could not meet another on equal terms they played one or more 'given men' from another county. This custom was kept up till a much later period. Another way of equalising two elevens was to 'bar' a celebrated batsman or bowler. Up at Lord's an eleven of right-handed players would oppose an eleven of left-handed ones. A team whose name all began with B on several occasions played the rest of England by way of variety.

[. . .] Matches were played until very late in the season at this time. Some we find recorded as having taken place after the middle of October!

Betting on matches was very common, and for years after I first came out the newspapers often quoted the betting at different stages of the game. It is needless for me to go over old ground and say how rough the wickets were at the time of which I write. Indeed, when we bear in mind that the wickets in most cases were prepared with a view of benefiting the bowlers rather than the batsmen and that there were no boundaries, we need not be surprised at the comparatively small scores which were made. Tall hats were the correct thing to wear when participating in a great match, although I believe that velvet caps, knee-breeches, and silk stockings were still sported by some. I have an old book giving the score of one match between Leicester and Sheffield which has a footnote quoted from 'Bell's Life' as follows: 'It would be much better if H. Davis would appear in a cricketing dress instead of that of a sailor.'

Playing a match for a large sum of money was very common, and single-wicket matches for sums of £10, £20, or even £50 were of frequent occurrence. As far as cricket in some of our remote villages goes, the contrast between 1828 and 1898 is not particularly striking. There were rough wickets then, and they are rough enough in all conscience now in many small places. Seventy years has not been long enough to impress the rustic mind with the fact that in order to play cricket correctly we must first take the trouble to have at least a fairly decent pitch to play on. We had plenty of cross-hitting and slogging in country matches years ago, and so we shall continue to have as long as we have bumpy unplayable wickets in our villages. If the members of some of our village clubs would devote an evening or two a week to the rolling and improving of their wickets, instead of always wanting to practise their batting and bowling, they would, I am quite sure, find their cricket soon begin to improve. I myself like to see a good innings played by a batsman on a *difficult* wicket; but there is a vast difference between a '*bad-good*' wicket (if I may use such an expression) and one which has never received any preparation whatever, and on which the veriest yokel is more likely to slog up 20 runs than one of the leading players of a county.

Slaves of the Lamp

ALAN GIBSON

Alan Gibson was a journalist and broadcaster.
From *Growing Up With Cricket* (1985).

～❧

MEMORY FAILS AS you grow older. This is not just a matter of age, but of the quantity of information it has to consume. When I saw perhaps half a dozen first-class matches a season, I could still recall much of the detail over many years. Now, the match is over, the report written and (much more difficult) telephoned. I am on the train back to Bath, day's work done. You dismiss it from your mind, and if some fellow traveller asks the score, have to look up your notes to be sure. If you think about cricket at all, it is to wonder where you are going tomorrow. Worcester? Damn. It means the 7.53 from Bristol, changing at Gloucester (an hour's wait) and still arriving at Worcester nearly an hour before the start of play. You can while away the time at Worcester by visiting the cathedral, and you can at Gloucester too (though it is a long way from the station, and there are never any taxis at the new Gloucester station). Besides, you cannot always be in a prayerful or architectural mood. The next train from Bristol leaves Bristol at 11.25, and does not get you to the ground until the middle of the lunch interval: that is, provided it isn't late, and you have remembered to ring up Golden Wings (one of the most reliable taxi firms I have encountered) to meet it and wait for it. Well, there will be good friends in the Worcester press box, who will 'fill you in' as the phrase goes. Besides, it might rain. Clouds there in the west you notice from the window. Hum, yes, risk the second train, and hope to Hennessy that Turner doesn't score a century before lunch, nor Gifford take a hat-trick. That's enough thinking about cricket for today.

～❧

Early Reminiscences

G. H. R. MOUNTIFIELD

From the Edmonton (Alberta) Cricket Club's Smoking Concert
programme of 1912.

⌇

DURING THE YEARS 1905 to 1909 there were only a few clubs within easy reach of Edmonton and it was no easy task to arrange matches on account of the difficulty of transportation. Fort Saskatchewan, which in those years boasted one of the strongest teams in the district, was only to be reached by road or steamboat.

[. . .] This antiquated craft reminded me of a torpedo boat (going down stream), the passengers congratulating each other on this very comfortable and expeditious means of transportation, no praise being too good for Admiral Hobson and his steam yacht. The Fort was reached in good time and a very enjoyable match was participated in. [A picture of a] large group in front of the Marquee was taken on this occasion, and it is very pleasant to notice among them such well-known supporters and players as Percy Belcher, St. George Jellett, Major Worsley, Eddie Slocock and many others.

The great feature of these visits to the Fort apart from the match itself, was the royal entertainment of the visitors by Major Strickland, who was the life of cricket during his stay in that town, and everyone who was fortunate enough to have visited there during his regime has the fondest remembrances of this gentleman and officer of the Royal North West Mounted Police.

After the game and dinner were concluded the members of the Fort club always entertained their guests to a lively smoker, and this occasion was no exception to the rule, when a very enjoyable evening was spent.

Steam was got up on the following morning and the passengers all embarked at about 8.30 when Hobby promised a swift and safe passage back to Edmonton of a few hours only.

This no doubt would have been accomplished if the current had not been running the wrong way, and it was soon realized that our torpedo catcher was worse than a 'tow barge' as there was no 'horse ahead doing his best'. Creeping up stream was no term for the expression of the progress made as on several occasions the 'Flagship' went down stream 'stern first'.

The climax, however, was reached when passengers and crew were commandeered to pack wood to feed the insatiable furnace, and keep up an appearance of a head of steam.

After a long and tedious voyage the landing below the bridge at Edmonton was finally reached and the weary passengers shouldered their bags and proceeded to their homes, only to meet on the way all the good people of Edmonton going to church.

Another memorable expedition to the Fort was undertaken in the celebrated 'Tally Ho' bus and four-in-hand, an offspring of Captain A. S. Weeke's livery barn, when a pleasant trip was to be expected.

A splendid gait was struck out of town for the first three or four miles, when it became apparent that the recent rains had not helped to grade the Fort road, which at no time was remarkable for its similarity to a billiard table and in consequence 'walking' became the order of the day whenever a bad piece of road was met with, and it was astonishing the number of bad places which had to be waded through.

Finally one of the leaders got mired and was so played out as to be absolutely useless, and after managing to reach the Fort expired in one of the stables of the R.N.W.M.P.

Village Cricket

GERALD HOWAT

Gerald Howat was a cricket writer and historian. He wrote *Village Cricket* in 1980.

❧

WHAT WAS THE game like for those village players of the pre-1914 era? Numbers aside, their problems were the eternal ones of village cricket: ground, transport, food and finance.

It is difficult for us to realise how important the horse was to those cricketers. The groundsman whose club owned its own horse would have to muck out the stables, feed and water the animal and put on its leather boots before beginning work on the outfield. It explains an entry in the accounts of Earlswood: '1879, £1 1s od to the saddler for boots' (for the horse!). Clubs in the mining areas would often borrow a coal-haulier's horse and return it in time for delivering coal in winter. One club recorded ruefully: 'Our horse wouldn't wear leather boots', while another sought guidance on how to give an injured horse a poultice.

Wickets were cut by a scythe and the outfield would be lucky if it saw anything more than a few sheep in the season. One club experimented with a mallet to flatten its wicket. While many pitches must have been rough, it was by no means the story everywhere. The club in North Wales who protested to their opponents in 1859 clearly expected something better: 'the ground was extremely bumpy, the creases not marked out, there was no table for the scorers, no tent, and worst of all, no refreshments'. The report added: 'The remarks were made in no unkind spirit because it is indispensable to render a cricket match what it should be.' A comment with which all cricketers would entirely agree. We like things to be ship-shape and admire a club which presents an image of good organisation and devoted care.

It would be unfair to those who gave such devoted care if one did not recognise the unsung groundsmen who did their best. The ground at Lascelles Hall was lovingly cared for, sown with lawn seed and white clover, and so well tended that its curator, John Lockwood, was soon called to serve at the Oval. For many years before 1914 (and as many after), Willie Scott, the groundsman at St Boswells in Roxburghshire, cycled six miles each way to care for the pitch. Against odds, many such Willie Scotts laboured south of the border as well.

The effect of poor wickets was twofold: scores were low and injuries were high. Low scores were the rule rather than the exception, and explain why matches were so frequently two innings apiece. When leisure was limited good cricketing time could not be wasted, and the second innings was taken just as seriously as the first.

How did those cricketers get to their matches, or even know they were going to take place? Newspapers and handbills were a common way in the eighteenth century of announcing sides, venue and places for teams to assemble. The more common device through much of the pre-1914 period was the simple one of telling players week-by-week and, in small communities, knocking on the doors of late replacements. One martinet of a captain required fifteen men to be ready and changed before he would inform four of them to stand down for the day. Fixtures were not arranged with the efficiency of modern club secretaries. In some cases the vicar would arrange them, and, no doubt, regular winter meetings with his fellow clergy in the rural deanery achieved much in that direction.

Players would be likely to travel by horse-brake, pony-trap or farm wagon. One club hired the local hearse on the principle that no one wanted to be buried on Saturday. At Holbeck in Yorkshire they chartered a corn-waggon. The poorer members of the Wirksworth side in Derbyshire went by horse-brake and the richer ones in their own carriages – an imposing cavalcade calculated to put the opposition into disarray! The cricketers from Bures in Essex had a well-planned route which allowed the horses to drink at the Doctor's Pond and themselves at the Red Lion, on their way to Great Bentley. Our ancestors were hardy travellers: the cricketers of Seaton Carew made an eighty-mile round trip on the roughest of roads by pony-trap to play Whitby in the 1850s. Many Yorkshire villages such as those used sailing vessels to make their way along the North Sea coast to play each other. As the cricketers of one Yorkshire village side disappeared into the gathering gloom, the last their hosts heard 'was a parting solo on the horn across the waters'.

From 1840 onwards a network of railways sprang up throughout the country. There is some evidence of their use by village cricketers and they became the means by which larger clubs established north-south cricket links in the nineteenth century. One Yorkshire village team's day began and ended with a four-hour train journey – home by 3 a.m.!

Later, the bicycle offered more prospects. The Blackheath cricketers found they could tie pads and bat to the crossbar and make their way in convoy. Many a village cricketer blessed an invention which, in its own way, created a major social revolution in Edwardian times.

~&

Disgraceful Scenes at Lord's

ROBERT LYND

Robert Lynd was an Irish writer. The game he is trying to see is the second Ashes Test in June 1921. From *The Sporting Life and Other Trifles* (1922).

⤚

'DISGRACEFUL SCENES AT Lord's'. That is the only heading that could do justice to the feelings of thousands of men and women who had bought tickets for the second Test Match, and who were still attempting to blaspheme their way into the ground nearly an hour after play had begun.

It was not the players, or the public, or the police who behaved disgracefully: it was the authorities at Lord's.

They had sold thousands of reserved seats, but had made no arrangements for admitting ticket-holders or for informing them where they could be admitted. They seemed to have kept the secret even from the police, who were as much at sea as anyone else.

I saw one old gentleman, with field-glasses slung round his shoulder, go up to a policeman in the crush and, holding out his ticket, ask: 'Where do I get in with this?' 'Nowhere,' replied the policeman, with the wild smile of a man reduced to desperation. It was very nearly the truth.

I arrived an hour early and was sent to the far end of a queue that appeared to be about a quarter of a mile long. One could amuse oneself by subscribing to a flag-day, or buying from hawkers souvenirs in the shape of a small cricket ball with a photograph of an Australian player let into it, or being deafened by a lean man who came up and whistled close into one's face with one of those distressing inventions that are supposed to imitate the songs of birds, or watching the *Chu Chin Chow* camels parading by, like turkeys that had tried to be born as horses, or listening to the endless chatter of men who explained that Douglas was a fine cricketer, but a bad captain, and who talked of English batsmen generally as though they were a lot of shivering schoolboys waiting to be caned by Mr Squeers.

After about an hour the rumour rippled along the queue that the ground was full except for ticket-holders. This meant the dropping away of some thousands of people.

The queue then advanced more rapidly, till when it was just within sight of the turnstile it was attacked on the flank by a rush and crossfire of persons who had the red tickets of members of Lord's.

To make things worse, a horse-policeman forced his way in and broke the queue up, and it in its turn became a mob. It gathered round the turnstile, while hundreds of people stretched their arms into the air, holding up their tickets, and yelling: 'Ticket-holders! Where do ticket-holders get in?'

It was a patient crowd, but the language was on the strong side. Ladies contented themselves with 'What the devils!' and 'Gracious heavens!' as the sun beat down on their delicate faces. Men thundered in growls, followed by vivid flashes.

Every now and then an elderly gentleman or a lady and her daughter would have to beat a way back out of the crowd in order to escape fainting. In any other country, or among the devotees of any other game, there would have been a riot. A man beside me said viciously: 'A football crowd would have had the gates down.'

Meanwhile, people in front were getting in at what seemed to be the rate of about one a minute. A cynical lady said that it was like a rich man trying to get through the eye of a needle. It was evident that they were examining every ticket-holder's passport and searching him for arms before admitting him.

New-comers would arrive and say to us, politely and hopefully: 'Would you mind letting us past? We've got tickets.' There would be a bitter and universal shout of 'We've all got tickets!'

After a time a merry-looking man looked out at us from a window in the back of one of the stands, and, framed in ivy, shouted out: 'England 58 for no wickets!' It was not true (as we afterwards discovered), but it cheered the crowd up.

Then King George arrived, and the gates opened and shut for him as if by magic.

After that a horse-policeman told us to line up against the wall in a queue. We did so, and sweltered in the sun for a little longer. Then he came and told us to go and form a queue at another gate. 'Queueriouser and queueriouser!' a punster in the crowd relieved his feelings by muttering. And even that wasn't the end of it, for one ultimately had to leave this for yet another queue at right angles to the wall, which crept into the ground between two banks of policemen, feeling somewhat like Swinburne's 'weariest river' that 'winds somewhere safe to sea'.

But when once you were inside the ground! Is there a more beautiful view in England, I wonder, than the view you get from one of the stands in Lord's on a fine day? There is the green and white of the field – as restful as a daisy field in Chaucer. But there is also at Lord's a noble and multiple idleness that takes the imagination, not to Chaucer, but to the South Seas.

It is a ground that one almost expects to be surrounded by palm-trees, and, surely, if one were on the roof of the pavilion, one ought to have a view of a blue lagoon and a distant reef keeping out the noise and strife of breakers.

∼❧

The 'How' and the 'Why'
We Crossed the Atlantic

R. A. FITZGERALD

R. A. Fitzgerald was Secretary of the MCC from 1863 to 1876.
From *Wickets in the West* (1873), the record of the first MCC tour of Canada
and the United States in 1872, which Fitzgerald organized.
W. G. Grace was in the touring party.

∼❧

WE WILL TAKE the 'Why' first. In the summer of 1871, two gentlemen interviewed the Secretary of the Marylebone Club at Lord's Ground. The one, Captain Wallace, of the 60th Rifles; the other, Mr. J. C. Patteson, of Toronto. They there and then unfolded a cricket-scheme, pointing out to the Secretary where Canada was, and explaining who the Canadians were. The precaution was necessary, as great ignorance prevailed in England at this time respecting its colony. The scheme amounted practically to this: Mr. Patteson was instructed on the part of the Canadians to invite an English Twelve to play a series of matches in the Dominion. The Twelve were to consider themselves as visitors, expressly invited by the several cricketing bodies in Canada. The Canadians proposed to defray all expenses connected with the voyage out and home, and generally to provide for the comfort and passage of the visitors throughout the Dominion.

It was hinted at the same time that the expedition might be extended to the United States, as Mr. Patteson expressed an opinion that a visit to

New York, Philadelphia, and Boston, would be hailed with satisfaction by the cricketers south of 49°.

The scheme was left in a crude state throughout the winter, and in the spring, when to think of cricket is less like suicide, the Secretary took measures to ascertain the feeling of his young friends about crossing the water with their cricket-bags. It took; he received flattering promises from more quarters than he expected; he had at least sixteen promises to go anywhere and do anything under his guidance. This was flattering but perplexing. The invitation was limited to twelve; his next step was to sound the note of public opinion, and though he met with objections in some quarters, he was advised generally, that an offer so made should not be rejected. He thereupon took it up in earnest. The cable announced his intention to the other side of the water, and a speedy reply expressed the satisfaction of the Canadians. The Secretary looked through his sixteen acceptances, and invited eleven of them to dine with him at Lords [*sic*] on July 2. All present swore a solemn oath – which we will not quote – that they would be true to the tryst; the day appointed for sailing was August 8. The original selection consisted of R. A. Fitzgerald, W. G. Grace, V. E. Walker, R. D. Walker, C. I. Thornton, A. Lubbock, A. N. Hornby, A. Appleby, Hon. G. Harris, R. A. Mitchell, J. W. Dale, R. D. Balfour. This list soon eliminated itself.

Mr. Thornton saw a picture in a shop window of a ship in distress, and read an article on sea-sickness, that did not convince him that he would be the lucky man in ten who escaped *mal de mer*. He excused himself accordingly. W. H. Hadow filled the gap. R. D. Balfour disappeared, and in his place C. J. Ottoway popped up; J. W. Dale then jacked up; and agony first fell upon the Secretary's mind. Bowling, it will be observed, was only represented by Appleby, and the more the manager thought of it, the less he slept; until one night he dreamed that W. M. Rose and lobs might be serviceable. He acted at once on the dream, and plucking the Rose from its blushing bride pinned him to the Twelve. C. K. Francis was next 'added to the list', very luckily – as a young lady afterwards remarked. All went merry as a muffin's man's bell until August 5. *Dies irae!* Ye Gods – three days only before starting and two vacancies suddenly occurred. The Messrs. Walker were struck down by illness. The Secretary has not much hair to lose, but he squandered that little in handfuls. What was to be done? Canterbury was at its height; there wasn't a day for weeks to come that hadn't its match; there isn't a cricketer, now-a-days, that is not claimed by at least three clubs. Into highways, into byeways, by dint of hansom cab, by wire and post, by everything that was sacred, in the name of everything unmentionable, drove, telegraphed, wrote, prayed, and swore the Secretary. His prayers or maledictions were heard, Edgar Lubbock and F. Pickering turned up trumps, but the Secretary was not sure that two more might not turn up at Londonderry after all. However fourteen were more to be desired than ten. Much eased in spirit, on August 7 the manager went down to Liverpool. The trysting spot was the Washington Hotel; twelve noon, on August 8, the hour appointed. Right glad was he to see half-a-dozen cricket bags in the hall, and more to come, according to the porter. Could it be? The Eleven were mustered. Farrands, the umpire, answered to his name, the expedition was a reality. The twelve apostles of cricket were committed to their work; a friendly company insisted on speeding their departure by a sumptuous lunch at the Adelphi. [. . .]

One toast only was proposed, 'Success to the Expedition', followed by Speech No. 1 of the Captain. These were very numerous in the sequel, and very like each other, but samples will be given anon. Half-an-hour after, the pilgrims stood on the landing stage, each with a large easy chair under his arm, and parcels various in either hand. A cheer from the crowd, and they were off on the tug. [. . .]

The S.S. Sarmatian, the last new vessel of Messrs. Allan's fleet, lay in midstream; up her side soon clambered the passengers; a whistle from the boatswain, and the tug loosed off, the last tie that bound us to England was severed.

❧

Alfred Shaw, Cricketer:
His Career and Reminiscences

ALFRED SHAW

Alfred Shaw was a famous England cricketer of the nineteenth century,
whom many regarded as the best bowler of his era.
His Career and Reminiscences was published in 1902.

❧

I THINK NO TEAM of cricketers can have had such an experience as we
encountered in travelling through New Zealand in the early part of the
year 1877. We left Sydney by the *Tararua* on January 16th. We should have
played a match at Greymouth on the way, but there was a danger that by so
doing we should be too late for the great anniversary day at Auckland. The
programme was, therefore, changed, and again we were threatened with legal
proceedings, which fell through on our promising to visit Greymouth later.
This we did on February 20th.

From Auckland we went to Wellington, and I refer to this match in order
to mention a bowling feat that was described at the time as unprecedented in
the Colony. I took 13 of the Twenty-two's wickets at Wellington for 11 runs.
Four of the wickets were taken in an over of four balls, three being clean
bowled, and one leg before wicket.

Our belated visit to Greymouth was the prelude to a most exciting
journey. On the second day of the match (February 21st) the players had to
be ferried across a lagoon owing to the bridge being partly demolished by
floods. From Greymouth we went by water to Hokitika, whence we drove
to Christchurch, a drive so attended with dangers and difficulties that it
was by the mercy of Providence we were able to accomplish it without loss
of life.

Hokitika was left in the coaches at five o'clock on the Friday morning,
and we expected to be in Christchurch on the Saturday night, and rest on the
Sunday before commencing the match with the Eighteen of Canterbury on
the Monday (February 26th, 1877). The Friday morning was bright and sunny,
but at mid-day rain commenced to descend in torrents, and continued falling
up to the next morning.

We had to pass through Otira Gorge, which we should have reached in daylight. Under ordinary circumstances a coach had to be driven over a shallow ford, and it was not a journey soothing to the nerves at the most favourable time. On this occasion our coaches made such slow progress that we reached the gorge in the darkness of midnight. Bad roads were responsible for the delay, for there could have been no foundation for the driver's humorous explanation that he 'hadn't such a lot of heavy fellows like us to drive every day'. The only other passengers, by the way, were a lady and an artist of Christchurch.

When the Otira Gorge was reached, instead of having a shallow ford to cross, we had to face a rapidly rising torrent then fully three feet deep. There was no question of turning back. The flood had to be faced; so in the coaches went. The first coach got through all right, but the second one, in which I was riding, came to grief in mid-stream. The four horses were dead beat, and fell down in the water. It was a most lugubrious situation to be in. The lights of the coach had gone out hours before, the horses were struggling in the swift stream, and we could feel ourselves as it were hemmed in by the forbidding sides of the deep and murky gorge.

'For God's sake get out and help me with the horses, or we shall all be drowned.' We did not need this exhortation from the driver to make us realise the desperate character of our plight. We jumped off the coach and were up to our waists in water immediately. Tom Armitage undertook to carry the lady passenger ashore, and he did so safely. The rest of us unyoked the horses, and literally pulled them to the bank, after which we waded back to the coach and got that out also. The danger was thus surmounted, but there was no doubt that we had all been in great peril; the water rose so rapidly that the next morning the gorge was found to be flooded to the height of ten feet.

[. . .] Our troubles were not ended when we had passed through the flood. We had to walk on, wearied and exhausted, and with saturated clothing, to find shelter for the night. We came to a little shanty flattered by the name of the Otira Hotel, but little more than a roadmen's shelter. Here the occupants of the first coach – who had been unaware of our exciting experience in the Otira Gorge, having driven straight on – had kindled a large fire, the sight of which was more welcome to us than I can describe. We had no clothing with us other than what we stood up in; the baggage of the entire team having been sent round by water in charge of Pooley, upon whom the trouble already described had not then fallen. There was no help for it but to divest ourselves of our saturated clothes, and stand before the fire in a nude state until we had dried them. The lady passenger, whom Armitage had so gallantly carried through the flood, was made as comfortable for the night as circumstance would permit by the woman who was in charge of the shanty. We cricketers slept on the floor in front of the fire as best we could.

The next morning we resumed the journey. The coaches had not been driven more than a mile out when further progress was found to be barred by a landslip, which had effectually blocked the road – a highway, I should mention, that had been cut by convict labour. There was nothing for it but to again seek the friendly hospitality of the Otira Hotel. This was on the Saturday morning. We had to stay there until the Sunday morning. The larder of the little establishment was not equal to satisfying the cravings of a band of hungry cricketers. One of the roadmen, however, proved equal to the emergency, for he went foraging in the adjacent hills, and returned laden with a real sample of fresh killed New Zealand mutton. Some of our party cooked it, and baked an apology for bread cakes, so we survived the day. George Ulyett has said that the bread cakes were cooked with the aid of a hay-fork. 'Happy Jack' always could draw a longer bow than any Yorkshireman who ever crossed the water.

The landslip was cleared by the Sunday morning, and we departed for Christchurch at five o'clock a.m. The result of all our experiences was that we reached our destination at half-past eleven on the morning of the match. The journey took about eighty hours to accomplish, and we were never in bed, and had had little or no sleep all the time. What would the new generation of cricketers say to an experience of this kind? We played from half-past twelve to five o'clock at night. That we should have the worse of the day's play may be supposed, when it is said we could with the greatest difficulty keep our eyes open as we stood on the field. A night's good rest restored our faculties. We atoned for our shortcomings of the first day, and rather disturbed local opinions by winning the match by 24 runs.

6

PITCH AND TOSS

Lord's on the Big Day

JIM FAIRBROTHER

Jim Fairbrother, head groundsman at Lord's from 1968 to 1984,
is readying the ground for play during the 1981 Ashes series.
From *Testing the Wicket*, published a month before he died.

~&~

SATURDAY. THE THIRD day of the second Test match between England
and Australia. England hold the Ashes but having lost at Trent Bridge
are one down with four to go. In reply to England's first innings total of 311
Australia are 10 without loss. And I am out in the middle dressed not in my
working clothes but in a dark suit to give the proceedings a bit of ceremony,
waiting by the wicket covers. Waiting on the weather.

The dove-grey clouds, among them an occasional evil-looking wad of
black, are sailing slowly over us from the north-west, almost directly over the
gap between the members' pavilion and the Warner stand.

The precious wicket itself and the immediate surrounds have been under
cover since the previous day. Alec Gull, my very capable number one, and our
permanent staff of six, buttressed by nearly a dozen additional helpers, mostly
MCC young cricketers, wait with me.

There is a steady flow of incoming spectators and I know that thousands
more are queuing right up St John's Wood Road and Wellington Place.
Obviously they have loosed the shackles of the working week for that's just
how they look – the young of both sexes in bright T-shirts and jeans or
slacks, their picnic lunches in bags slung over the shoulder or carried in
shiny little picnic cases. Their outbursts of laughter and buzz of talk reach us
from all over the ground as they settle on the terraces or on the grass behind
the boundary boards – three or four thousand are accommodated there on
this big day.

These days several matches every season are big occasions; the NatWest
Cup Final, the final of the Benson & Hedges competition and, if Middlesex
are in the running for the title, the last Sunday John Player league match.
Club and village cricketers play the finals of their national competitions here
too and these are always well attended. The University and Eton and Harrow
matches are still part of Lord's rare tradition.

But a Test Match, particularly with the 'old enemy', has a pull of its own. Even people who seldom watch cricket, except perhaps on television, come along to try to get in, if they haven't wheedled tickets out of their cricketing friends beforehand. And that's why, as I shuffle about in the middle, I am keeping my fingers crossed. Personally I want everyone here to enjoy the skills and excitement of the game, not to have to worry about whether the conditions are fit to play.

Up to now the summer has been so utterly predictable in its unpleasantness: a soaking May, with match after match abandoned, and in June, except for a day here and there, hardly a glimmer of sun through forbidding clouds. And yesterday the familiar demons of rain and bad light had done their best – or worst – to fell a fascinating tussle.

Today we know already the local forecast, received as usual from the RAF weather bureau at Northolt, that we must expect drizzle – but it shouldn't last for more than half an hour. Expectation of some rain is why we still have the covers on and are ready for action when it comes, immobile as we may look while we wait and see.

Ah, here it is. A slight breeze fans it gently and wetly across our faces. The clock tower tells us it is still only a quarter to eleven. So if this is all we are going to get the start of play need not be delayed. But now the umbrellas are going up. Spectators are hastening not strolling to their seats and for positions on the grass. Trying not to worry too much, I watch an Aussie supporter lope in, parading his felt hat with those little bobbles dangling from the brim to keep off the bush flies. And now here's a plump fellow garbed in a Union Jack and waving a similar flag. (Sad to report that sometime later we saw him being gently conducted out of the ground by a policeman, excessive patriotism or over-imbibing having prompted him to run across the playing area and interrupt play.)

Out here in the middle we can feel the tension building up. Will we be able to make the eleven-thirty start as scheduled? It is now ten past the hour and the drizzle is thickening. Could even the RAF weather experts be wrong?

We now have extra flat sheets to extend cover of the bowlers' run-ups. I have a word with Alec and he calls on a few more ground-staff boys to join us. I signal the tractor driver to drag out the extra covers.

The forecast was so positive that the rain would last no more than half an hour that I am still fairly optimistic the game will re-commence on time.

But the minutes tick by, the rain, though gentle, continues and I don't have to look around to know that the lads share my feelings. Slight but persistent rain is perhaps even more exasperating than a brisk shower. The conditions are so nearly right yet we have to stand about like mugs as if the whole situation is somehow our own doing. We are always aware that the spectators regard us as interlopers between them and the players. If we weren't here the game would magically begin.

As it happens, the drizzle is lessening . . . and almost ceases. The clouds appear to lift, it becomes a little brighter. We move around in relief.

However, enough rain has fallen to compel us to get those extra covers on, for any more of it, with the bowlers' longer run-ups uncovered, will certainly mean further delay to the start. The covers have been unhooked from the tractor and we get to work unrolling them.

Groans from the crowd are audible.

Our caution is justified when another black cloud sends down what, despite the RAF, feels like steady rain. The umbrellas in the crowd, which had scarcely shown wetness, are soon glistening and the rain is dropping off them. Somebody fetches my anorak for which I am very grateful.

It is eleven twenty-five, the moment when I should be setting the stumps and waiting at the wicket to hand over to the umpires, approaching down the pavilion steps. Instead, however, we are still battling to get those extra sheets finally rolled out. They are very heavy, I can assure you, and when we have a real downpour and they have collected a lot of water, even our tractor puffs and blows in its efforts to tow each one to its match site behind the advertisement boards at the Nursery end.

By now Colonel Stephenson, MCC secretary to cricket and my immediate boss – a genial and generous man, though he will chip me for saying it – has joined us. The red rose in his buttonhole strikes a brave note. As if he has commanded it, the rain gives over, but for good?

More waiting and then the empires, Ken Palmer and Don Oslear, walk out, but with no white coats over their blazers. Over the public address system the crowd has just been informed that now it has stopped raining, and in view of Northolt's forecast of no further rain, play will begin as soon as the pitch has been cleared.

So, with a wary glance up at the heavens, we get on with removing everything that such a short time ago we had rushed on to the table. Ken and

Don are inspecting the mobile wicket covers to make sure no water has crept in underneath them.

Colonel Stephenson puts his back into it with the rest of us – a line of more than a dozen men and lads, rolling up each flat sheet as we trudge over them.

A few weak cheers accompany our efforts but I think I know what is being said. 'What a silly arrangement. How primitive! And it's taking so long. There must be better ways of covering and uncovering the wicket. Know what they do at Edgbaston? They've got a huge tarpaulin operated mechanically that covers the whole ground – and it takes only a few minutes.'

How I long to be able to tell them that Bernard Flack, Warwickshire's head groundsman, is by no means certain that his £50,000 polyethylene cover is the final answer. Removing any cover which might bear a million gallons of water is the tricky part of it. It might take only nine or ten minutes for two men, aided by hydraulic motors, to unroll it, but the bigger the cover, the more men you need to remove it and the greater the risk of some of that water spilling on to the wicket. A great innovation, certainly, but with our big drop from the Father Time stand to the Tavern it will be doubtful if we can ever use one, though of course we went to the demonstration and are closely watching the results in actual match use.

And I am sure others are piping up with: 'Why aren't they using the Whale? That new roller thing from Australia. They've got it on loan from the Oval – trust the Oval to be way ahead of sleepy old Lord's. And the Surrey groundsman Harry Brind's with them to operate it. Come on, don't bother with those ridiculous sheets – next time leave the table as it is and just have the Whale to mop it all up.'

True enough, Harry and the Surrey CCC have been as co-operative as ever. And yesterday, Friday, the second day of the match it was used on the outfield, particularly the Tavern side, which, as I've said, is always our problem. The machine is another excellent innovation and of such practical use to us that we already have one on order, having emerged from what our questioner suggests is a permanently comatose state.

Now it is almost five minutes past noon. Don Oslear and Ken Palmer emerge from the pavilion at last in their white coats, to be followed soon after, and to a loyal cheer, by England in the field, looking quite sprightly. Then Graham Wood and John Dyson, sober and with every appearance of confidence though one knows quite well that even world-class batsmen are combating butterflies in the stomach at the thought of the savage deliveries that will meet them from the morning-fresh fast bowlers.

The white gate is closed behind them; the match is on.

Trent Bridge Ground-Keeper

RICHARD DAFT

Richard Daft was a well-known cricketer of the mid-nineteenth century who played for Nottinghamshire and the All England XI, 'in his best day the most graceful of bats'. William 'Billy' Walker was groundsman at Trent Bridge from 1877 to 1893 and a popular personality. From *A Cricketer's Yarns* (1926).

A FTER HIS APPOINTMENT to the charge of the Trent Bridge Ground, Walker effected a great change in the wickets on that enclosure. Years ago the wickets would not wear at Trent Bridge, but thanks to an application in winter of a special kind of marl or clayey soil, which Walker has procured at different times from a certain part of Nottinghamshire, the wickets at Trent Bridge became second to none.

This preparation of his Walker always designated as 'hair oil'. Some years ago he was invited to inspect the Old Trafford cricket ground at Manchester, and, having strongly recommended an application of the Nottinghamshire 'hair oil', several truck loads were afterwards despatched to Old Trafford. William returned from Manchester, speaking in the highest terms of the Lancashire executive, and of 'the princely manner in which they had treated him' during his visit.

William's manner of speaking of his wickets is rather amusing. He always talks of the wicket as if it were himself; consequently his conversation when on this subject is apt to be very puzzling to strangers. 'I'm better this match than ever I was. They'll never be able to wear me out; I shall be just as good on the third day as I shall be on the first.' Again, 'So-and-so can never get any runs except when he bats on me.' These and such-like are the remarks William makes when speaking of his favourite subject. He has visited most of the leading cricket grounds in England, and declares that he has seen nothing to surpass his own. And indeed the Trent Bridge as it is now is a ground to be proud of. Some years ago when Notts County played Blackburn Rovers at the Oval, William availed himself of the opportunity of going up to town, and of 'killing three birds with one stone', as he put it. That was first to visit Lord's in the morning, then to come down to witness the football match and inspect the Oval in the afternoon. I had come up to town the day before myself, and met William's train about eleven o'clock the next morning, at King's Cross, and having seen him safely in a train on the Underground on his way to Lord's I proceeded to transact some business in the city and went down in plenty of time to the Oval before the match began.

There was a crowd of thirty thousand people to witness the encounter, and I had told William to be sure and be on the ground very early or he would never be able to see anything of the play. Just before the game began I saw Scotton in the pavilion, who told me that he had just come straight from Lord's in a hansom and that Walker had been there some time, and was so interested in the ground and its surroundings that he believed he had altogether forgotten about the match at the Oval. I was sorry to hear this, as I was particularly anxious that he should see the other great Metropolitan ground and the football match as well, but came to the conclusion that now this was not to be expected. I was pleased to find out afterwards, however, that our groundsman had been put in a hansom at Lord's at the last moment, sent off at full speed to the Surrey enclosure, had been taken to a snug seat in an excellent position, through the kindness of Mr. Alcock or one of the Committee, and had consequently seen the game in the most comfortable manner possible.

Recollections of Lord's and the Marylebone Cricket Club

WILLIAM SLATTER

William Slatter joined the Lord's ground staff in 1863 and rose to be head groundsman. His *Recollections* were published in 1914.

❧

I HAVE OFTEN HEARD the remark that the match wickets of to-day are greatly superior to what they were 40 years ago, and considering the rough usage the ground had in those days, I think they ought to be.

The ground was used for practice in all parts when no match was in progress; sheep were allowed to wander about wet or dry, over the match ground (if any one part more than another could be called the 'match ground'), and if the turf was at all soft they made holes with their trotters often two or three inches deep, which remained for the rest of the season if the turf dried soon afterwards. These holes were often hidden by the grass, which was much longer than it is at the present time; we had no improved mowing machine, nor a three-ton roller. The old hand roller (which is still in existence) was the only roller that we had for the purpose of making wickets. Then again, the wickets at the present time are selected and prepared three or four days beforehand, but in those days the pitch was selected by the two umpires an hour before the match was due to start. After the selection was made and the creases marked out or cut, the ground between the wickets was simply rolled by the roller previously mentioned which was trundled along by two or three boys for 15 or 20 minutes. Could it be expected under these conditions that pitches played so easy as they do now?

Another big disadvantage the batsmen had then was there was no boundary – all hits were run out – and I often think that 50 runs obtained forty-five or so years ago is as good as a century obtained at the present day. Neither could it be supposed that the out fielding portion could be in that state of perfection as it is now. Practice and matches took place, as I have previously stated, all over the field, and the whole ground staff consisted of my father with the assistance of one man and a boy – or in the season of about four boys; these boys having to clean the ground every morning where the sheep had been; roll the wickets; longstop while practice was going on; set out the forms (what there was of them); mind the sheep, which were kept in one corner, until a paddock was made for them in the north corner; hold horses; water the ground; and do other work of that kind.

Besides these here were several bowlers who had the privilege of getting a living on the ground by bowling to all comers at so much an hour. They did not often get engaged before eleven or twelve o'clock; so before that time they had to give their services in doing the work on the ground free for this privilege. One or two of these bowlers were at times found work at a very poor rate in the winter. Old Elmer, better known as 'Norfolk' (I believe because he came from that Shire), and George Hutt who was known as 'Cambridge George' (for the reason that he came from Cambridge) – the latter was a somewhat fast underhand bowler, who, when he happened to bowl one straight ball, threw up his hands and shouted. This practice at times so surprised the batsmen that they became puzzled and were bowled out. The bowlers, as a rule, were paid at the rate of 2/- per hour; the longstop 1/-; and the fielder 6d. I have myself fielded or longstopped for six or seven hours after doing the usual morning's work. On match days the boys were, as now, allowed the privilege of selling match cards, only one or two receiving wages.

Equestrians were allowed to enter the ground on match days. The horses often being left in charge of the 'elder ground boys' (who were then, as now, often married men). Ropes were attached to the trees at the rear of where 'A' enclosure is now, and the reins of the horses were fixed on the rope between the trees. In this way two 'boys' would perhaps have as many as thirty horses during the afternoon, some coming late and others going away early; and a shilling was expected if they remained any length of time. These 'boys' have been known to share 15/- each in one afternoon by these tips (Lord's in those days being nearly all 'tips'). As many had to depend on this kind of payment for their services (even those that received wages had such a small amount), it was often impossible for them to make both ends meet without gratuities and tips from the members and visitors. Even my father who was groundsman (and everything else) did not receive more than 21/- per week, 7/- of which was repaid to Mr. Dark on account of rent.

One of these 'big boys' is still alive and in a good way of business, and when I saw him a few months ago, he spoke of the money he had collected in this way in a short time on match days, but he also spoke of the days when he had to work hard for nothing.

One of the smaller boys was trusted one day to take charge of a horse belonging to one of the members. He had not been leading the horse up and down the path on the north side of the pavilion for more than about ten minutes, when a loud clapping and applause was made for a fine catch. This frightened the horse which started jumping about. The boy also became frightened and let go of the reins, and the horse had a free gallop across the field, tearing it up very much as it had been raining the previous day, and the ground was soft. The holes made were forked up, filled in under the turf with fine soil, rammed and rolled, and very little was seen of the damage the next day. This was not the only time that horses had broken loose, but on other occasions the ground was hard, or they were kept to the outskirts or paths.

Over fifty years ago it was thought a big staff when five or six professionals were engaged at Lord's. In 1859 (as far as I can remember) they consisted of Nixen, Chatterton (who, by the way, was an underhand bowler), Jimmy Dean (the Plough Boy), Martingal, Harry Royston, and at that time during the season, Sam Dakin. The staff was greatly increased after 1864, although a slight increase had taken place previously. Jimmy Grundy came, I think, in 1861, and Tom Hearne in 1863.

Being a boy in the pavilion in that year, one of the members gave me a pair of discarded flannels, and Tom Hearne, who was a tailor by trade, and filled up his time between his turn to bowl on practice days with his needle, cut them smaller and made them to fit me.

The Gatekeeper

R. C. ROBERTSON-GLASGOW

After playing first-class cricket from 1920 to 1937, R. C. Robertson-Glasgow became a cricket correspondent and author. From *More Cricket Prints* (1948).

❧

AMONG THOSE WHOM the war relieved of a regular profession was the Pavilion gatekeeper; I mean the man who lets you out to bat.

He who stops you coming in was still there, probably because there is nothing else in the world that he can do. He has grown old in the business of prevention. He knows to a nicety what sort of deception will be practised at the Members' Entrance, discerning afar between those smaller invaders who will seek to ooze in under the shadow of a corpulent member and those who put one foot on the mat inside and remark, in easy tones: 'Oh, Mr. Culpepper said he would sign me in,' and who may be overheard at intervals for the rest of the day discussing Mr. Culpepper's incomprehensible absence or his still more perplexing non-existence.

This janitor of exclusion remained at his post. In war his work was more intricate, because wider and more democratic was the passage to the mysteries within. All the same, he stuck to certain standards, and he told me one day: 'Chaps without a collar or tie I do not let in.'

But the man who let you out vanished, and will only return with bananas, benedictine, and rubber handles for bats. I know, because I wrote to one who has let me out to many a snick and swat, and he said that he, and, he was quite sure, his fellow-artists, were not going to be 'brought out for an odd Saturday for any old bunch of hit-and-missers who wouldn't care what you told them about the bowling'.

I understood. He had attended for the first summer of War in a straw-hat and his old chair by the wicket-gate; but his pride had been hit. His professional advice had been questioned, perhaps derided, by some flailing sergeant who batted by numbers, bowled a mechanised medium, and, opening the gate on his own, shattered the ceremony of fifty summers and passed, unforgivable, on his ignorant road.

For there were, and will be again, subtly various ways of opening that wicket-gate. In deference to the first pair of batsmen he laid it open as soon as he saw them coming from the dressing-room, and he smiled on them as one who smiles on prosperous travellers who go a long journey. If one of them returned unexpectedly early, he still kept a silence, at once surprised and tactful. But, if Nos. three and four also came back somewhat empty, he put two and two together; ratiocination, it is sometimes called; and he began to offer advice which, in its brief simplicity, embraced the whole art of batting. If spin was the source of trouble, he said: 'What you want to do is to stop 'em breaking. Play 'im on the dap.' If speed prevailed, he said: 'Hit 'im back past his whiskers. No bowler never likes that.'

For the last two batsmen he kept an entirely different line. I think he knew that, in their case, all technical suggestions were superfluous. They had no batting to discuss. So he stuck to merely secular affairs, observing in offhand tones: 'There's a good Picture at the Regal to-night,' and, on one occasion, 'Mrs. — is expecting again.'

But he would soon return to business; for, if you looked round on your way to the crease, you would see that he had not only opened the gate, but also left it open.

❧

A Cricketer on Cricket

W. J. FORD

After a brief first-class career, W. J. Ford (1853–1904) became a schoolmaster. *A Cricketer on Cricket* appeared in 1900.

❧

PASSING FROM THESE few words of preface to the business in hand, I find that the first question for consideration is, – 'Should the visiting side be given the choice of innings?' There is no doubt that every cock crows best on his own midden, and that, to take an example, Middlesex is generally seen at its best at Lord's, and Surrey at the Oval, and that the choice of innings would, if accorded to the visitors, to some extent discount the disadvantage of playing on a foreign ground. Personally, however, I believe in the retention of the element of luck to a reasonable extent, and should be very sorry if the interesting little ceremony of tossing the halfpenny were abolished. All games that are worth playing, except those of the type of chess, owe their popularity to the occasional freaks of fortune: golf would be tame without bunkers; whist without 'honours'; billiards without flukes; and remembering that there are a certain number of cases when the option of batting or fielding puts the captain in a large quandary and when the wicket is at its best for the fourth innings, I say once more, 'Let things stand as they are.' The argument is more sentimental than logical, of course, but then there is more of sentiment about cricket than there is of logic. There is a further and very delicate point, which I only wish to mention in a subdued whisper, and it is, that if it were known beforehand which side would certainly bat first, there might be a temptation to 'cook' a wicket. Mind, I do not suggest or think that there is the slightest chance of such a piece of rascality, but wickets have been tampered with before now, and such a thing as a dishonourable groundsman might some day be found. On the whole, then, let us keep the present rule, especially as the doctrine of averages always holds good, though no cricketer can underrate the depression that settles on a side when fortune has been, not fickle, but consistently unkind.

❧

Winning the Toss

R. E. S. WYATT

R. E. S. Wyatt was an able all-rounder of the 1920s and 1930s who captained
England fifteen times. From *The Ins and Outs of Cricket* (1936).

&

THE TEAM HAVING been picked and an initial policy decided upon, the
next duty of a captain is to win the toss. This is, of course, entirely a matter
of luck, but in cricket 'the luck of the game' is always an important factor and,
as all gamblers are superstitious, one may be pardoned for having a sneaking
regard for the ridiculous idea that some coins are luckier than others. I have
a half-sovereign which has brought me amazing luck in test matches but is
useless in county matches. I hope this admission of the ownership of such a
rarity will not be taken as an innocent's invitation to international crooks!

In Barbados we had a West Indian dressing-room attendant of the
name of Shepherd, whose keenness and interest in the game has never been
surpassed. One day he quite reasonably announced that winning the toss
was just a matter of luck, but Patsy Hendren, a great leg-puller, more or less
convinced him that there was a lot of skill attached to it. Consequently, as I had
won the toss on the first two occasions, he followed me out on to the ground
and watched me intently. I won a third time and this convinced Shepherd
that, by following the coin carefully to the top of its flight, it was possible to
gauge which way up it would fall on the ground. He felt sure that I was a great
expert in the art, which was doubtless one of the most desirable qualities in
a captain! After that he always had a bet of a bottle of rum that I would win
the toss, and as I was lucky seven times running, and only lost the toss twice
during the tour, I had several letters from dear old Shepherd thanking me for
another bottle of rum, with which he had just celebrated an M.C.C. century
or bowling feat. He was a great fellow with a wide knowledge of cricket and
his enthusiasm was unbounded.

&

Bumpers, Boseys and Brickbats

JACK POLLARD

Jack Pollard was an Australian journalist and sports biographer who wrote about a wide range of sports. *Bumpers, Boseys and Brickbats* was published in 1971.

❧

THE 1953 SEASON in England provided some fascinating data for collectors of that old cricket chestnut – how to win tosses. Australia's captain that year, Lindsay Hassett, distinguished himself by winning the toss in all five Tests, which touched off some intriguing stories about the pennies used, how Hassett called, and linked his luck with Army training in wartime two-up matches.

The English were much impressed by Hassett's skill in winning tosses, for many years earlier they had themselves set a very high standard in this art when Dr W. G. Grace was around. Grace tossed the coin and called, 'Monkey,' picked it up and informed the opposing skipper 'We bat, then.' The only captain I have been able to find who had a remote chance of winning tosses against the doctor was Blackham. When Grace was in Australia in 1892, Blackham produced a very old and battered coin. When he spun it Grace called 'Man' but the coin turned up 'Woman' and Grace looked at it in disgust. 'That's a pretty sort of coin to toss with,' he said. 'You have to toss first and then take it into the light to see if it's man or woman.' Blackham remained unruffled. 'We bat, doctor,' he said.

When English cricket writers were harassing Hutton in 1953 for his unforgivable failures to win the toss, Jack Fingleton came up with a good suggestion in the London *Sunday Times*. It would have been worth emulating if you had been an English captain, I thought.

'Australian captain Joe Darling lost every toss he once had in England against F. S. Jackson,' wrote Fingleton. 'When next they met, at Scarborough, the Australian astonished the natives by presenting himself at the opposing dressing-room clad in underpants only. "Why, Joe," they said, "what is this?" and Joe said, "Well I can't beat him at tossing so I want to wrestle him for first innings this time."'

❧

The Toss at the 2011 World Cup Final

VIC MARKS

Former Somerset and England cricketer Vic Marks is the cricket correspondent of the *Observer*. This is an extract from his report on 3 April 2011 about the World Cup Final between India and Sri Lanka.

IT IS NOT OFTEN that the toss is a remarkable event in a cricket match, but it was here. With microphone in hand the host Ravi Shastri was his usual ebullient self, saying something along the lines of 'this is the greatest match in the history of mankind'.

Mahendra Dhoni tossed the coin. No one quite heard what Sangakkara called. Shastri announced that the coin, specially minted (and soon available from the ICC via auction – they try not to miss any opportunity for making a bit more dosh), had come down displaying a head. Then there was confusion since Sangakkara was certainly not volunteering that he had called 'tails'. Briefly the captains stared at one another.

Swiftly the match referee, Jeff Crowe, demanded another toss, which was undoubtedly won by Sangakkara. The whole episode was an embarrassment to the affable Crowe. In the final between Australia and Sri Lanka four years ago in Barbados he did not know when the game should finish. Here he could not get the game under way properly.

So had Sangakkara pulled a fast one? One snippet for the prosecution: if Sangakkara had called heads the first time around surely he would have made much more of a fuss when there was the suggestion of another toss? He, like Dhoni, was very keen to bat first. Instead, he was all equivocation. Being a lawyer, Sangakkara will have an articulate defence, albeit a soft-spoken one, I suppose.

7

DRINKS BREAK

The Light and the Dark

C. L. R. JAMES

C. L. R. James (1901–89) was a distinguished Afro-Trinidadian
historian and writer. From *Beyond a Boundary* (1963),
frequently cited as the best book on cricket ever written.

⤳

A S I LOOK BACK, all sorts of incidents, episodes and characters stand out
with a vividness that does not surprise me: they were too intensely lived.
What is surprising is the altered emphasis which they now assume. A Chinese
would land in the island from China unable to speak a word of English. He
would begin as a clerk in a grocery store in some remote country district.
[. . .] But this man, after about fifteen years, would be seized with a
passion for cricket. He did not play himself but he sponsored the local village
team. He would buy a matting for them and supply them with bats and balls.
On the Sunday when the match was to be played he provided a feast. He
helped out players who could not afford cricket gear. He godfathered very poor
boys who could play. On the day of the match you could see him surrounded
by the locals, following every ball with a passionate intensity that he gave
only to his business. All night and half the day his shop was filled with people
arguing about the match that was past or the match that was to come. When
the team had to travel he supplied transport. The usual taciturnity of the local
Chinese remained with him, except in cricket, where he would be as excited
and as voluble as the rest. You could find people like him scattered all over the
island. I didn't find it strange then. Today he and such as he are as intriguing
as any of my cricket memories. I don't believe that, apart from his business and
his family life, he had any contact whatever with the life around him except his
sponsorship of the local cricket club.

⤳

The Experimental Matches

WILLIAM DENNISON

William Dennison was a cricketer and writer of the mid-nineteenth century.
From *Sketches of the Players* (1846).

❧

FOR THE LAST three years there has not been so great an interest excited with the lovers of the manly game, as within this month (June, 1827), on account of the grand match which has lately been made between All-England and the County of Sussex, for 1,000 guineas a side, to be decided by three trials. The two first have been played, and both ended in favour of the county, – at Sheffield, by 7 wickets, and at Lord's, by 3.

On the part of England, there are one or two men from the neighbourhood of Sheffield, who have displayed great skill, and convinced the cricket world that the *South* must not, as heretofore, presume to wear the wreath for ever. On the part of Sussex there are some very fine players; but their victories have been, undoubtedly owing to a singular, novel, and perhaps we may say, unfair manner of bowling, by the *overcast* from the arm, instead of the *underhand* and graceful mode of the Old School. There has been considerable discussion on this point, – whether it could be allowed, and whether it shall be continued to be practised. The writer of this, an old cricketer, really shakes with fear of its adoption, as it certainly gives birth to the hope of gaining a wicket by *chance*, by a *wild twist*, instead of the fine *steady length*, as shown us in former times by Lumpy, Harris, John Wells, etc. It is true, these men could *twist*, but there was not that space taken for the chance, as at present. The general complaint of the hitting now being so much superior to the bowling, can alone justify the experimental and it is on that account it has been brought forward. Other means have been suggested to produce more equality, and to shorten the game; such as *four* stumps, increased length, and narrower bats; but this has been the one adopted, and the effect is certainly imposing. Indeed, it appeared in these matches, that there were only *two* men capable of playing against it with confidence, and to understand it, Saunders, and Mr. Ward, – although many runs were made by others.

The outcry against the hitting has not, in our opinion, sound reason on its side; nor is it borne out by comparative facts; at least the superiority is not more positive than in former times. Casting back the memory for twenty years or more, the difference will not be found so great. Who, in modern days, excel Tufton (now the Earl of Thanet), Beauclerk, Beldham, Robby, the Walkers, Fennex, and *throw over* Lambert with many others, – old Aylward, Jack Small and his active son? They had better bowlers to beat off, than these days supply. Where is the old Shepherd, and Harris, Wells, Fenner, Clifford, Bullen, Boxall, and (in the very *slow* school), Walker, and the Reverend Lord? The more there is written, the less the conversion; indeed, a challenge is offered for these heroes, and with a defiance to that excellent judge, the worthy Secretary to the first club in the kingdom, to produce a superior list. The single instance of the great favourite of the day is potent; but still he stands alone; and after all, though wonderfully powerful, steady, and safe, there is wanting that peculiar finish so prominent and so particularly pleasing in two or three of the above. The matches were as long, the runs quite as many, and three days were often employed without regret or murmur. It is difficult to account for the new-fashioned fancies, and wishes to have the game shortened; you may try to get the *hitting* into *slashing*, and the *bowling* into *throwing*; but in such a revolution you will lose all the fine science. You will gain *time*, but you will lose good *taste*.

Since writing the above, the following declaration, signed by nine of All-England, has been promulgated:–

'We the undersigned do agree, that we will not play the third match between All-England and Sussex, which is intended to be at Brighton, in July or August, unless the Sussex players bowl fair; that is, abstain from *throwing*.

T. Marsden

W. Ashby

W. Matthews

W. Searle

J. Saunders

T. C. Howard

W. Caldecourt

F. Pilch

T. Beagley.'

This declaration was afterwards withdrawn, and the third match was played.

Cricket at the Universities

S. J. SOUTHERTON

S. J. Southerton was editor of *Wisden* from 1933 to 1935.
From the anthology *Bat and Ball* (1935), edited by Thomas Moult.

STILL, UNIVERSITY CRICKET provides the historian with numberless notable features. That god of former days, W.G. Grace, did not go to either University, but had he done so, what records would he have created? At the time when he was of the age to be an undergraduate he was not only the outstanding batsman in the world, but he was a great bowler as well, and it must always be a matter of regret that circumstances did not conspire to enable him to go to either Oxford or Cambridge. And in mentioning 'W.G.', one instinctively calls to mind that his eldest son, W.G. Grace, jnr., was at Cambridge. If the truth be told, young 'W.G.' was not quite up to the standard of the average University cricketer. He had a rather stilted, awkward style in batting, but he took a few wickets with his somewhat angular action in bowling. Still, he was given his Blue, and thereby hangs a very sad and tragic story.

He played for Cambridge in 1895 and 1896, scoring in the first year 40 and 28 and taking one wicket. In the following season, when Oxford, left to get 330 in the last innings, hit off the runs for the loss of six wickets, I was a witness to one of the most heartbreaking scenes it has ever been my lot to encounter. 'W.G.' jnr. had been bowled by J.C. Hartley for nought in the first innings, and when he went in a second time, his mother and sister were sitting in the grand-stand just next to the press box. It was quite obvious to anybody watching them that they were both highly strung over the question as to how Grace would acquit himself. For the second time in the match he was bowled – on this occasion by F.H.E. Cunliffe – without scoring, and as he was making his way back to the pavilion, I glanced at Mrs. Grace and saw tears coursing down her cheeks. Her sorrow was intense, for on the ground on which her famous husband had achieved so many triumphs, the son, in the greatest match of his career, had twice failed.

Lord Harris in India

A. A. LILLEY

A. A. (Dick) Lilley (Warwickshire and England) was the leading
wicketkeeper of his era and played thirty-five Tests for England.
Twenty-Four Years of Cricket (1912).

⤳

IN SPEAKING OF cricket in India, I am reminded of a story told by Dr.
Pavri, the Parsee cricketer. The moral tone of Parsee cricket has remarkably
improved, says Dr. Pavri, during the past fifteen years, but before then it was
not considered as being opposed to the spirit of the game if strategy were
resorted to to win a match. About twenty-three years ago he was playing for
a Parsee Club against a regimental team, and the best batman on the Parsee
side went in, but was dismissed without scoring. Six wickets had fallen for
only 30 runs, and the position was becoming serious, when this batsman put
on a different dress, tied a handkerchief round his head to further disguise
his identity, and went in to bat again. This time he made a substantial score,
and won the match. He was afterwards found out, however, and received a
salutary lecture.

⤳

Cricketers

SAMUEL REYNOLDS HOLE

Samuel Reynolds Hole was Dean of Rochester from 1887 to 1904 and a noted horticulturalist. From *The Memories of Dean Hole* (1893).

ॐ

IT IS RARELY GIVEN to a clergyman to effect a complete transformation of character upon the cricket-field, as it was to one, who is now very highly esteemed in love for his works' sake, as a suffragan bishop, but he may exercise a very healthful influence. In the case to which I refer, the parson, who frequently played cricket with his parishioners and neighbours, was surprised and grieved to notice that one of those who joined in the game had a manifest dislike of his presence. The cause, whether some anti-clerical feeling, evoked by those agitators who tell working-men that they are robbed and priest-ridden, or from some other prejudice, he never knew; but the aversion was obvious, and on one occasion was conspicuously displayed by the proprietor, who placed himself at the beginning of an over by the side, and within a few feet, of the ecclesiastic who was going to bat, and contemptuously replied to a remonstrance and warning of danger, 'I'm not afraid of nothing as the likes of you can do to me.'

There came a loose half-volley to leg, and the batsman hit it with all his strength. His malignant adversary, anticipating results, fell just in time to the ground, or he would in all probability have been stretched there in woeful plight. He was a miner, and shortly after this escape he was very badly hurt by an accident in the mine. Then the clergyman, to his surprise, received an invitation to go and see him, and after several visits he had the curiosity to inquire the motives which had dispelled his antipathy. 'Oh,' said the miner, *'that hit o' yourn to square leg for six converted me.'*

ॐ

8

THE PROFESSIONAL LIFE

County Round: April–May

DICKIE DODDS

Dickie Dodds was an opening batsman who played for Essex from 1946 to 1959.
From *Hit Hard and Enjoy It* (1976).

&

WHILE MUCH HAS been written on Test cricket, many people have asked me what the life of an ordinary county cricketer was like. We will live through an imaginary season.

County cricket before the advent of the 'one-day game' was a comparatively uncomplicated affair. The season started early in May and went straight through to the end of August, with one three-day match following another. Occasionally there was a gap with no fixture, but the impression was of four months' continuous cricket. It was a wonderful way of life for those who had the good fortune to play then.

I can still almost taste the atmosphere and feeling and smell of those early April days when the Essex players reported for their first nets of the new season. After the constraints of indoor winter jobs, and long dark winter evenings, it was a joy, and gave a marvellous feeling of freedom to be in flannels and run on the newly-mown turf. And there was the inviting sight of the freshly rolled and cut net wickets – the green of the turf set off by the glistening white of the bowling and batting creases.

In those days we would begin straight away with net practice. The opening batsmen would be asked to pad up, and a little self-consciously we would go to the crease (for we had spent the winter in anonymous activity and had got out of the habit of being looked at) and take guard. The bowlers were no less self-conscious, wondering where their first delivery would pitch, if at all. And so, creakily, it would all begin – another summer of history to be recorded in *Wisden*.

Those first seasons after the war seem very carefree in retrospect. I am sure we were not as fit as we should have been. In Essex, at any rate, physiotherapists, trainers and managers were unknown.

But it was not long before the county moved with the times, and instead of nets we began the season with weight-training and had a full-time physiotherapist to repair the damage to muscles unaccustomed to such violence.

Perhaps I should have done better had I been fitter. I made a serious attempt to achieve this once. I had spent the winter in Stoke-on-Trent. The Port Vale football ground was not far from where I lived and as the season grew nearer I decided I would burst on the cricket scene as the fastest man in the county. Port Vale were glad to let me train on their ground and every afternoon I used to run round their pitch.

The only result of all this activity was that I damaged both achilles tendons and played the whole of the next season with them strapped up and in much discomfort. I was never much of an enthusiast for pre-season training after that.

After a week of nets or sometimes two – depending on when Easter was since we always did a stint of schoolboy coaching during the holiday period – we would have our first practice match. Traditionally this was against Halstead, which is a town on the eastern side of Essex. Their beautiful ground is in a meadow on a hill on the outskirts of the town. The pavilion has a thatched roof. There are tall fir trees on one side and the other is wired off from the park-like field beyond, where cows lazily graze.

The opposition were mostly farmers and occasionally they would import a well-known player or two to stiffen up the side. One such man had a bowling action that had brought him notoriety and a large crop of wickets. As we drove to the ground, those who batted low down the order would pull the legs of their companions higher up, who were going to have to gain their early-season confidence against the projectiles this man delivered on the never very certain Halstead pitch.

Whenever I drive past the Halstead ground I recall with pleasure those springtime games and the fun we had. Once, when Tom Pearce gave the ball to Ray Smith and asked what he was going to bowl, Ray said, 'Well, at this time of the season, skipper, I think the main thing is to try and hit the pitch.'

Provided the weather was good, it was not long before we had had enough of nets, and practice matches, and were anxious to get going on the real thing.

Our first three-day match of the season was often against Cambridge University. It was a fixture that made a pleasant start to the summer. One would motor up through the lovely East Anglian countryside, wondering what fortune the day would bring. By supper-time one might have 50, 80 or even 100 runs to one's name, or five wickets, with the glow and promise of a bumper season ahead. Or it might be a low score and the suspicion that this was going to be the year all cricketers dread when nothing goes right.

Cambridge is especially beautiful at this time of the year. The cherry blossom is blazing, the daffodils, wallflowers, and the fresh green of the willow trees give their spring-time dressing to the lovely buildings.

Fenner's, the University cricket ground, is always a picture. An artist groundsman of the highest skill was in residence there: Cyril Coote, reputed also to be the best shot in the county. He produced superb wickets with the ease of an Academician executing a portrait.

I am told that when it was recently decided to build a new pavilion at Fenner's, the suggestion was made that it should be put in a position which would have meant moving the 'square' on which the pitches are prepared. When Cyril was asked about this, he is said to have replied that it would be easier to move King's College Chapel. So the new pavilion stands in a place which enabled Cyril's 'square' to stay put.

He and his wife prepared the meals we had in the pavilion. If one felt one was sufficiently senior a player to approach him for his views he would give shrewd judgements on the current crop of cricketers at the University.

Lunches at this match were always interesting. The two teams sat with each other. I would look at and talk to these young men and try and foresee which would be household names in a few years' time – men like May, Bailey, Insole, Marlar, Dexter, Sheppard.

Although so close to Essex, Cambridge was classed as an away match, which meant we would be staying at an hotel for the first time in the season. Sometimes we stayed at the Boar's Head and sometimes at the University Arms. The latter adjoins the famous Cambridge greensward, Parker's Piece, where Jack Hobbs learned his early cricket. This stretch of turf can accommodate half-a-dozen cricket matches. Crossing this from the hotel one comes to a small lane off which the Fenner's ground is situated.

The feeling of the players at the end of the first day of a new season is a mixture of relief and satisfaction – a bit like after the first day of term at school. In the dressing-room after close of play, the players usually sink on to the bench where their clothes are hanging and have a drink; beer for most, soft drinks for some. Then there are the quick changers and the slow changers. But for almost all cricketers it is surprising how soon their thoughts switch from the activities of the day towards the activities of the coming night.

Haircut

PHIL TUFNELL

Phil Tufnell (England and Middlesex) played forty-two Tests for England between 1990 and 2001. From *What Now?* (1999). 'Gus' is Angus Fraser, 'Embers' John Emburey and 'Gatt' Mike Gatting – Tufnell's Middlesex colleagues.

BY THE TIME we clocked on for duty in the spring of 1990, Gus had returned from the West Indies with stirring tales of exploits on and off the field. Whereas my own experience of the Caribbean during the England Young Cricketers' tour had been, largely, a piss-up, this all sounded suspiciously like what every cricketer is in the game for. Given two chances of upsetting the odds against Viv Richards and company, one of which barked, the team had nearly pulled off a major upset, returning as glorious losers of the 2-1 rather than the usual 5-0 variety. At the same time they had obviously enjoyed themselves as well, and tales of rum and ginger tickled up what you might call my thirst for action. I decided that I really did want to play for England, after all. But I was determined that it should be on my terms.

In the immediate short term I was helped in my ambitions by the fact that Keith Medlycott hadn't really advanced his claims during the tour. Not that he had had much opportunity, for neither he nor Eddie Hemmings – who had been chosen because Embers had signed up on Gatt's rebel tour – played in any of the Tests. Then when the England selectors started looking around again, the playing conditions in place for the 1990 season could have been made for me. First, the return to low-seamed balls meant that the practice of relying on trundlers to tuck in on helpful wickets was about to disappear. Secondly, the summer was hot and dry, bringing the twirlymen into the game even more.

I began the season in far from auspicious form when, on the first day back at pre-campaign training, the club physio sent me home to get some sleep. But I ended up playing in twenty Championship matches. Embers, who, along with Gatt, was available all summer because of the five-year ban imposed on them for their involvement in the rebel tour to South Africa, played in all twenty-two. We bowled very nearly 2,000 overs between us, took 122 wickets (Embers 57, me 65) and Middlesex won the title. Wallop.

Sending down that many overs and being that involved, it was inevitable that I developed as a bowler more quickly during this season than at any other time during my career. I started to use my brain more, picking up on people's abilities and weaknesses, setting certain field placings, laying little traps and so forth. I was varying my pace more, and my flight, and I was bowling with good control. I also started to realize that, in order to take wickets, you don't have to turn the ball square – just enough. But the thing that really swung it for me, so I am reliably informed, came about halfway through the season with the rearrangement of my coiffure.

The hair was long again now, and a bit unmanageable, to be honest. On occasions the top used to flop across in front of my eyes, so that after I had delivered the ball, I was blinded momentarily in the follow through. By the time we turned up at Lord's for a Championship game against Worcestershire – in which, incidentally, I came up against Ian Botham for the first time, which was a bit oo-er – it was obvious I couldn't go out to field with the barnet flailing in the breeze. I didn't fancy asking one of my sausage-fingered colleagues to have a crack at trimming it, so the only thing I could think of was to try and tie it up at the back in a pony tail.

I'd be lying if I said I was unaware of the possibility that this might cause a stir. Who could say what effect the sight of my pony tail might have on the MCC members in the Long Room? As I walked through cricket's Holy of Holies on the way out to field, I could almost hear the spirits of the giants of the game, some alive, some long gone, calling to me from their portraits. Douglas Jardine in particular was plainly unimpressed. Mind you, judging by that cap he used to wear he is a fine one to talk.

Perhaps I couldn't hear it for the hair covering my lug-holes, but the game seemed to pass without too much piss-taking. Inevitably, though, the powers-that-be wasted no time in jumping on me again about the usual subjects – my general appearance and approach, etc. – and, as usual, I found it all difficult to get to grips with. Attitude. That was the word I kept hearing. My attitude was wrong.

I never quite saw it like that. In some ways I felt my attitude was too right for some people. Whatever I got up to after clocking off was my business, but the fact was that there was no one with a better attitude than me where it mattered, on the field, trying my hardest to get batsmen out.

There may have been some people at the club who felt that things came a little too easy for me. Perhaps they wanted to see me graft a bit more. The truth is that, had I played the game by their rules, I would have had a much smoother ride. But I just couldn't see that there was more to playing cricket at this level than bowling. The cream and brown snakeskin shoes, the hair, the ear-rings and all the rest . . . what did they matter as long as I was doing the job, taking wickets and helping the club win the Championship?

After the degree of success he enjoyed as England captain in West Indies and a good start to the international season on their return – including his 333 against India at Lord's – Graham Gooch was firmly in the driving seat. Having been left out of the squad for the trip to the Caribbean, David Gower was back in favour now, although seemingly on sufferance, but pony tails and scruffy gits with too much lip did not fit into Gooch's scheme of things.

His greatest friend in cricket, and in life come to think of it, was Embers. Schoolboy cricketers together, mates on early tours, they had the kind of relationship that makes wives suspect their husbands might be on the turn. So whenever Embers perked up on matters pertaining to Gooch and England, everyone in the dressing room listened with more than usual interest.

One day he mentioned my name in that context. 'Look, Cat,' he said. 'I think you have got a good chance of playing for England. You are bowling well, better than any other left-armer in the country, and they are definitely looking.' So far so good. 'But,' he continued, 'you've got to smarten yourself up and buck your ideas up. That means lose the pony tail.'

I knew it was coming and I knew I probably did need a haircut. But I wanted to be the one who decided when to do it, not them. By now I had worked myself up into a bit of serious rebellion. I dug my heels in. 'I like the pony tail. If they don't want to pick me, that's their problem.' I thought no more about it, and when we went to Uxbridge a fortnight later for the next Championship match, against Yorkshire, it was still there. As soon as Embers saw me he took me to one side. 'I'm pretty sure that a couple of the selectors are coming to watch you in this match. That thing has got to go. I'm serious.' And so was I. 'Bollocks,' I told him, or words to that effect. 'I'm sorry, but why does everyone seem to be more bothered about my hair than my bowling?' Too far gone now, I wasn't budging.

Very soon, however, the matter was taken out of my hands in dramatic fashion. During the lunch interval, Gatt tapped me on the shoulder and said, quietly: 'Tuffers, can you come with me for a minute?' Obviously he wanted to have a chat about tactics, the way I was bowling, or a ploy to attack one of their batsmen in a certain way. I duly followed him out of the pavilion and out of earshot of the opposition for the passing on of the secret plans. But he carried on walking. In fact he speeded up to such a lick that by the time I caught up with him I was virtually running.

Then he pounced. He turned, grabbed me, frogmarched me to his car and bundled me in. He drove me down the road into Uxbridge High Street, dragged me out of the car and into the barber's shop and, in the manner of the Master of Ceremonies at Madison Square Gardens, announced: 'Short back and sides.' I've never been so humiliated in my life. There was I, slumped sulking in the barber's chair having all my hair cut off while Gatt, like a pissed-off dad teaching his naughty little boy a lesson, sat reading the newspaper to make sure I didn't leg it. We were both still in our cricket gear. Job done, he took me back and made me play without another word.

From then on to the end of the 1990 season, little whispers started being heard. There were a few mentions in the newspapers and the like. I wasn't bowling any differently to how I'd been bowling before the haircut, but there was definitely a change of mood in the dressing room as well. 'Tufnell for England,' one or two of the boys would jokingly chant after a good spell. Except that it seemed to be more than a joke. I kept grooving along the way I had been, paying no real attention to the rumours. Around early September, the squad for the upcoming England tour to Australia and New Zealand was announced. *And I was in it.*

Get your hair cut, play for England. Simple.

❧

One Hundred for Eddie

MARCUS TRESCOTHICK

Marcus Trescothick made his debut for Somerset in 1993 and played seventy-six
Tests for England between 2000 and 2006. The Test match referred to is England v.
Australia at Headingley in 2001. From *Coming Back to Me* (2008).

B Y NOW I WAS firmly established as the man in charge of looking after
the ball when we were fielding. It was my job to keep the shine on the new
ball for as long as possible with a bit of spit and a lot of polish. And through
trial and error I had finally settled on the best type of spit for the task at hand.

It had been common knowledge in county cricket for some time that
certain sweets produced saliva which, when applied to the ball for cleaning
purposes, enabled it to keep its shine for longer and therefore its swing. As
with most of the great scientific discoveries, this one happened quite by
accident. While at Warwickshire, Dermot Reeve noticed that his bowlers
somehow had the ability to keep the ball swinging far longer than any team
they faced. The problem was no one in their side knew why. By process of
investigation and elimination he realized the reason was that the player in
charge of polishing and keeping the ball clean was his bespectacled top-order
batsman Asif Din, or rather, what he did to keep his concentration levels up,
chewing extra-strong mints.

It took a while for word to get around the circuit but once it did the sales
of sweets near the county grounds of England went through the roof.

I tried Asif's confection of choice but couldn't get on with them. Too dry.
Then I had a go at Murray Mints and found they worked a treat. Trouble was,
even allowing for trying to keep one going as long as possible I still used to
get through about 15 a day and the taste soon palled. Still, at least I never had
to pay for them. Once Phil Neale came on board as our operations manager
it was one of his jobs to make sure the dressing-room was fully stocked at all
times. We even tried taking them on tour a couple of times until we realized
that they didn't work as well on the Kookaburra balls used overseas as the
Dukes we used back home.

On the first day of the match in Leeds, an unfortunate fielding incident
almost gave the game away to the Aussies for the first time, as I dived to

gather the ball at square leg, I landed on my side and a shower of Murray Mints spewed out of my trouser pocket all over the grass right in front of the umpire. Fortunately, neither he nor the two batsmen seemed to take much notice as I scrambled on all fours trying desperately to gather in the sweets before they started asking awkward questions.

Batting Orders

MIKE BREARLEY

Mike Brearley (Middlesex and England) captained England on thirty-one occasions, losing only four times. From *The Art of Captaincy* (1985), which won the Cricket Society/MCC Book of the Year Award.

OCCASIONALLY IT IS necessary to convey a message directly to the middle. The captain may have to whistle or clap his hands to attract the attention of the batsmen, especially when they are aware that a change in policy unwelcome to their personal interests is to be expected. At other times the batsmen themselves look up to the dressing-room for instructions. 'Are we still going for the target?' they may need to know. Or the umpires are debating about the light: 'Should we come off if they offer us the option, or stay on?' When umpires are debating about the light, the captain must always take responsibility for at least part of the decision. He must make it absolutely clear to the batsmen whether as a matter of policy he requires them to stay on or come off, or whether the decision rests with them and their personal confidence or lack of it. Clear signals are essential in all these cases.

Sometimes the captain can even convey a subtle message. In the Headingley Test in 1981 the pitch favoured the bowlers. Having allowed Australia to score 403-9, we lost wickets cheaply. Botham went in to bat, and started to play shots. He tried to force Lillee off the back foot and missed. He looked up to the players' balcony and saw me. I grinned broadly, and gestured that he should have tried to hit it even harder, thereby conveying, I hoped, my pleasure at his uninhibited approach and an unqualified approval of his continuing in an extravagant vein. Or a captain may wish to suggest to one batsman that he restrain or indeed unleash the other. It is worth having a signal that means that one batsman should talk to the other at once, for either purpose; the one I favoured was a rapid movement of thumb to and from fingers, like a glove-puppet.

All these broad gestures are necessarily public. If the plan calls for secrecy the time-honoured means of delivering it is with a batting-glove taken on to the field by the twelfth man. However, this ruse takes nobody in, especially when the batsman himself has to be informed by the fielders that the glove is on the way; and though they will not know the content of the note (unless he tells them) they know that it is a note, and will soon infer its import.

Not all such semaphore and note-carrying is about tactics, incidentally. Jack Simmons of Lancashire is more likely to be concerned that the twelfth man gets him a double portion of fish and chips for lunch. And notes may convey assignations, exam results, even the birth of a baby.

During the Adelaide Test of 1955, Hutton was alarmed to see Cowdrey play one or two reckless shots not long before lunch. So he sent out the twelfth man, Vic Wilson, with a message. In Hutton's words: 'To the surprise of all, Wilson in flannels and blazer walked calmly to the middle and, under the curious gaze of fielders and umpires, produced and offered two bananas to Colin. "What the hell are these for?" he demanded. Wilson replied: "Well, after seeing a couple of wild shots from you just now, the skipper thought you might be hungry. It rather suggests he is keen for you to stay out here batting and get your head down."'

In South Africa in 1965 I was acting as twelfth man while England batted in a Test at Johannesburg. Bob Barber and I happened to be in the middle of a chess game. When he called me on to the field during his innings, ostensibly for some dry gloves, his purpose was to inform me that his next move was Queen's pawn to QB4.

❧

Random Reflections

FRANK CHESTER

Frank Chester was a Test umpire from 1924 to 1955, standing in what was then a
record number of forty-eight Tests. From *How's That!* (1956).

❧

ALL UMPIRES HAD one difficulty in common in the first years after the
last war – particularly 1946 – in finding somewhere reasonable to stay on
our travels around the country.

Clubs should have realized that umpires are every bit as important to a
game as players and that they have to be accommodated like anyone else, but
we had to take pot luck in finding somewhere to sleep. It was a nightmare
getting fixed up. After a tiring day in the field it was no joke tramping around
a strange town searching for a bed. I know of one umpire who solved the
problem by resorting to an air-raid shelter and found that he had as a sleeping
partner an amateur taking part in the match. In the middle of the night they
were joined by a third person – a Fleet Street sports writer who had been sent
to cover the match.

I shall not forget Whitsun of 1946 in a hurry. With Harry Lee I was at
Derby for the Warwickshire match. No hotel was available after tramping
around until midnight. I was making for the railway station waiting-room
when I met a police officer, who said he knew a boarding-house which had a
vacant bed. My heart slumped when I found the room; it was a musty attic, yet
the charges were no different from an hotel; there was nowhere to sit except
on the rickety bed.

The next day being Whit-Sunday, I caught the first 'bus to Nottingham,
where I succeeded in getting a meal and a drink. When I returned to Derby, I
tried to get to sleep by compiling my list of players for the following winter's
Australian tour. I could only get as far as eight.

On the Monday evening I went in search of a quiet drink but found
queues outside the pubs; when one customer came out another was allowed in.

Without being too harsh on the town of Derby in that year of more
grimness than grace, I must confess I was never more pleased to begin
my homeward journey. Harry Lee had been wise enough to make a prior
arrangement to stay at Nottingham.

❧

Fox on the Run

GRAEME FOWLER

Graeme Fowler (Lancashire and England) played in twenty-one Tests. His diary *Fox on the Run* appeared in 1989. It is December 1984 and England are on a tour of India.

NORTH AND CENTRAL ZONES 186 AND 176-3; ENGLAND 377 (ROBINSON 138, COWDREY 70, MOXON 42). MATCH DRAWN

ONE TROUBLE WITH not playing is it means perpetual nets. We have to be seen to be doing the right thing. I'm lucky in that I am a great 'net' person anyway. I always have a net whenever possible, because I feel they do me good. Not everyone is the same. Some people positively hate them.

The other trouble is that it gives you more time to be introspective. Very often sportsmen become blasé about their life-style, their surroundings and the places they visit. But that can be a necessary response. If you reflect too hard on where you are and what you are doing, the pain might strike the back of your eyes as you realize you'd rather be elsewhere with someone else.

When I married Stephanie, our prospects were of a Lancashire first-team player and a biology teacher. Within twelve months I was waving goodbye wearing my England touring blazer. Now after over three years of marriage I am on my third consecutive tour, and she is a college lecturer. Our lives have changed utterly. This year I have spent over seven months in hotel rooms; she has had over seven months on her own. In the remaining five months, I have probably spent two months seeing her night and day, and the rest of the time at home consisted of leaving one another at 8.15 a.m. and not meeting again until 8.30 or 9 p.m. Not exactly what we envisaged when we got married, expecting a fairly normal existence and the constant companionship of someone we loved. Is it any wonder that sports marriages are always under pressure?

I do miss her. I try to keep my feelings repressed, which is the way to cope through tours anyway. I never allow myself to look forward to anything, because that means you can never be disappointed. Taking everything at face value means relative safety, and so does just doing the everyday things. Eat, sleep, drink, watch and play, and no more. It is a strange existence, strange to have to catch your emotions, bottle them and throw away the bottle, but it helps you to cope. For me it is essential. But at the back of the mind there is always the nagging knowledge that I am missing her and my home life.

And little things catch you off guard. Out here the day's fielding can be brightened for me by a passing butterfly. There are some beautiful species flying around, the type you see adorning lounge and hallway halls in England. But every time I see one I think of Stephanie, because she adores flora and fauna. She is annoyingly well informed on the subject, but her love of nature instantly comes to me when I spy anything. She would love to see the butterflies, and I would love her to see them and share her excitement. But these little subliminal reminders catch you off guard and leave you with a lump in your throat or a smile trying to hide over-full eyes.

When I was a kid I would never have thought that an England cricketer could cry for any reason. This one can when the stream builds up and gets too powerful. Some day I might know if I am soft, or whether I have taken matters in my stride and coped. Out here I am Foxy the England star, not Graeme the husband. The latter is stored away, because letting him out of the bottle is too painful. But this England cricketer is not superhuman. He is an Accrington lad who has achieved the top level in cricket. I am still just an Accrington lad, though. Thank God!

And After

C. B. FRY

C. B. Fry played many sports at the highest level, representing England
at cricket and football, as well as holding the world long jump record.
This excerpt from *Life Worth Living* (1939) centres on the England/Australia/
South Africa Triangular tournament of 1912.

～&～

OUR FINAL MATCH with Australia at the Oval was a proper final. It was
a straight knock-out fight, the other two matches having been drawn.
The preliminary atmosphere was tense. The Press was on one of its pessimistic
and critical wavelengths. A rival evening paper explained my incompetence
in two columns. The weather enhanced the situation. So much rain fell that,
although the first day was fine, the field was quite unfit for play. A crowd of
30,000 was sitting expectantly in the sun looking at a wicket which they did
not know was a quagmire. The junior groundlings had been slowly proceeding
to and fro with the pent-houses.

Early in the afternoon Syd Gregory, the Australian captain, came to me
and proposed that for the sake of the crowd we should make a start. The
officials at the Oval were becoming anxious at the crowd's disappointment.
Now this was a good gamble on the part of little Syd. The wicket was bound
to be wet even if we played, not on the prepared pitch, but on another. Syd
knew that his side was done against our bowling unless he had the luck to win
the toss with a chance for his batsmen on the wicket while it was in its easier
state, and a chance for his bowlers if they got us on a drying sticky wicket. I
knew that with equal conditions of a mud wicket my team was bound to win.
So with the rubber depending on the one match I refused to start until the
turf was genuinely fit.

We did not start until late in the afternoon, and then I won the toss.
Thanks to Jack Hobbs, Rhodes, and Frank Woolley, who made 177 runs
between them, we registered the fine total in the conditions of 245. When I
walked out to the wicket I was unanimously booed by our 30,000 supporters.
The news had got around that I was the captain who would not start earlier.
Sidney [*sic*] Barnes and Frank Woolley easily accounted for our opponents for
a total of 111. No Australian batsman except Kelleway made double figures.

Our two heroes took 5 wickets each for 6 runs apiece. Frank Woolley made the ball break away with his left-hand finger-flip, and Barnes was quite unplayable. Had the Australians been able to play him they would have made fewer runs. In our second innings we lost Rhodes and Spooner quickly. Then Jack Hobbs and I attacked the bowling as in 1909 at Edgbaston. After making 32 by sheer hitting Jack Hobbs punched a long-hop into the stomach of point. Having again been booed properly on my way to the wicket, I was very much on the job, and with the help of Johnny Douglas the other end I may say that I performed in quite the right sort of way on the bowling. I think I should have got a century instead of 70 odd if I had not divoted the turf in attempting a full drive. No one else made runs and our total was 175.

I started the Australian second innings with Sidney Barnes, but I saw in a couple of overs that he was not the Barnes of the first innings. Great bowler as he was, he was liable at that stage of his career to be stiff and angular at the start of his second attempt. He had a slight rheumatic tendency, especially in damp weather. So I said to him, 'Barnes, what about trying the other end?' This brought on Frank Woolley, and he and Dean of Lancashire bowled the side out for 65 runs. Glorious victory. Immense applause. And in ten minutes down came the rain.

Just when we were finishing them off, Jennings, I think it was, one of the good Australian batsmen, in trying desperate measures, hit too soon and projected the ball vertically above himself to the height of a steeple. I shouted 'Wicket-keeper!' and Tiger Smith stood arms akimbo. Rhodes was at silly mid-on. I shouted 'Wilfred!' and the immobile Wilfred looked benignly at the sky. I shouted 'George!' to Hirst, who stood star-gazing at silly short-leg, like the Royal Observatory. The ball was well on its way down, so from silly point square I projected myself and arrived just in time to pouch it about a foot from the ground with a dive. I regard the catch as almost a fluke, but it looked all right as I casually tossed the ball into Wilfred's disobedient tummy.

This added the last straw to the growing burden of my popularity. But when the crowd gathered round the pavilion and shouted for me I would not go on to the balcony, because I felt that the time for them to cheer was when I was walking out to bat as captain of my side to try to win the match on a foul wicket. Ranji was in our dressing-room and he said to me, 'Now, Charles, be your noble self.' But I said, 'This is not one of my noble days.' All the same it was a great match, and I never saw the Australians again till 1921.

A Cricket Pro's Lot

FRED ROOT

Fred Root (Derbyshire, Worcestershire and England) was a fast bowler who played first-class cricket from 1910 to 1932. *A Cricket Pro's Lot* was published in 1937.

~&~

To GIVE AN opponent a 'toffee-ball' to enable him to score the important single run when his score is 49 or 99 is practised by many bowlers.

I had my initiation into this 'freemasonry' of cricketers in my very earliest days. It proved one of my many early disappointments, a disappointment which I could not reconcile myself to, or thoroughly understand for many years, but which was considerably alleviated by an experience I had later on. One of my first matches for Derbyshire was against Surrey at the Oval, when Tom Hayward was in his glory. As a raw country boy and a worshipper of cricketers, Tom was my hero. Incidentally his presence at the crease, with myself at first slip, filled me with awe. All the Derbyshire shock bowlers, including Cadman, Warren, Tom Forester, and Morton, had bowled for what seemed to me to be hours at Hayward, and a Lancashire League bowler – Noah Buxton – had been warned (at the instigation of Tom Hayward) that he 'cobbed them'. For the sake of his league career he had been taken off after his second over, never playing county cricket again, although being allowed to get hundreds of wickets in the league.

At lunch time Hayward had scored 94. After the interval I was put on to bowl and Hayward said to me, 'Have you ever got a wicket in first-class cricket?' Truthfully I answered, 'No, sir!' Tom immediately gave me hope. 'All right, sonny,' he replied, 'as soon as I have got my century you can have mine.' Thinking I might not be trusted to bowl many overs, and absolutely longing to be credited with the dismissal of so great a batsman, I promptly and purposely bowled him two full-tosses, which he just as promptly dispatched to the boundary. His hundred obtained, I gasped when this hero of mine continued to mete out drastic punishment to my bowling. I lost my faith in human nature when he approached his second century.

Poor Tom dropped 100 per cent in my estimation and I spent many sleepless nights wondering how such a great cricketer could so flagrantly have let me down. To make matters worse, Tom had caused me to chase many a mile from first slip to fine leg after his leg-glides. When after one of the balls he had tickled towards the gasometer I turned round to see the batsmen running their fifth run, so kicked the ball over the boundary thinking to save a run. Instead, the umpire signalled an additional boundary, and the scorer added nine to Hayward's total. However, as I have already remarked, I was young and inexperienced then-a-days, and later – years later – I realized what had happened and that I had been blaming the idol of Surrey crowds unfairly. It was this way. Playing for Worcestershire against Hampshire at Southampton we found Jack Newman on a real 'glue-pot' of a wicket. He was making the ball turn square. The only possible way to stop a typical Worcestershire rot seemed to me to be to play Jack's bowling with my pads. This I proceeded to do, stylishly shouldering arms with my bat. Imagine my chagrin when a particularly vicious off-spinner hit the flap of my leg-guards, flew up over my shoulder, ran along the whole length of my bat and finished up in the safe hands of Phil Mead at first slip. Parry – who was umpiring – called 'over' in a tone which, by intuition, told me he had not seen the incident. On the spur of the moment I walked down the pitch and did some 'gardening', then returned to my crease. Walter Livesey – the Hants wicket-keeper – informed me I was out and Phil Mead – ever an old soldier – sat down. A nasty moment was relieved when Newman appealed to Parry with the usual 'How's that?' to which the surprised rejoinder was, 'Not out; he never even played at the ball.' Naturally, the Hampshire players did not relish my apparent lack of sportsmanship in not walking out, and I became rather ashamed of my action. To placate Newman – who was always a really good sport – I broke the icy silence by telling him how sorry I was, and that I would get out as soon as possible, but in a manner which would not be apparent to either the crowd or to my own captain, who would probably have been averse to my action in throwing my wicket away. From that moment I simply slashed carelessly at every ball I received. Much to my astonishment I 'connected' magnificently, scoring 86 in a very short time, thereby placing my team in a very strong position. I was honestly trying to get out every ball. In quieter moments of guilty shamefacedness I remembered Tom Hayward at the Oval some sixteen years previously. He was vindicated in my thoughts.

❧

Cricket with the Lid Off

A. W. CARR

A. W. Carr captained Nottinghamshire and England during the 1920s and 1930s.
Cricket with the Lid Off was published in 1935.

O NE OF THE strangest things that has happened in my cricket career took place in 1929 when Notts played Hampshire at Southampton. At the end of the second day's play Hants wanted just one run to win the match. They wanted to go on and finish it off that evening, but I would not agree. If it had happened to rain hard during the night and next day, play might have had to be abandoned and we should have saved the game instead of losing it. My argument is that in a case of this sort each side ought to abide strictly to the rules.

However, it did not rain during the night, and next morning there was the extraordinary sight of two Hampshire batsmen, Alec Kennedy and Crease, coming out to make one run. There were one or two spectators on the ground and they saw me start the bowling in, to quote a local paper, 'a well-tailored dark suit' and the rest of the Notts team wearing their ordinary clothes and hats and two of the team, Barratt and Voce, fielding in overcoats.

9

KEEPING COUNT

The Men in White Coats

TERESA McLEAN

Teresa McLean was the first woman to win a cricket Blue for both Oxford and Cambridge. Her book *The Men in White Coats* was published in 1987.

❧

IN ALL EARLY cricket an umpire's main responsibility towards batsmen was to stand where they could touch his staff with their bats to score notches (runs). That is why the umpire at the batsman's end is shown in all cricket pictures right up until the early nineteenth century standing at leg slip, where his staff was in easy reach, not at square leg, to which position he gratefully retreated when staff touching stopped being the means of scoring notches.

Short notches were favourite causes of dispute and it took a brave umpire to call one if he thought the batsman had not run the full length of the pitch. Notches and short notches were signalled to the notchers, or scorers, who sat on the field of play with long hazel sticks into which they cut a notch for every run scored and a deep notch for every fifth or every tenth run, to make adding up easier at the end.

The notchers, like the umpires, retreated gradually as batting improved, until they reached their present position outside the boundary ropes. In 1727 there were, as yet, no boundaries. Every notch had to be run and the number of notches scored could be shouted to the notchers without a signal. Long after the introduction of the popping crease, batsmen continued to hit the umpire's staff to score a notch.

[...] In 1744 a score-card appeared for the first time, though most scorers still notched up the score on sticks. A Kent scorer recorded all the individual scores in a Kent/England game, all the byes, which meant all the extras – mainly overthrows, and gave the names of a catcher and stumper as well as a bowler. It was thirty years before such a detailed card was seen again.

The growing interest in cricket and the ever increasing betting on it created a demand for details of individual scores. There were bets on everything: how many runs a batsman would score, how he would be out, when, to whose bowling, at which end. By 1773 the best score-cards recorded how all the wickets were taken, not just the ones that were bowled and caught, with the occasional run-out. Scorers at sophisticated games kitted themselves out in smart clothes, moved out of the field of play and sat at tables, watching for umpires' signals and writing the score. Most cricket was pretty rough, and so were its notchers, but by 1775 scorers were second only to umpires as status symbols at clubs like the Star and Garter.

Knowing the Score

KEITH BOOTH

Keith Booth is a writer and the principal scorer for Surrey.
His book *Knowing the Score* appeared in 1998.

❧

THE FASTEST RECORDED authentic hundred – i.e. disregarding those scored in contrived circumstances to expedite a declaration – is by David Hookes who achieved it in 34 balls. How this compares with earlier efforts by (say) Gilbert Jessop around the turn of the century, who recorded hundreds in 40 and 42 minutes in 1897 and 1907, we do not know and never shall.

Instrumental in crystallising the thinking in the minutes v balls issue was the advent of limited overs cricket and money. When the John Player's County League began in 1969, there was a prize of £250 for the fastest 50. It was won by Keith Boyce who clocked 23 *minutes*. Then, someone, somewhere must have said that the measure of time was less valid than that of balls received and in 1972 the prize went to Glenn Turner who made 50 from 32 *balls*. There was still an element of unfairness in that the prize was restricted to televised matches, but that is another story . . .

Bill Ferguson was recording balls received somewhat earlier and in the statistical appendices to Douglas Jardine's book about the 1932–33 'bodyline' tour *In Quest of the Ashes* includes tables of runs scored and balls received by each batsman against each bowler in each Test and over the series.

Roy Webber in the 1950s demonstrates that it is possible to calculate balls received, but does not maintain a cumulative record and the statistic does not form an integral part of the system. It began to do so when Bill Frindall redesigned the Ferguson system in 1966 and for media scoring has done so ever since.

Official records, however, have been slower to catch on. We have seen how limited overs cricket accelerated the inclusion of balls received, but it did not become a feature of first-class records until later. Wisden makes no mention of balls received in Robin Hobbs's 44-minute hundred against the Australians at Chelmsford in 1975 and in The Oval Test match scorebook the first record is as late as 1984. Mike Ringham, who scored for the Australian touring team in 1985 (and two earlier tours), recalls that in that year he was helping county scorers come to terms with the concept of recording balls faced.

The history of the Walter Lawrence Trophy, one of the Ridley Awards, presented for the season's fastest first-class century, parallels the chronology outlined above and illustrates this stuttering progress towards using balls faced rather than time at the crease as a measure of the speed of scoring. Oozing with nostalgia, the list records the first winner as F.E. Woolley with a hundred in 63 minutes for Kent against Northamptonshire at Dover in 1934 and continues to 1939 when L.E.G. Ames recorded one in 70 minutes.

The award then died and was not resurrected until 1966 when it was restricted to Test Matches and calculated in terms of balls (First winner: K.F. Barrington against Australia at Melbourne – 122 balls). It then reverted to all English first-class cricket in 1977 and the speed of scoring was again measured in minutes. (As the late Harry Sharp, player and scorer for Middlesex for many years, was fond of reminding his colleagues: 'We didn't have balls in my day!') Only in 1985 are balls introduced and the first two winners are, perhaps unsurprisingly, I.T. Botham and I.V.A. Richards.

That nostalgic diversion serves to illustrate that, while linear scoring systems have provided the facility to record balls faced for some time and media scorers have used it, it has only recently replaced time batted as the official method of measuring speed of scoring.

Opponents of linear scoring have argued that there is too much to do at the end of an over, especially when a wicket falls on the last ball. It is certainly true that the demands are greater than under the traditional system, but, on the other hand, more information is immediately available and there is usually time while the players are changing over to record the information. And the sky will not fall down if the changed statistics resulting from an over with extras, wickets and boundaries to more than one batsman are not entered until half way through the following over.

Most scorers have established a routine of a tripartite check with their colleague of runs from the over, cumulative runs against the bowler and total. Periodically – perhaps every ten overs or so – the batsmen's totals and balls received are compared to ensure that any discrepancies can be rectified before they are continued too far down the sheet. At the Foster's Oval, the almost invariably accurate manual scoreboard is directly opposite the scorebox and any discrepancies in the total and batsmen's scores are usually noticed pretty quickly. The scoreboard operators are among the most efficient in the country, but it is easy enough to miss the umpire's bye or leg-bye signal, especially when it is given in the opposite direction.

Scorers vary as much in their approaches to cross-checking as they do in their personalities: some do no checks at all, preferring to leave it all to the end of the innings; others check at the end of each over. Personally, I prefer to adopt a middle route and check occasionally when the opportunity is available.

There is a certain bonhomie about the county scoring circuit with virtually all scorers on good terms and willing to help one another with cross-checks, calculation of statistics etc. Byron Denning of Glamorgan has a complicated system of numbering the balls of the over by the names of towns running east to west through South Wales – and if that were not sufficiently confusing, he does it in Welsh. I believe the origins of this labyrinthine scheme lie in the coincidence of Porthcawl rhyming with fourth ball and the mythical superstructure has been built on either side. Thus, the first ball is Cas Newydd (Newport), the second Caerdydd (Cardiff), the third Pen-y-Bont (Bridgend), the fifth Castel Nedd (Neath), the sixth Abertawe (Swansea) and the seventh, where there is one, Llanelli. Clem Driver has attempted to devise a rival scheme based on the towns of the Essex coastline, but could find nothing between Clacton and Southend.

Just as runners bore non-runners with talk of courses and PBs, so do scorers bore non-scorers with talk of scoreboxes, their accessibility, the view of the playing area therefrom and the quality of the catering on the grounds of the county circuit. They have even ritualised it and established a 'Standards League'. Until his retirement from the county scene, Bill Peterbridge, Yorkshire's 2nd XI scorer, used to invite scorers to mark on a scale of one to five, the scoring position under accessibility, assistance, communications, comfort and viewpoint, and the ground under atmosphere, catering, hospitality, ease of access and car parking.

Scores Real and Imaginary

W. E. W. COLLINS

W. E. W. Collins had a brief first-class career of seven matches in the late nineteenth century. From *Leaves from an Old Country Cricketer's Diary* (1908).

❧

ONCE AGAIN, THE man who is always thinking about his bowling or batting average not only loses half the enjoyment of the game but lacks the true spirit of a cricketer, and deserves to be relegated to the golf-course. Still, in years gone by I used to be not a little amused by the care which a certain gentleman of my acquaintance took to ensure that he should be supposed to be playing up to his reputation. It was his habit to send to a weekly paper the scores of the matches in which he played, and according to the 'authorised version', which eventually appeared in print, he was in country cricket among the best all-round performers of the day.

'Hulloa,' he would remark as he unrolled the score-sheet, 'this won't do. Only nineteen runs and two wickets. That's not good enough for F. C—. Now, just look here! That greedy great creature, Brown, has gone and got forty-seven runs. Hang Brown! he's no good, never saw a worse innings in my life; he ought to have been out a dozen times over; he'll have to part with some of that little lot. Besides, forty is just as good as forty-seven, so I think we'll give my old friend F. C— that odd seven. Then there's Jones – fourteen. Who the devil is Jones when he's at home? He won't see the "Field", you bet. He may think himself deuced lucky to be allowed a run at all. However, he shall keep the four and I'll have that ten. That's thirty-six anyhow. But, hang it all, if I'm not a better bat than Brown I'll eat my hat, and he's got forty. Oh, I say – extras seventeen, that looks bad, don't it, and besides, I'll vow I touched one of those byes that went to the boundary. What an ass their umpire was! And that Winchester boy really did not keep wicket half badly. Young talent ought to be encouraged, and he'll be awfully pleased to see some of the byes knocked off. Well, we'll call it four byes instead of twelve, and I may as well have that odd no-ball while I'm about it. The bowler won't mind, and somehow forty-five looks better in print than forty-four. It's half-way on to fifty, isn't it? Well, here goes, F. C— forty-five. And now about wickets. F. C— two? Here, I say, old chap, you got four, don't be greedy, give me one and then we shall be quits.

And here's Walker got a wicket. One wicket is no good to any man. I'd rather get none than one, wouldn't you? I think F. C— may as well have Walker's little lot. And then there was a silly beast who got run out. I'll bet he'd rather have been bowled. Leastways we'll chance it and call him bowled. There now, that's better, F. C— five wickets and forty-five runs. Good old F. C—, deuced fine player still, eh!'

And that, possibly, was the opinion of sundry of those enthusiasts who make it their business to follow the doings of great men in the columns of the sporting papers.

Funny tricks are occasionally played by the scorers themselves. Some twenty years ago I was playing at Vincent's Square against the Westminster boys. As it happened, theirs was a very poor side, and we won our match pretty easily. Small thanks, however, to the scorers, two small collegians with very few inches and no conscience at all between them. Probably, through wholesome fear of ulterior consequences, they credited their own heroes with their proper or even more than their proper quota of runs, but they employed a process of subtraction and division, varied by occasional fits of absence, bodily as well as mental, when we were batting. I only scored a single figure myself, and so was not a material sufferer; but even so, I would just as soon have had the nine runs which I really did make as the three which they were generous enough to allow me. But when a hard hitter who had been piling up runs at a tremendous pace retired after a solid hour's batting, he was considerably disgusted to find that the telegraph board showed thirty odd as the result of his exertions.

'But please, sir, I wasn't scoring all the time,' pleaded one of the small culprits when tackled on the subject.

'Nor was I,' chimed in the other.

'Well, where are the fellows who were scoring, then?'

'Please, sir, I don't know,' and there is no getting beyond this *ultima ratio* of the small boy.

'Well, I'll vow that I got a hundred, and I shall count it a hundred in my average,' announced the victim; and it is to be hoped that in this resolve he found consolation.

I may say that if on that occasion we found the gallery at Vincent's Square moderately sympathetic, some of their personal criticisms savoured of candour rather than of courtesy. Ours, as it happened, was a side without a wicket-keeper, but a good-natured veteran, built on rather substantial lines, good-naturedly volunteered to 'stand back' with the gloves. It was unfortunate under the circumstances that he should have brought his newly-married wife to watch his prowess; still more unfortunate that he should have found her a seat where every remark of the gallery – they don't talk in whispers at Vincent's Square – was all too audible; most unfortunate of all that the first ball of the match should have been steered just out of the gentleman's reach, and that he was enforced to run after it. For I never yet met the wife who really relishes hearing her husband saluted as 'fatty', and in that case 'fatty' was quite the least objectionable term applied to the panting runner, some of the gallery preferring to particularise.

I had more reason for posing as an aggrieved party when in a match in Northants upwards of a quarter of an hour's really hard hitting on my part was rewarded by the addition of two runs both to my own score and our total. Having looked at the score-sheet at lunch-time I happened to know that I had got sixty-seven runs, and at the time of my final dismissal was quite prepared to believe that I had made well over a hundred, and I had been not a little surprised that the gallery had not in any way shown their appreciation of the fact. As it happened, both telegraph board and plates were second-hand articles, and the figures were so illegible at a distance that nobody in the field ever thought of looking at them. When, however, I passed the scoring-box, *en route* for the pavilion, I found the small telegraph boy in the act of returning my score as sixty-nine. On entering the box to lodge a protest, I found that the one and only scorer, a valet who had been pressed into the service in the absence of the regular official, had in the first place counted on a whole hour's interval, then added an extra five minutes on his own account, and had finally got to work again in the last over of my innings. As we had supplied the scorer, and as his omissions did not affect the result of the match, things were left in *statu quo*.

A Yorkshire Cockney

ALAN GIBSON

Alan Gibson was a journalist and broadcaster.
From *Growing Up With Cricket* (1985). The then world record partnership of 555
by Sutcliffe and Holmes took place against Essex at Leyton in 1932.

I SAW A GOOD deal of this famous partnership. Every moment when I was not at school and play was on, I was on that balcony. I refused to go downstairs to eat. Mother was inclined to make trouble about this, but I had the support of father, who was an enthusiast himself, and promised to 'keep an eye on me' – so long as he had his meals up there too. Think what it meant to me, the little Yorkshire exile, when my very own heroes came and did this to the Londoners! Who were the Frenchmen now? At the end of the first day – I do not have to look this up – Yorkshire had scored 423 for no wicket. I remember the swift, silent running between the wickets (very different from modern Yorkshire practice) and the huge pull for six to mid-wicket with which Sutcliffe reached his 150. Next morning I raced back from school again. No wicket had fallen. It was about one o'clock that the 555 was reached (the previous record had been 554, made by two other Yorkshiremen, Brown and Tunnicliffe in 1898). The cheering was rapturous, none more than mine. There was a big crowd by now, many Yorkshiremen having travelled south during the night. I saw Holmes and Sutcliffe stride down the pitch towards each other, majestically, and shake hands. Life, I felt, had not anything to show more fair, though I did not put it that way; and I am not sure that it has had.

However, I soon learnt that bliss does not long remain unalloyed. Next ball, Sutcliffe, taking a wild swish at Eastman, was bowled. By this time I was in the ground itself, nobody bothering to keep children out in all the excitement. Holmes (224 not out) and Sutcliffe (313) were assembled to be photographed under the scoreboard. Suddenly the total on the board moved back to 554. There had been a disagreement between the scorers about a no-ball. Had they only equalled the record, not broken it? There was a time of agonised suspense, and then the board moved back to 555. There has been much research into which was the true figure, none of it, I think, conclusive. I would not be surprised if both were wrong; we shall never know. Before modern scoring techniques were invented, in the first place by Arthur Wrigley, and then developed by Roy Webber, Bill Frindall, Irving Rosenwater and several more – scoring in first-class cricket was haphazard. It was commonplace for one scorer to 'take a stroll around the ground' for half an hour, and then fill in his book from his colleague's, while the colleague in turn took his stroll. Something like this, I expect, had happened at Leyton. I like the story that it was a little parson (Essex grounds have always seemed to harbour a lot of parsons) arriving with his own scorebook, meticulously kept, who settled the argument.

Recollections of Lord's and the Marylebone Cricket Club

WILLIAM SLATTER

William Slatter joined the Lord's ground staff in 1863 and rose to be head groundsman. His *Recollections* were published in 1914.

❧

THE SCORING IN those days, as now, was done by the professionals, but it was done on a stand made of iron rods framed up with a wooden seat and back, about seven feet from the ground. The scorers rested the score book on their knees and if the rain came on suddenly they often got wet with their book, before they could scramble down from their perch and seek shelter under the old sheds, where the Grand Stand now stands. The score board was attached to this stand on the right hand, and the scorer on that side had also to put up the figures. This scoring stand laid about for some few years after the score boxes with the board each side were erected, but what eventually became of it, I do not know.

[. . .] No accommodation was made at Lord's for the press until the Grand Stand was erected. Previous to this, the reporters had to stand their chances of getting a seat anywhere, and I believe that they had to pay entrance to the ground just the same as any other visitor. There were shrubberies at each end of the pavilion, and Mr. Knight, the only recognised paper representative in those days (1861–64), (and a nice old gentleman he was), attended to his business on the ground and not in the refreshment bar. He has stood all day in the bushes inside the rails, being the only place to view the cricket on a crowded day, with no score board or slips to tell him the state of the game, and having to score the whole doings of the match in his own notebook. He had no refreshments from lunch time until 7 o'clock when stumps were drawn with the exception perhaps of a cup of tea which I have taken to him when I have had the chance. I have never heard him grumble, and he reported only what he saw and knew. On an ordinary match day you would find Mr. Knight sitting on one of the forms among the general spectators. I believe I am correct in saying that he reported cricket for 'Bell's Life in London', the leading sporting paper of that time, which is now, I understand, incorporated with the 'Sporting Life'.

A Summer Saturday

HAROLD C. WOODS

From *Cricket in the Long Grass* (1995), a memoir of village cricket in Hertfordshire in the years before the Second World War. The names of places and people are fictitious.

As MOST OF the cricketers worked until noon on Saturdays there was little time available for all that had to be done before the official start of play time of 2.30 p.m. Some, like the Bates brothers for example, lived in the outlying hamlets and may have several miles to bike home from their place of work – have a quick dinner, smarten up, and don the whites – then bike off to the cricket field. The sacred meadow was somewhat tucked away, on part of the Squire's large estate, on the outskirts of Shappley; in fact, it bordered onto the long drive leading to the Manor House itself, so that the magnificent chestnut trees forming the avenue also became one of the boundaries behind the bowler. Like most village cricket fields – its first and primary purpose was to provide a pasture for cattle – and the tiny mown rectangle, cut in there in the middle, would today look as incongruous as a tennis court on the African veldt. Consequently some form of strong protection was required to prevent the cows from meandering all over this tempting patch, which, quite naturally they desired to sample. The fence, therefore, was both high and strong – made of heavy six-foot wooden posts bearing three strands of barbed wire. There were concrete sockets every few yards around the 'table' to accommodate the posts and the whole affair constructed in two 'L' shaped halves – each having about a dozen posts and being joined at diagonal corners with iron screw-bolts; so some ten men were needed to dismantle and drag one half up to the top boundary near the spinney, then drag the other half down to the ditch/boundary at the bottom. It was not unknown for members of the visiting team to lend a hand in this operation – although this might depend, to some extent, on certain umpiring decisions at the last meeting! The fourth direction, opposite the giant chestnuts, enjoyed no natural lines of demarcation, and was therefore deemed unlimited.

Whilst Jim helped with the small secondary fence of chicken wire (which, in this case, was there to keep rabbits out rather than chickens in), two lesser mortals were despatched to the nearby Lodge-keeper's cottage to borrow the good lady's well scrubbed scullery table and, hopefully, two chairs for the benefit of the scorers. The wooden box of numbers, and the stand for their portrayal, were fished out from under the hollybush which served as changing-room, toolshed, and clothes rack. The club bag arrives – balanced, fore and aft, on the handlebars and seat of Bill Miller's bike. More men appear, in dribs and drabs, from various directions – over stiles, through hedges, and, more circumspectly, on bikes down the road. The visiting team were biking the five miles from Menin and arrived, more or less, together about a quarter to three; some wearing ordinary trousers through fear of getting black chain oil on their precious whites which were rolled up and tied onto the carrier with the usual piece of hairy 'Binder String'. These particular blokes repaired to the uninviting corner behind the hollybush where the necessary change could be affected in some measure of privacy from the highly interested eyes of the various giggling schoolgirls in the vicinity. In the meantime, George and Jack Bates had finished mowing and marking out the creases – pitched the stumps, and returned their equipment back to the all-enveloping holly bush. Eventually, at about three-o'clock, when all the fielders had rolled, and enjoyed their final pre-match 'fag', all is ready for battle – and the two umpires, resplendent in freshly laundered white milking coats, make their stately way out to the middle; whether they walk out together with a friendly chat – or separately in stony silence, again depends on what transpired when the two teams last met.

Having won the toss, Bill decided on first knock so Jack Bates and Fred Owen get padded up as best they can from the sorry-looking five pads available in the bag, here again – binder string, that constant friend and companion of the countryman, is much in evidence where straps and buckles have suffered damage over the years. These two openers can enjoy the privilege of wearing a pad on each leg if they so desire – a luxury obviously denied the rest of the side, unless, of course, both men are dismissed quickly, in which case some of the more fussy ones may 'double up'. The introduction of that piece of equipment known, strangely, as a 'Box' has not yet reached Barfordshire, so all in all, padding-up is not a very complicated affair.

Jim takes his seat of office at the table and, under the guidance of the captain, fills in the batting order and other relevant details. The order will need to be fairly fluid because Bob Green has had trouble with a scythe during the week and is reduced to wearing a carpet slipper on his damaged left foot, so if he goes to the crease at all it will be as a temporary enforced left-hander. This small hiccup in Bill's plan of campaign is offset, to some extent, by the news that one of the visiting side will be late because he has suffered a 'Puncher along be 'Unny Lane'. Thus, with the sun beaming *its* approval on the proceedings so far – Charlie who has been shovelling away the worst of the 'pancakes' round the edges of the wicket area, gave it up as a rather pointless exercise and threw his shovel under the bush.

The distant church clock strikes once – 'ar parst three then Wal, yearse, jist struck ar parst be the church', observes George to Big Wally-Stanton as they indulge in another leisurely 'roll' and light up.

There is little time for young Jim to daydream about the possible time, in the vague future, when *he* would be one of the white-shirted demi-gods now engaged in battle – because wickets fell at a rate which demanded his full attention to the all-important book and instructing the lesser 'Hobble-De-Hoy', whose duty it is to change the appropriate numbers on the 'Telegraph' board.

The lush long grass, with patches of two-feet high thistles and nettles, in the outfield ensured that only the lofted blow is likely to bring much reward; any stroke played along the ground stopped dead at the edge of the mown 'table' and is rarely likely to produce more than a scampered single. Later in the season, especially during a hot dry summer, things may improve in this respect, in that the cows would consume more of the dwindling grass faster than it could grow, thus close cropped areas would appear here and there, allowing the ball to bounce and possibly roll.

The Shappley innings follows a fairly normal pattern, with runs keeping just ahead of wickets, at Ten for Six; then comes a flurry of runs from the bat of Alf Marsh who has simplified batting by using a powerful golf-like swing regardless of the line or length of the delivery. To-day he 'strikes oil', so to speak, and clobbers a six and two fours over long-on before missing a straight 'shooter'.

Thirty-three all out is a handsome enough total and will just about allow both sides to speculate on victory during the tea interval.

As the players wander off to the village-hall a quarter of a mile back into Shappley — where tea will have been prepared in typical village style, Jim is faced with the most arduous and only disliked part of the day — for the cows were already advancing menacingly towards that succulent looking, temporarily vacant, rectangle — and armed only with a cricket stump in each hand he races out to begin his hour-long battle with these fifteen four-legged enemies of cricket. Sometimes he received some assistance from one or two other boys who might also be looking for a free jam sandwich brought back by the players, but, today he is fighting alone and dashes madly around in desperate attempts to keep the pitch inviolate; as he bashes one intruder on the nose with his stump two more are stealthily encroaching elsewhere so that he is forced to run and shout continuously to prevent their cruel hooves from injuring the sacred turf.

Suddenly, and for no apparent reason, the enemy seemed to lose interest and withdraw in disorderly manner. With great relief Jim fetches the shovel and sets about removing the worst of the steaming new deposits that had appeared — especially on the bowler's run-ups and the 'keeper's normal territory; there was unmistakable evidence, too, of at least one successful trespasser — at Silly Point, (or Short Mid-On as the case may be), evidence which demands frenzied attention for removal before the men's return — otherwise the lad's protective efficiency may be questioned and his reward accordingly reduced. Fortunately, on this warm July day, the players' stroll back after the interval is somewhat desultory, so he just has time to sprinkle some fairly fresh grass mowings over the offending stains — thus hoping they will escape notice before returning to his seat at the scorer's 'throne'.

Brother George slaps down two slices of well buttered and well jammed new currant bread onto the scoring book then turns his back to lean on the table to roll another 'homemade' in company with his team-mates. Having finished the delicate operation and got 'steam up' once again he suddenly said, 'Ullo, wot we got 'ere then?' and withdraws from his open shirt front one of the delicious triangular iced cakes which were an extra product of the local currant-bread baker.

'I wunder 'ow *that* got there?' says George. 'Well blow me if there een't another one? They musta' cre'p in there summow.' Jim munches quietly away at his second jam sandwich – supplied this time by the Captain, hoping, of course, that he might be in line for an iced cake.

'I carn't eat 'em,' announces George, 'I've 'ad anuff, anybody warnt 'em afore I give 'em t' the sparrers?' Right behind his broad back young Jim holds his breath, knowing full well that as a mere schoolboy he was not authorised to answer the general question posed by George; in any case, he was beginning to suspect that it was all a hoax perpetuated by his elder brother who had, in fact, carefully nursed these iced delights all the way back from the tea table especially for the young scorer; Jim's suspicions are soon proved right when all the other men vowed they were 'Bustin' and couldn't eat no more'; so George, with a broad grin, turns and puts the rather battered looking items onto the scorebook with the words 'P'raps the scorer can find a 'ome for 'em, eh Jim?' The Menin scorer had, of course, enjoyed an official tea with the players so all is well for the hard-earned reward to be consumed at leisure.

Subsequently the visitors innings gets underway; their openers prove sound and solid, ten runs come without loss and things look black for Shappley – although it must be pointed out that Alf, the main strike bowler, is below par due to his brand new, dark blue, braces which have not yet 'worked in' and consequently restrict his usual rhythm. Fortunately Wally at the other end discovers a patch of daisies and dandelions just short of a length on a line of off-stump and, in the space of three accurate overs, swung the match by reducing the opposition to Nineteen for Seven – and eventually, with the last man being run-out, Menin muster only Twenty-nine. Several of them are most disgruntled at this dubious end to the game and, without stopping even to change trousers, they climb the fence, mount their steeds and speed off with angry shouts of 'Yew jist wait 'til yew come over our place, tha'sall'. The rest are more philosophical – with one or two even helping to drag the fences back then agreed on a pint and postmortem at the 'Dog and Duck'.

All in all, a fairly typical day and very much to Jim's liking.

10

IT'S NOT CRICKET

W. G. – Too Clever to Cheat?

SIR DEREK BIRLEY

From *The Willow Wand* (1979) by Sir Derek Birley, a distinguished educator and writer, who also wrote the award-winning *A Social History of English Cricket* (1999).

❧

ONE OF THE canons of 'playing the game' is that the umpire's decision is inviolable and always unquestioned. Anyone coming upon cricket for the first time in the winter of 1977–78 would need a large pinch of salt to swallow that. Listeners to the BBC radio commentaries from Pakistan could regularly hear the faultless accent of Henry Blofeld communicating scepticism about the standard of umpiring based on the expressions of doubt by various England players before they left the wicket.

Nor is this just modern decadence. In a county match in 1875 William Oscroft refused to leave when given run out, and only submitted after much debate and the lapse of half-an-hour. Lord Harris wrote of another county player: 'Jupp loved batting and was quite difficult to get to leave the wicket if there was a chance of the umpire deciding in his favour.' In one match on his local ground he was bowled first ball. 'He stooped, picked up and replaced the bails, and took his guard. "Aren't you going out, Juppy?" asked the opponents' captain. "No," said Jupp, "not at Dorking"; and he didn't.'

But the code expects more than that the player shall leave the crease promptly without demur. He is required on occasions to own up to things the umpire may not have seen. In first-class cricket, for instance, he is supposed to 'walk' without waiting for the umpire's decision if he has edged the ball to the wicket-keeper. Now there is no doubt that 'walking' does occur (though probably more often when batsmen have just made a hundred than when the snick comes first ball after three successive ducks) but the custom owes as much to convenience and prudence as to virtue. It sometimes happens that a faint edge is neither seen nor heard by an umpire: if it is known by batsman and wicket-keeper to have happened, but the appeal is rejected and the batsman remains, and bad feeling is created. In English county cricket since the teams play each other so regularly they find it convenient to operate a sort of knock-for-knock agreement. It seems likely that the convention had its origins in the predominance of amateur captains amongst whom the bonds of similar schooling, upbringing and class feelings made 'playing the game' important and whom history had set above the lowly umpire. Significantly the code is not associated with league cricket, where they tend, especially in the north, to think it foolish to try to do the umpire's job for him. Nor is it by any means so universally accepted in Australia where the special conditions of English county cricket do not exist.

This difference has frequently led to unpleasantness. There are those who solemnly maintain that the whole course of post-war Test cricket was altered because of failure to observe the code. On the 1946–47 tour of Australia Bradman, they say, should have 'walked' on the first morning of the first Test when caught in the slips. Australia had lost two wickets cheaply while Bradman put together 28 not very sparkling runs, when, according to Bradman, 'came the most debated incident of the series. Voce bowled me a ball which was near enough to a yorker. I attempted to chop down on top of it in order to guide the ball wide of the slip fieldsmen. Instead it flew to Ikin at second slip. In my opinion the ball touched the bottom of my bat before hitting the ground and therefore it was not a catch.' The fieldsmen thought it was. As one English writer put it: 'The batsman did not move and, after a pause, Ikin appealed, only to have it refused.' He went on: 'All those to whom I have spoken and who were there assure me the catch was a fair one and Bradman was out, but the umpires ruled otherwise.' There were in fact other opinions, mostly Australian. But the England captain Hammond was incensed and at the end of the over said to Bradman: 'That's a damned fine way to start a Test series,' meaning that he should have 'walked'. But Bradman stayed, went on to make 187, and Australia won the series and held on to the Ashes until 1953.

Another Australian captain, Richie Benaud, explained the problem: 'It had always been drummed in to me that as soon as an appeal is made I must look at the umpire and if he says "out" or "not out" I must obey that decision instantly and without any display of emotion. Consequently when the business of "walking" came into vogue it proved a difficult assignment for me.' He goes on to describe an occasion when he moved without waiting for the umpire. 'For an instant I thought I had hit the ball and started to move to the pavilion . . . I was a couple of yards from the crease when I realised it had flicked my shirt – but there is no going back once you have started to move.'

This was in 1960. F. S. Trueman appears to have encountered Benaud before he had taken to 'walking'. He tells us: 'At Lord's in 1956, I had Richie caught behind first ball, and he was given not out. He went on to score 97 . . . . Some years later he told me the ball went off the edge of the bat, flicking his shirt, and went to Godfrey Evans, but Richie, by immediately rubbing the arm where the ball had brushed his shirt, got the decision.'

The television cameras reveal in close-up that 'walking' is by no means normal behaviour and that many players try to avoid errors on the part of the umpire: when suspected of having been caught off their gloves they may well rub their forearms vigorously. The England captain, Brearley, seemed likely to rub a hole in his shirt, near the shoulder, when in the fifth Test at Adelaide in 1978–79 he was given out caught at the wicket. Fred Trueman will also know that it is not only in Australia that cricketers are not used to 'walking'. There may be interesting variations in certain northern leagues. Young cricketers in Yorkshire are likely to be taught that it is very poor policy to let a fast bowler know that he has hurt you, even, or perhaps especially, if he has; but two exceptions may be allowed. If you are hit on the knuckles and there is an appeal you can rub your elbow, and if you are hit on the leg you can rub yourself high on the thigh.

In the second case the advice may also be to jump about a bit as well (as an aid to the umpire in reaching a correct decision about l.b.w.). It is interesting to note that, in contrast with the doctrine of 'walking', nobody seems to expect players to leave their feet in position after the ball has hit their pads. The difference between this and catches behind the wicket may be that with an l.b.w. decision only the umpire can see exactly what the position is. Another incident involving Bradman in the 1946–47 series has been amusingly described by the Australian writer, Ray Robinson. It happened in the third Test. That was the Test in which Wright felt sure he had Bradman (3) when the batsman moved in front of the stumps and tried to force to the on a shortish ball which leapt through too quickly for him. The bowler turned to appeal for l.b.w., both hands raised supplicatingly, and Evans supported him with gloves eagerly aloft. Umpire Scott ruled against them. As if to provide circumstantial evidence of the correctness of the ruling, Bradman walked aside rubbing a place on his anatomy which was too high for the ball to have hit the wicket.

Bumpers, Boseys and Brickbats

JACK POLLARD

Jack Pollard was an Australian journalist and sports biographer who wrote about a wide range of sports. *Bumpers, Boseys and Brickbats* was published in 1971.

❧

FROM THE BEGINNING of the nineteenth century cricket matches were monopolised by professionals. Only infrequently did amateurs appear to challenge the pros' supremacy. One of the most notable of these was the Reverend Lord Frederick Beauclerk, the fourth son of the Duke of St Albans, a descendant of Charles II and Nell Gwyn, and one of cricket's greatest punters.

Lord Frederick was a batsman of skill, for he sometimes hung his gold watch on a stump and defied bowlers to hit it. He became a dictator at Lord's where he was the only person permitted to bring in a dog. Often he ordered from the ground people he did not like.

Much of Lord Frederick's penchant for gambling was emulated at Australian cricket grounds of the time. The activities of betting men at important matches worried our administrators. Despite placards in the pavilions warning spectators against betting, the practice was very difficult to curb. Bookmakers treated cricket matches as an ideal place to continue their business on non-race days.

Lord Frederick was a great gambler on single wicket matches in which side bets often reached vast sums and the morality of the game was continually suspect. He would bet on anything from whether a batsman would hit the ball out of Lord's to the time an innings would occupy. Even the most assiduous of modern punters like Don Tallon and Keith Miller would have been hard pressed to match him.

'His Lordship, like many a younger son before him, took Holy Orders, but we are bound to admit that he never seems to have allowed his clerical duties to interfere materially with the claims of cricket,' says Harry Altham. 'For 35 years, elegant in white stockings, bankeen breeches, a scarlet sash, and a white beaver which, when frustrated, he was apt to dash to the ground, he was an outstanding figure in the great matches, and for nearly 20 more as a critical spectator at Lord's where his word has become virtually law . . .

'Unfortunately, Lord Frederick's cricket had another side to it. He openly avowed that in match-making cricket was worth 600 guineas a year to him and, though this does not necessarily imply sharp practice, it is not easy to reconcile with a presidential speech of his in 1838 when he spoke of cricket as "unalloyed by love of lucre and many jealousies". It was, alas, not his habit to count the game beyond the prize and there were times when batting with a rival he could hardly be induced to run the other's notches, and when, if he lost a match or failed himself, he would try to bribe Bentley, the official scorer, to suppress the score.'

John Sparkes, an eminent player of Lord Frederick's day, tells of the lengths Lord Frederick would go to win bets in this story from *The Cricket Field* by the famous cricket reporter, the Revd James Pycroft: 'When the noble Lord drew himself in the guinea lottery for runs, and was in with me, he would not run any runs hardly but his own if he could help it in order to get the lottery. Lord Ponsonby, who had drawn my name, once promised me two guineas if I got most runs; but Lord Frederick went backwards and forwards to the scorers to count his notches and mine, and the end of it was that he got 64 and I got only 60. Though he did give me a guinea, Lord Ponsonby would have given me two, and I call that kind of thing which Lord Frederick did "cheating" and nothing more or less.'

Another great player, E. H. Budd, offered to back himself to carry any man at Lord's on his back and run 60 yards with him while an opponent ran 100 yards. The bet was taken by a 'very gentlemanly prime fellow' named Val Kingston who nominated a 20-stone passenger for Budd. Even so Kingston only won the bet by cribbing 10 yards on Budd at the start of the race while Budd's passenger was saddling up.

Mary Russell Mitford records how Lord Frederick took himself off in the middle of the second innings of one match so that the last two batsmen played without him. 'By this means his side lost and the other could scarcely be said to win,' said Mary Russell Mitford. 'So be it always when men make the noble game of cricket an affair of bettings and hedgings, and maybe, of cheatings.'

It was of Lord Frederick that this verse was written:

> My Lord he comes next, and will make you all stare
> With his little tricks, a long way from fair.

During Lord Frederick's reign at Lord's, E. H. Budd once hit a ball clean out of Lord's original ground, a feat against which Thomas Lord had bet someone 20 guineas; but on Budd's claiming the money with the intention of dividing it amongst the players, 'Lord was shabby and would not pay'.

In front of the pavilion at Lord's at every great match sat men ready, with money down, to give and take the current odds upon the play. Many well-known bookmakers were in their midst, men who resorted to all kinds of skulduggery to keep their money safe. The bookmakers even made trips into Hampshire and the near-London counties specially to corrupt players. They transacted most of their business, however, at the Green Man And Still, the cricketers' pub in Oxford Street, London, where all visiting players lodged.

One of the unsavoury offshoots of the gambling which accompanied most important matches of the time was that it frequently caused fighting among spectators. After a court action in which a defendant had been found not liable to pay a betting debt which he had incurred at a cricket match, the Judge commented, 'It is, to be sure, a manly game, and not bad in itself, but it is the ill-use that is made of it by betting above £10 that is bad and against the law.'

Bills announcing forthcoming cricket matches invariably mentioned side-stakes, and although many of these may have been exaggerated to draw the crowds, there is little doubt that huge sums of money changed hands at some matches. One match between the Old Etonians and The Gentlemen of England at Newmarket was reliably reported to have had almost £20,000 in side-stakes on it. Commenting on cricket betting, *The Gentleman's Magazine* said, 'It is a notorious and shameless breach of the laws, and gives the most open encouragement to gambling.'

With the bookies' financial assistance, the professional cricketers of the day lived it up at a rate 'five guineas for a win and three guineas for a loss would never have paid for'. Many a young county player fell easy victim to the free drinks and the purse of the bookies they met in London. There were few first-class players so the bookies only had to 'fix' one or two outstanding cricketers to be certain how a match would end.

'If gentlemen wanted to bet,' James Pycroft reported, 'just under the pavilion sat men ready with money down to give and take current odds, and by far the best men to bet with, because if they lost it was all in the way of business; they paid their money and did not grumble. Still they had all sorts of tricks to make their betting safe. One artifice was to keep a player out of the way by a false report that his wife was dead.'

By far the most corrupt cricket of the time were the single wicket matches. Altham's *History of Cricket* describes one match, a double-cross, in which the bowler refused to bowl within the batsman's reach (wides did not count) while the batsman refused to make any stroke for fear he might score and so lose his money.

At Lord's a dinner party was disturbed by a brawl out in the middle of the field. It was in the midst of a Surrey v. England match which everyone expected the powerful Surrey side to win. Much to the experts' surprise the bookmakers were laying seven to four against Surrey. The two principals were ordered to be taken into the pavilion when alarming accusations they made floated through the open windows. Both men were in a rage and they were ordered to stand on opposite sides of the table.

'You were paid to lose the Surrey match.'

'You were bought over at Nottingham.'

'Who missed the catch at Bury?'

'Ay, and who bowled at anything but the wicket in Kent?'

MCC members who had lost money on the matches discussed found the taunts 'falling in so accurately with painful recollections as to matches won and lost against all reasonable expectation, the committee had no choice left open to them'. The two players were warned off Lord's for life.

Although many blamed the 1879 riot at Sydney Cricket Ground on betting men, Australian cricket has nothing in its past to equal events like those at Lord's in the era of Lord Frederick Beauclerk.

❧

Radcliffe – Spilling Blood for Victory

HARRY PEARSON

Harry Pearson is a writer and journalist. *From Slipless in Settle* (2010), which won the Cricket Society/MCC Book of the Year Award. Middleton CC play in the Central Lancashire League.

෴

(PAUL) ROCCA HAD made it into the Middleton first team when Eric Price was the professional at Glebe Road. Price was born in Middleton and played county cricket for Essex. He was a typical English medium pace bowler and he'd been on the receiving end of a famous hammering from Don Bradman's 1948 Australians. At Southend the tourists had posted two hundred before lunch on the first day, Bradman thrashing Price for five consecutive fours and reaching his century in seventy-four minutes.

'They scored 721 in a day and Eric finished with 0–156 off twenty overs. Though, of course, the way he told it if it hadn't been for a few poor LBW calls and a couple of spilled catches he'd have got five for twenty-seven and they'd have been all out for ninety-two,' Rocca said with what I'm pretty sure was a chortle.

Cricket in Lancashire had an edge to it, Rocca said. 'When I played cricket in the army during my national service people from down south were surprised by how competitive I was,' he said. 'But that was the way cricket in the leagues was always played. It was hardnosed, played to win. Mind you, there wasn't any of this sledging.'

Not even from Cec Pepper? I asked.

Paul Rocca sucked in his cheeks and raised his eyebrows. 'Well,' he said, 'you know. Pepp was Pepp.'

Many people believe the Australians invented sledging. In fact, some even go so far as to lay the blame at the steel-toed boots of one bloke, Cecil George Pepper. Pepper was a man who lived up to his name. He was so fiery it's a wonder his cap never caught fire. Rocca had played with and against him on many occasions.

Pepper was regarded as one of the finest all-rounders of the post-war years. But he never played test cricket for Australia. This was because he had roundly abused Don Bradman in a Sheffield Shield match at Adelaide in

1946. The exact wording of Pepper's verbal onslaught is not known, but since he taunted another batsman who had played and missed at his leg breaks throughout an eight-ball over with the words 'You can open your fucking eyes now, mate, I've finished', reacted to a loud blazer worn by the Indian batsman Vijay Manjrekar by yelling 'Jeez, where'd you get that jacket, off the back of a bloody horse?' and responded to a spectator criticising his, to borrow a phrase from Brian Close, frequent invocations of the conjugative verb in a Central Lancashire League match by smacking him in the mouth, we can probably hazard a guess that it didn't include any quotations from Proust.

Cec Pepper was born in 1916 in Forbes, New South Wales. He was built like an Edwardian bobby, with a meaty face and even beefier forearms. He was a hard-hitting lower middle order bat and a dynamic bowler of leg spin. He made his name as a teenage prodigy in grade cricket with Parkes, hitting 2834 runs, and took 116 wickets in a single season.

When the Australian Services team toured England in 1946 playing a series of 'Victory Tests', Pepper outshone even the brilliant Keith Miller. His amazing hitting in a game at Scarborough, in which he sent the ball sailing across the sky above the boarding houses and into Trafalgar Square, is the stuff of legend. 'Pepp could have been one of the all-time greats,' Paul Rocca said as Ken Skewes smacked the ball over the heads of the Radcliffe fielders and it bounced into the wall of the gents' toilets beneath the scoreboard.

Bradman, though, was known as 'The Don' and in the post-war years he ruled Australian cricket like the Boss of Bosses. After the Adelaide business word soon came down to Pepper that he would never play for any Australian team Bradman was involved with. Pepper decided to come to England instead. Alley, a man very like Pepper in temperament, felt similarly wronged by The Don. Bradman had assured Alley he would be picked for a tour of New Zealand and the future Colne and Blackpool pro had gone out and ordered several fresh sets of whites for the tour, only to learn via the wireless that he hadn't actually been selected.

Keith Miller, or so it was rumoured, had been deprived of the Australian captaincy by Bradman. After The Don retired from playing and became a selector everyone expected the charismatic former fighter pilot eventually to take charge of the national side. He didn't. It was said that this was because in the game against Essex in which Eric Price had been so severely mauled, Miller – feeling that Australia were simply humiliating weaker opposition and having been commanded to bat by his captain – deliberately got out for a duck. Nobody defied Bradman and got away unpunished. He vetoed Miller's appointment as successor to Lindsay Hassett, insisting on Ian Johnson instead. When I asked a veteran of the leagues what he made of this suggestion he said it sounded highly plausible. 'I played with a lot of Australians,' he said, 'and the impression I formed was that, while they all agreed Bradman was a genius as a player, most of them regarded him as a right little prick.'

Miller almost went into the leagues himself. He signed a contract to play for Rawtenstall in the 1947 season, but, allegedly under pressure from Bradman, later reneged on the deal. The Lancashire League charged him with breach of contract and put him on the blacklist with 'Bagger' Barnes. Bradman, incidentally, had been offered a contract in the Lancashire League by Accrington during the winter of 1931–2. After some thought he turned it down, because 'The Accrington offer would of course have involved me in becoming a professional cricketer, which I did not want to do.' Well, quite.

After his problems in Australia, Pepper, in his own words, buried himself in league cricket. He signed up for Rochdale in the Central Lancashire League in 1947 and did the first double of a thousand runs and a hundred wickets in CLL history. After two seasons he moved on to Burnley in the Lancashire League where he did the double again, one of only three men ever to do so (the others were Vijay Hazare and Colin Miller). Shortly after his arrival in Lancashire the veteran league professional George Pope had told the Australian that 'The important thing as a pro is that when you are on the field you project your personality.' League crowds liked big characters and Pepper was about as wide as would fit.

'As a bowler I'd put Pepp on the same level as Shane Warne,' Paul Rocca said. As a batsman he was one of the biggest hitters around. During the 1946 Victory series he'd almost hit the clock at Lord's. He'd struck a six during the Commonwealth XI tour of India that sailed straight out of the massive Wankhede Stadium. At the SCG he smacked the ball from number two ground over the stand to number one ground, a distance estimated at 140 yards from strike to first bounce.

Pepper was a roaring success at Burnley. Unsurprisingly he also fell foul of the authorities and had to write a letter of apology to the League President after some of his more ribald remarks had carried through the walls of the dressing room and into a function suite where an awards dinner was being held. After five seasons at Turf Moor the Australian returned to the CLL, playing for Radcliffe, Oldham, Royton and Worton.

On the field Pepper bristled with purpose and aggression. Anybody who didn't match up was likely to feel the rough edge of his tongue. Despite the fact that he was a spinner, Pepper expected to open the bowling. On one occasion the skipper of the side decided to hold him back and bring him on first change. After a dozen overs the batting side were sixty for no wicket and the captain threw the ball to the Australian. 'You're on now, pro,' he said. Pepper shook his head and threw the ball back. 'You bowled them in. You can fucking bowl them out.'

The umpires in particular suffered. During one Central Lancashire League game he rapped one off the batsman's pad. 'How's that?'

The umpire shook his head. 'Not out.'

'Not out?' Pepper asked in an apparently calm tone.

'Yes,' the umpire replied, 'it would have missed leg stump.'

'You are quite right, umpire,' Pepper said genially. 'It *would* have missed leg stump. It would not have hit the off stump either.' He paused for a moment to fill his lungs with air and then bellowed at a volume that rattled the windows in the clubhouse 'IT WOULD HAVE HIT FUCKING MIDDLE STUMP.'

Not that Pepper got everything his own way. In a game umpired by Harry Wood, a rejected shout for caught behind saw Pepper give vent to various colourful expressions relating to Wood's eyesight and parentage. When the Australian took his sweater at the end of the over he apologised for his outburst. 'No need to worry,' Wood replied, 'in the heat of the moment we all say things we may later regret.' In the next over Pepper had a large shout for LBW. Wood stared at him. 'Not out, you fat, bald, Australian bastard,' he said. Pepper enjoyed that immensely and it was apparently Wood who persuaded him to take up umpiring when he retired from the game in 1964.

Pepper was on the first-class umpires list until 1979, but though he was well respected in the county game he was never appointed to umpire a Test match. It was said that this was because the authorities thought he was a racist.

Pepper was great friends with Frank Worrell and Colly 'Mighty Mouse' Smith, and he also reputedly helped Radcliffe pro Gary Sobers financially, but some of his reported remarks, particularly to Indian and Pakistani players, don't read too well.

Cec Wright, who'd come up against Pepper when pro-ing for Crompton, said that he had always got on with the Australian: 'In the clubhouse he was good company, very friendly. What he said on the field was a different thing. When he crossed the boundary ropes he did what he thought would help his side win. I took no notice of it myself. It was just nonsense, you know?' Like Paul Rocca, Cec Wright is a man of unimpeachable niceness. It's hard to imagine everybody would be quite so forgiving.

Pepper made his home in Lancashire and died in Littleborough in 1993. In old age he was as forthright as ever. When Ian Botham was destroying the Australian attack during the 1981 Ashes series Pepper was asked what he made of him. 'Ian Botham?' he said. 'I could have bowled him with a cabbage with the outside leaves still on it.'

Alfred Shaw, Cricketer: His Career and Reminiscences

ALFRED SHAW

Alfred Shaw was a famous England cricketer of the nineteenth century, who many regarded as the best bowler of his era. *His Career and Reminiscences* was published in 1902. The tour of 1876/77 was the first England tour of Australia to be accorded Test status.

I T IS SOMETIMES said now-a-days that betting is unpleasantly prominent in cricket of a certain type, notably League cricket, and this more particularly in Lancashire. In first-class English cricket the taint is fortunate, almost unknown; in Australian cricket, while betting is still too prevalent, there is no comparison with the condition of things that prevailed when I first made its acquaintance on this tour. It was on the occasion of our first defeat at Sydney by New South Wales (fifteen players), on December 7th, 8th, 9th and 11th, 1876, that I had my first experience of what betting on cricket in Australia meant.

The local newspapers were perfectly frank, alike in admitting the existence of the evil and in regretting it. *The Australasian*, on December 16th, 1876, wrote that 'in proportion to the population there is probably no part of her Majesty's dominions in which betting is more extensively pursued than in this colony.' A writer who adopted the pseudonym of 'Censor', in specially referring to one match with fifteen of New South Wales, on the dates just mentioned, said:–

'I do not like to mention the word "betting" in connection with cricket, but, truth to tell, there is a large amount of wagering over the match, the Sydney players being well supported at 6 to 4, and 7 to 4. Several commissions have arrived in Melbourne from Sydney to accept that price, and now 6 to 4 is hardly to be had.'

The craze for betting was not without its influence upon some of the English players, for one or two regrettable matters cropped up that it will be my duty to refer to later on.

As events turned out, though we scored 122 and put out the New South Wales fifteen for 81, making the price 2 to 1 on England, we lost the match by two wickets. This result sent the local populace into ecstasies, while I fear one patriotic daughter of the Old Country suffered great tribulation. For, while the match was in progress, Lillywhite received a letter from a lady imploring his team to make every effort to win this match, 'as it would not be safe for any Englishman or woman to walk the streets of Sydney if New South Wales were victorious!' Methinks the lady in her love for the Old Country, misjudged the nature of the Sydney sportsman's enthusiasm and underrated his gallantry.

This success of New South Wales followed Trickett's splendid victory over Sadler, on the Thames, for the title of champion sculler of the world. Betting apart, had not our New South Wales cousins an excuse for an excess of enthusiasm? They had 'licked England on the water and on the cricket field', and though they had had the advantage of four extra men in the latter contest, it was our pleasure to accept the defeat, and not remind them of their lost sense of proportion. We could do this with all the more grace in that the match had produced a little matter of £3,000.

Jack Selby, during the tour, put his sprinting powers, and capacity for effecting a *coup*, to good account. He arranged numerous matches with town and up-country pedestrians, most of which he won – when it was necessary he should succeed. It was in Selby's nature to dearly love 'a plant', as the sporting term goes.

It cannot be considered surprising that in quarters where betting was rampant, as was the case in Australia at this time, some of the members of our team, who needed very small encouragement to back their opinions and statements at any time, should be led to participate in enterprises they had better have eschewed. One of these enterprises had most unpleasant consequences to one member of the team, and it led to the side being deprived of his services for the last few weeks of the tour. The victim was Ed. Pooley. He has referred to the incident in 'Old English Cricketers', but the real circumstances have never been detailed until now.

We were playing at Christchurch against Eighteen of Canterbury, on February 26th, 27th, and 28th, 1877. In a discussion as to the prospects of the match that occurred in an hotel bar at night, Pooley offered to take £1 to 1s. that he named the individual score of every member of the local team. It is a trick familiar to cricketers, and in the old days of matches against local eighteens and twenty-twos it was not infrequently worked off against the unwary.

How safe it was for the nominator of the individual scores can be judged from the bowling record which had been credited to me at Auckland shortly before. In 55 overs, of which 30 were maidens, I took 18 wickets for 39 runs, while in the second innings Emmett obtained 7 wickets for 8 runs.

Another incident, which caused much amusement, showed the helplessness of some of the twenty-twos. One of the players was a gentleman whose skill was not equal to his enthusiasm, and his wife made a bet with him of a suit of clothes to a silk dress that he did not make a run. He came to me and told me he must win, and I agreed to bowl him a slow long hop on the leg side to enable him to get the run. When he came in I bowled him just the one he wanted, but he put out his leg in the act of attempting to hit, mistimed the stroke, and the ball hit his leg and rolled into his wicket, so he was bowled, and his spouse became the richer by a silk dress.

But to return to Pooley's bet. The bet being accepted, Pooley named 'a duck' as the score of each batsman on the local side. A fair proportion of 'ducks' was recorded, and Pooley claimed £1 each for them, while prepared to pay 1s. each for the other scores. The man with whom the bet had been made said it was a catch bet on Pooley's part, and he declined to pay. The man's name was Ralph Donkin. His refusal to pay led to a scene of disorder, and brought Pooley's services with the team to an unpleasant end.

We had to go next to Otago, and at the close of the match there Pooley was arrested on a charge of 'having at Christchurch maliciously injured property above the value of £5', and also of assaulting Donkin. For the assault he had £5 and costs to pay. In the other charge he had as partner in trouble Alf. Bramall, a supernumerary attached to our team. The two were committed for trial, bail being allowed of £100, with two sureties of £50 each.

We never saw Pooley again during the tour. He and his companion were tried before the Supreme Court at Christchurch on April 6th, 1877, and found not guilty. The local public thought he had been hardly used in having been taken away from the team. They subscribed £50 for division between Pooley and Bramall, and in addition they presented Pooley with a gold ring. The old Surrey wicket-keeper had to make the journey back to England alone.

In justice to him it should be stated that he was not the only, and possibly not the chief, participant in the row that followed the bet.

The Mohali 'Fix'

SHAHARYAR M. KHAN

Shaharyar M. Khan is a former Foreign Secretary of Pakistan, UN Special Representative and chairman of the Pakistan Cricket Board. He was manager of the Pakistan team that toured India in 1999. From *Cricket: A Bridge of Peace* (2005).

❧

AT THE BREAKFAST table in the hotel restaurant, I had noticed that a large number of former Pakistani Test players had also gathered for the match. Former captains, Majid Khan, Intikhab Alam, Wasim Bari, Asif Iqbal, Ramiz Raja, were all at the hotel and later in the Pakistan enclosure at the stadium. We were also joined by Pakistani Board officials, journalists and commentators.

At breakfast, a Pakistani official had come up to me and whispered in all seriousness that the Mohali match had been 'fixed' between the players on both sides and the gambling mafia. They had selected the Mohali match because it did not affect the outcome of the triangular series and was, therefore, not under the scrutiny of officials and others on the lookout for betting scandals. National patriotism was not at stake.

I, of course, had been aware from the onset of the tour, of the damaging shadow of the betting scandal hovering over the Pakistan team. Wasim Akram, Saleem Malik, Ijaz Ahmed, Mushtaq and Saqlain were under particular pressure but other members of the team also felt the stress of the scandal during the tour. I had looked hard at possible evidence of interaction between our players and the betting mafia but had found none. While not discounting the possibility of our players having indulged previously in deals with the betting mafia, especially in meaningless tournaments in Toronto, Sharjah and Singapore, I was convinced that this scourge to the good name of cricket had not seeped into the conduct of the Pakistani team during its high-profile visit to India.

There were three reasons why I was convinced that the team on this tour was clean and free of any betting scandal. First, there had been so much publicity about match fixing that no player in his senses would risk his career and even a jail sentence by indulging in betting during a tour that was under constant scrutiny. Secondly, because of the Shiv Sena threat, security was so tight that contact – even telephone contact – by the players would have been immediately discovered and betting attempts brought to light. Thirdly, I found the team so committed, so spirited, so patriotic and so disciplined that the very thought of individual gain at the expense of team and national honour when playing India seemed unthinkable. I did receive a call from a Pakistani fan stating that Saleem Malik had been talking on the phone to a known mafioso but I dismissed the accusation as a personal vendetta because Malik had not even played in the match that he was supposed to have fixed.

I, therefore, disregarded the whispered warnings at breakfast, which my informant substantiated by stating that Ajay Jadeja and Moin Khan – the acting captains – were seen breakfasting together. I disregarded this as evidence of duplicity immediately, as the two teams were socially on good terms, and whenever they stayed in the same hotel, the players mingled freely at meal times. Srinath, Harbajan Singh and the younger Indian players were special favourites with the Pakistanis as were Afridi, Shoaib and Ijaz with the Indians. International stars like Wasim, Tendulkar and Waqar also knew each other well and were often seen chatting together. Jadeja and Moin having breakfast together was, therefore, quite normal and I discounted the dark implications of the two acting captains* hatching a betting deal over a conspiratorial breakfast.

As we moved to the ground after lunch, several retired Pakistani Test cricketers and Board officials came up to me with more 'evidence' of a betting

*Wasim Akram later decided to play and captained Pakistan at Mohali.

fix during the match. They all conveyed the 'agreed scenario' to me, which ran as follows: India would bat first, regardless of who won the toss. They would then be bowled out for a relatively low score on the best batting wicket in India. This would push all the betting money on Pakistan. Then, Pakistan would make a good start, pushing bets further on Pakistan. There would then be a collapse so that India would win the match unexpectedly, leading to a massive clean-up by the betting mafia. Even our commentators and journalists seemed to be aware of the agreed script, in which our team were supposedly willing conspirators and ready for a substantial pay-off. Their patriotic spirit was also not being tested because the result of the match had no bearing on the contestants for the final.

I heard these accusations of a fix with disbelief for reasons I have already stated. Above all, to think that this disciplined, spirited team would stoop to such levels was unbelievable. If true, it would destroy my assessment of their character and patriotism. Accordingly, I remained stubbornly unconvinced of any match-fixing deal. I considered it based on scandal-mongering to which, I regret, many Pakistanis, even educated ones, lend a receptive ear.

The match began after lunch and, true to the match-fixing script, India batted first and on an excellent wicket were bowled out for 196, a low score considering Pakistani bowlers were not at full throttle, the lightning outfield and batsman-friendly pitch. Throughout the Indian innings, I kept receiving more messages of a fix, this time even senior Indian cricketers joining in. Even Minnoo turned to me and said 'Don't you know the match has been fixed'. She was the only messenger of foul deeds that I could turn against and I told her that she was talking nonsense. She replied, 'You seem to be the only one who believes in your team's innocence. Everyone else is convinced that there is a fix.' By now even Nino Qazi, forever flaunting her huge green flag, had dismay and horror written all over her face.

Silently, I was beginning to have my own doubts, which increased when the match-fixing script was being played out exactly as predicted. The Pakistan openers failed but Ijaz and Inzamam, supposedly the principle [*sic*] conspirators, dug in confidently. The collapse was expected to follow. Even the staunchest defender of the team's honour – myself – was now riven with doubt. Perhaps, I had been wrong all along. These cricketers were unpatriotic, money-mad; they would sell their grandmothers for the extra cash. They had no pride in playing for their country and I was just a diehard optimist. Our veteran cricketers knew their young colleagues. The final straw came when my own Assistant Manager, Mian Munir, took me aside and, looking extremely solemn, told me that he too believed that the match had been fixed. All I could say was 'Mian Sahib, I have been told so by others. What can I say? There would have to be an inquiry.' I then gloomily sat down to watch the remainder of the match-fixing script unfold. So far, it had been word perfect.

Ijaz and Inzamam were together and batting freely. I expected them to hole out and for the rest of the team to capitulate but Ijaz and Inzamam played maturely, sensibly and with immense composure. The partnership prospered and soon these two magnificent players – supposedly up to their ears in betting bonanzas – smacked the Indian bowling to all parts of the ground, leading to a comfortable seven-wicket victory for Pakistan! The match itself was not important but I was relieved, vindicated and overjoyed at my faith in the team. I never breathed a word of the scandal to any of them because it would have been demeaning to their patriotism and fighting spirit to even suggest a fix. I, nevertheless, cherished this win as much as any other during the tour for essentially non-cricketing reasons.

So there was no betting fix at Mohali, the storm had been nothing but hot air – a cloud of malicious scandal-mongering, sensationalism and vicious maligning of our players. I wondered how and why people – educated responsible people – went to such lengths to perpetuate these false rumours. Were our journalists yearning for another shameful scandal? Were our former Test players – many of them captains – envious of their young successors? Were the Board members falling for these malicious rumours so that they could get their revenge on player power raising its head? All these explanations do not stand up to scrutiny. They cannot justify such complete credibility to what was the floating of an absolute falsehood. It made me wonder if the previous accusations of betting had any base at all, except acts of vengeance by discarded players, sensation-seeking journalists or Board members who wanted to get back at their own players.

My Tour Diaries

ANGUS FRASER

Angus Fraser, the former Middlesex and England fast bowler,
played forty-six Test matches from 1989 to 1998. His *Tour Diaries* appeared in 1999.
The Jamaica ODI was part of the 1993/94 one-day series against the West Indies.

WE THEN LOST a one-dayer in Jamaica which was notable, as far as I was concerned, for me being sent off the field by my captain! I'd bowled my allocation of overs, not particularly well, in a rain-affected game in sweltering heat after returning from my hand injury, and Atherton said: 'You've bowled your overs, what are you doing out here?' I replied, 'I'm playing, that's what.' I'd just taken a good catch, too, but he said, 'We'll get you off and get a good fielder in your place. You pretend you've got hamstring trouble.' So out came the physio and I had to lie on my back having my hamstring stretched, pretending I was injured. Then, when I went off, I sat in the dressing-room on a towel of ice in case any West Indians stuck their heads around the door. The irony was that after I went off, the wheels came off and we lost! My alleged lack of mobility in the field has led to other captains suggesting this course of action, but apart from on that occasion, I've always told them to p*** off.

The English Game of Cricket

CHARLES BOX

Charles Box's *The English Game of Cricket* was published in 1877. This extract focuses
on a Kent v. Hampshire game in the mid-nineteenth century. Hampshire have won
the toss and put Kent in. But where is Kent's star batsman?

THE MATCH PROCEEDED. The wickets of Kent were lowered with more or less ease, and 126 runs were registered. The absence of Evelyn bordered upon mystery; even to his parents, who had come to see the match, and who not only regarded his absence with surprise, but alarm. Hampshire went in, and whether from superior skill or fortune, or both united, their runs came fast – faster – exceeding fast; and when the last two men quitted their wickets they had more than doubled the innings of Kent, scoring 260.

In the interval of rest the multitude talked over the events of the morning. Sad, sulky, and almost fierce were the Men of Kent, but to their honour, far as they were from home, they would not even talk of a surrender. The play had commenced early, and was to be continued late, in order that the game might be concluded in as short a time as possible, and 'play the match out' was the general cry. No substitute for Evelyn had been proposed, for such was the confidence placed in his skill, that his party would not have taken any other player, or even two, whilst even the forlorn hope of his arriving before the close of the second innings remained to them. His veteran sire, though not without unpleasant misgivings that some accident had befallen his son, cheered his countrymen by recalling to their minds the infinite variety of the game, and that a match is never won till it is lost.

Once more Kent sent in two champions. Both played with caution, but not with timidity, and when the ninth man had succumbed to the adverse bowler, they had only two to tie. The game, though so gallantly contested was, however, lost – at least so thought both the out and in-side; but in gloomy despair Kent awaited the allotted ten minutes for the absent player. When just five of these had been numbered with the times gone by, the rapid clang of a horse's hoofs when at its utmost speed attracted the crowd; and while yet two minutes of grace remained, the absentee appeared at a racing pace. In an instant his eagle eye and quick ear perceived the peril of his county, and, leaping to the ground, he threw off his coat, seized a bat, and rushed to the wicket. His partner was a safe and steady player, and of good judgment. Evelyn had the ball, played it, and in another minute Kent are *tye* and *four* on. Hope began to revive, but formidable odds presented themselves. Jack Styles played well up to him, but the force, confidence, and skill of the young squire surpassed description. The red-hot balls of Elliot at Gibraltar were scarcely more terrible to his foes, and certainly not more cheering to his friends, than the red and not cool ball of this great match, urged by the vigorous arm of this astonishing cricketer. At last, when Sykes was out, he quitted his post with honour with 45 runs from his own bat, gained in marvellously quick time, and the whole day's play stood thus: Kent's second innings, 182 – total 308, being 48 ahead of the rival county.

Play now ceased for the night. Kent were still sensible that they had an uphill fight to win, but they, too, felt that Evelyn was a host in himself, and despaired not. Hampshire was still confident, but Evelyn was now surrounded by inquiring friends anxious to know the cause of his strange absence. It was, of course, unintentional and unavoidable, but he had been made the victim of a base and ingenious hoax, doubtless by some who had heavy bets against Kent. A letter, most plausibly composed, led him to believe the scene of action changed to a distance of sixty miles off across country. He had only discovered his error in time to arrive at the eleventh hour.

Cricket in the Fiji Islands

PHILIP A. SNOW

Philip A. Snow played cricket for Leicestershire Second XI in 1936 and 1937. Subsequently he was a colonial administrator in Fiji, for which country he played five first-class matches. His memoir *Cricket in the Fiji Islands* was published in 1949.

~❧

FROM THE TIME of the return of the team from Australia, cricket was scarcely played on the island of Taveuni in the province of Cakaudrove for another twenty years. The reason is a rather remarkable one. Just after his Australian tour, Ratu Kadavulevu took the team to Taveuni to play what corresponds closely to a festival match.

In addition to the cricket, in which rivalry would be keen as two old competing states, Bau and Cakaudrove, were opposed to each other, there would be a vast amount of eating. Only those who have seen the enormities of food presented on such ceremonial occasions can accurately visualise the extent of food presented on this event in honour of Ratu Kadavulevu. The chiefly Cakaudrove dish – snakes – were offered and had to be eaten by the Bauan chiefs who would normally never touch them. Great ceremonial accompanied every part of the visit; etiquette was at its highest. The cricket began. Ratu Lala, Tui Cakau, the highest chief on Taveuni and of great status throughout Fiji (Tui Cakau means King of the Reefs), though not so omnipotent as Ratu Kadavulevu, went in to bat first. This was not due so much to his possessing the greatest ability among his side at the game, which he did not, but to his being of the highest rank. He received a trial ball, as everyone opening an innings does in Fiji whenever Fijians are playing together (and indeed when everyone is playing unless a European is there to point out that the custom died out in the early part of this century). He was out to the next ball, the first one after his trial ball. It is not narrated whether an attempt was made to give him any runs at the beginning. Although of such semi-divine status, which would certainly have accorded him the privilege of some easy runs if he had been playing amongst his own tribe or clansmen, it is unlikely that the Bauan chiefs would have made this gesture on the cricket field. The omission to do so, or at least the fatal error of taking Ratu Lala's wicket, was a diplomatic gaffe on the part of Bau. For Ratu Lala pulled up the shattered stumps and called away his followers from the ground. The match ended abruptly on the first real ball – the earliest abandonment possible in any cricket match. Not only that, but Ratu Lala prohibited the miserable game from being played again in his domains. This prohibition lasted for very many years, and it cannot be said that even after his death the game has flourished or regal consent been more than lukewarm on Taveuni. If the score could be found, it must have a most picturesque appearance. It can be presumed that, if it were kept (probably the scorers had not fidgeted into position by the time of the end of the game), it was torn up by regal command. One can imagine the score to be:

Cakaudrove v. Bau at Somosomo
Taveuni, 1908

Cakaudrove
First Innings

The Tui Cakau, b Samu	0
Joni Tomasi Koka, not out	0
Extras	0
For one wicket	0

Bowling

	O.	M.	R.	W.
Samu	0.1	0	0	1

Match abandoned on account of high dudgeon of High Chief.

11

HEROES

Everybody's Hero

SIR IAN BOTHAM

Early heroics from the great England all-rounder in
Somerset's Benson & Hedges quarter-final against Hampshire at Taunton in 1974.
From *Head On: The Autobiography* (2007).

I MADE MY COUNTY Championship debut against Lancashire at Taunton
on the opening day of the 1974 season, and once more it was not a particularly
auspicious start. The wicket was damp and the skies overcast, and I was out for
13, steering a short-pitched delivery into David Lloyd's huge hands. When we
took the field, conditions had improved and I was entrusted with only three
overs, taking none for 15, as the Lancashire openers, Barry Wood and David
Lloyd, put on 265 for the first wicket. Lancashire had the better of the game
but it ended in a rain-affected draw. I doubled my highest score to 26 in the
next game against Sussex, but still didn't take a wicket, and finally broke my
duck in our third game against Gloucestershire, though match figures of one
for 91 and innings of 2 and 1 scarcely suggested a star in the making. I hadn't
done myself justice and, though bitterly disappointed, I was not surprised
when Brian Close told me that I would be returning to the second team to
continue my cricketing education. My only consolation was that he made it
clear that it was only a temporary exile, and it only increased my determination
to make it count the next time I was picked for the first team.

I sat out the next two county games and I was only picked for Somerset's
Benson & Hedges quarter-final against Hampshire in June 1974 when our
first choice, fast bowler Allan Jones, was ruled out with a leg strain. The call
to join the first team came just a few hours before the game. I packed my kit
and hurried to the Taunton ground. The dressing room in those days had a
concrete floor, reached by a narrow, precipitous flight of steps. The green floor
paint was so chipped and scarred by players' spikes that it was down to the
bare concrete everywhere except under the benches. A doorway led to another
room with some less-than-fragrant urinals along one wall and a communal
plunge bath against the opposite wall. Beyond that was a little physio's room
with a couple of couches that were used far more often for sleeping than for
treatment; Somerset didn't even have a physio in those days. On hot days

Merv Kitchen's mountainous dog, Thumper, which went everywhere with him, would lie panting on the cold concrete floor between the dressing room and the bathroom, an immovable obstacle that you somehow had to negotiate if you wanted to use the loos or have a kip in the physio's room.

It was a perfect summer's day, scorching hot, with the sun glinting from the gilded weather vane on top of the church spire and hardly a breeze stirring the trees in the churchyard. There was a tremendous atmosphere and a capacity crowd, the biggest I had ever seen, let alone played before, with the gates closed long before Brian Close won the toss and put Hampshire in. They made a solid start until I bowled their finest batsman, the South African Test star Barry Richards. Our wicketkeeper Derek Taylor was standing up to the stumps – practically an insult to someone who considered himself a fast bowler – and Richards stayed at the crease for a few moments, unable to believe that the ball that had bowled him had done enough to hit the stumps without rebounding from Derek's pads. I took another wicket without addition to the score, and with Graeme Burgess chipping in with a couple more for no runs, Hampshire had collapsed from 22 for none to 22 for four. They recovered well to 182, thanks mainly to Trevor Jesty's 82, but I was reasonably pleased with my bowling and fielding. That was just as well, because I'd been picked as a bowler and was well down the batting order, at number nine. By the time I walked out to the wicket, windmilling my arms to loosen up and taking some deep breaths to calm my nerves, the game was as good as lost. We were 113 for seven, needing 70 runs from the last fifteen overs, and with only three wickets to take, Hampshire were long odds-on to go through to the semi-final.

The last of our recognised batsmen, my unofficial mentor and bowling coach Tom Cartwright, was at the crease and he walked over to me as I came out to the middle. 'All right young 'un?'

I nodded.

'Don't try to knock the cover off it straight away. Play yourself in, we've still got a few overs in hand.'

Unfortunately Tom immediately departed, caught at mid-on for a duck, and was replaced by Hallam Moseley, a definite tailender. I farmed the strike as much as I could and with an odd boundary and a few nudged ones and twos from me and a few lusty blows and flying edges from Hallam we had whittled the target down to 38 runs by the time the lightning-quick West Indian fast bowler Andy Roberts returned to the attack. I hadn't played against him or even set eyes on him before that day but I was well aware of his fearsome reputation. He had been terrorising English batsmen all season and had put several of them in hospital with broken arms and broken jaws.

He'd removed a couple of our batsmen in his first spell – I think he scared one of them out as much as got him out – but I had no intention of showing him too much respect. I was well set by now and when he dropped one short, I was on it at once, swivelling to hook it over square leg for six. Roberts stood there, hands on hips, glowering at me – and he had a very penetrating stare, his eyes burning holes right through me – then snatched the ball as it was returned from the boundary and stalked off back to his mark.

We now needed 32 runs. I told myself to put the last ball out of my mind and play the next one on its merits. Tapping my bat lightly, I settled at the crease and watched Roberts running in again. I saw the ball as it left his hand, the sun glinting slightly on the polished side, the white stitching along the seam a few degrees from the vertical. I didn't see it again until it was about a foot from my face. In those few tenths of a second some part of my brain had recognised that this was another short one and I had rocked on to the back foot, shaping to hook this one too, but there was one crucial difference: this was the fastest ball I had ever faced. Halfway through the shot, I realised I was way too late on the ball. Before I had fully digested that alarming fact, the ball had smacked into my face, and in those far-off days batsmen did not wear protective helmets.

In an instinctive act of self-preservation, I'd thrown up my gloved right hand towards my face and that absorbed some of the impact, but the ball still smashed my hand into my mouth with savage force. I dropped my bat and backed away, cursing and spitting blood, then realised that I was not just spitting blood, but bits of teeth as well. Two teeth had been knocked clean out and another two broken off at the gum line. Even more alarmingly, they were on opposite sides of my mouth, and the ones in between were noticeably looser than they'd been a few moments before. My right eyebrow was also cut where the ball had ricocheted on to it after striking my hand, but that was a minor problem – I didn't even notice that until the next day.

I was staggering around the pitch and so groggy that I almost slumped to the ground. Peter Sainsbury, the Hampshire left-arm spinner, ran up to me and said, 'Are you all right?'

'Fine,' I said, though it was more an instinctive than a considered reply. Meanwhile, as good fast bowlers should, Andy Roberts paused at the end of his follow-through only to give a quiet nod of satisfaction and fix me with another of those meaningful, penetrative stares. Then he turned to pace back to the end of his run-up, ready to deliver the next thunderbolt. As he did so, I spat out the last fragment of tooth, took a few sips from the glass of water that the physio – actually the twelfth man – had brought out, and then let him assess the damage. Believing that the game was now lost, he and some of the crowd wanted me to retire hurt to avoid further punishment, but doing that had never entered my mind.

The doctor who examined me after the game told me that I had suffered mild concussion from the blow, which might explain the curious sense of detachment I felt as I brushed off the twelfth man's restraining arm, picked up my bat and walked back to the crease. The umpire held out his arm for an unduly long time, partly to ensure the twelfth man had left the field before play resumed, but partly also, perhaps, to give me time to change my mind before unleashing Andy Roberts once more.

I declined the opportunity. I felt no pain from my teeth then – perhaps I was still in shock and certainly the adrenalin was pumping – and I was strangely calm and relaxed as I watched Roberts moving in, accelerating smoothly as he approached the wicket, the arm whipping over and the ball arrowing towards me. This one was a very full length, noticeably slower than the previous delivery, but still fast enough and with a little late inswing to help it spear in towards my toes. But I had already gambled that he would follow such a vicious short-pitched delivery with a yorker, and I managed to get enough bat on it to clip it away for three runs through mid-wicket. Normally I blanked out the crowd and was only dimly aware of the noise they were making, but this time there was no mistaking the roar that went up as I began to run.

I really must have been mildly concussed because while I was running the three runs, I had a curious floating sensation, as if I was hovering a few inches above the ground. As I stood at the non-striker's end, I muttered to myself, 'Come on, you've got to snap out of this.' We now needed 29. I kept farming the strike as much as possible and we had put on another 22 runs – I hit another six and even whacked Andy Roberts for a couple more fours – making our partnership worth 63 from thirteen overs, when Hallam missed one ball too many and was out for 24. There were now just 7 runs needed to win from sixteen balls but our last man, number eleven Bob Clapp, was walking to the wicket, a sight that usually had bowlers and fielders licking their lips in anticipation, and the bartenders taking the towels off the beer pumps. Bob was a very useful bowler and no slouch in the field, but his career batting average was in the low single figures – to misquote a famous football manager, he was often lucky to get none – but on this occasion he did all that was required, blocking, leaving or playing and missing without losing his wicket, while I kept sneaking singles and then a three in which Bob had to dive full-length to make his ground and avoid being run out. He later told me that he reckoned he'd been run out by a good twelve inches. Had there been a third umpire using slow-motion replays in those days, the game would have been over there and then, but luckily the umpire at the bowler's end had to use his own judgement and he gave him not out.

Those watching must have found the tension almost unbearable, but my concentration was now so total that I was no longer aware of their existence, though my nerves must still have been jangling for, having brought us to within two runs of victory, I then played and missed three times in a row against Herman before connecting with a flowing drive to a half-volley outside off-stump. As I saw it speeding away, beating the despairing dive of the cover fielder and smacking into the boundary boards, I raised my bat over my head and heard the loudest roar I had ever heard. I'd scored 45 out of the 70 we'd made with the last two wickets to win the game. Bob Clapp was nought not out, and if he never played another innings in his life, he had fully earned his winning bonus with that one. We ran from the field together as the crowd poured across the boundary ropes, forming a backslapping gauntlet that we had to pass through to reach the safety of the pavilion.

I was on the biggest high of my life so far; we'd won the game and I collected the Gold Award for player of the match, though perhaps I should have shared it with Andy Roberts. If he hadn't smashed my teeth, we might never have won. I needed some emergency dentistry, but that could wait for now. The broken teeth were not yet sending out pain signals so I showered and changed, then went straight to the Stragglers' Bar to join in the celebrations. People I'd never seen before were wringing my hand, slapping me on the back and offering to buy me drinks, but I took most pleasure and satisfaction from the quiet nod of approval I got from the Somerset captain, Brian Close, as he caught my eye across the bar. He then followed it up with some no-nonsense cricketing advice. 'Know why you got hit?' he said, immediately answering his own question. 'Because you took your eyes off the ball. Your head can move faster than any other part of the body, so providing you actually know where the bloody ball is, you can always get your head out of the way.'

As I was pouring my first pint over my smashed teeth and swollen gums, two old Somerset professionals, Bill Alley and Kenny Palmer, called me over and gave me some more fatherly advice. 'Today, you're everybody's hero,' they said. 'Just remember that tomorrow they'll have forgotten you again.'

I thanked them for their wise words, though in truth I didn't want anyone raining on my parade that night, but in time I came to appreciate how right they were; as the old saying goes, today's headlines are tomorrow's fish and chip wrappers. Those headlines also gave me a small problem when I strolled into my local, the Gardener's Arms, later that evening. Expecting at the least a pint on the house and a bit of mild hero-worship, I got a cold shoulder instead. 'The usual, please,' I said as I approached the bar.

I would have had a warmer welcome from an iceberg. 'And just what is your usual?' the landlord said.

'You know what it is,' I said. 'The same as it's been for the last year and a half.'

He gave me another frosty glance, then picked up the evening paper and dropped it on the bar in front of me. The headline read: 17-YEAR-OLD SOMERSET YOUTH PLAYS A BLINDER. Then, as now, the legal drinking age in Britain was eighteen. There was a beat of silence, then he winked and said, 'Must be a misprint. The usual then?' and pulled me a pint. In fact it *was* a misprint. I'd been eighteen since the previous November . . . though I'd also been a regular at the Gardener's for rather longer than that.

When the pub closed, Dennis Breakwell, Viv Richards and I went on to a club and were drinking till two in the morning. When I woke up the next morning I was in agony and for once it wasn't the hangover to blame. My jaw and the lower half of my face were a mass of bruises and the inside of my mouth looked like an out-take from *The Texas Chainsaw Massacre*. I went straight to a dentist and he patched up the hole where one tooth used to be and put temporary crowns on the broken ones, and gave me some powerful painkillers.

My next call was at a newsagent to pick up the papers. The sports pages were full of my exploits, swelling my head even further. BRAVE IAN'S

GOLDEN DAY, BOTHAMS UP, YOUNG BOTHAM THE SOMERSET HERO, and so on. I read them all several times before reluctantly handing them over to my mum for the scrapbook she had already started to house my cuttings. To swell my head even further, I received a case of champagne from a Somerset supporter living in Devon, with a note reading 'In appreciation of your great "recovery innings" today, the best I've seen since I started watching cricket in 1912'.

My mum soon had to buy another scrapbook because that narrow, impossibly dramatic victory had catapulted me into the public eye and given my fledgling career an enormous boost. From a nobody, I was now an overnight sensation. *The Sun* included me in a feature on 'Young England hopefuls' and whenever and wherever I played for the next few weeks, crowds were turning up to take a look at this new prodigy. I could sense and hear a definite buzz when I next went out to bat – but had that been my only moment of fame, I would have faded from public view as quickly as I appeared. I had now set a standard for myself and every time I took the field I would be expected to live up to it. I was still only a novice, feeling my way in professional cricket, but everyone – spectators, reporters and commentators, as well as opponents – was now aware of me and what I could do. I had to live up to the billing. Had I been left entirely to my own devices, my swell-headedness could easily have been my downfall, and I was lucky that two men in particular, Tom Cartwright and Brian Close, had the time and the patience to coach, cajole and encourage me through this crucial period in my career.

❧

Ranjitsinhji's 154 Not Out

A. A. LILLEY

A. A. (Dick) Lilley (Warwickshire and England) was the leading wicketkeeper
of his era and played thirty-five Tests for England. He was a batting partner of
Ranjitsinhji (aka 'the Prince' and 'the Jam') during his famous innings of 154 not out
in 1896, made on his Test debut and including a century before lunch.
From *Twenty-Four Years of Cricket* (1912).

❧

THIS MATCH WAS also memorable for Ranjitsinhji's second innings of
154 not out, which I have always considered the most brilliant exhibition
of batsmanship I have ever witnessed. This was the first century of the season
made against the Australian team, which included E. Jones, the greatest fast
bowler Australia ever sent to this country. In the first innings Ranjitsinhji
made 62 and I succeeded in making 65 not out – the highest score – and I well
remember the effort it cost me. We were all out for 231, and followed on 181
behind Australia's total of 412.

It was then that the Prince made his great innings. Mr. Jones was bowling
his fastest, making the ball rear face high in very dangerous fashion; but the
higher Jones made the ball rise, the more easily the Prince appeared to score.
I stayed with him some time, but what was hard labour to me seemed to him
the easiest thing in the world. He repeatedly brought off his wonderful leg-
strokes, and not merely his placing on the leg side, but his cutting of those fast
rising balls was little short of the miraculous. He stood straight up to them,
forcing them away on the leg-side or cutting them as the case might be, when
most other batsmen would have been more than satisfied in getting safely out
of their way.

I was discussing this particular innings with the Jam when he was last in
England, and he explained that it was desirable to get straight in front of such
balls, in order to get a more perfect and unbroken sight of them. I perfectly
agreed that the theory of this was quite correct, but the particular circumstance
seemed to me an exceptional one to put into practice. It would be a bad day for
the batsman, if, when standing straight up facing those rising balls, he should
happen to miss one, and I said so to the Jam. 'As a matter of fact, Dick,' he
said, 'I did miss one. I felt some blood trickling down my neck, and when I

put my hand up to feel what it was, I found it had split open the soft part of my ear.' A desperately narrow escape of prematurely closing a brilliant career.

[. . .] As a batsman pure and simple, Ranjitsinhji unquestionably was greatest of all. He stood upon a pinnacle. I remember very well a remark once made by Clem Hill that very tersely and comprehensively described him. The occasion was the Test match at Manchester in 1896. The Prince in this game scored 154 not out in the second innings, as I have already briefly described.

Of all the many brilliant exhibitions I have seen him give, this stands clearly out to me as the greatest. He seemed to have placed the ball just where he liked, and those terrible express deliveries of E. Jones were treated with apparent contempt.

It was at the conclusion of play, when I was having a chat with Clem Hill, that I remarked what a fine batsman Ranjitsinhji was. 'A fine batsman, eh!' said Clem Hill. 'He's more than a batsman – he is nothing less than a juggler!'

[. . .] The opinion I hold with regard to this particular innings I know is not accepted by Ranjitsinhji himself; and when he returned to England in 1907 as the Jam of Nawanagar, he told me he preferred the innings he subsequently played at Nottingham under conditions which he considered more disadvantageous than at Manchester, and so correspondingly enhanced the value of the score.

Ranjitsinhji was a batsman of infinite resource. There is no stroke known to cricketers that he did not execute to perfection, and the ease and style in which all his scoring strokes were made rendered his stay at the wickets a source of the keenest pleasure to all experts, a delight to the spectators, and an education to the student.

The particular stroke which he made so famous, and which will always be associated with his name, was the 'glide' on the leg-side. I believe that this particular stroke was his own invention, for in my early days batsmen always 'forced' the ball away when pitched on the leg-side, or else played it more squarely. But Ranjitsinhji, with a simple flick of the wrist, just slightly altered the course of the ball to very fine leg. To such perfection did he develop this stroke that he very seldom made any mistake about it. I have seen many other batsmen attempt to play it, and have also frequently seen them lose their wicket in trying it. It is so very fine a shot to make that it must necessarily be attended with a considerable amount of risk.

The Prince so perfected the stroke that he not only made it when the ball was pitched on the leg-side, but even when it was pitched in a line with the leg-stump. This has proved quite fatal to other batsmen, who have paid the penalty by being given out leg-before-wicket. The stroke calls for simultaneous rapidity of wrist and feet movement, and also quickness of sight. But Ranjitsinhji was dexterity itself, and his style, in its way inimitable, was ever a leading characteristic of the world's pre-eminent batsman.

It was of course a heavy loss to English cricket when his accession as ruler of the State of Nawanagar compelled his return to India. He revisited us, however, in the late autumn of 1907, and during the following season again donned the pads, and, though he had been absent for three years from the cricket field, he more than once demonstrated that he still retained that skill with which he was wont to delight us. Although in the first few matches he played part in for Sussex in that season of 1908 small scores only resulted, he soon found his form with the advent of congenial weather, and the ultimate outcome of the ten matches in which he assisted Sussex was, that he once again headed the batting averages of his old county with the fine average of 65 for 13 innings. This was eloquent testimony that he had preserved his batting powers after so long an absence. It further demonstrated, if such were necessary, how great was the loss occasioned by his retirement.

The Wicket at Melbourne

FRANK TYSON

Though he played relatively few Tests, Frank Tyson (Northants and England) is generally acknowledged as one of England's most destructive fast bowlers. In *A Typhoon Called Tyson* (1961) he described the fifth and final day of the Melbourne Test of the 1954/55 Ashes series.

THE STAGE IS SET for the final act. Australia want just under 200 in the fourth and final knock; already the cracks are beginning to reopen and the wicket is less reliable. Can Australia score the runs? I was confident in my own mind that they could not.

As we took the field, we were joined by a spectator, who made his way round the whole field in a series of kangaroo-like hops while we watched with

Anglo-Saxon detachment. The two white-helmeted policemen who were in hot pursuit finally captured him and led him off. I later learnt that he was a regular performer during the football season.

Each little detail crowds back on me from the past, for this was destined to be a great innings for me. The game restarted, and for a while Favell went on his own gay way. I was trying so hard that it hurt. Every last ounce of speed was being called out. Morris was batting more phlegmatically, as if he sensed that this might be his last Test opportunity to 'come good'. When the Australian score had reached 23, I banged one down on the line of Arthur's leg-stump and the left-hander, shuffling across his wicket, fended the ball too strongly off the line of his pads. It popped up towards Colin Cowdrey at very square silly mid-on, and I held my forehead in anguish as I felt that the ball would not reach the fieldsman. But no, Colin flung himself forward to take the catch in his right hand, inches from the turf, and my anguish became jubilation. First blood to England. Miller should have been the next batsman, but instead Benaud succeeded his vice-captain at the wicket. Miller was being kept back for the effort of the morrow. The light was still excellent in spite of the late hour, and the sun was very bright. Hutton brought on Appleyard, bowling from the Richmond end, and Favell overreached his aggression at last. He stepped out to drive the slow bowler, but only succeeded in making a half-volley into a yorker. It hit the top of the middle stick. Harvey and Benaud continued sedately until half-past five, when Australia needed 165 to win the game with eight wickets standing. The match was poised for the following day.

January 5 was a red-letter day for me. Let me reproduce the cryptic entry in my diary:

'Perhaps the luckiest and certainly the happiest day of my life. I bowled out Australia before lunch!'

This was the day I had dreamed of, the fulfilment of my ambition to go out on to the field and to bowl out the Australian batsmen just as quickly as they came in.

Sixty thousand people saw us take the field, and most of them, chatting amongst themselves, were agreed that 165 was not beyond the powers of the remaining eight wickets. They little thought of the surprises the day had in store, and, anticipating a full day's play, they had brought picnic lunches to the match. By twenty minutes past one, I had bowled out the Aussies and the game was over. The 60,000 lunches were all wasted.

I took the ball, gave it a vigorous rub and turned to take the first over from the Richmond end. It was the first time I had bowled from this wicket; the ground sloped up to the city end, and the wind was slightly in my face. Even from the end of my shorter run, the umpire seemed to be miles away, but I told myself that this was no time for worrying about small details. It was the moment for action. Slowly I moved into my run, and gradually as ball succeeded ball the pace of my first over increased. The seventh ball pitched on Harvey's legs and the left-hander shaped as if to leg-glide it. He had reckoned without Godfrey Evans. The stumper's feet twinkled over the first two yards before he launched himself to cover the remaining distance in the air and clutch the deflection to his body like a long-lost brother. At the end of my follow through, I could scarcely believe my eyes. It did not seem possible that Godfrey could have caught it; but the proof lay in the evidence of Neil making his slow way back to the pavilion.

If ever there was a turning-point in a match this was it. Before, it had seemed possible that we could bowl out the Aussies. After that catch, and the heart it put into the whole side, I never doubted for one moment that we *should* bowl them out.

At the other end Brian Statham had Miller in trouble as soon as he came in, and it was only with difficulty that he kept out a 'creeper'. Runs came slowly: only 10 from the first four overs. Bad balls were few and far between, and Richie Benaud, a naturally aggressive bat, was dying to get on with the game.

The first ball of my third over was exactly what he had been waiting for: well short of a length and outside the off-stump. It was a rank bad ball, and only bettered by an even worse shot. Richie went for the hook, only to find that the ball was too wide of the off-stick, and his wild swing merely succeeded in deflecting the ball via the bottom edge of the bat on to the middle and leg stumps. It was the stroke of a man relieved to find a ball he could hit, who then never even watched the ball or kept his head down. For my part I accepted my luck with incredulity. This was really my day.

Hole scored a single off the third ball he received and this brought Miller face-to-face with me. I have always been in awe of Keith. He has always impressed me as a complete man; charming, adventurous, and accomplished. I have feared him on the cricket field because he was one of the few men in the world who could turn the tide of a game in the space of a few overs with either bat or ball. Being a fast bowler, this has given me cause to hate him more than most players when he takes up the bat. At Melbourne on this wonderful day I was determined that Keith should have no scope for his batting talents. Trudging back to the end of my run, I summoned up the sinews to hurl him down a real thunderbolt. Scuffling and pawing the earth, I measured my distance to the wicket, found my stride and moved off, dipping my feet first, only to rise to my full height as I delivered. My left hand balanced the sky like a tray, and my right arm described an arc, hesitant at first, but full as it gained momentum. My left leg crashed down and my body catapulted the ball down, following up, airborne and crouching. It was, without doubt, the fastest ball I ever bowled, and reared from the line of the off-stick. Keith's defensive prod failed to reach the pitch and the leap of the ball caught the shoulder of the bat. From where I stood, the catch seemed to be soaring over the slips, but at the last minute the skipper thrust up a hopeful hand. Smack! The ball hit flesh and I clutched at the sky as the catch was pushed upwards. By Hutton's side, compatriot slip Bill Edrich was on his toes with anxiety and as the ball came down behind the English captain's back, Bill dived to get his hands beneath it. Miller had gone and half the Australians were out for 87!

For a while Hole and Archer held us up. Short-pitched balls and bouncers did not trouble Graeme, and Archer was soon indulging in his favourite square-cut. One swashbuckling boundary hit the pickets at point and bounced half-way back to where I waited at the bowling crease. Australia were only three short of the century when Hole fell to Brian Statham. He edged a ball which moved slightly off the wicket and Evans took the catch gratefully.

Maddocks came and went in quick time. The very first ball I bowled to him was a yorker, and because he was on the back foot, anticipating a short-pitched delivery, he could do little but come down very hard on it. He seemed mesmerised by the ball, and both he and I watched breathless and tense as it spun from outside the off-stick, slowly, ever so slowly, on to his wickets. There were only three more wickets to fall! Two balls later I trapped Lindwall, again expecting a short ball, and moving into his wicket to be leg-before to one well up on him.

I was bowling in a daze. This was not happening to me. It was as if I were watching another bowler. Never before had I bowled like this, I was making the ball swing, in Australia! The ball which had dismissed Ray Lindwall was an outswinger which the fast bowler had tried to force away on the leg-side.

I collected my thoughts and came back to the job in hand. There were only two more men to deal with. The Australian total stood at 98 for eight wickets. Their cause was, at first glance, hopeless.

Archer could make nothing of Brian Statham, but luck was not with the Lancashire bowler. Throughout this memorable Wednesday morning he had toiled without reward, but for the wicket of Hole. The batsmen played repeatedly at him but without edging the ball. Then Fortune smiled briefly on him. A Statham yorker hit Archer on the toes, skittling the Queenslander from his feet. Another yorker found its mark; 110 for nine! One run later, it was all over. Bill Johnston took a single and faced up as I made my way back to my mark for the fifty-first time that morning. I was tired but what did that matter! With victory so close, I could bowl for another hour-and-a-half. Just one more ball, Frank, one more and we are home and dry!

To a ball going away from him, Big Bill proffered a bodyless bat. As the ball left the edge and climbed steadily towards the stand where Mr Menzies was sitting, Godfrey snapped up his third catch of the morning. It was all over and my body sagged with relief. Suddenly I was very, very weary – but also very, very happy.

The third Test was ours! The crowd surged over the fence and the players hung back waiting to applaud the bowlers as they entered the pavilion. I paused, waited for Brian Statham, put my arm around his shoulder and we passed into the dressing-room together. It was not a sentimental gesture, even less a mark of sympathy for a morning's atrocious luck. It was my way of saying thanks.

Fast bowlers always hunt in pairs and only a fellow-bowler can appreciate what it means to have the support of Brian at the other end. A batsman facing two really fast bowlers quickly realises it requires a great deal of concentration, application and guts. There is a respite when a side has only one quickie. With a fast bowler at each end, there is no escape: no running to the other end. I had taken seven for 27, but it might easily have been Brian who returned the figures. For my part, I prefer to say that we took nine wickets between us.

❧

The Cricketers of My Time

JOHN NYREN

John Nyren (1764–1837) was a cricketer and writer.
The Cricketers of My Time appeared in 1833.

ABOUT THE PERIOD I have been describing, Noah Mann joined the Hambledon Club. He was from Sussex, and lived at North Chapel, not far from Petworth. He kept an inn there, and used to come a distance of at least twenty miles every Tuesday to practise. He was a fellow of extraordinary activity, and could perform clever feats of agility on horseback. For instance, when he has been seen in the distance coming up the ground, one or more of his companions would throw down handkerchiefs, and these he would collect, stooping from his horse while it was going at full speed. He was a fine batter, a fine field, and the swiftest runner I ever remember: indeed, such was his fame for speed, that whenever there was a match going forward, we were sure to hear of one being made for Mann to run against some noted competitor; and such would come from the whole country round. Upon these occasions he used to tell his friends, 'If when we are half-way, you see me alongside of my man, you may always bet your money upon me, for I am sure to win.' And I never saw him beaten. He was a most valuable fellow in the field; for besides being very sure of the ball, his activity was so extraordinary that he would dart all over the ground like lightning. In those days of fast bowling, they would put a man behind the long-stop, that he might cover both long-stop and slip: the man always selected for this post was Noah. Now and then little George Leer (whom I have already described as being so fine a long-stop) would give Noah the wink to be on his guard, who would gather close behind him: then George would make a slip on purpose, and let the ball go by, when, in an instant, Noah would have it up, and into the wicket-keeper's hands, and the man was put out. This I have seen done many times, and this nothing but the most accomplished skill in fielding could have achieved.

Mann would, upon occasion, be employed as a change-bowler, and in this department he was very extraordinary. He was left-handed, both as bowler and batter. In the former quality, his merit consisted in giving a curve to the ball the whole way. In itself it was not the first-rate style of bowling, but so very deceptive, that the chief end was frequently attained. They who remember the dexterous manner with which the Indian jugglers communicated the curve to the balls they spun round their heads, by a twist of the wrist or hand, will at once comprehend Noah's curious feat in bowling. Sometimes when a batter had got into his hitting, and was scoring more runs than pleased our General, he would put Mann in to give him eight or twelve balls, and he almost always did so with good effect.

Noah was a good batsman, and a most severe hitter; by the way, I have observed this to be a common quality in left-handed men. The writer of this was in with him at a match on Windmill-down, when by one stroke from a toss that he hit behind him, we got ten runs. At this time the playing-ground was changed from Broad-Halfpenny to the above-named spot, at the suggestion of the Duke of Dorset and the other gentlemen, who complained of the bleakness of the old place. The alteration was in this, as in every other respect, for the better, Windmill-down being one of the finest places for playing on I ever saw. The ground gradually declined every way from the centre: the fieldsmen therefore were compelled to look about them, and for this reason they became so renowned in that department of the game.

At a match of the Hambledon Club against all England, the club had to go in to get the runs, and there was a long number of them. It became quite apparent that the game would be closely fought. Mann kept on worrying old Nyren to let him go in, and although he became quite indignant at his constant refusal, our General knew what he was about in keeping him back. At length, when the last but one was out, he sent Mann in, and there were then ten runs to get. The sensation now all over the ground was greater than anything of the kind I ever witnessed before or since. All knew the state of the game, and many thousands were hanging upon this narrow point. There was Sir Horace Mann, walking about, outside the ground, cutting down the daisies with his stick – a habit with him when he was agitated; the old farmers leaning forward upon their tall old staves, and the whole multitude perfectly still. After Noah had had one or two balls, Lumpy tossed one a little too far, when our fellow got in, and hit it out in his grand style. Six of the ten were gained. Never shall I forget the roar that followed this hit. Then there was a dead stand for some time, and no runs were made; ultimately, however, he gained them all, and won the game. After he was out, he upbraided Nyren for not putting him in earlier. 'If you had let me go in an hour ago' (said he), 'I would have served them in the same way.' But the old tactician was right, for he knew Noah to be a man of such nerve and self-possession, that the thought of so much depending upon him would not have the paralysing effect that it would upon many others. He was sure of him, and Noah afterwards felt the compliment. Mann was short in stature, and, when stripped, as swarthy as a gipsy. He was all muscle, with no incumbrance whatever of flesh; remarkably broad in the chest, with large hips and spider legs; he had not an ounce of flesh about him, but it was where it ought to be. He always played without his hat (the sun could not affect *his* complexion), and he took a liking to me as a boy, because I did the same. Poor Noah! his death was a very deplorable one. Having been out shooting all day with some friends, they finished their evening with a free carouse, and he could not be persuaded to go to bed, but persisted in sleeping all night in his chair in the chimney-corner. It was, and still is, the custom in that part of the country, to heap together all the ashes on the hearth for the purpose of keeping the fire in till the next day. During the night my poor playmate fell upon the embers, and being unable to help himself, burned his side so severely that he did not survive twenty-four hours.

A Hobbs Innings

DUDLEY CAREW

Dudley Carew was a journalist and film critic. The Hobbs innings
took place during the Surrey v. Cambridge University match
at the Oval in June 1926. From *England Over: A Cricket Book* (1927).

THERE WAS ONLY half an hour left for play but very few of the crowd made any movement to depart. After the excitement and incidents of a long innings, it is pleasant to relax for a little and watch two batsmen do no more than play out time, and when one of those batsmen is Hobbs, one's pleasure takes on a keener edge. Between them they scored twenty-two tranquil runs, but Hobbs was tired and played the bowling meditatively as though he were thinking, not of the day, but of the triumph which was to be his on the morrow.

The ordinary occasional spectator of cricket too often meets with the maddening experience of seeing his favourite batsman bowled just as he arrives on the ground, or, on the only afternoon he can get off in the week, of having to watch the tail batsmen of a side in which he has no interest. It is seldom that the little hour of their leisure coincides with an hour of greatness on the part of a great cricketer, but one of these shy, rare hours was caught by the thousand or so people who gathered at the Oval on Thursday morning. For Hobbs made 108 and in his innings he exhausted all the art and variety of batsmanship. The bowling was by no means negligible; at times it was very good, but it made no difference to him. He played his innings as an actor plays a part in a play he has written himself, working up to a climax, relapsing into quietness, bursting out into sudden nervous energy, doing everything at the prompting of his own spirit rather than at any outside dictation. Up to the time he reached his fifty he batted as though he were filled with a divine fury. Time and again he would play that lovely on-shot of his, leaning back on the stumps and pivoting on his right leg, and when the field was altered he would smash the ball to the exact part of the field which had just been left unguarded. He did not seem to be thinking of runs; indeed, it was almost as though he wanted to be got out. His was the impatience of the master with the pupil, who cannot with all the paints and canvases in the world at his command, approach a sketch he scribbles with the stump of a pencil on the back of an envelope. He scored 15 runs in one over from Enthoven, who pitched the ball up to him gallantly, reached his 50 and then, as though realising that, however inspired his strokes were with danger and adventure, he could not get out, relapsed into cool and untroubled defence.

Sandham had meanwhile gone quietly on with the work of building up his own century. Sandham has carried self-effacement to a fine art. There is nothing crude or glaring about his batting; he works in cool monotones, never attempting the heroic, but seeing that everything he does is in perfect taste. And yet every now and again brilliance breaks in startlingly. Over after over Sandham will play with a sedate correctness, and then suddenly he will produce a perfect off-drive or a vicious hook, and then before the ball has been returned from the boundary he will have withdrawn into himself again and one is left to wonder whether one did not doze in the sun and see, in a momentary dream, that vivid flash of activity.

At a quarter past one, Hobbs reached his hundred and was out almost immediately afterwards to an unfairly good catch by Dawson who was fielding deep at cover. After luncheon A. Jeacocke was bowled by a good ball from

L. G. Irvine, but Shepherd then proceeded to hit the Cambridge bowling all over the field. There is more than a suggestion of Tom Hayward about Shepherd, both in build and in stance at the wicket. When one sees Shepherd play one of his hard driving innings – and he can drive as soundly and whole-heartedly as anyone in England – one always wonders how it is that he never played for England. Like P. A. Perrin in another age he will probably go down as the best batsman of his time who did not have that honour. In thirty-five minutes he made 42 runs and was then bowled by Meyer; Sandham, after he had reached his hundred, became infected with Shepherd's pugnacity, and finished his innings in a blaze of fours.

At tea-time Surrey were 87 runs on with five wickets to fall, and it became a question of how many more they could make before stumps were drawn. Fender and Peach hit hard, but rather streakily. To see them in together when Surrey are on top and wanting runs quickly is usually a noble and thrilling sight. The very contrast they make grips the imagination, Fender, tall, dark, with twinkling ferocious glasses, disdaining footwork and swinging firm-footedly at the ball at one end, and, at the other, Peach, small, cheery, with slightly bow legs dancing out of his crease and making the ball suit the effervescence of his temperament. On this day they both got runs, but not as grandly as one could have wished. However, they raised the Surrey score to the eminently respectable total of 463 and gave their side the lead of 176 runs. There was still time for Cambridge to begin their innings, but the clouds which had been gathering ominously on the horizon all the afternoon had spread over the heavens and begun to drip gentle and reluctant rain.

We in the pavilion told ourselves that it was a pity, but that we should have a great day's cricket to-morrow. It would be a good test of the stability of the Cambridge team. And so, cheerfully, because we had seen Hobbs at his best, and because we had another full day before us, we caught trams and buses and taxis to our homes. But the clouds did not vanish as an ogre in the night. They drooped over London all the next day and poured rain down with a kind of melancholy persistence. There was no need to go to the Oval; one could only sit staring at the blind panes musing over one more spoilt day, and wondering what would have happened had the sun shone and Dawson and Seabrook taken their way to the wickets.

❧

Fights for the Ashes 1882–86

GEORGE GIFFEN

George Giffen was a leading Australian all-rounder of the late nineteenth century.
In this extract from *With Bat and Ball* (1898), he recalls playing in the famous
Test in 1882 when Australia narrowly defeated England.

WHAT ARE 'THE ASHES'? Nothing more or less than the ashes of
English cricket. A London paper immortalised them when the 1882
Australian Eleven defeated England at Kennington Oval; and ever since
newspaper writers have alluded to test matches between representatives of
England and Australia as the Fights for the Ashes. Until 1882 there were no
ashes. In 1877 an Australian Eleven defeated eleven representative English
professionals at Sydney, but although that contest has always been regarded
as the first of a series of half a hundred test matches, no one for a moment
considered that Lillywhite's team thoroughly represented the mother country.
England's supremacy was unquestioned, and continued so until the 1882
Eleven so sensationally won at the Oval. Since then there have been many
gallant fights for the ashes, and numbered amongst them are some of the
greatest games recorded in the annals of cricket.

Who would ever have imagined twenty years ago that cricket matches,
mere games after all, would have excited such intense, such thrilling, such
world-wide interest, as we have seen in recent times, when the representatives
of the two countries have faced each other? The issue of a battle, on which
depended the fate of a dynasty, could scarcely have been awaited with greater
anxiety. Certainly its every phase would not have been described with greater
attention to details. It has been my privilege to bear arms in many of these
historical cricket battles, and as I have written these reminiscent pages, my
blood has warmed within me at the recollection of some of the thrilling
situations in which I have stood alongside my comrades.

The greatest match which had until that time been played – and for
many years no other game led to such sensational incidents, certainly there
has never in an international contest been a more remarkable finish – was
the one test to which the Australian Eleven of 1882 submitted. Prior to that
engagement we had a very fine record, and English Press and public, although

probably they felt that the reputation of England was secure enough, were not by any means over-confident about the issue of the great event. Any way England placed a magnificent Eleven against us at Kennington Oval, when the fateful day arrived. Just look at the array of cricketing giants – W. G. Grace, Hornby, Steel, Studd (who had the best batting average against the 1882 Eleven), Lucas, Alfred Lyttelton, Barlow, Barnes, Ulyett, Peate, and Maurice Read. It is questionable whether at the time it would have been possible to materially strengthen that combination. We, however, suffered irreparable loss from the inability of George Palmer, through illness, to play, Sam Jones, who was the one unsuccessful player of the tour, being but an inefficient substitute for the Victorian bowler.

From the commencement of the game it was evident that we were in for a titanic struggle. The Englishmen, who had been sent into the field, bowled with splendid precision, and fielded magnificently. Who could wish for finer all-round play than was seen when Peate and Barlow sent down more than a dozen successive maiden overs to Murdoch and Bannerman? Not a loose one from either of them, while the way the ball came back on the treacherous wicket put the batsman through a severe ordeal. Small wonder that we had 6 wickets down for 30! Blackham and Garrett then made 27 between them, and the total reached 63. Dicky Barlow's bowling was responsible for our downfall; we ought to have made at least 100. When Spoff yorked W. G.'s leg stump we were in great feather, but good hitting by Ulyett and Maurice Read, and a clever innings by Steel, gave the Englishmen a lead of 38 on the first hands, which had been completed on the first day.

I am free to admit that Fortune smiled upon us on the Tuesday morning when for a little while we had the wicket fairly easy, as the result of a shower of rain. This gave us a golden opportunity, and fortunately for us we had the man for the moment in Hugh Massie. Never on a slow wicket have I seen a batsman do a grander bit of hitting. Only for twenty minutes or so was the pitch really easy, but in that time Massie had got his eye in, so that when the ball did begin to bite he could bang away with as great certainty as before. It is worth noting that the only fair, genuine chance given during the great match came from Massie's bat, and it cost England 17 runs – 10 more than we won by. At last A. G. Steel came on and bowled Massie, but our hitter had given us a chance in the game. If one praises Massie's hitting, what can be said of Murdoch's batting, for long before he had completed the putting together of his 29 the wicket was as difficult as bowler could wish. W. L. M. demonstrated then how great a batsman he really was, and I only once felt sorrier to see a man run out, than I did when Murdoch, after seeing seven of us out, was run out through a bad call of Tom Garrett's. One read at the time a good deal about the bad luck of the Englishmen – Steel and Lucas in playing the ball on, and Lyttelton in being caught off his glove – but no commiseration was expressed for our great batsman in his misfortune.

England needed 85 runs to win. Would they get them? As we excitedly discussed our chances during the interval, Spofforth said they wouldn't. Spoff's faith in himself and Murdoch's cheery assurance inspired the rest of us, and we filed out of the dressing-room to make the effort of our lives. When the Demon had bowled Hornby and Barlow with only 15 runs scored, we felt assured of victory, but the hitting of the Champion and Ulyett changed the complexion of the game, which then appeared to be gradually drifting away from us. Ulyett did not bat particularly well, but W. G.'s innings was a masterpiece. They were, however, separated at last, and with 53 up both had been sent to the right about.

Now began a tremendous struggle. Boyle maintained a grand length, Spofforth was well-nigh unplayable, and the fielding was perfect. The English batsmen were in the pickle Barlow and Peate had had us in on the previous day. Gradually we tightened our hold on the game; and the moment, I fancy, it was really clenched was when Steel was dismissed without scoring. So long as he remained, we could not feel perfectly safe. The situation was one of those trying ones in which I think the batsmen invariably appear at a disadvantage. A bit of fearless hitting might have snatched the game from us, but after Lyttelton and Lucas went, none of the great English batsmen could muster up the courage to have a bang, and, considering the magnificent way in which Spofforth was bowling, there was some excuse for them.

I remember on our way to England in 1882, Spoff had figured in a fancy dress ball as Mephistopheles; but, aided by art on that occasion, he did not look half the demon he did when at the Oval on that Tuesday afternoon he sent in those marvellous breaks, almost every one of which, if it had passed the bat, would have hit the wicket. The later English batsmen have been blamed for their want of nerve. One gentleman in the pavilion is said to have remarked, 'If they would only play with straight bats they would be sure to get the runs,' to which his companion, a lady, replied, 'Would they really? Couldn't you get them some?' But their failure was pardonable. If W. G. had been at one end and Murdoch at the other, Spofforth might have been beaten, but I doubt it. Irresistible as an avalanche, he had bowled his last 11 overs for 2 runs and 4 wickets. The finest piece of bowling I have ever seen! Nevertheless, as I have said, the English batsmen were blamed, even ridiculed, and it was at this time that the London *Sporting Times* created the ashes, by publishing the following 'In Memoriam' notice:–

IN AFFECTIONATE REMEMBRANCE

of

ENGLISH CRICKET,

Which died at the Oval,

on

29th August, 1882.

Deeply lamented by a large circle

of sorrowing friends and acquaintances.

R.I.P.

N.B. – The body will be cremated, and the

ashes taken to Australia.

Such a scene of excitement as ensued after the match I have seldom seen on a cricket ground. While the tension had lasted the spectators rarely gave vent to their feelings, and when Peate, the last man, was caught they seemed unable for a moment or two to realise that England had actually been beaten. That great crowd was like a man stunned. But they soon forgot their sorrow to applaud us, and we had cheer after cheer from those healthy British lungs. A small coterie of Australians, who sat in the pavilion, were wild with joy; and I remember Mrs. Beal, the mother of our manager, running down the steps, and I being the first who came along, although I had contributed as little as anybody towards the victory, found her arms around my neck and a motherly kiss implanted upon my brow.

Caste: Up from Serfdom

RAMACHANDRA GUHA

Ramachandra Guha is an Indian writer, journalist and cricket historian. Palwankar Baloo (1876–1955) was a Dalit ('Untouchable') who played very successfully for the all-Indian team that toured England in 1911, and later became deeply involved in politics. From *A Corner of a Foreign Field* (2002), which won the Cricket Society/MCC Book of the Year Award.

～❧

THE NAME 'PALWANKAR' denotes the bearer's place of origin, the village of Palwan, on the Konkan coast, north of Goa, a land washed by the sea and watered by the monsoon, celebrated for its fish and its Alphonso mangoes. In rural Maharashtra people of all castes, when asked to assume a 'surname' (a category that did not exist before the British came to India) simply take the name of their village and add a suffix. Thus Palwankar means 'of the village of Palwan'. There might even be Brahmins with this name, but we know that Palwankar Baloo was a Chamaar, a caste that lies almost at the bottom of the Hindu social hierarchy. The caste's name comes from the Sanskrit word for leather, 'charman', and the people of the caste work with leather, as tanners and dyers, and as the makers of shoes, bottles, tents and saddles.

The Chamaars, wrote one authority, 'are by birth doomed to illiteracy' and a 'lamentable and abject poverty'. They undertook tasks vital to the clean castes, yet despised by them.

Palwankar Baloo was born in July 1875, in the town of Dharwad, deep in the Deccan Plateau and at least 500 miles south-east of his native village. His father worked there but soon after his birth appears to have taken a job in Poona. He was employed in the army; one account suggests that he worked in the ammunition factory in the suburb of Kirkee, another claims that he was a sepoy in the 112th Infantry Regiment. It was in Poona that Baloo and his younger brother Shivram learned to play cricket, with equipment discarded by army officers. The boys also went, briefly, to school, but were soon withdrawn to help augment the family income. Baloo's own first job was at a cricket club run by Parsis. Here he swept and rolled the pitch, and occasionally bowled to the members at the nets. For this work he took home 3 rupees a month.

In or about the year 1892 Baloo moved a step upwards, from the Parsi cricketers of the city to their European counterparts. These were congregated in the Poona Club, set up a few years previously in a wooded estate known as Edwardes Gardens. The club, typically, has no documents of its history, except for the original lease agreement signed between its promoters and the Bombay Government in March 1886. This granted, for a period of ninety-nine years and an annual rent of 13 rupees and 12 annas, an area of almost 14 acres for 'various annexed means of public recreation and amusement'. The 'public' meant, of course, the white public, but the state placed limits even on its chosen elite. Lessees could build on the land or mould it as they wished, but lessors reserved the 'liberty to search for, dig and carry away minerals and to sink all necessary pits and shafts and to make and erect all necessary erections, machinery, roads and other conveniences and things for the purpose'.

No gold was ever found on the premises, and what digging was done was for sporting purposes alone. When I visited the club, in July, during the monsoon, the trees were in leaf and the cricket ground was in prime condition. The original pavilion, built in the 1880s, overlooked play from wide mid-wicket. It is a charming little stone building, with coloured pillars on the verandah and a shingled roof. In 1999 I could walk into the pavilion unchecked, but I don't suppose Palwankar Baloo ever entered it himself.

At the Poona Club Baloo had his salary increased to 4 rupees a month. His duties included rolling and marking the pitch, erecting the nets and, when required, marking the tennis courts as well. To these routine tasks was later added an altogether more pleasurable one: bowling to the members. It was, it seems, a Mr Tross who first encouraged Baloo to bowl to him. He might, after play ended, have seen the ground boy bowl a ball or two into an empty net, and recognized his talent. Baloo had taken as his model a Captain Barton, a left-arm bowler with a smooth, flowing action. Soon Baloo was bowling on a more or less regular basis to the members of the club, valuable practice for the matches they would play against other teams of expatriates.

At this time, the leading English cricketer of Poona was Captain J. G. Greig. He was known as 'Jungly' because that was how his forenames, 'John Glennie', sounded if spoken quickly. Greig was a small man with supple wrists and quick feet. A master of the square cut, for years he was regarded as the best white batsman in India. Like other small men – Don Bradman and Sunil Gavaskar most obviously – he had an appetite for runs that was gargantuan. Framji Patel wrote that you will never catch Captain Greig napping, even after he has made his hundred. He is always on the *qui vive*. He goes on piling up his big score without fatigue. His pose at the wicket is ideal, giving him a full view of the bowler's hand, as well as of the flight of the ball, which as a rule he watches with 'feline insistence'. He is quiet, but deliberate. For his small stature he has any amount of courage, resource and staying power.

Every day Greig would arrive at the Poona Club an hour before anybody else, and command Baloo to bowl to him. Thus he would perfect his technique, and thus the Indian would improve his bowling. There is a nice story, undocumented but therefore all the more appealing, that Greig paid Baloo 8 annas for every time he got him out. At this rate, if the bowler was successful once a week he would have doubled his salary each month.

Baloo once told his son that although he had bowled for hundreds of hours at the Poona Club, not once was he given a chance to bat. In India, as in England, batting was the preserve of the aristocratic elite. One consolation was that by adding bowling to his other duties Baloo had his salary tripled. And his control of spin and flight was honed to perfection by the thousands of balls bowled to Jungly Greig and his less gifted colleagues.

Like his ancestors, Palwankar Baloo came to make a living working with skill and care upon a piece of leather. Slowly, word of his talents with the cricket ball reached the 'native' part of the city. There was a pioneering Hindu club, which sought to challenge the Europeans of Poona. Should they call upon the services of the Chamaar bowler? The question divided the Hindu cricketers. Some Telugu members were keen to include Baloo, whereas the local, Marathi-speaking Brahmins were not. At this stage J. G. Greig jumped into the fray. He gave an interview to the press suggesting that the Hindus would be fools to deprive themselves of Baloo's services. It was not that Greig had the instincts of a social reformer – his commitment to his race was scarcely less strict than the Poona Brahmin's commitment to his caste – but, rather, that he wished to test his skills against his net bowler in the fierce heat of match competition.

In the event, Baloo was invited to play for the Poona Hindus, but at a price. On the field the upper-caste cricketers touched the same ball as he, but off it they observed the ritual taboos. At the tea interval, that ceremony sacred to cricket, Baloo was served liquid outside the pavilion, and in a disposable clay *matka*, while his colleagues drank in white porcelain cups inside. If he wished to wash his hands and face, an Untouchable servant of the club took a kettle out into a corner of the field and poured water from it. Baloo also ate his lunch off a separate plate, and on a separate table.

But he took plenty of wickets all the same. Due chiefly to Baloo's bowling the Poona Hindus defeated the Poona Europeans and other local sides as well. On one celebrated occasion they visited the inland town of Satara, to play against its white-only Gymkhana. The hosts had instructed their groundsmen to roll the wicket for a week, so that it would blunt Baloo's spin. Baloo still took seven wickets, and his team won easily. In one account the bowler was then serenaded on an elephant through the streets of Satara. In another account he was garlanded at a public function on his return to Poona, the garland lovingly placed around his shoulders by the great scholar and reformer Mahadev Govind Ranade. It was also Ranade who told his fellow Brahmins that if they could play with Baloo, they must drink tea and break bread with him too. A little later, Baloo was praised at a public meeting by a Brahmin nationalist even more celebrated than Ranade, Bal Gangadhar Tilak. This, writes one chronicler, created 'a stir, because in those days a person from the backward community did not have an honourable place in society'.

The Three Pears

A. A. THOMSON

A. A. Thomson was a writer and journalist. One or another of the seven
Foster brothers played for Worcestershire from the end of the nineteenth century
to the 1930s. From *Cricket Bouquet* (1961).

WORCESTER AT ITS best is among the most enchanting spots in the world, and Worcestershire cricket was one of the glories of the Golden Age. If it has not been so glorious since, the change may well have been due to those changes which have taken place generally in the world at large rather than in the pleasant western county. Worcestershire rose grandly to the upper reaches under the aegis of the illustrious brotherhood of the Fosters. It is an ancient pleasantry that Worcestershire at the turn of the century was known as Fostershire. In the seven sons of a country parson lay something virile, civilised and indestructible in the history of nineteenth-century England. Worcestershire folk regard the Fosters as the greatest of cricketing families, though Northamptonshire admirers of the Kingstons might dispute the claim and the men of Gloucestershire might scorn it. But if the Graces were Himalayas the Fosters were at least Alps. The Worcestershire in which they flourished was an integral part of the larger landscape of English country life. How else could you have had three wicket-keepers named Straw and Bale with Gaukrodger intervening? With authentic names like these behind the stumps, you might happily hope to find Snug and Joiner at point and Flute and Bellows-mender at cover. Something of the magic of the *Dream* must have gleamed over Fostershire cricket: honest, earthy, rustic English magic, but magic nevertheless, to be found in a 'wood near Athens', or an enchanted cricket ground on the bank of the Severn. The Fosters were a truly remarkable body of cricketers; for, of them all, four (G.N., M.K., N.J.A. and B.S., who, being an actor by profession, lived in London and played for Middlesex) were good; two (say H.K. and W.L.) were very good and one (R.E., the third brother in age) was undeniably great. Their batting was of the polished, cultured kind which history has associated with the Malvern school; indeed, the Fosters were the firmest builders of the renowned Malvern tradition. Three of them played regularly in Worcestershire's first season among the top people and in an early game of that summer R.E. and W.L. each scored a century in each innings.

Mr. W. L. Foster c Webb b Baldwin .	.	142 not out	172
Mr. R. E. Foster lbw b Steele .	. . .	134 not out	101

As a record of fraternal solidarity it is unlikely to be beaten.

On one occasion five brothers played in one eleven, and for twenty-seven years, until M.K. retired, there was always one Foster to show the flag. When the greater ones among the Fosters had departed there was nobody who could repeat their Malvernian brilliance until the coming of C. F. Walters, who came from Glamorgan and played for five seasons with an elegance that recalled the golden age of R.E.; his strokes were graceful, elegant and almost insolent in their effortless ease. Along, too, came the Nawab of Pataudi, not so dazzling in action as were his two princely predecessors, Ranjitsinhji and Duleepsinhji, but sound in defence and progressively attractive when well set. In the years since the second war Worcestershire have been represented by modern teams extremely talented and well equipped for the county cricket of the day, with excellent batsmen like Kenyon, Dews, Horton and 'Laddie' Outschoorn, a lively incomer from Ceylon. It is no fault of theirs that, not being Fosters, they seem to lack what the old Scottish poets called *'the glamourye . . .'*

If the Fosters were the Alps, R.E. was Mont Blanc. Cricketers, as we are agreed, are ordinary men, like you and me, and, apart from especial skills in their own game, their general interests are as widely varied as their personalities. As individuals they are far from equal: one died a devoted Christian missionary in an Africa far darker than it is today; and two were hanged for murder. As for their skills, they are rather like those tested in a schoolboy's examinations: there is first of all an O level and all must pass that; otherwise they would not play first-class cricket at all. Then there is an A level, comprising the cream of county warriors, players of sterling value like Jack Robertson or Don Kenyon or Vic Wilson, who have their reward in general esteem and a well-deserved benefit. But over and above the line of high talent and dutiful service there are a few who play their parts on a wider stage, whose heads are among the stars, and whose names are as fresh when those who saw them as boys are old men. Of such are Trumper and Ranji, Jessop, Hobbs and Bradman and a few, a very few, others. Among this select company, selected by the gods themselves, was Reginald Edward (Tip) Foster.

His career was slight, for he played only a few full seasons; it was short, for he died young. From Malvern he went up to Oxford and in his second year he hit up 171 in two and a half hours, the highest score till then in any University match. Three times since then that record has been eclipsed by higher scores, but those who surpassed him in runs came nowhere near him in brilliance. After a dazzling half-century against Lancashire he was picked for the Gentlemen instead of W.G., dropped for the first time in thirty-five years. Foster acknowledged the honour by hitting a century in each innings. These hundreds were not gauges arrogantly flung in the faces of the enemy. The second of them was like a prolonged storm of summer lightning. Every ball was attacked, not by wild hitting, but by true strokes dazzlingly executed: glorious on-drives, diamond-fine late-cuts and imperial off-drives from wrists slender but steely. There was a moment in time at which Foster had scored 95 while his partner, C. B. Fry, the most prolific of scorers and wholly unhandicapped by diffidence, had made 19. This game was a classic – perhaps the classic – among Gentlemen v. Players matches, and after a titanic struggle before the Players won by two wickets, it had gone through every dramatic situation. If any innocent author had presented for publication a story based on a fictional match containing scores like those of this match, he would incontinently have been thrown down the editorial stairs. In the game 1,276 runs were scored in three days against the cream of amateur and professional bowling and the winning hit was made in the last over by a young Yorkshireman named Wilfred Rhodes. Besides a 98 by Abel there were four centuries: one by Hayward, one by J. T. Brown and two by Foster, but Foster's second was infinitely the most scintillating. Only Ranji, said Fry, could match Foster's instantaneous co-ordination of eye and hand.

In 1901 he played regularly, gathering a rich harvest of runs and averaging 55; the next season he came in late, but this made little difference, for he scored a fierce hundred against Derbyshire early on. Then after a further summer in which he had very little practice, he received an invitation to go to Australia with Warner's 1903–04 team. It was the first Test of the series at Sydney which gave Foster his final and indisputable claim to immortality.

If fate had been so cruel as to restrict me to only one cricket match in my whole life this would be the one of my choice. It had every thrill of dramatic action from the first ball to the last and, despite the absence of Grace, Hobbs and Bradman, numbered among its twenty-two participants a bigger proportion of the unchallengeably great than have ever appeared on a cricket field since. Which the same I am free to maintain.

Everybody over a certain age knows the story: how the Australians won the toss on a plumb wicket, lost three wickets for ten, and were rescued from destruction by an Ajax-like act of captain's defiance by M. A. Noble. England began almost as disastrously and then came Foster. He started quietly for him; first with his county colleague Arnold and then with Braund, he fought back with courage and resource. The bowling was good; the fielding was razor-keen but, though Foster, by his own standards, was performing modestly enough, fours flowed from his bat like the glittering plumes of a mountain cascade. 'You couldn't set a field for the chap,' said Noble. Such late-cutting, such cover-driving had never been seen, and they were hardly seen then, averred the connoisseurs on the Hill, because they came so perishin' fast. Nobody, was the universal verdict in Sydney, had ever batted better; only Trumper ever batted so well. In the middle of the innings England suffered a slight collapse. When Braund left, Hirst, of all people, was out for a duck, and two more wickets fell cheaply, but Foster's innings flowed serenely on. His bat was a royal sceptre and the fielders were his slaves. For the ninth wicket Relf joined him as a stubborn companion and when Rhodes came in at 447, there began a last-wicket stand that has remained for well over half a century the finest of its kind. Foster went on batting like an angel of light and Rhodes showed the mettle which was in a few years to promote him from No. 11 in the batting order to No. 2. When Foster was caught at last, he had scored 287, the highest total ever made by an Englishman in Australia, and incomparably the finest as a work of art.

In the next two years he played only a limited number of games, but when he took the time off from business, or even from hospital, he could walk to the wicket and bat as if he had been practising for months. Cricketers capable of doing this are rare in any age. Major R. M. Poore of Hampshire could do it. I have no doubt that Bradman could have done the same, if he had made up his mind to do so. The only man capable of such a feat today is the Reverend David Sheppard, and what is more, I think that he could tell you why.

In 1905 Foster turned out against Kent, having not touched a bat until August Bank Holiday, and scored 246 not out. This would have been a remarkable feat for any kind of batsman, but for a daring, quick-sighted, quick-footed attacker like Foster, depending on instant accord of eye and limb, it was almost miraculous. At Taunton he repeated the feat, totally unrehearsed, a week later in the following year. By the time he had passed his third fifty on his way to 198, Somerset bowlers were complaining of the eternal injustice of things: a man who could bat like that ought to be made to operate with one hand tied behind him.

When he captained England against South Africa in the dismal season of 1907 it seemed that his brilliance had become dimmed and from then on he had less and less leisure at his disposal for cricket. In 1910 he played only once, but to describe his innings of 133 against Yorkshire as a gem would be an understatement. It sparkled like a gay selection from the crown jewels.

He died in 1914, three months before war broke out, a victim of diabetes, for the cure of which insulin had not been invented soon enough. A melancholy light plays forever over the names of those like Foster, Trumper or K. L. Hutchings, who enriched all cricket, though they perished ere their prime. They could not know that their time was so short, yet with some sort of superhuman generosity they gave of their best to the fullest stretch of their powers and beyond.

Plan of Pavilion Seating on the Worcester Ground

MCC

From *Cricket at the Breakfast Table* (1909) by the pseudonymous MCC.

❧

H. K. Foster	W. Foster	S. S. Foster	A. H. Foster	J. K. Foster
R. E. Foster	X. Foster	T. U. Foster	B. T. Foster	K. L. Foster
S. N. Foster	Y. Foster	U. T. Foster	T. F. Foster	S. T. Foster
W. Foster	T. P. Foster	S. Foster	J. N. Foster	J. P. Foster
A. B. Foster	A. T. Foster	S. M. Foster	M. D. Foster	P. A. Foster
B. D. Foster	W. S. Foster	A. M. Foster	B. A. Foster	N. A. Foster
P. Q. Foster	G. R. Foster	L. Q. Foster	F. S. Foster	Y. T. Foster
D. Foster	J. T. Foster	R. Z. Foster	E. P. Foster	A. N. Foster
E. Foster	N. H. Foster	T. Y. Foster	X. Foster	Y. M. Foster
F. Foster	H. P. Foster	A. C. Foster	Z. Z. Foster	O. R. Foster
C. Foster	A. I. Foster	C. M. Foster	R. S. Foster	E. Foster
N. Foster	I. P. Foster	M. O. Foster	S. N. Foster	F. O. Foster
M. Foster	I. F. Foster	N. P. Foster	P. R. Foster	S. T. Foster
N. Foster	J. L. Foster	F. Z. Foster	R. R. Foster	E. R. Foster
O. R. Foster	O. O. Foster	E. T. Foster	R. X. Foster	S. Foster
P. Foster	L. Y. Foster	N. T. Foster	N. T. Foster	S. E. Foster
Q. Foster	L. & N. W. Foster	U. W. Foster	U. P. Foster	A. T. Foster
T. Foster	S. W. Foster	W. X. Foster	V. F. Foster	S. Foster
U. Foster	M. R. Foster	A. W. Foster	F. O. Foster	S. T. Foster
W. Foster	P. P. Foster	R. R. Foster	R. S. Foster	X. Foster

John Jones

❧

12

'ONE OF LIFE'S BEST EXPERIENCES'

My Tour Diaries

ANGUS FRASER

Angus Fraser, the former Middlesex and England fast bowler, played forty-six
Test matches from 1989 to 1998. His *Tour Diaries* appeared in 1999.
On England's 1995/96 tour of South Africa, the team plays a game in Soweto
Township and Fraser worries that the team is being used politically.

B UT IT WAS fine, and this turned out to be the day we met Nelson
Mandela. We were told that he might well pop in sometime during the
game and we were all looking forward to that, but we didn't expect it to be on
the first day and, consequently, I didn't have my camera on me. I really wished
I had brought it when he arrived, because there are few heroes in this world
and he is definitely one of them. My knees went weak when I met him, it was
just the most amazing thing. I've never seen so many people so focused on one
person. Nobody took their eyes off him. Nobody spoke to each other while he
was at the ground. Who knows how Atherton and Stewart, who were batting
at the time, managed to concentrate on the game and stop themselves getting
out, because it was like a god had walked into the ground and was among
us. Everyone, without exception, was aware that someone special was in our
midst.

I didn't know what to say to Mandela when I was introduced to him. He
told me, because of my size, that I was intimidating him and that he didn't
know how their cricketers felt about playing against me. He then asked if
I was enjoying the country. I just muttered that I was pleased to meet him.
He's actually taller than you think and also looked really well for his age, and
considering all he has been through in his life. He just seemed such a gentle,
kind, lovable man. Then he, famously, said to Devon [Malcolm], 'I know you,
you're the destroyer,' a reference to Devon's nine wickets at the Oval in 1994.
It must have been unbelievable for Devon.

I felt privileged to be there. Lunch lasted a lot longer than usual and then
the president did a lap of the ground with Devon while a group of us followed
them in a huddle, walking five yards behind. Mandela was like a magnet and
we just wanted to watch him and hear what he had to say. And if we were
thrilled, I can only imagine what it must have been like for the children of

Soweto to have the great man among them. Soon after, he was back in his car and away. One of life's best experiences was over and the cricket seemed a total anti-climax after that.

Lord's

RACHAEL HEYHOE FLINT

Rachael Heyhoe Flint (Baroness Heyhoe Flint) captained the England women's cricket team from 1966 to 1978. The occasion is the first Women's One Day International at Lord's in 1976. From *Heyhoe!* (1978).

WE STAYED AT the Westmoreland Hotel, on the perimeter of Lord's, for the night before the match, but despite the comfort of the place I hardly slept at all. Once again, the nerves that many refuse to believe I possess were forcing themselves forward. I was so concerned that the day to come should be the greatest possible success, for I knew that this, more than any other occasion we had ever been part of, was a searching trial of women's cricket.

I got up early for breakfast – just toast and coffee: butterflies wouldn't have let bacon and egg settle! I then looked forward to the first thrill of the day – an unhindered passage through the famous Grace Gates at Lord's. Many was the occasion that I had had to plead my way through – I reckon it's easier to get into Fort Knox than Lord's – but not this time. I drove my car up to the gates, all required passes glued to the windscreen, and as the gateman waved me on I raised my cine-camera and recorded the moment – I almost shouted out 'Hallelujah'!

Inside the pavilion, men seemed to be stationed on every corner of every stairway, just to ensure that we didn't encroach on forbidden territory. We were shown warily into our dressing-room and my first impression was how incredibly antique the room looked.

Perhaps I was looking through domesticated female eyes at a male domain, but to me the cranky old wash-basins, floors of erupting linoleum, torn chair and not-so-sweet-smelling loos merely emphasised what an age-old place Lord's is.

It wasn't until I stepped out on to the player's balcony that the aura of the ground really hit me. This was the balcony that I had viewed so many times from below, staring at idols of the male game. Now it was our place, I must say I felt extremely proud.

Our two attendants, women of course, brought in some English roses – surely an innovation for the day, I thought: Greig and Brearley don't order these, do they? Then it was time to toss up, and my first walk of the day into the centre of the arena.

I lost the toss which ironically turned out to be a stroke of good fortune for England. Australia, a match up in the one-day series, elected to bat first. They had not bargained for the early movement of the ball in the Lord's atmosphere, which was just as well, for neither had I. I would have batted first, too!

In a way, I was pleased that we were forced to field, for at least it meant that I would be the first woman ever to step on to the Lord's turf in a playing capacity. That meant more to me than I can say, even if I did do it wrong. Instead of turning left at the foot of the stairs, I opted to go straight on, out through the double doors, then along the pavilion frontage to the steps on to the grass, simply because no one had told us if we were allowed into the Long Room or not. The last thing I wanted to do at such a late stage was commit an irretrievable *faux pas*.

There were quite a few spectators in the ground early on, as well as plenty of cameramen. One of them asked me to raise my arm in a victory salute as I walked on. I refused, intent on doing nothing that could possibly offend the Lord's authorities who had finally shown us the green light.

My feelings as I actually walked on the pitch were of elation, pride, misgivings and extreme nervousness. I felt goosepimples appearing as we walked out to the middle and I know it sounds rather like Angela Brazil, but I could have easily cried.

I was surprised how cosy it was at Lord's compared with the wide open vastness of Old Trafford and the Oval, the concrete coolness of the Edgbaston Test Ground, and the extreme width of Trent Bridge.

I was surprised how much the field sloped from one side to the other and it took some time for us to adapt to the speed with which the ball ran down to the Tavern. Fortunately, it took the Australians longer to adjust to the complete occasion. We dismissed their most dangerous bat, Lorraine Hill (who had scored 1,000 runs, including five centuries, on the tour), inside the first over, and never really looked back.

Eventually we were left to score only 169 in our fifty overs, and were given a start which virtually guaranteed us victory in the game. It was not, however, likely to be quick enough to give us the fastest overall scoring rate in the series, which matched against Australia's win at Canterbury three days previously, would have won us the St Ivel Cream Jug. So, I was left with a decision – do we go for the win at Lord's, or risk everything – and possibly lose – by throwing the bat and try to take the series? I put it to my team, and they supported my secret personal view by opting for the win at Lord's. We did so comfortably, by eight wickets, but some officials annoyed me again by showing some resentment at the fact that we had not brought home the trophy.

When I went in to bat I scuttled nervously through the Long Room, smiling a pale thank you to the shouts of good luck. I reached the middle, took guard and surveyed the Australian field placings; I then drew breath to relax. The cloistered silence clung all around like a blanket; there was an air of expectancy. Suddenly from out of the reverent hush came Benjamin's piping tones – 'I can see you Mummy,' and I smiled, drew breath, relieved. I was relaxed and ready!

For me, the greatest part of the occasion arrived at its climax. I had been batting with Chris Watmough when she struck the winning runs, and the crowd, which had built remarkably to about 8,000 during the day, stood to a man (and woman) and roared approval as we came off.

In the pavilion, age-old members creaked to their feet, shouting 'Encore!' and 'Bravo!' Cheers rang through the Long Room as I ran up the pavilion steps two at a time. It was the sort of moment that made me want to call for an instant 'Match of the Day' replay. Champagne flowed in our dressing-room – a gift from the *Sunday Telegraph* for my 179 at the Oval; we drank out of teacups!

Sadly, though, it was all over, and a day that had been planned for so long, and caused me so much personal aggravation, had to end with a disappointment. With thousands of happy, patriotic spectators waiting outside for the presentation, the establishment insisted that the trophy and awards should be handed over in the Long Room, where there was barely room for even the teams and officials. Lord's said bleakly that there was no precedent for making a presentation on the pitch. Had they forgotten every male cricketing cup final? Not even the players' relatives were allowed into the Long Room to share with us all the thrill of the whole occasion – they were left outside in anti-climax, waiting like the peasants outside the castle. It seemed to me very sad that Lord's should show such an unsympathetic lack of public relations, for many of our supporters had travelled hundreds of miles to be with us on Ladies' Day there.

The Sentiment of the Ball

A. E. CRAWLEY

A. E. Crawley was a schoolmaster, journalist and anthropologist.
From *The Book of the Ball* (1913).

WHAT WE ARE aiming at is to get some idea of the fascination of Ball Games, and particularly of the extraordinary pleasure one feels in achieving this play or that. The sensation, especially, of hitting a ball clean and true with the appropriate implement deserves far more scientific attention than it has received. Typical cases are the half-volley hit to square-leg at Cricket, the drive at Golf, the force to the grille at Tennis, the Lawn Tennis smash. These are 'full' strokes, and half their sweetness is in the follow-through. The complete sensation can be analysed from start to finish; to describe it is less easy. For it is unique; there is nothing in life resembling it; and the man who lacks this experience has not truly lived.

To begin with, such a stroke makes you realize, what no scientific imagination can, the meaning of that double essence of the world and of life which we call matter and motion. It envelops you in practical dynamical things; it connects you up with mass and movement; it forces reality into your bones. This is not mere fancy. The pleasure of the ball player is a radiation from his 'muscular sense'. The term might perhaps be improved, but it has to cover so much that its vagueness may be excused. All sensation is pleasurable when normally satisfied, especially in the spontaneous freedom of play. There is pleasure, then, in the appropriate satisfaction even of sight, with its accompanying muscular sensations. But the bigger work of the muscular sense is in dealing with weight, mass and resistance, texture, friction, vibration and velocity. A stroke is like a wave; there is a preliminary flow of movements; the climax is the hitting of the ball; the follow-through is like the fall of the wave. Both the pitching of a ball and the striking of it include a similar series of bodily movements, releasing energy and giving a pleasurable feeling, as the tension is relieved and the muscular functions are satisfied by a rhythmical orgasm. They are more alike still, because a hit is mechanically identical with a throw. The chief difference is that at the climax of the hit the movement has to overcome the resistance of a mass either at rest or in motion. The shock of impact, graded down by absorption into both bat and ball, whose respective substances are harmonious in texture and resilience, gives a unique sensation of resistance overcome, of weight released, of force repulsed. All sense of touch is, at bottom, sense of pressure, but here and there it is specialized, and we have what are called 'acute sensations'. As distinguished from these, muscular sensations are called 'massive', because they interpret weight, resistance, and so forth. But this feeling in the muscles – almost in the bones – is as intense, though different in quality, as the most poignant sensation ever generated in the mucous membranes of men.

The relief of pressure and the overcoming of resistance constitute a dynamic form of the pleasure received from a work of art. In both, the nerves are stimulated to function; the discharge of their energy produces pleasure, which we call pleasure of the eye, the ear, the imagination, or the muscles. Something similar happens, if we may put it so without being fantastic, to the bat and the ball, to the bullet and the gun. Their interchange of blows means compression and restitution, deformation and restoration; potential energy is released, and, if the ball and the bullet, the bat and the gun, feel nothing, the shock raises their temperature.

❧

Goodbye to the Razor-edge

FRANK TYSON

Though he played relatively few Tests, Frank Tyson (Northants and England)
is generally acknowledged as one of England's most destructive fast bowlers.
From *A Typhoon Called Tyson* (1961).

IF I HAD MY life to live over again, I would not ask for success alone, sweet
though it is. I should only want to be allowed to bowl fast once more. To
those who have bowled quick, really quick, there is no comparable feeling in
the world. The sudden clutch of suppressed anticipation as you mark out your
run: the hesitancy that blossoms into arrogant confidence as, from a shuffling
slow start, the stride quickens, lengthens, and becomes smoother; two yards
from the wicket now and time to give it everything you've got; the body
swivels, left hand plucking at the clouds, right arm swinging in a deadly, ever-
quickening arc as the batsman appears in the sights over the left shoulder; the
left leg is raised high, ready for the final plunge and the body is poised and
ready; crash! – the skull shakes and the muscles of the body jar screamingly,
as the front foot thumps down like a pneumatic-hammer and the ball rockets
on its way at the cringing batsman, pursued as if by an avenging angel, by the
bowler's flying body. What power there is in bowling fast! What a sensation
of omnipotence, and how great the gulf between this sublime sensation and
ordinary, mundane everyday existence!

A Personal Perspective

CHRISTOPHER MARTIN-JENKINS

Christopher Martin-Jenkins is a well-known cricket broadcaster and journalist.
From the introduction to *Ball by Ball* (1990).

POTENT AND NOSTALGIC as the half-remembered smell of the music
room which housed the old brown radio set on which I first heard cricket
commentaries, the voices of the BBC commentators of the 1950s return to me
now as I contemplate that good fortune. Sounds echo back into consciousness

when I conjure up the scene of a musty room on the second floor of my prep school, St Bede's in Eastbourne, looking out across the playing field to the English Channel, a vacant blue plateau seen through a wide gap in the bank beyond the cricket pitch. Across that gap many a dirty British coaster butted its way through the mad March days, but on one particular morning I recall, the *Queen Mary* herself might have escaped my notice as I fixed my attention on the wireless perched on a cupboard opposite the tinny piano on which I never produced anything more original than 'Chopsticks'.

It must have been during the short break between lessons and lunch, which I would have normally spent outside with a bat and a ball. Word had got round that something of national importance was happening and I listened anxiously, along with other cricket-besotted boys, as the match-saving stand between Willie Watson and Trevor Bailey developed. Lord's, 1953: England v. Australia. It was the greatest salvage operation since Dunkirk and that had been three years before my time. The tension seemed all the greater for the measured nature of John Arlott's deliberate description, each word he uttered apparently savoured for a moment, like wine, on the tongue. That rough Hampshire burr was almost melancholy at times but it was fuelled by an agile mind with a seemingly limitless vocabulary at its disposal.

I had only been at the school for a month or so. Cricket had been my sanctuary from the start. I pity children who now have to start their schooling with the long Michaelmas term instead of the months of sun, ice-cream and cricket. Isn't it always the summer days that we recall when we think back to the best aspects of school life? I know that, when I was an eight-year-old boarder at St Bede's, the pain of being wrenched from home and parents had been eased, indeed forgotten, by a game of cricket with my elder brother and his friends on the first evening in my new surroundings. The passion for cricket remained throughout my schooldays and although, unlike Carlisle Best, the Barbados and West Indies batsman, I never actually commentated when I was playing in a serious match, informal games in the garden, on the beach or against school walls were always accompanied by a running commentary from me.

❧

A Day at the Home of Cricket

TOBY PULLAN

Toby Pullan is fifteen and wrote this article especially for this book.

❦

LORD'S IS A VERY special occasion for our family. It is the day when everyone gets involved, male or female. For the mothers, making picnics and relaxing in the sunshine (or rain) is the order of the day, and of course from time to time, making the odd remark such as 'Who is winning?' or 'When is it England's turn to hit?' However even their heads may turn from their magazines as they see the young six-foot-five Stuart Broad thundering in from the boundary! For me watching the cricket at Lord's is an exciting experience where you can admire your favourite players from thirty yards away, rather than through a television screen. There are moments that make your heart skip a beat and there are times when you can just sit back in the sunshine and watch England get on top of a rather mediocre bowling attack – both occasions being equally enjoyable. However Lord's is primarily the day when the middle-aged man comes into his own. The dads whip on their egg and bacon ties as quick as a flash and waltz around talking to old friends, or commenting on the day's play with people they have never met before. The wine list is as good a line-up as any England batting order!

The Lord's ritual starts the second the family is all on-board the train from Haywards Heath to London Victoria with their strong coffees and sticky cinnamon whirls. It is a perfect chance to read up on the latest news on the squad and get to grips with the opposition's strengths and weaknesses. When we all arrive at the ground there is always something missing, whether it be last year's TMS headset or the picnic rug that should have been with the umbrella. However, after a few minutes faffing about looking for the missing items, they will always appear at the bottom of the bag, or even sometimes wrapped around someone's neck. We then attempt to navigate our way through the crowds towards the Tavern Stand where one of Grandpa's friends will have usually reserved us seats. It doesn't matter how many times I go to Lord's, the second I enter through those gates I always get this tingle in my chest knowing that there is not a place I would rather be in the world – apart from batting out there myself of course. I do not know whether it is the jazz band busting out upbeat solos that makes me feel excited, or simply the people around me. The place has a special atmosphere not just from the cricket, but from the incredible setting itself. Indeed, you just want to take a little time to soak it all in before the actual play starts. When I do take my seat I am hit with a buzz of mutual anticipation from everyone inside the ground. This brilliant sensation that covers the whole ground is what planted my original thrill and love for Lord's.

It's not really the cricket that I remember from when I first went to Lord's; I recall thinking, 'Why is everyone standing up and clapping?' It is the sheer size and brilliance of the place – the cheering, the chatting, and the laughter. In fact, the only cricket statistic that I can recollect from my early trips is that Rob Key made a Test hundred against the West Indies in 2004, when I was seven. Now that I am a little older and more of a cricket fanatic I go to Lord's to watch every ball of the game, but it is most definitely a day that the non-cricket fan can enjoy. I have known many hardcore cricket fans just watch an hour of cricket and then sit out on the champagne lawn drinking and chatting with old mates all day – not that I think that is a good thing of course. Why not give your ticket to a cricket fan like me who will actually watch the cricket?!

So, in conclusion, I believe that Lord's is a place of great meaning, from the grand old pavilion to the hallowed green turf. From the minute you enter the stands you can tell the seat you are sitting on is very special and has been sought after by many members of the British public. These sorts of things are what make Lord's so memorable; the fact that it's fun, social, historic, and most of all full to the brim with amazing cricket moments and wonderful memories that will never be forgotten and will always remain at the Home of Cricket.

The Book of the Ball

A. E. CRAWLEY

A. E. Crawley was a schoolmaster, journalist and anthropologist.
The Book of the Ball was published in 1913.

THE BALL IS a natural symbol of man, and the more appropriate because Ball Games play so important a part in modern civilization. They form the pastime of the majority of the people; their exercise improves the physique of the race, and their morality its social life.

More than one modern poet has personified bat and ball and described their mutual attraction and repulsion in terms of love and strife. Players themselves are always personifying them – now one and now the other. Living metaphors in abundance are used in the language of Ball Games. The ball 'talks'; it has 'devil' in it, like a human demoniac; it is 'killed', and is 'dead'.

In the psychology of games the Ball represents nearly every human activity, desire, idea, and volition. Just as the bat is an extension of the player's arm, increasing its radius and multiplying its accuracy and force, and is therefore a kind of solidified will-power, so is the ball an artificial focus of concentration. This is its first meaning: a universal centre of attention, gathering into itself, like a 'receiver', every movement and idea of the players. Then, in turn, it radiates out what it has received. Every game is thus a sort of planetary process or solar system; the ball is the central atom in the molecule – the sun surrounded by its planets. But, without using metaphors, we may put it that the ball receives the player's will, literally. It leaves the pitcher's hand, charged with his intention; it is a shell whose explosion executes his message. As regards the bat, there may be two processes: the bat may simply represent a throwing apparatus, a means of carrying the player's intention to the required place; but when at the same time it defends the player, the bat is both armour and gun. The act of defence is also the act of offence. During the defensive-offensive hit, the energy with which the ball was charged may be altered in character in the same way as its destination is changed. It is a curious coincidence that an india-rubber ball acquires, when struck, a negative electrical charge, and loses its potential.

Then, again, the Ball as a go-between and intermediary between the opposing players receives the knocks of competition. It represents the enemy;

you vent your feelings and exert your strength on a substitute; when you smite it, you are smiting him by proxy. You are even smiting his head. 'There is certainly,' writes Dr. Chance, 'much in a human head that reminds one of a ball.' There is something ball-like about a skull, and something skull-like about a ball. A 'bald' head is one that has become a ball; it is 'balled'.*

The humorist, seeing two such heads at a natural angle, exclaims, 'What a lovely cannon!' The brachycephalous man is 'bullet-headed'. In French slang each of three words for ball – *boule*, *bille* and *balle* – means the human head. The ball surmounting the cap worn by some Lacrosse teams is doubly appropriate. Old pictures of St. Denys, the patron saint of France, represent him after decapitation carrying his head in his hands to the spot where he wished to be buried. In the course of an interesting attempt to derive the word 'Tennis' from Denys, Dr. Chance observes that this figure of the saint might have been compared by the fanciful with a Football player carrying the ball. In some such way St. Denys might have come to be patron saint of all Ball Games. As a bowler, he would have bowled 'with his head'; the idea is not unknown in literature; and the picture is worthy of the Wiertz museum. Certainly, Ball Games need a patron saint. Hunting has its St. Hubert. For a god of the Ball the Scandinavian Thor might be suggested, with his 'hammer' of ball-lightning – Miölner. The figure of the Viking god would be additionally appropriate, because the word for 'ball' in all European languages is derived from the northern Teutons, whose Viking blood, whether Scandinavian, Anglo-Saxon, Danish or Norman, flows in our veins. Latin and Italian even, as well as French, took the word from the Teuton tongue.

Dr. Gilbert Slater asks pertinently: 'What is it that makes the action of knocking a little white ball with a crooked stick so soothing to the nerves of the middle-aged clerk or sugar-broker? So far as I know no one has given the answer. . . . The very word "club", used by the golfer to denote his crooked stick, conveys it. The little white ball represents nothing less than the skull of your enemy. When you smite it with brassy or cleek, your nerves thrill to the very stimulus which maddened uncounted generations of your ancestors through ages of palaeolithic savagery in tribal warfare. It is, probably, on some of your earliest visits to the links that you best realize this, when, again and again, you open your shoulders and strike with repeatedly increasing vigour,

*This derivation is challenged by some.

and still that little white ball grins back at you from the spot where it lies on the turf. There is, in fact, an elementary pleasure in the mere striking of a ball cleanly and effectively. This forms what we may call the primary constituent in the charm, not of Golf only, but of Ball Games in general. The intensity of this particular pleasure varies in proportion to the closeness with which the sensations of primitive contest are copied. Thus it detracts somewhat from the pleasure of Golf that the symbol of the enemy's skull lies motionless; the Tennis player, the batsman at Cricket, the Association footballer, all aim their blows at objects full of motion and apparent life. On the other hand, the pleasure of the act of striking is intensified in Golf from the bone-like hardness of the Golf-ball, and the equal hardness of the wood or metal club with which it is struck. In comparison, the soft Tennis ball and springy Racket are insipid. Cricket here does not compare ill with Golf, and I think it offers on the whole a keener thrill than Golf can to the batsman who hits hard and successfully. But Cricket is chancy and fraught with frequent disappointments.'

Baseball and Cricket retain the two chief methods of dealing with the Ball in their purest and most primitive form. These are the throw and the hit. Whenever we pitch or bat a ball, we are doing something which has been practised by countless generations of ancestors.

[. . .] The pleasure of catching a ball is fascinating, and still more when the ball is spinning. We may think of the primitive hunter catching rabbits or young birds with his bare hands, or of the modern boy 'tickling' trout. The spin of the ball makes it like a living creature struggling out of the hand. The kitten playing with a ball is fascinated by its motion; it answers to the touch of her paw. Animals probably identify movement with life and immobility with death, as a thousand stories show. And the kitten's ball is a symbol of the mouse. It seems to be living; it seems to struggle. When she grips it with both paws, she feels the pleasure of a 'catch'. The whole business is made more realistic when the ball is of wool, which has a suggestion of fur.

Club Cricket and Umpires

RICHARD DAFT

Richard Daft was a well-known cricketer of the mid-nineteenth century
who played for Nottinghamshire and the All England XI, 'in his best day the most
graceful of bats'. From *A Cricketer's Yarns* (1926).

✥

W E HAVE HAD many pleasant matches and some rare fun at Matlock
altogether. Our match was always a great event there, and we were
always treated in the most hospitable manner possible by the home team, who
entertained us at a most sumptuous luncheon, and a dinner in the evening
when we were playing two days. Seldom, I think, were such lunches given
as those we had at Matlock. The Bakewell puddings we used to have there
I particularly remember. Tom Foster, our umpire, was wonderfully partial to
them. Once at Matlock we had a very young player with us who sat next to
Tom at lunch, and who, after the second course, handed him a plate of cheese-
cakes, saying, 'Will you take a cheese-cake, Mr. Foster?' Tom, shaking his head
and casting on the young man a look of pity for his ignorance, replied briefly,
'Pass the "Bakewell",' and, after having helped himself to a large piece of his
favourite sweetmeat, he turned to the youth and said solemnly, as though he
were giving him a piece of advice which would be of use to him through
the remainder of his life, 'My lad, never put anything in front of a Bakewell
pudding!'

✥

The Memories of Dean Hole

SAMUEL REYNOLDS HOLE

Samuel Reynolds Hole was Dean of Rochester from 1887 to 1904 and
a noted horticulturalist. *The Memories of Dean Hole* was published in 1893.
Thomas Barker (1798–1877) played first-class cricket for Nottinghamshire
from 1826 to 1845 and then stood as an umpire for twenty years.

❧

TOM BARKER WAS the first distinguished cricketer with whom I was
acquainted, and on an eventful day, when I had accompanied my father to
a meeting of our County Club at Southwell, which Barker attended as a paid
bowler, and when my seniors were leaving the ground and going for lunch to
the pavilion, he said to me, 'Now, my little man, I'll give you a ball.' I took up
a bat, and went with my heart in my mouth to the wicket; for Tom was a tall,
dark man, and bowled at a terrible pace; but he favoured me with a ball which
was exquisitely slow, and which, in the most awkward manner imaginable, I
spooned up into the air; and he called out, 'Bravo, bravo!' and I was bound to
believe him; and we parted to our mutual satisfaction.

Then, on the Trent Bridge Ground at Nottingham, I saw all the great
heroes play: Fuller Pilch, with his long reach, grand defence, and powerful
hitting; short, stout Lillywhite, who was the only round bowler, until Redgate
(in white breeches and stockings) followed his example, with twice his amount
of speed, and round bowling became the rule. I saw Alfred Mynn, with his
tall figure and handsome face, hit a ball which he could not resist, in practice
before the match (the biggest hit I ever saw, or shall see!), over the booths,
over the Bingham Road, and some distance into a field of potatoes on the
opposite side thereof; and we stood gazing as it rose, as rustics gaze at a rocket,
and then relieved our oppression of astonishment with that universal note of
admiration, 'Oh!'

And here I must relate an incident, which created such an intense
excitement as I have rarely seen, and which was followed by a discussion, never
to be solved, whether it was the result of intention or of accident. There was to
be a great match between Nottingham and Kent. Mynn had recently made a
big score, over one hundred runs, off Redgate's bowling at Leicester (in which
operation, playing without pads, he was sorely bruised, and for some days

was unable to leave his bed), and William Clark was absorbed by one anxious ambition, to bowl him, or get him caught. He walked about the ground before the play began, and murmured at intervals to a friend of mine, who reported the interview, 'If I can only get him – if I can only get him!' The ground was cleared; Mynn and his colleague went to the wicket, and the umpire called 'Play.' Then Clark bowled, and Mynn seemed to prepare to hit, but changed his mind, and quietly blocked the ball half-way between wicket and crease. Clark bowled again with a similar result, but the ball was stopped much nearer the wicket. A third ball came, but the batsman went back so far that as the ball fell from his bat, a bail fell also! For two seconds there was a profound silence; there might have been nobody, where many thousands were. We Notts men were mute with amazement, dumb with a joy which hardly dare believe itself. The 'Lambs' could not utter a bleat. Then they roared like lions! They left their seats and, not satisfied with shouting, they danced and capered on the sward!

Sports and Pastimes

WILLIAM HOWITT

William Howitt (1792–1879) and his wife Mary (1799–1888) wrote prolifically about a wide range of subjects. From *The Rural Life of England* (1840).

BUT, IN TOWN and country, it is the noble, and as Miss Mitford, the fair historian of rural life, justly calls it, the true English game of cricket, which shews whither the mind of the people is tending, and what will be the future character of English popular sports.

This game seems to have absorbed into itself every other kind of ball-game, trap-ball, tip-cat, or foot-ball. Foot-ball, indeed, seems to have almost gone out of use with the enclosure of wastes and commons, requiring a wide space for its exercise; but far and wide is spread the love of cricketing, and it may now be safely ranked as the prince of English athletic games. I will here describe a match of this fine sport, which was played on the 7th and 9th of September 1835, between the Sussex and the Nottingham Club, and the thoughts which it produced in me at the time.

The Nottingham Club challenged the Sussex to a match for fifty guineas a-side; and played first at Brighton, where the Sussex men were beaten, who then went to play the Nottingham men on their own ground. The match commenced on Monday, September 7th, and was finished on Wednesday the 9th, about half-past four o'clock. Tuesday having been a wet day, there was no playing. The Nottingham men beat again, having three wickets to go down. A more animating sight of the kind never was seen.

On Sunday morning early, we saw a crowd going up the street, and immediately perceived that, in the centre of it, were the Sussex cricketers, just arrived by the London coach, and going to an inn kept by one of the Nottingham cricketers. They looked exceedingly interesting, being a very fine set of fellows, in their white hats, and with all their trunks, carpet-bags, and cloaks, coming, as we verily believed, to be beaten. Our interest was strongly excited; and on Monday morning we set off to the cricket-ground, which lies about a mile from the town, in the Forest, as it is still called, though not a tree is left upon it, – a long, furzy common, crowned at the top by about twenty wind-mills, and descending in a steep slope to a fine level, round which the race-course runs. Within the race-course lies the cricket-ground, which was enclosed at each end with booths; and all up the forest-hill were scattered booths, and tents with flags flying, fires burning, pots boiling, ale-barrels standing, and asses, carts, and people bringing still more good things. There were plenty of apple and ginger-beer stalls; and lads going round with nuts and with waggish looks, crying – 'nuts, lads! nuts, lads!' In little hollows the nine-pin and will-peg men had fixed themselves, to occupy loiterers; and, in short, there was all the appearance of a fair.

Standing at the farther side of the cricket-ground, it gave me the most vivid idea possible of an amphitheatre filled with people. In fact, it was an amphitheatre. Along each side of the ground ran a bank sloping down to it, and it, and the booths and tents at the ends were occupied with a dense mass of people, all as silent as the ground beneath them; and all up the hill were groups, and on the race-stand an eager, forward-leaning throng. There were said to be twenty thousand people, all hushed as death, except when some exploit of the players produced a thunder of applause. The playing was beautiful. Mr. Ward, late member of Parliament for London, a great cricket-player, came from the Isle of Wight to see the game, and declared himself highly delighted. But nothing was so beautiful as the sudden shout, the rush, and breaking up of the crowd, when the last decisive match was gained. To see the scorers suddenly snatch up their chairs, and run off with them towards the players' tent; to see the bat of Bart Goode, the batsman on whom the fate of the game depended, spinning up in the air, where he had sent it in the ecstasy of the moment; and the crowd, that the instant before was fixed and silent as the world itself, spreading all over the green space where the white figures of the players had till then been so gravely and apparently calmly contending, – spreading with a murmur as of the sea; and over their heads, amid the deafening clamour and confusion, the carrier-pigeon with a red ribbon tied to its tail, the signal of loss, beating round and round as to ascertain its precise position, and then flying off to bear the tidings to Brighton, – it was a beautiful sight, and one that the most sedate person must have been delighted to see.

13

ON TOUR

Heyhoe!

RACHAEL HEYHOE FLINT

Rachael Heyhoe Flint (Baroness Heyhoe Flint) captained the England women's cricket team from 1966 to 1978. The tour to New Zealand took place in 1969. Her autobiography *Heyhoe!* was published in 1978.

NEW ZEALAND GAVE me a chance to try out a different but very vital type of tactic, in one friendly match we were playing. The game was staged at North Shore, very near to the docks. We were out fielding in this particular encounter when a row of bronzed British naval officers appeared on the boundary and gave great vocal support. So, as captain and being in charge of tactics, I immediately moved a fielder out so that she stood right among the handsome 'fellers' on the edge of the field. She knew the tactics and we all knew the tactics, and when the next wicket fell our deep fielder came running in to the cluster of players in the middle of the field and reported, 'There's a party on the ship tonight – how many want to go?' This proves that women place as much importance on tactics while touring as men do!

Fox on the Run

GRAEME FOWLER

Graeme Fowler (Lancashire and England) played in twenty-one Tests. His diary *Fox on the Run* appeared in 1989. It's October 1984, and he has just arrived in India as part of the England touring team. 'Jabba' is Mike Gatting, 'Giff' is Norman Gifford.

31ST OCTOBER. We had a good flight. Club class, but I spent about four hours in the galley, playing cards while Jabba ate cheese and peanuts, so it was enjoyable. The BA crew were pleasant. I didn't even see the film between the time in the galley and knocking back red wine.

The arrival, though, was unusual. There was no one to meet us, which was a complete mystery to anyone who has been here before. I expected hordes of people clambering everywhere, but not a sign of anyone, not even the usual official party. We did arrive at 5.13 a.m. local time, which might have had something to do with it. At the hotel, however, we were met by three musicians dressed up as Mexicans, who welcomed us with 'Home on the Range'!

We went straight to bed, and when we woke up it was to the news that Indira Gandhi had been shot by Sikhs. The first reaction was one of incredulity, followed by horror, shock, etc. But as the day went on and tales began to come back to the hotel of what was happening in Delhi, we began to wonder where that left us. Everybody is in chaos. The tour is in limbo. Do we carry on or do we fly home?

1ST NOVEMBER. The fighting in the streets is getting worse. Our hotel is away from the centre, so we are a little detached from it. The people from the Imperial Hotel, which is right in the city centre, were evacuated out here because they were virtually under siege. Four of the press, including Graeme Morris, were set upon last night – from all accounts their hard journalism was antagonistic to the locals.

Even from our hotel we can see the city burning. It is eerie, because all we can do is sit by the pool, work out in the hotel gym, relax and wait. As Vic Marks put it, 'While Delhi is falling, so far I've played bridge and had a sauna and jacuzzi.' I reminded him we'd also played chess.

Needless to say, there was no question of practising. We did not do so as a mark of respect; had we practised, we might have encouraged some ugly scenes.

We had a meeting with the tour management this evening. A twelve-day mourning period has been decreed, so there is no chance of any cricket in that time, which means the original tour schedule is already out. So there is no point in our being here, quite apart from the possible danger. How strong that is is difficult to tell. [Team manager] Tony Brown, I thought, was a bit harsh in putting down some people's legitimate fears, directed in the main at Allan Lamb. The news has come in that two hotels have been burnt down, that Sikhs are being killed, and that the road to the airport is blocked, which does not add to one's composure. But everything is in limbo at the moment, and the mood among the players is fragile, to say the least.

2ND NOVEMBER. We left the hotel to go to the High Commission for a practice on coconut matting. It was hardly first-class practice, but it served to relieve the boredom. Vic was struck in the face trying to catch a skyer from Giff during fielding practice. He didn't need stitches, but he ended up with a sore black eye and a small cut. In the evening we went back to the High Commission again to play darts and snooker and to have a drink with the people there. We got back to the hotel after midnight and had a laugh at the NBC news reporter who was stationed outside our hotel. He was useless and I couldn't stop laughing at him.

3RD NOVEMBER. Today is the state funeral. Mrs Gandhi is being cremated. Millions of people have gathered, and it is being transmitted live on TV. Half of the commentary is in English, half in Hindi. There is some Hindi on at the moment, so I've got Barbra Streisand playing. I'm watching with Vic. From the window, I can see a lot of the lads are trying to pass time away round the pool.

The latest news is that we may be going to Sri Lanka, but it isn't official yet. Frantic negotiations are taking place to try and salvage some kind of tour, but nothing can happen here until the official period of mourning is over; so even if the tour can start with a new itinerary then, there is no point in our being here in the meantime. The High Commission think the violence could get worse – the death toll has risen to 700 – and many of the press, who have been here before, are very sceptical about any cricket being played at all.

4TH NOVEMBER. We travelled to Colombo on the President of Sri Lanka's plane. It was pretty short notice, and we had to split our baggage to take essentials with us, but it was a great relief and not a bad trip – there were only forty of us on the Tri-Star, so we had plenty of room. We managed to get some Swan lager, which made for a pleasant journey. The President, who had been at the funeral, introduced himself, and didn't seem a bad bloke.

We arrived mid-evening and it was pouring down. As soon as we got here we found the bar full of New Zealand cricketers on their way to Pakistan. It was good to see them and have a drink and a chat and swap stories.

❧

Cricketing Reminiscences and Personal Recollections

W. G. GRACE WITH ARTHUR PORRITT

W.G. was twenty-four at the time of the tour to Canada and the USA
in 1872 and already known as 'The Champion'. He says about the experience,
'it stands out in my memory as a prolonged and happy picnic'.
These *Reminiscences* were published in 1899.

❧

O N THE EVENING of the first day of the match we were banqueted, and I made my first appearance as an after-dinner speaker. I had to reply to a toast to 'The Champion Batsman of Cricketdom' and our Captain Fitz, in his amusing book, 'Wickets in the West, or the Twelve in America' records my maiden effort as follows: 'Gentlemen, I beg to thank you for the honour you have done me. I never saw better bowling than I have seen to-day, and I hope to see as good wherever I go.'

We had another dinner on the second night, this time at the St. James's Club, the members of which kindly invited us to be their guests. The people of Montreal took a very keen interest in all our movements, and large crowds assembled to watch the match. The newspapers paid great attention to all our doings. Their reports of the matches were very funny, if not very accurate. Neither the reporters nor the spectators seemed to understand the game very thoroughly, and we were often amused at the excitement when a catch was made off a bump ball.

From Montreal we travelled to the Dominion capital, Ottawa, where we took up our quarters at the Russell House, and were very well looked after by the proprietor. Canadian hotel-keepers seem to keep their bars open all night, and I was awakened about half-past two one morning by an exciting discussion which was going on in the bar. Recognising the voice of Farrands, whom we took out as our umpire, I listened to the conversation, and overheard a gentleman bragging about his own cricketing abilities, and declaring that he had scored freely off Freeman's bowling. Farrands would not listen to this assertion, and bluntly told the man that Freeman would knock him, bat and ball, right through the wickets in a couple of overs. I believe that if I had not made my appearance and pacified the disputants, who were getting very excited, a row would have been inevitable. I poured oil on the troubled waters, and when I left the scene of the controversy Farrands was enjoying the hospitality of his antagonist.

Next day we commenced our match against twenty-two of Ottawa, and again we won a single innings victory. The wicket was certainly better than it had been at Montreal, and as I was in good form I made 73, the top score of our innings. Rose and Appleby did the mischief with their bowling against the twenty-two. Of course, we were entertained in Ottawa – we could not move anywhere in Canada without being entertained, as the people were so hospitable. Once more I was called on to reply to a toast, and once more I cannot do better than quote Fitzgerald's report of my utterance: 'Gentlemen, I beg to thank you for the honour you have done me. I never saw a better ground than I have seen to-day, and I hope to see as good wherever I go.' I have a lively recollection of this particular banquet, because among the delicacies of the menu was a haunch of bear. Naturally, never having tasted this rarity, we all thought we would sample it. It looked all right, appetising enough in its way, but it was terribly tough and the taste was abominable. I quite believe that the haunch never came off a wild bear; in fact, I think it was a relic of some poor superannuated show animal whose dancing career was ended. It was quite impossible to get one's teeth through it, and though the taste for bear may perhaps be cultivated, like the taste for olives, I fought shy of the delicacy ever afterwards. While in Ottawa we were asked, as everybody who visits Ottawa is asked, 'to do the slides'. Shooting the slides really means sliding down the rapids of the Ottawa River on a lumber raft. We were comfortably assured that there could be no danger, as the lumber was always firmly secured when picnic parties were doing the shoots, and so most of the party accepted the invitation. It is exciting work for the first time, and makes a pleasant diversion, but it is a pastime of which one soon tires. As Fitzgerald said, the peril all told is not equal to a real slide on a bit of orange-peel on a London pavement.

Journeying via Lake Ontario, one of the most amazing of Canada's inland seas, we next stopped at Toronto, where we found a well-prepared ground ready for our encounter with twenty-two of Toronto. The interest in our tour was even keener here than at Montreal or at Ottawa, and the crowd of spectators was greater than had hitherto been attracted by our matches. A flower-pot stand, with accommodation for 2000 onlookers, had been specially erected for the occasion, and much better accommodation was provided for the cricketers than we had previously enjoyed. For the first time, for instance, we found soap and towels provided in the pavilion for our use, and as the climate was sultry we greatly appreciated the thoughtfulness which prompted this provision. I recollect this match principally because I was lucky enough to make my first century in Canada on this occasion – my share of the English score of 319 being 142. Again we were easily victorious, winning for the third time in three matches by an innings. Against Rose and Appleby's bowling the Toronto twenty-two compiled only 97 in the first innings and 117 in the second. The match excited great interest. One gentleman, who had come down from the country to witness the encounter, got himself introduced to me in order to offer me a couple of young bears to take home to England. I could not quite see to what use I could apply the creatures when I got them home, so I declined the seductive offer.

At Toronto we had another banquet – that goes without saying. This time the members of the Royal Canadian Yacht Club were our hosts. Here I perpetrated my third speech, reported by Fitzgerald thus: 'Gentlemen, I thank you for the honour you have done me. I have never seen better batting than I saw to-day, and I hope to see as good wherever I go.' Our visit to Toronto was made extremely pleasant by the hospitality of the people. We were entertained somewhere and somehow nearly every night. The Toronto Club invited us to a banquet, and of course I had to get on my legs again to respond to a toast. Fitz reports my fourth speech as follows: 'Gentlemen, I have to thank you for the honour you have done me. I never met such good fellows as I met to-day, and I hope I shall meet as good wherever I go.' I may say that my speech was received with rapturous applause. Mr. W. H. Smith, afterwards the leader of the House of Commons, was present at this banquet, and also spoke. Hospitality was literally showered upon us. Indeed, the people seemed unable to do enough to make our visit pleasant and memorable. The Lieutenant-Governor gave a ball in our honour, and an excursion was arranged by Mr. and Mrs. Cumberland to Lake Simcoe, and Couchising. Altogether, we did not get much breathing time between a constant succession of festive and social engagements. To finish up the week's sojourn, the Toronto Club organised a scratch match of teams selected from the English twelve and the Toronto cricketers. I captained one side, consisting of six Englishmen and five Canadians, and Fitzgerald captained the other, which was similarly constituted. Like most scratch matches it was productive of excellent fun, although the play was not of the order of strict cricket. My eleven made 168 (of which Lord Harris made 65) and 119, and Fitz's side scored 165 and 63. I ran out to meet a ball in my first innings and got stumped, and in the second innings, just when I was well set, and scoring freely, my opponents, who thought they had had enough of me for that day, bribed the umpire to give me out LBW, and I retired discomfited, much to their amusement and my own disgust.

Throughout our stay in Toronto the weather was splendid, and we were reluctant to leave the city when the day of departure came. Leaving Toronto, and still travelling westward, we made a short stay at London (Ontario), where we played a match on the old Barracks ground against twenty-two of London. We made 89 and 161, and they compiled 55 and 65, Appleby and Rose proving invincible with the ball. There was no lack of entertainment for us in London, whose citizens were not going to be behind Toronto, Ottawa, and Montreal in their welcome to us. Our last sojourning place in Canada was Hamilton, where we had the experience of finishing a match in the dark, to which our opponents consented, so as to expedite our departure for Niagara. By this time, of course, the summer was rapidly waning, and the evenings shortening, and as there is no twilight to speak of in Canada, darkness fell suddenly upon us while we were playing. It was so dark that we could hardly see where the ball went and I remember I bowled the last man out with an underhand sneak. We gave the twenty-two of Hamilton a thorough beating, for while we made 181, they only managed to put together 86 and 79. The captain of the Hamilton team entertained us at his house, and a large company assembled in our honour. Again I was made spokesman of our team in response to one of the toasts, and if Mr. Fitzgerald does not misreport me I said: 'Gentlemen, I have to thank you for the honour you have done me. I have never seen prettier ladies than I have seen to-day, and I hope I shall see as pretty wherever I go.' The Canadian tour was a triumphal success in every way. Never did twelve cricketers work together in greater harmony and with more perfect esprit de corps. From the day we left the Mersey to the day we got back to Liverpool there was not a single hitch, nor one moment's bad feeling. I have spoken since to several members of the twelve, who have subsequently been to Australia, the Cape, and the other places, with cricketing teams, and they all with one accord say that they never experienced such a harmonious tour. I attribute the credit for this very largely to the man we had as our captain. Poor old Fitz smoothed all the rough places with his unfailing tact, geniality, and businesslike ability; and looking back at the tour, over a vista of nearly thirty years, it stands out in my memory as a prolonged and happy picnic. Most of the cricketers we encountered in Canada were gentlemen who had gone out from England and settled in the Dominion for business and professional purposes. I have every reason to believe that our visit had a beneficial effect in the direction of cultivating cricket sentiment in Canada, though the Canadians have not gone ahead with the game as the Australians have. The batting of the teams we met in Canada did not attain a high standard – they seemed incapable of facing our bowlers, and fell victims to easy balls, which ought to have been severely punished – but nothing else could perhaps be expected. It must be said, however, that we met some excellent bowling, and that the fielding of the Canadians was very creditable. It is a curious fact that while we were in Canada Fitzgerald never lost the toss, and yet with one exception we beat our opponents by an innings and some runs to spare.

As in the case with most travellers seeing the Falls for the first time, our first impressions of Niagara were in the nature of a disappointment. We were disposed to discount the majesty of the great cataract – like the Irishman who, when asked if he did not think it was wonderful that so many million tons of water should go pouring over the precipice, replied, 'Wonderful? No! for, begorra, what's the hindrance? It might have been wonderful if it had gone up the precipice.' But this feeling soon vanished, and the awe-inspiring grandeur of the Falls grew upon us and increased day by day until we left the vicinity. Of course we visited all the points of interest, and amongst other things were photographed, with the Horseshoe Fall as a background. The photograph hangs in my room as I write, and conjures up many happy reminiscences of our Niagara experiences. Several of the influential Canadians, who had feted us during our visits to the cities of the Dominion, accompanied us to Niagara, and stayed at the Clifton House Hotel, where we had taken up our quarters. Some of the younger members of The Twelve thought it would be only right if we showed our appreciation of their kindness by returning their hospitality in some small way which would be agreeable and enjoyable to all; so we gave a ball at the hotel, but unfortunately – or as some of us thought very fortunately – the ball took place on a Saturday night, and dancing had to stop at midnight.

Leaving Niagara on September 16, we crossed into the United States, and entered on the second portion of our tour. We took train first to Albany, and then steamed down the Hudson to New York. We were not greatly prepossessed by our first glimpse of New York. The first thing that struck me in the city was that each hotel – we stayed at the Brevoort House – had its own oyster-bar. We found this exceedingly convenient, and soon became good customers, for the oysters were excellent. We opened our tour in America with a match on the Hoboken Ground in New Jersey against twenty-two of the St. George's Club. To reach the ground from New York we had to cross the river, and for the first time in my life I saw a vehicle driven on to a ferry boat, and then driven off on reaching the other side. For this match we had an excellent wicket – it was prepared by Stubberfield, the old Sussex professional, who had an engagement out there – and we had another easy victory, our score being 249, of which I made 68, while our antagonists totalled only 66 and 44. In the first innings Rose and Appleby did all the bowling, and in the course of some chaff some one said that I could get the St. George's men out even quicker than Rose. Anyway, I went on bowling with Appleby in the second innings, and we succeeded in getting rid of the entire twenty-two for 44 runs. Great interest was evinced by a certain section of the people in this match, but cricket was not then, as it is not now, a very popular game in New York. George and Henry Wright, the famous baseball players, were included in the St. George's twenty-two, and were the best scorers of their side, while, of course, their fielding was – as the fielding of all baseball players is – simply magnificent. Our visit to America was the third which had been paid by English cricketers – George Parr having captained a team which visited the States in 1859, and Willsher having taken out another team in 1868. Some of the comments of the New York newspapers were extremely amusing. Ottaway, for instance, was described as 'a tall, lithe, sinewy man, with a splendid reach, and an eye that can detect at a glance the course about to be pursued by the invading sphere of compressed leather'. We were just as hospitably entertained in America as in Canada, and at one of the banquets in New York they made me make another speech. In the words of Fitzgerald again, my speech runs:– 'Gentlemen, I have to thank you for the honour you have done me. I have never tasted better oysters than I have tasted here to-day, and I hope I shall get as good wherever I go.' I think it is rather too bad of Fitz to have perpetuated my first utterances in this way, but I daresay that the reports are not libellous. I make no pretensions to oratory, and I would any day as soon make a duck as a speech.

Line and Length

FRANCES EDMONDS

Frances Edmonds is a writer and expert in cross-cultural communication.
Here she joins her husband, England cricketer Phil Edmonds, on the 1986 tour
of the West Indies and recalls the previous winter tour to Sri Lanka, India and
Australia in 1984/85. From *Another Bloody Tour* (1986).

❧

I JOINED THE TEAM in early February, at Hyderabad. India is the most
fascinating, delightful and often distressing place. Tours to the Antipodes
are all very well, but basically Australians and New Zealanders are just the
same as us, except, of course, that they operate in fewer polysyllables. India,
on the contrary, is a disturbing amalgam of the alien and the familiar. It is a
country of violent contrasts: ostentatious wealth juxtaposed with the most
horrendous poverty; affluent tourists and even more affluent Indians immured
in sumptuous hotels, the one emotionally incapable of dealing with, and the
others inured to, the mutilated beggars, the maimed children, and the sheer
force of Indian numbers.

Cricketers are deified in India. Certainly the team was never subjected to
the usual aggravations of travelling in that country. No 'OK' flight reservations
which suddenly become 'wait-listed', because a few 'Men from the Ministry'
want seats. No interminable waits for baggage at the other end. No infuriating
dealings with the relentlessly inefficient Indian bureaucracy at check-in desks.

All these nightmares I experienced when I left the glorious fold, and
travelled on my own to Goa for a week. None of these headaches, however,
for our pampered heroes. The team had its own bearer, Govind, who collected
their luggage from one hotel, and made sure it turned up at the next. Their
Goanese travel manager, Charlie, ensured that they boarded every plane at the
very last minute, and were whisked away by coach immediately on arrival. The
scheduled flight from Nagpur to Delhi was re-routed to put down at Agra, so
that the England team could see the Taj Mahal. One player, however, declined
the treat. Mike Gatting had seen that old mausoleum before, and besides,
'The House of the Rising Moon' was an excellent Chinese restaurant in Delhi.

It is no wonder that four months of such preferential treatment and the
almost degenerate ease of hotel existence can spoil a man. When Phil returned

home and started demanding steak sandwiches at two in the morning, I was obliged to knock him into line pretty smartly. Men, as the ancient Serbian proverb runs, must be treated like horses. Allow any sort of deviant behaviour to persist and they are ruined for life. Unsellable, too.

A piece of advice, by the way, for ladies travelling in India. Look after your own laundry. Remember that clothes are what an Indian dhobi breaks stones with. Now, this sort of treatment is perfectly acceptable for jock-straps (rancid) and cricket socks (sweaty), but it is hardly appropriate for your brand new collection of Christian Dior lingerie (*écru*), as I learned to my cost in Delhi. To see the fruits of an entire day's shopping in the Avenue Montaigne boiled to the colour of cabbage and the consistency of a combat jacket is enough to make a strong woman cry. On the sartorial front, incidentally, a Sanyo travelling steam iron now seems an essential piece of kit for the tour to the West Indies. The Trinidadian Unions, it would appear, are refusing to carry our bags. Presumably, next, they will be refusing to iron our clothes. Touring, quite frankly, just ain't what it used to be.

The England team in India was a very personable bunch. Many of the old-hand correspondents said (though I noticed that few of them actually wrote) that the degree of team spirit, bonhomie, and general affability was due more to the absence of specific individuals than to the presence of anybody else in particular. (I cannot recollect that Matthew Engel ever mentioned this, however, so it probably was not true.)

Pat 'Percy' Pocock (the off-spinner of Surrey and England) would indubitably rate as one of my favourite tourists. Tedious transfers by bus were often alleviated for me by Percy's cheerful chatting in pidgin Spanish, a dialect he has no doubt acquired around the 19th hole at La Manga club, and which is somewhat restricted to an in-depth vocabulary of beverages alcoholic. My own dear husband would sit totally incommunicado, his Walkman clamped firmly on his head, lost in the sort of catatonic trance rarely seen in cricket circles since Bob Willis retired from the game, listening intently to Beethoven. I felt he was acting like an absolute pseudo. His Walkman might well have been playing Beethoven, but his briefcase was full of Tina Turner. I would accuse him of being pretentious. 'Pretentious?' he'd muse quizzically. 'Moi?'

Rooming arrangements for the men on tour are bizarre, to put it mildly. Apart from the captain and the vice-captain, the Test and County Cricket Board has decided in its infinite sagacity, or perhaps its infinite parsimony, that team spirit is best served by players sharing rooms. Not, of course, the same two players sharing together for the entire five months. There are too many professional cricketers sporting single earrings nowadays. No, there is a judicious rotation of roommates so that everyone gets a thoroughly good dose of everyone else's most nauseating habits and infuriating idiosyncrasies. Probably a jolly good dose of anything else going around as well. Thank God for penicillin.

My arrival in Hyderabad was greeted with almost audible sighs of relief from those who had been obliged to share with Phil. The man is an almost total insomniac, and listens to the radio (if possible, Radio Four or the World Service) all through the night. In the early stages of marriage this produced a most disturbing effect. I would wake up at 9 am and already know the news verbatim. I began to believe that I was some twentieth-century Cassandra, and wondered whether this sooth-saying gift could be focused more profitably on the results of the 2.30 pm at Catterick. It was only several years later that I realized I had been assimilating the information subconsciously at 4 am, 5 am, 6 am, 7 am and 8 am.

Originally, I encouraged Phil to wear a radio ear-piece, but the noise still just reverberated around his bony cranium, unhindered by much hirsute muffling. I am constantly being woken up to the sound of the World Service broadcasting in German. It would not be so bad if he understood a single word of German, and yet the awkward blighter resolutely refuses to turn the radio off. It is truly staggering that no one on the team has ever slugged him. And when people wonder why there are no little Edmondses, I lay the blame squarely at the feet of Alistair Cooke. I refuse to get intimate to the stentorian tones of *Letter from America*. Just in case certain heavy sleepers in the team can cope with incessant radio, Phil insists on sleeping with the curtains open too. In India the light streams in the bedroom window at about 5 am, inevitably waking any slumbering inmate. A weary Allan Lamb had the temerity to complain, and was immediately fined by the 'Social Committee' for selfishness in wanting the curtains closed. Poor Jonathan Agnew (would that he were here with us in the West Indies) was obliged to cover his side of the bedroom's lighting arrangements with a cocoa-pot cosy, since Edmonds also likes to read until about 3 am.

My Tour Diaries

ANGUS FRASER

Angus Fraser, the former Middlesex and England fast bowler, played
forty-six Test matches from 1989 to 1998. His *Tour Diaries* appeared in 1999.
The Antigua Test match took place in April 1994.

IT'S NOT USUALLY good for the game when one side gets close to 600 and
then the other matches it and there is barely time for another innings. The
fifth Test in Antigua came into that category, but it was a game that will go
down in history because of the contribution of Brian Charles Lara. We were
on the receiving end of the highest individual score in Test history.

Richie Richardson wasn't playing in the match, so Courtney Walsh took
over and immediately put an end to the previous dithering by winning the toss
and saying 'We'll bat.' I thought, 'There's a typical bowler. No p****** about.
Now he can go and put his feet up!' The pitch looked flat, but we actually had
a good start and got rid of Phil Simmons and Stuart Williams early. It raised
our expectations, but we were soon brought back down to earth and the match
became very hard work.

I actually felt I had bowled pretty well and got through 23 overs in the
day, but I was tired by the end of it simply because there was no way past Lara's
bat. It was the same after the second and the third days, too, as he just went
on and on. It was an absolutely chanceless innings as he progressed to 164 by
the end of the first day, 320 by the close on day two and then went on to better
Sir Garfield Sobers's previous best of 365 by 10 runs before Caddick had him
caught behind. Lara never slogged, went at the same tempo throughout and
displayed incredible concentration. After each 50 he just raised his bat and
carried on, and he didn't put a foot wrong until after he went past 300. Then I
beat him a couple of times, went down the wicket and said, 'I don't suppose I
can call you a lucky bastard when you've got 300 on the board.' He just smiled
at me and carried on.

We were always aware, from an early stage, that he was going for the
record and that the West Indies were going to give him the chance to get it. A
score of 375 out of 593 for five declared is amazing, particularly on an outfield
that was on the slow side. Lara is the best batsman I've bowled at, no question.

People like Border and Richards were great, but even they were a little more limited in what they were capable of doing than he was.

Lara had such a range of shots that he can make you look stupid. Having such a good eye, he can score freely and gets away with most indiscretions on the strength of it. The goal was there for him that day and he just played and played and played until he reached it. The big moment came when he pulled Lewis for four, and some amazing scenes followed immediately afterwards. We weren't aware of what was going to happen, but the ground was suddenly full of people and Sobers was on his way out to the middle.

We all congregated in the middle because we knew the ground would take at least 10 minutes to clear and just watched while Lara kissed the ground and hugged Sobers. I thought it was a bit too much to set up a scene like that. We said to each other, 'I thought you just raised your bat when you reached a landmark.' Darrell Hair was the umpire and we asked him if the time lost would be taken into account when our over-rate was calculated. He said, 'How much time do you want?'

By this time there were hundreds of people on the outfield and the umpires were desperately trying to keep them off the wicket because we still had to bat on it. They all moved away, but there was one bloke walking up and down the pitch looking to see if there was any damage to it and Hair went up to him and pushed him out of the way, telling him to p*** off. Then he discovered it was actually the groundsman inspecting his beloved wicket.

❧

14

'SO OVER TO THE CRICKET AT...'

So Over to the Cricket At . . .

JOHN ARLOTT

John Arlott was an outstanding writer, journalist and broadcaster, possibly best known for his distinctive cricket commentaries. From *Concerning Cricket* (1949).

❧

EACH DAY, EACH time in each day of each season, as the cricket commentator comes to the microphone, the puzzle is set afresh. It is a jigsaw whose ultimate design he can never foresee, which he can never complete, but which he must try to build with pieces suddenly handed to him, varying in size, in shape, even in significance – some of them not really belonging to the picture at all. The ideal cricket commentary can never be broadcast – even television can never give it – but the commentator must always aim at it.

It is a Test Match at Leeds. The atmosphere is as heavy as a Turkish bath. Runs are coming at no more than thirty an hour from Hutton and Washbrook, but the batsmen have not given a chance nor suggestion of a chance. The two bowlers, Rowan and Mann of South Africa, are dropping the ball 'on the spot' with a regularity which, to the casual eye, seems monotonous – but it is not monotonous or Washbrook and Hutton would not be watching every ball with such care. There is little or no movement in the crowd, no cheering, no jeering. The commentator feels what is happening. In a tiring atmosphere, where the ball will move in the air, and against bowling relentless in the perfection of its length, Len Hutton is going to make a hundred in his first Test Match in Yorkshire. Ball after ball is played meticulously, calmly, safely in the middle of the bat. There is an echo in the mind of that moving poem by Wilfred Owen which built the atmosphere of imminent dramatic events about the refrain 'But nothing happens.'

On the far side of the field spectators are sitting on mud, watching cricket after their own hearts with the grim intentness of the Yorkshireman. How shall the commentator put into words this apparent inaction, this sultry heaviness of the air, the steadiness of the batting, the grim relentlessness of the bowling? Shall he do it by bald, blunt statement, which must prepare his listener for minute after minute of *numerically* dull play? Or can he show the true nature of this tug-of-war – the tightness of the bowling and fielding, the grim, experienced, technically perfect batting of Hutton and Washbrook?

How can he show that the work of these two batsmen has the quality of deep knowledge and experience to be found in the oldest of the crafts of the country? How shall he convey the suddenly acquired steadiness of Rowan whose nerves have, until now, failed him at crucial moments? How shall he convey the bland, placid, almost lazy guile of Mann's bowling? Better perhaps to rely upon the word 'again' – used again and again – of bowler, of the batsman's negative stroke, and then to announce, with as near as possible the tone to be associated with an automatic reckoner, the slow, inexorable, single-by-single progress of Hutton's score.

Or perhaps it is a day on a small cricket ground remote from the centres of Test Match cricket. Two counties far removed from the struggle at the top of the Championship table are playing the match down to a friendly draw on a warm weekday afternoon before a handful of spectators – old men too tired to go home – or with no home to go to – and small boys, to whom all cricketers are gods and their actions memorable. Two steady if uninspired batsmen see, in the easy wicket and the relaxed state of the game, an opportunity to build their season's averages towards the levels of respectability. A bowler, who has sighed these many years for relief from doubling the parts of spearhead and solid body in his county's attack, bowls steadily away, just short of a length. Then, because he bowls as a man should bowl, some slight gust of wind, some variation or irregularity in the wicket lets the well-delivered ball beat the bat. The wicket-keeper (with the neatness of Haydn Davies if the commentator's luck is out) suddenly interrupts that mild, restful afternoon which will know no headlines tomorrow and which even the spectators are following through a sunny haze. With the minutest movement of the hand which holds the ball he removes one bail and looks enquiringly at the umpire. And the batsman is out – just as the commentator's voice has taken on the uneventful lull of the afternoon. Explanation is not easy.

I have spent five seasons with touring sides – Indians, South Africans, Australians, Englishmen, New Zealanders – season-long, country-long, with cricketers in trains which never hurry, talking, taking tea with them through interminable Sunday afternoons at Sheffield, or Cheltenham, or Swansea, and coming to know them as men. Thus you come to know how much success means to them, how deeply they feel about the things they do, the things they try to do, on a cricket field. But how much of that human being can you put into your radio-drawn picture of a bowler who has just been punished for 30 runs in four overs? Easy enough to hail the maker of a century or the man who takes six wickets for 20 runs. But how difficult to show the worth of the man who has bowled hard to find the edge of a Test Match batsman's bat, and found it, only to see the catch drop short of second slip. Two overs later he is taken off with figures of 0 for 40 – and little credit.

All these things may be handled with critical appraisal, with flashbacks to other games, or the player's great record and in the due solemnity with which so many people regard this richest and fullest of all games. But imagine Douglas Wright and Eric Hollies, two good bowlers whom the course of the game requires to present themselves at the crease as batsmen, going out to bat on a green-topped wicket at Manchester. Runs do not matter to England in the least, the time factor is of no importance in the game. Pimsoll and Tuckett are bowling well, moving the ball through the air and off the pitch. Even in Birmingham, even in Hollies' heart, Eric Hollies is not believed to be a good batsman; Douglas Wright, with a broad grin and a bat at an angle more remarkable than technically desirable, may hit his fours on perfect wickets – but not often. One remembers Sydney Barnes' story of the batsman who 'was not batting well enough to get out'. Twenty cricketers playing in this match – and most certainly including the two batsmen – regard the Wright-Hollies partnership as not without humour. Shall the commentator, then, ponderously record ball after ball striking bats handled with less craft than optimism, treating every ball bowled as of earth-shaking importance because this is a Test Match? Or shall he enter into the humour which is there? If he does, his levity will offend some of his listeners – though not the men of whom he speaks!

Even television can give only a *picture* – it cannot capture the *feel* of a cricket ground, the warm humanity of the men who play the game – nor that feeling of tension which will seize a crowd at a moment when the scoreboard appears to bear figures no more significant than those of five minutes earlier.

I may, perhaps, be forgiven for saying that I believe that this cricket, which is spoken of as a game, is transmuted by many imaginations into something more – a fine art perhaps, or a pattern whose unpremeditated grace can sometimes hold the quality of ballet; or an arena where the minds and the emotions of thirty thousand people can be bound up with the muscular reflexes of a man in white flannels.

I cannot say these things lest they should prevent me from stating the precise score, which Mr. Smith, who has just dashed panting into his sitting-room to switch on his set, is so anxious to hear. It is not enough for Mr. Smith, nor for Mr. Brown, who has been at his loudspeaker ever since I began to talk, that I am enjoying myself, I have a duty to them both.

I ought to be a television receiver, a second-by-second news reporter, a painter – to capture the impressions as distinct from the photograph of the play – and a poet – to catch the atmosphere of controlled strife and deep strategic exercise of a mellow craft. I can never be this many-sided paragon – no commentator ever will be. One day, when the picture becomes *half* complete, I shall know that I am dreaming.

And now, with the score, significantly speaking, exactly where it was before I started, I am returning you, reluctantly, to the studio.

Radio: A New Career

ALAN McGILVRAY

Alan McGilvray was an Australian cricketer and for over fifty years a cricket broadcaster. This extract is from *The Game is not the Same* (1986), and the series is the Australians' tour of England in 1938. Charles Moses was the producer of the Australian Broadcasting Commission cricket broadcasts.

RADIO OF THE day was not sufficiently advanced technically to rely on direct broadcast from England. Short wave transmissions were occasionally receivable, but they had not at that stage developed procedures to bounce the signal off the ionosphere with any reliability. Moses decided we had to do something ourselves. His *modus operandi* was to establish a commentary team in the ABC studios in Market Street, Sydney, who would re-create what was going on in England.

Their information would be provided by a cable service specially provided from England. The effect would be the same. The commentators would describe the scene as if they were watching with their own eyes. The only thing that would be different was the fact that the eyes had to be on the other side of the world. Those eyes belonged to Eric Sholl, an ABC employee with an eye for detail who worked in the Sydney office.

He was despatched to send back the cables according to an elaborate code. Outside our studio, a team of five or six decoders would put the cables into readable form from which the commentators would operate. The cables covered everything we would need to paint a word picture of what was happening. Sholl would tell us about the weather, the crowd – even the traffic getting to the ground.

He would keep us totally informed as to where every player was on the field. Any time the field changed, he would fire off a new cable, and each over, he would send a cable with a complete run down on every ball – where it pitched, what the batsman did, where the ball went, who fielded . . . absolutely everything.

In the studio, every possible step was taken to set up an atmosphere for the commentators. A large photograph of the ground, for instance, was suspended in front of us so we had a mental picture of the scene, and the best chance possible for adding some colour into our broadcast. There were four commentators involved, Vic Richardson, Monty Noble, Hal Hooker and myself. Richardson and Noble had been to England, so they could identify with each of the grounds. Hooker was a fine Sheffield Shield player, but never quite made the international arena.

Since Vic and Monty knew the scene best, we left most of the background descriptions to them. Vic knew where all the cathedrals were, what the pavilions were like, where the noisy section of the crowd would congregate. But if we were stuck, there was always that faithful photograph to fall back on.

We had a scorer and a records man, who could keep track of events and turn up whatever figures we needed to kick things along. And there was the all-important sound effects man.

He had a series of recordings which would provide the applause and crowd noises. We had to make a quick judgment as to whether a shot was a good one or not, whether a player would be loudly cheered as he left the field or mildly applauded, whether the crowd would take umbrage at an umpire's decision. Accordingly we would signal the sound effects man for wild cheering, loud applause, booing or gentle clapping, depending on how we thought it would be.

How closely we judged the scene we could never know. But after a time the sound effects man was an artist at what he did, and in all my experience of international cricket I doubt I have ever known a crowd more animated than that which Australians knew through the England tour of 1938.

The most basic sound effect of all we provided ourselves. This was the charismatic crack of leather on willow, the marvellous ring of bat on ball that has so enraptured cricket followers through the generations.

This we provided with a pencil. A spanking drive through the covers, hit with a presumed high back lift and a poultice of flourish, would require a very firm bang on a round piece of wood on the table. Defensive taps and more gentle strokes were handled with appropriately proportional force. This led to occasional difficulty. Sometimes our enthusiasm to describe the shot meant we would have told the world all about it, suddenly remembered the pencil, and had the crack of the stroke arriving somewhat belatedly. Other times the effects man would get in first with the crowd cheering before the shot came. Co-ordinating mind, voice and pencil through some long and arduous innings must have been every bit as hard as coping with Farnes, Verity and Co, as our batsmen were doing.

Sound effects were not the only area in which our enthusiasm initially made it tough for us. The information we were fed came at the end of each over, covering that over in entirety. We would work our way through the six balls, then look for the new cable and the new over.

At first, we were finding an extraordinary delay between the end of an over as we described it and the next cable.

'Where's the telegram?' we would plead as we thrust ourselves into long and arduous fill-in chatter, sometimes to take up several minutes.

Some simple arithmetic eventually forced on me the realisation that I was whipping through in two minutes an over that the bowler in England was taking four minutes to bowl. Since the cables couldn't come any quicker than the balls were being bowled, we soon learned to take more notice of our stop watch and spread each over to more realistic lengths.

But the mistakes and the rough patches were surprisingly few. As we grew accustomed to this rather revolutionary method of describing a cricket match, we became extremely polished at it. We got faster as time went on, and in the end I think it was every bit as colourful and comprehensive as the real thing became in later years.

The key to everything of course, was the information with which we were supplied and the slick work of those who decoded it. The raw cables, sent at the end of each over, were masterpieces of improvisation.

A typical cable would begin: 'BRIGHTENING FLEETWOOD HAMMOND FULL FIRSTLY TWO HASSETT'.

[. . .] The decoders would get hold of that, and the message would come into us in slightly fuller form.

First of all we would establish that the weather was brightening and Fleetwood-Smith was the bowler. 'HAMMOND FULL FIRSTLY TWO HASSETT' would come back 'Hammond batting, first ball pitched up, driven, Hassett fielded, ran two'.

[. . .] So we would work off that information, add a touch of atmosphere, try to imagine the scene, and come up with something like this:

'In comes Fleetwood-Smith, he moves in to bowl to Hammond and Hammond comes down the wicket and takes it on the full and he drives it beautifully past Hassett who moves around behind the ball and fields brilliantly just before it reaches the boundary rope, and meantime they've run through for two.'

The second ball we'd read: 'HAMMOND, FLEETWOOD-SMITH, FULL TOSS, UPPISH STRAIGHT DRIVE, ALMOST CHANCE, FOUR.'

We'd get that out something like this: 'Hammond again moves down the wicket and hits it beautifully past the bowler. My word, that carried. That was almost in the hands of Fleetwood-Smith, but it went just past him and although he put a hand out he didn't get near it and it raced past him for four. But it was certainly past him round about knee high.'

A fair bit of imagination was called for, although we were desperately careful not to be so carried away as to significantly risk the accuracy of the reports.

A cable which read 'HAMMOND SWEPT BARNES FOUR' might end up, 'Hammond sweeps him. He's really got on to that one and Barnes is tearing around the boundary to cut it off, but I don't think he'll get it, and he doesn't, and the ball just beats him over the boundary rope for four.'

Barnes's race around the boundary, of course, would be greeted with some enthusiasm by our sound effects man, who would bring an excited cheer from the crowd, reaching its peak as we nominated the boundary. He really became quite expert at producing a crowd reaction fitting for each event, and timed to perfection.

We could operate with quite remarkable efficiency on fairly skeletal information. We always knew where everybody was in the field, for instance, so with brief information on the rough direction of a shot we could assume a likely scenario as far as the fieldsmen were concerned. And the advantage of having men like Richardson and Noble involved, men who knew their cricket and their cricketers backwards, was that they could read the game with singular clarity.

Their knowledge of how the Australian players, particularly, thought and performed, their habits and their idiosyncrasies, allowed them to gauge reactions and assume trends of play with extraordinary accuracy.

There were, however, times when we were confronted with absolute disaster. Occasionally the flow of cables from the Post Office would be interrupted for one reason or another. When the delays were long we would simply announce a loss of communication and cease operations until they resumed.

But when the loss of contact was brief, or while we thought it would be brief, we tried to tough it out. We might slip in a few balls to mark time. We were always careful in such crises, however, never to advance the score beyond what we knew it to be. Any of these 'fill-in' deliveries would of necessity be insignificant, 'back-to-the-bowler' stuff.

And we filled the gaps with some of the most horrendous discussion. We used to get quite animated. We would be locked in heavy discussion and quite lively argument on subjects that were only imagined.

'He really should be moving forward to those deliveries that are pitched up to him and having a bit of a go,' Vic might offer. 'Well, I don't know about that Vic,' I would reply. 'The bowling's pretty tight and I think the batsmen are quite right in being cautious and taking their time.' The verbal battle would ensue. We would argue the point hammer and tongs, completely oblivious to the fact that neither of us really knew how the batsmen were approaching it, or whether the bowling was good, bad or indifferent. But we became so involved in the broadcasts we almost convinced ourselves we were there. It is quite amazing how the mind and the imagination can take over completely in such circumstances.

Charles Moses fed this line by brain-washing us as much as possible into feeling like we were there. He insisted, for instance, that we lived the nights as if they were balmy English summer days. We kicked off at 8.30 pm Sydney time each evening, and were required to take morning tea at 9.30 pm.

Moses insisted we had 'lunch' at 10.30 pm. Lunch would be sandwiches, fruit, etc, as if we were schoolboys and our mothers had packed them for us. Moses monitored everything, shaping our attitudes and our approach to the point that, in the end, whether we were in Manchester or Sydney made precious little difference.

Only rarely did it go badly wrong. I recall one occasion when the cable came through identifying one of the Australians simply as 'MC'. There were two 'Macs' in the Australian team, Stan McCabe and Ernie McCormick, and at this particular time both were batting.

The cable came through announcing that 'MC' was out. Which 'MC', of course, we had no way of knowing. I quickly switched off the mike and looked at Vic.

'Who'll I give it to?' I pleaded.

'Oh, give it to Stan,' Vic responded. 'He's got his hundred and he'll be throwing the bat at anything.'

In I plunged. 'McCabe steps into the drive. He's lofted it . . . it's in the air and I think he's gone, yes he's out, McCabe is out. And what a glorious innings it was.'

On I trekked into the unknown, rolling along valiantly as the picture unfolded in my mind. I described McCabe's standing ovation. I had him clapped all the way to the pavilion. The sound effects man had a field day.

Then came the next cable. It was McCormick who had gone, not McCabe.

I could do nothing but launch into abject apology. I explained exactly how the error occurred. It was one of the more embarrassing moments of my broadcasting career, but explaining the error quickly and honestly served only to enhance the credibility of the broadcasts.

The ABC, and Moses in particular, were concerned that there should be no dishonesty involved. We were seeking only to inform in as colourful a manner as possible, not to 'con' people into believing the commentaries were the real thing.

That particular error was made infinitely worse by the fact that the innings I so prematurely ended is remembered to this day as one of the finest innings ever played in Test cricket. It was the first Test of that series, when our broadcasting techniques were far from finely tuned. It was played at Trent Bridge, Nottingham, and McCabe's final scoreline read, c Compton, bowled Verity, 232. So stunning was the performance that his skipper, Bradman, still recalls it as the finest innings he ever saw.

Bradman was so enthralled at the time that he went to the dressing room and summoned the whole Australian team to the verandah. 'Come and watch this,' he demanded. 'You will never see anything like this again.'

Of all the innings I could have picked to make a mistake and end prematurely, it had to be this one. It was the only really calamitous error we made through the whole of the synthetic Tests exercise. In many ways it was sheer bad luck, for the whole operation was geared to be scrupulously honest.

Quiet Studio

MICHAEL SIMKINS

Michael Simkins is an actor, writer and Sussex supporter.
He is attending the Sussex v. Lancashire NatWest Trophy Final at Lord's in September 1986. From *Fatty Batter* (2007).

❧

THE WAY I LOOK at it, there can only be one result, a huge and humiliating defeat for my team at the hands of a side who have systematically crushed us under their heel for over a decade. Particularly as Lancashire have playing for them today Clive Lloyd, a player whose murderous hitting has been described by no less than the great John Arlott, doyen of commentators, as 'like a man knocking a thistle top with a walking stick'.

If only I could come up with stuff like that.

But when the umpire's finger goes up to send the world's most destructive batsman loping back towards the pavilion for a big fat duck to give Sussex their third wicket in as many overs, I break my own golden rule to keep my mouth shut and nearly blow my cover. Leaping to one's feet and bellowing like a circus elephant running amok in a shopping arcade is obviously among the permitted code of conduct. But surely the day can't get any better than this?

In fact, it's hardly begun.

It's after I take a wrong turning on my way back from the gents' that I see it. Slap bang in the centre of the balcony, a tiny white-painted hut a few yards along with three simple letters painted on the door. *TMS*. The combination of a permanently open bar and the warm autumnal sunshine had all but driven the purpose of today's quest from my mind. But now I've stumbled upon it by accident. The small side door opens to the hut and Peter Baxter, *TMS* producer, steps out. Behind him, crammed together with his colleagues like an oversized gnome in a potting shed, I snatch a glimpse of Johnners' proboscis-like nose. The door swings shut again. Baxter loosens his tie, takes a few lungfuls of fresh air and perches on the handrail to watch the remaining balls of the over.

This is the moment. If I don't seize my chance I may not get another one. I've had four pints of Theakston's, and, after all, Dad wouldn't have lied to me about his friendship. Would he? Not for all those years?

'Excuse me. Would it be possible to speak to Brian Johnston?'

Baxter turns his head and smiles amiably back. After all, I'm a member. There's no need to panic. I'm not going to pull out a machete or ask him if he knows God loves him.

'Is he expecting you?'

'Um . . . not exactly. I'm the son of an old friend of his.'

Baxter checks his watch. 'He's just finishing his stint on mike, but I'll go in and ask if you like. Who shall I say it is?'

'My name's Michael. Michael Simkins. My dad was Benny Simkins. They were in the war together . . .'

'Just a mo. I'll push a note under his nose.' He smiles pleasantly once more, quietly opens the door to the commentary box and disappears inside, offering another tantalising glimpse of the mighty Johnston unclamping a set of headphones from his monstrous ears.

What have I done? My mate made me promise not to open my mouth, and yet here I am trying to strong-arm my way into the *TMS* box on the basis of a completely dubious story probably invented by Dad to keep his youngest son amused in the long afternoons on Lancing seafront. I've staked my entire day on a piece of improbable fiction from a man anxious to press his cricketing credentials on a son who palpably worshipped him. Of course my dad would try to suggest he was best buddies with one of the voices of cricket. Wonderful in its way.

I'm just about to retreat in panic when the door to the hut opens and the huge figure of Brian Johnston fills the tiny doorway. He wears a cream suit, an MCC tie and his trademark correspondent's shoes. He shoots out a huge mottled hand, flecks of cake crumbs and marmalade still clinging to the finger ends.

'Benny Simkins!! Good God, I haven't heard from old Benny for years. Wonderful musician, and told the filthiest jokes in the whole British army. And his lovely wife, Peggy. It must be over thirty years ago now. And you're his son! Lovely to meet you, Michael – come in and meet the others.' Before I can speak he ushers me up the steps and into the commentary box.

The following forty minutes pass in a dream. *TMS* is everything you could ever hope for, except with more cake. The tiny cubicle is full to bursting with excited middle-aged men, not only the commentary team but various friends, celebrities and hangers-on who, like me, have managed to blag their way in for a few precious minutes in this cricketing Shangri-la.

One by one Johnston introduces me in gleeful hushed whispers, each one accompanied by, 'He's the son of the filthiest joke-teller in the British army.' Christopher Martin-Jenkins says how nice it is to meet me, David Lloyd says, 'Good on yer, son,' former Sussex captain John Barclay assures me it's his absolute pleasure, and Henry Blofeld even calls me his dear old thing. Bill Frindall also behaves exactly to type, complaining that I'm standing in his light and not to open the door without looking first as the wind disrupts his papers.

Moments later I'm handed a glass of champagne followed by a large slice of fruitcake covered with marzipan and frosted with icing. The cake emerged from a white cardboard box and was apparently a gift from Doreen in Shrewsbury. And there I sit, eating cake and drinking Veuve Clicquot, while far below Sussex add 137 for the second wicket.

It must be nearly an hour later when the four pints of Theakston's start to make their presence felt. In any case, I don't want to overstay my welcome. I had planned to delicately bring up the purpose of my visit, but with live commentary taking place it would plainly be inappropriate to ask for extensive career advice. Now I've made contact I can drop Brian a line asking for some help and take it from there. I lean across to indicate that I'm going now and rise from my stool. But he signals for me to linger a moment longer.

With that he pulls from his coat pocket a tiny set of clockwork plastic feet, silently winds the key on the ankle, and just as David Lloyd is about to do his end-of-over summary, Johnston leans across and sets them trundling across the desk in front of him. My last memory is of seven middle-aged men spluttering with barely suppressed glee while the eighth sits frowning at me as I open the door to leave.

I stumble uncertainly down the steps again and stand with my hand gripping the guardrail. My head is spinning. That's what I want to do. I want to be a cricket commentator. To spend my days opening cakes from Doreen and playing practical jokes on my chums and watching cricket over a glass of bubbly.

Insect Bites and Missing Luggage

ADAM MOUNTFORD

Adam Mountford is BBC Radio's cricket producer. This extract is from a blog he sent in March 2011 during the ICC Cricket World Cup in India.

❧

INTO MY THIRD week at the 2011 ICC Cricket World Cup – and from Bangalore to Chennai to Chittagong . . . sometimes with luggage!

THURSDAY 3 MARCH. The morning after the night before! Producer Steve Houghton makes his way to the Ireland team hotel in Bangalore to try to coax hungover Irish heroes onto the radio after the remarkable victory over England. Record-breaking Kevin O'Brien agrees to appear on 5 Live Breakfast and Radio 4 Today programme. Although he says he has no intention of following the likes of Eoin Morgan in trying to play for England, he does fancy getting a contract to play in the Indian Premier League.

The rest of the TMS team has the rather unenviable task of travelling to Chennai with the defeated England side. Journeys like these are always rather tricky as you are not quite sure what to say to players after a dramatic defeat like that. Graeme Swann is selected as the official team spokesman at the airport and starts by taking the mickey out of myself and Aggers for our choice of pastel-coloured polo shirts. 'You look like a pair of children's TV presenters,' he jokes before going on the offensive. 'All those former players in the commentary boxes forget they used to make the mistakes on the field that we did last night,' he says.

Overall, the mood on our short flight east is pretty good and the journey goes to plan with the plane on time and luggage in tow. Word reaches us as we travel in a minibus from the airport to our hotel that Pakistan are struggling in their match against Canada in Colombo. Surely not another World Cup shock on the cards?

We are all anxious to catch up with the action when we arrive at the hotel and we gather in the bar to see the conclusion to the match. The room is decorated with the flags of the 14 competing teams and the hotel staff are all decked out in cricket gear. There is a big screen in the corner and a huge poster alongside urging everyone to enjoy all the World Cup action in the hotel. But Aggers notices that the match being shown is actually an old one involving Pakistan. Ironically, Salman Butt is batting.

This may be an official ICC World Cup hotel but guests are unable to watch the matches because the subscription fee has not been paid! Instead, the choice of entertainment is either a restaurant with an out-of-tune saxophonist or a bar playing the greatest hits of the Bellamy Brothers on a continual loop. Well, I say the greatest hits . . . When I hear the words 'If I said you had a beautiful body, would you hold it against me?' for the eighth time, I retreat to my room in protest.

FRIDAY 4 MARCH. Set-up day at the MA Chidambaram Stadium. The last time we were here was for the remarkable India v England Test match that took place a few days after the Mumbai terror attacks. Graeme Swann took two wickets in his first over in Test cricket, Andrew Strauss scored centuries in both innings to put England in a strong position before Virender Sehwag and Mumbai-born Sachin Tendulkar led India to a huge victory total.

The ground is almost unrecognisable from 2008 following an amazing amount of redevelopment in time for the World Cup. There are new umbrella-style covers on top of the seating areas reminiscent of the Mound Stand at Lord's, while the media facilities have been revamped. A certain amount of last-minute drilling is taking place in the TMS commentary box but I am thrilled that our broadcast lines have been fitted and work first time.

While things are going relatively smoothly in Chennai, I find out that one of our other producers, Tim Peach, is battling against the odds in Dhaka to get commentary of Bangladesh v West Indies on air. This is the first time Tim has been on a cricket tour and everything had worked perfectly at the Sher-e-Bangla stadium for days. But on the morning of the actual match, all the broadcast lines fail. It adds to a growing tale of woe. Commentators Simon Hughes and Simon Mann suffer a nightmare journey to Dhaka the day before the game, delayed at a mosquito-ridden Kolkata airport for nearly 10 hours.

Tim manages to find a way of broadcasting just as the first delivery of the match is about to be bowled, gathering the commentary team around a laptop. But having gone to all that trouble, the match is over in less than three hours. Tim and the team do a remarkable job to get the commentary on air but I receive a forlorn-sounding text from Tim later that night. It read: 'Quite a day. Now computer broken, phone broken and voice broken. Have to get up in two hours to fly to Colombo.'

SATURDAY 5 MARCH. The day before England's match against South Africa in Chennai and I get to the ground early because our reporter, Alison Mitchell, is unwell and I have some press conferences to cover. Firstly, International Cricket Council chief executive Haroon Lorgat responds to the incident in Dhaka, where stones were thrown at the West Indies team bus. We had learned about the incident as it happened, thanks to some fairly colourful tweets from Windies batsman Chris Gayle.

Then it is the turn of South Africa captain Graeme Smith to address the media. The highlight is the moment a journalist's mobile goes off – the ringtone is a loud sheep noise. I go to our commentary box to send the interviews . . . only to find that the broadcast lines that were working perfectly yesterday are now as dead as a dodo. I spend the next six hours getting them working again.

Back at the hotel, I get a text from Tim Peach, who has made the long trek from Dhaka to Sri Lanka. 'Arrived in Colombo. Luggage. Voice missing and it is raining. Going to spend the evening counting the insect bites on my legs.' A couple of hours later, my phone beeps again. It's another text from Tim: '74 bites on my left leg . . . 39 on the right.'

SUNDAY 6 MARCH. Arrive at the stadium at 7 am to get things ready for the commentary team ahead of a 9.30 start. We record the toss interviews shortly before going on air. Host Nasser Hussain remembers the first name of the South African captain . . . something he failed to do when he came across Graeme Smith as England captain. Then we watch in disbelief as England lose two wickets in the first over of the match. England stutter to 171 all out, a total that looks woefully short as South Africa stroll to 63 without loss in 15 overs.

It looks like we are in for a fairly low-key match. In fact, the only real drama takes place at the back of the TMS commentary box, where a large number of angry-looking officials have gathered. Like a naughty school child, I am summoned by the angriest of these officials, who starts to shout at me. At first, I don't have any idea what the problem is but eventually work out that he is upset because of two bottles of water that have been brought to the ground from our hotel by Vic Marks and our cricket organiser, Shilpa Patel. The water, I am told, is not the official brand recognised by the ICC and, much worse, is apparently manufactured by a rival organisation to one of the ICC's main sponsors. Having offered huge apologies and thrown the offending items into the bin, we just about avoid being removed from the ground. The ICC are rightly concerned about the threat of ambush marketing but to make such a fuss about two bottles innocently brought to the ground seems a little extreme.

Suddenly there is some excitement out in the middle as England start to fight back, reducing South Africa from 124-3 to 127-7. Unbelievably, England pull off a six-run victory and have now been involved in the four best matches in the tournament. After the match, Sir Geoffrey is in excellent form on the TMS podcast. On struggling South Africa batsman J. P. Duminy, he remarks: 'His footwork is all over the place . . . I've seen giraffes crouching down at water holes show better footwork than he did today.'

MONDAY 7 MARCH. Not sure I get any sleep as my alarm goes off at the unearthly hour of 5 am ready for our journey from Chennai to Chittagong. I also realise that my phone is full of messages about a rumour that Kevin Pietersen is flying home because of a hernia injury. Fortunately, I know the England team are also getting an early flight, so, as I carry out some last-minute packing, I make an urgent call to the team media manager, who tells me that an announcement will be made in the next hour or so. Confirmation that KP is out of the World Cup comes via a text message from the ECB just as I put my luggage through the X-ray machine at Chennai airport.

I manage to call the office and get the news out on Twitter before putting my phone through the security checks. Then there is a mad rush to file a report to BBC Radio 5 Live as I attempt to get on a plane. While I argue over excess baggage charges at check-in, Aggers is writing a 30-second voicepiece on his laptop. After clearing security, he tries desperately to find a quiet corner to record his report into a small tape machine. He has to find a rare 30-second gap between airport announcements and just manages to get the last word in before the next 'bing bong'.

Meanwhile, Alison Mitchell is firing up her laptop ready to send the Aggers voicepiece online. We are called onto the bus waiting to take us to our plane but Alison is not giving up. She continues to try to send the piece, balancing the laptop on a seat. Only 75 per cent of the file downloads, so Alison crouches down on the tarmac by the plane in an effort to get the final part through. Just as the cabin assistant shouts that final passengers have to board the flight, the download is completed and the report is on the radio less than five minutes later. It never ceases to amaze me what you can do with technology these days. We change flights at Kolkata airport and Aggers manages to grab a word with England coach Andy Flower. That interview is also sent on the laptop, while Aggers chats live to 5 Live Breakfast, standing in the check-in queue.

More drama follows. Because we are taking a small plane to Chittagong, we are told that all the baggage cannot fit on the plane and a heated debate begins about whose luggage is more important. I decide to sacrifice my cases on the condition that I am given assurances they will arrive at my hotel in Chittagong later that evening. As I wave goodbye to my bags, all I can hear in my head is the Three Degrees singing: 'When will I see you again?' At 2 am, I am pacing around my room in Chittagong like an expectant father still waiting for my bags – and the thought strikes me that I may have to borrow a pair of underpants from Aggers. Fortunately for me – and for Aggers – I am eventually reunited with my own boxer shorts.

There is also an added benefit to staying up late. I discover that Test Match Special has been named Radio Programme of the Year at the Sports Journalists' Association Awards. This is a real honour, especially as we were up against such excellent programmes as 5 Live Sport and the brilliant commentary of the Ryder Cup.

TUESDAY 8 MARCH. We are staying in the same hotel as both the England and Bangladesh teams. Security in and around the hotel is very tight. It is not just the cricketers who have armed guards, there are several soldiers in the corridor where the TMS team are located. It is rather odd exchanging pleasantries each morning with a man wielding a Kalashnikov rifle.

Today, one of the heroes from Sunday's Chennai victory, Stuart Broad, is nominated for media duties at a press conference at the hotel. With Broad running more than an hour late, we find out that he has suffered a side injury. Later that day, he becomes the second England player to be ruled out of the World Cup in successive days. It is a real blow to Broad, a player we got to know well when he joined the TMS commentary team in Perth during the Ashes series.

WEDNESDAY 9 MARCH. Set-up day at the Zohur Ahmed Chowdhury Stadium ahead of the Bangladesh v England match. The journey to the ground, located 20 minutes or so outside the centre of Chittagong, is always enjoyable. Brightly coloured rickshaws and an amazing array of market stalls populate the route. Chittagong houses one of the largest ship-breaking yards in the world – a graveyard for huge vessels. Thousands of dismantled bits of boat are sold at stalls across the city. Nothing goes to waste, from doorknobs to toilets. Even the last drops of oil from a tanker's hold are drained and resold.

When I arrive at the stadium, I am again amazed at the extensive redevelopment work. There are new stands and a completely revamped media centre. Although the work to the ground is very impressive, it is a shame we no longer get as good a view of the surroundings as we did when England toured here last year. Then, we could see mountains, animals and even the beach from our commentary box. I get back from the ground in time to see Simon Hughes on local TV. Simon is no shrinking violet but tonight has met his match. He is on the panel alongside the legendary Navjot Singh Sidhu, famous for his 'Sidhuisms' like: 'Statistics are like miniskirts – they reveal more than what they hide.'

The Middle Men

ALAN McGILVRAY

Alan McGilvray was an Australian cricketer and for over fifty years a cricket broadcaster. From *The Game is not the Same* (1986).

ONE OF THE best accolades I ever had as a cricket commentator was the puzzled look on one of my colleagues in Brisbane after I had called a dismissal. 'Goodness Mac, you've got good eyes,' he said, shaking his head in undisguised awe. He was not the only commentator through the years who was rather astounded by my speed in picking up something on the field. I would occasionally nominate the bouncer before it was bowled, explain with certainty that the finest of nicks was the ball flicking the pad, nominate a man out before the umpire's finger was up.

Before I sound like I'm singing my own praises as some sort of eagle-eyed fountain of knowledge, I have to concede some inside information. Most of those quick assessments of what had taken place were conveyed to me, quickly and certainly, by umpires with whom I had developed a comprehensive communications system. In the days of Col Egar and Lou Rowan, undoubtedly the best umpires I ever saw, as many as twenty signals were in operation. They kept me fully informed, quickly and accurately, on every eventuality. The signals were for each other, but they took me into their confidence and made sure I could see them.

A ball would go to the keeper rather sluggishly, and the batsman would be given out. Col Egar would casually turn so that I could see him, and nonchalantly rub away at his thumb. The message was clear – the batsman had been caught off his glove, and I could tell the world quickly and surely, without the often inconclusive aid of a TV replay.

Hands together might mean the ball had come off the pad, a touch of the ear might mean it went from bat to pad. Whatever the circumstance, Col or Lou would let me know pretty quickly, and the commentary was much better for it.

Throughout my time in radio I have also made a study of the idiosyncrasies of umpires. More often than not they telegraph their decisions before they actually make them. If I could read their intent, and get in with the decision before they did, I could call a man out before the crowd realised, so the swell of their roar built up behind me. That added so much drama to the broadcast. Egar, for instance, always drew his feet together, as if standing to attention, before he raised his finger to signal a batsman's demise. As soon as those legs came together, I knew. 'He's gone,' I would say, beating the finger and beating the crowd.

It was an almost foolproof system, and one which I never let on about, lest Egar unconsciously changed his *modus operandi*. Other umpires had a habit of crouching before they gave a decision in the affirmative. Others let their hands drop to their sides first. Reading them, I reasoned, was one of the biggest aids to my broadcasting technique.

Rowan and Egar were most conscientious about our communication system. They thought it important their actions were quickly understood, for a start. And they said it relaxed them. Physically nominating the basis for each decision somehow crystallised it in their minds, and made them feel better. I made a point throughout my career of getting as close as I could to the umpires. With that pair it was very easy. They were great men with a great love of cricket, and our morning chats before play became a ritual.

For much of my career, too, I had considerable help from the players. Keith Miller would touch his forehead as he turned to bowl, thereby alerting me to the fact that he was going to let fly a bouncer. I was ready for it. Often I would get in first. A rub on the right side of his nose would nominate the inswinger, a rub to the left side would nominate the outswinger. I could call with certainty so many of the deliveries he bowled, particularly those that were in any way different. So it was with several players.

Occasionally we would get down to working out specific scenarios. I recall one such occasion in South Africa, where the Australian spinner Johnny Gleeson worked on a plan to dismiss Graeme Pollock. He reasoned that Pollock played away from his body a lot, and that if he bowled two or three of his stock deliveries, which would be the off-break to the left-hander, and tried to push him back, he might then be vulnerable to the floated wrong-'un. I happened to be having breakfast with Johnny as he mulled over his plan, and we determined he would need a gully fieldsman as well as a slip if it were to work properly. Off he went to see the skipper Bill Lawry, and duly returned to announce that all was in readiness. The plan was set.

Next day he had started an over to Pollock when he looked up to the commentary box and signalled that Plan A was in operation. The first ball went as scheduled, then the second, then the third. All was in readiness. Gleeson gave me the thumbs up and I began to describe the trap that was being laid. Alas! As Gleeson turned to bowl the ball he had planned for, Lawry pulled the gully away and stuck him somewhere else to fill a hole. Gleeson stopped in his tracks and turned to me, arms spread as if to decry the best laid plans of mice and men. I described Johnny's anguish at not having the fieldsman he wanted. As a broadcaster, I was able to give an insight into the play that not even all the players were able to appreciate.

15

LUNCH INTERVAL

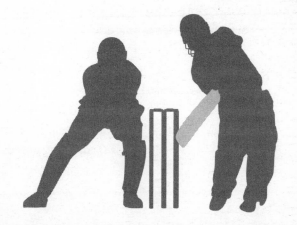

Cricket Scores 1730–1773

H. T. WAGHORN

H. T. Waghorn was a cricket historian and statistician.
Cricket Scores was published in 1899.

SEPT. 1734. A great cricket-match was lately to have been played between the gentlemen of London and Croydon, but the latter having been regaled with a good dinner, &c., gratis, withdrew, and have not since been heard of; and the former, desirous of playing one match before the season is expired, do challenge to play with any eleven men in England, with this exception only, that they will not admit of one from Croydon; not that they object against them as good players, but as men they have an ill opinion of: having so lately had the credit of feeding the hungry, they would not expose themselves to the reflections of sending the naked empty away.

The Pick of the Bunch

A. W. CARR

A. W. Carr captained Nottinghamshire and England during the 1920s and 1930s.
From *Cricket with the Lid Off* (1935).

I GIVE JIM IREMONGER, the Notts cricket coach, most marks for bringing out what was really there to be brought out in Larwood, and myself most of the credit for nursing and handling him. He was born a bowler, but Iremonger taught him how to make full use of his talent and I saw to it that he did.

I confess that when I first saw him I thought that he was too small to be a fast bowler in big cricket. I thought he would not last in a first-class game. He was, from the start, very quick off the ground, but he seemed to lack stamina. However, I could see with half an eye what there might be in him, and I decided that the best way to deal with him was as if he were my own son.

And now I will give away a secret – a secret which perhaps Harold Larwood himself does not know: I made it my business to see that he took to beer.

Now this matter of drinking and playing first-class cricket successfully is a ticklish one on which, as an authority in the matter, I shall have more to say presently, but of one thing I am pretty certain in my own mind: all really fast bowlers need beer to help them keep going. You cannot be a great fast bowler on a bottle of ginger-pop or a nice glass of cold water. Your fast bowler is in much the same case as your harvester and your navvy; he uses up an immense amount of physical strength in hard out of doors exercise and he must have something to give him a kick.

Beer is best. A pint too much may make him slightly tiddly for a little while, but only for a little while. He very quickly perspires it out of his system. When I have particularly wanted to get Larwood's tail up in order to get a quick wicket or two for Notts I have seen to it that he has not wanted for a drop of beer.

Diary of a Cricket Lover

VERNON COLEMAN

Vernon Coleman is a former GP and author of over a hundred books.
This *Diary* appeared in 1984.

❧

SATURDAY 5TH MAY

AT TRENT BRIDGE today I met a good friend of mine whom I have not seen for years. He is now working as a general practitioner just down the road in Leicestershire and although he is a member at Grace Road he prefers the atmosphere at Trent Bridge. I do not think this is meant as any sort of a slight on the Leicester club but is rather a tribute to my friend's past. He studied medicine in Nottingham and spent a good deal of his six years in the city watching cricket rather than tending to patients. Going to Trent Bridge for the day reminds him of his days at medical school.

My friend, whom I will call Dr H, for the very good reason that neither his first name nor his surname begin with the letter H, had brought with him a large picnic hamper. It was one of those old-fashioned whicker [*sic*] hampers and it seemed to contain just about every delicacy known to man. There were four different kinds of pâté, three different types of cheese (including an excellent Stilton and a very fine Brie), a loaf of French bread, an excellent mixed salad, a large plastic container filled with strawberries and another filled with cream and a whole host of other tit-bits designed to titillate the palate and satisfy the stomach. In addition to the food, there was also an excellent bottle of claret, a bottle of dry white, and a bottle of champagne to go with the strawberries.

I did not take much persuading to share this feast.

I cannot remember exactly when we started our lunch but I suppose that it must have been somewhere around noon. And if it is difficult to say just when we started, it is even more difficult to say when we finished. All I can say with any certainty is that we finished the last of the strawberries and the last of the champagne just as the official luncheon interval came to an end.

It was at that point that my friend produced a large flask of black coffee. I thought that this was an excellent idea and I told him so with great enthusiasm. I am not all that good at coping with wine for lunch and three bottles shared with just one person is more than enough to damage my faculties and send me off to sleep.

The afternoon was quite extraordinary. I honestly cannot remember anything about the cricket. Without looking up the fixture in the calendar I cannot even tell you who was playing whom or what the competition was. And I never did find my scorecard although I am sure it must be somewhere. By half past two I knew that I had drunk far too much; I was determined to sober myself up for the evening. Oddly enough, however, by three I felt worse than I had at two. I decided that the wine was having a delayed effect and I drank another large cup of black coffee. By four I felt worse than I had at three. And I drank more coffee.

By half past five there was absolutely no coffee left in the flask and I remember feeling a good deal worse than I had at four.

With some slurring I congratulated my friend on the state of his liver. He had drunk hardly any black coffee at all but seemed far less inebriated than I. I commented on this extraordinary fact as an example of the way that one body will cope with insults far more effectively than another.

My friend seemed slightly confused.

So I explained yet again that I was impressed that he had managed to stay sober without drinking heaps of black coffee.

It took my friend the best part of ten minutes to stop the tears pouring down his cheeks and to halt the hysterical laughter that threatened to tear his body in half.

When he did finally manage to stop himself laughing long enough to talk he explained that what I had thought had been plain black coffee had been Russian coffee, strongly laced with vodka. While I thought I was sobering myself up I was busy getting absolutely plastered. I left my car at the ground, my friend gave me a lift to the station, and I finally got home by train and taxi.

Cricket in the Fiji Islands

PHILIP A. SNOW

Philip A. Snow played cricket for Leicestershire Second XI in 1936 and 1937. Subsequently he was a colonial administrator in Fiji, for which country he played five first-class matches. His memoir *Cricket in the Fiji Islands* was published in 1949. This extract begins with the final part of a report submitted by the Hon. Adolph Brewster Brewster, administrative officer in the 1880s.

୶

'AT NADARIVATU THE game was played *en règle*, and everything went smoothly until the village clubs came up for matches. One of the set ideas of the latter was that the crack bowler was the bowler and by prescriptive right. In fact, he was regarded as the Lord High Bowler, and as soon as the over finished he went on again at the other end.'

It is only fitting to round off Brewster's anecdote by stating that although secret societies of Luveniwai, a Water-Babies sorcery cult, have sprung up in the interim subsequently from time to time they have not again allied themselves to the game of cricket.

Brewster's brother, Alex B. Joske, managed the Fijian team touring Australia in 1907–8.

A story is told by an early writer which illustrates the spread of the game and the shallow, superficial surface where cricket rivalry lay over smouldering, tribal feeling. He wrote: 'A cricket match played on one occasion at Nagigi on the south side of Vanua Levu, which began in good humour and nearly closed in wild tragedy, proves how near the surface lie passions that in olden days led to fierce, inter-tribal wars. The Navatu men, who were good scorers and proud of their fame, challenged the Natewa tribe to send their best men. The Natewans took the field and began to play with some glint of fortune and show of courage. But they were sadly beaten. The other side, elated with their victory, flung taunts and jeers at the defeated team and told the Natewa men, who lost their temper over it, to go home and put up their fighting fences. This was taken cheerfully up and the two teams, supported by friends, now confronted each other in deadly earnest. They fought hand to hand, confining themselves to the use of fists and feet, and many were badly injured on both sides. Friendly mediation, however, later prevailed.'

[. . .] Isolated as many of the smaller islands are within the Fiji Archipelago, it does not come as a surprise to find that the cricket in some of them has developed along highly individual lines. In a few of the remote islands, especially those in the little-visited Lau Group, what most forcibly impresses one at the present day is the 1870-ish character of the institutions of the game. Their chiefs were possessed, before the cession of the entire Archipelago in 1874, of tremendous power, often benevolently exercised. This power was thought by Fijians to render their states immune from defeat at cricket. A headmaster of the Lau Provincial School, who was a most detailed observer of Lauan life and later became Director of Archaeology, Cairo University, has recorded that the 'village of Lakeba is said to be hard to beat at cricket, because it is the dwelling-place of Roko Sau, who is endowed with miraculous efficacy (mana)'. The high chief did not have to play to confer immunity from defeat; his existence anywhere about was sufficient. A descendant of the Roko Sau (the Tui Nayau) in 1940 hit me for the biggest six I have ever seen: it was honestly, if temporarily, lost in the sky. His team's win was never in doubt at any stage: no one could remember when, in fact, the team had last lost. Although the descendants of high chiefs have surrendered some of their atmosphere of divine right in the passage of time and through contact with more democratic society, they still cling firmly to many of their rights. One of them is the right to bat first. This they exercise often with some skill for the chiefs were for long the only exponents of the game. When this privilege of batting has been used, they often exercise another right, that of disdaining to field or bowl or take any further part in the game.

While a chief is batting it is not unusual to see the captain of the opposite side go up to him in a crouching posture of respect and ask him humbly whether he can change the bowling against him. A chief more than usually inclined to autocratic moods would be quite likely to reject the suggestion if he happened to be enjoying the present pair of bowlers. He would therefore have every chance to get his eye in. The first ball to him would be a trial ball. Anyone who questioned the existence of this right (practised even to-day wherever Fijians play among themselves) would be looked at as though he were ignorant of the finer points of the game.

Another trace of chiefly influence over the cricket can be detected when a chief (or occasionally a European administrative officer) is batting. There will always be among the spectators a person of the herald or ambassador caste. Each chief and administrator had, and still has, a herald whose function it is to act as mouthpiece for the chief, receiving or making in his name any presents or, on his behalf, rendering or replying to any speeches. He also acts as a kind of court jester, his express and hereditary duty being to keep the chief amused or flattered. The chief's herald will call out from the crowd at the end of each over that the chief has been batting in, 'Good batting, sir.' A little later, so as to impress the chief that he really knows that it is good batting and that he is showing his pleasure because the bowling is difficult and the fielders hard to elude, 'Good bowling and good fielding, too, indeed.' Completely defensive play by a chief against fast bowling which puts his royal person in danger is always appreciated by the herald: 'You are shutting the door well, sir. That's right, sir, keep the bulamakau out of the door.' Bulamakau (pronounced bull-a-ma-cow) is Fijian for a bull which so often corresponds with a batsman's impressions of a fast bowler tearing up to the wicket to him. The shutting-of-the-door simile only too often aptly describes the batsman's reflex action to safeguard his wicket when there is nothing else to be done.

Fijian umpires consider themselves undressed for their occupation if they do not carry a bat as the outward sign of their arbitrary status. They adopt a more conversational attitude towards batsmen in the serious moments of the game than their European counterparts. When they are giving guard, they invariably inform the batsmen: 'Middle and leg. One to come. Now hit this ball into the ocean.'

Fijian batsmen tend to accept the fact of their being out with more surprise than most players of the game. When the wicket has been broken or a catch taken they look undisguisedly miserable at the moment of dismissal and start to walk as if in a trance away from the wicket, regardless of direction. They then invariably turn back to the wicket where they look dubiously at the stumps or the fieldsman who has committed the offence. Finally, and reluctantly, the irrevocability of it all makes itself felt and they walk with trailing bat and feet to the pavilion that means obscurity after limelight. The whole process upon dismissal takes up to seven minutes which in a clockless environment matters not at all.

When a fielder has made a catch, his custom is to throw the ball up in the air to an enormous distance in his immediate reflex of excitement.

Viliame Mataika, in one of the matches against Auckland in 1948, delighted the crowd with a throw from first slip (where he took a hot catch) to outside the boundary and over where long-off might have been standing.

Against Canterbury in the same tour, Ilikena Bula intrigued the crowd. He dropped a most difficult catch in the outfield and was clearly crestfallen. He later missed another hard one and, although barefooted, expressed his disgust by punting the ball from long-on back to the bowler. Another chance came his way, quite the hardest of the three. He held a spectacular running catch not far from the ground, and then threw the ball from long-on to the fence behind third man to express his exuberance.

It often happens that the fieldsman to whom the last ball of an over has gone returns the ball to the next bowler, not by a throw but by kicking it from underneath so that it travels without a bounce to him.

Julius Caesar

WILLIAM CAFFYN

William Caffyn was a highly regarded cricketer of the mid-nineteenth century.
Julius Caesar (1830–78) played first-class cricket between 1849 and 1867.
From *Seventy-One Not Out* (1900).

THE WORD 'BRILLIANT' may be used very appropriately when describing the batting of my fellow-countryman Julius Caesar. He was one of those hard clean hitters whom it is so delightful to watch. Although only about 5 feet 7 inches, 'Julie' was very powerfully made. He may be described as 'a big man in little room'. He had a wonderful knack of timing the ball, which had a great deal to do with his success as a batsman. He was not much of a cutter, – those who set themselves for a driving game seldom are, – still he had a good hard cut past cover-point, which he often made use of. The on-drive was his best hit, and he was also noted as a leg-hitter. He appeared at Lord's in 1850, and I believe was engaged by Clarke for the All-England Eleven about the end of the following year, with which he remained until Clarke's death, and continued to play under the captaincy of George Parr, when he succeeded to Clarke's office.

'Julie' was a first-rate boxer, and exceedingly fond of the noble art. He was of a peculiarly nervous temperament, and, laughable as it may appear, was always afraid of sleeping in a room by himself at a strange hotel, for fear some one might have died in it at some time or other. When playing, I have frequently shared a double-bedded room with him, and when sound asleep have often been awoke by his calling out that he was sure the house was on fire! Poor 'Julie' seemed to have a fixed idea that every hotel *must* be burnt down sooner or later, and always refused to be put higher than the first floor. I shall never forget once sharing the same room with him at Hereford. The streets were very quiet, it being almost morning. All at once I could hear a drunken man come staggering along, bawling something out by way of a song, as I thought. 'Julie', however, who was half asleep, felt sure that some one was calling out 'Fire!' He at once called out to me, but I pretended to be asleep. 'Billy, the confounded place is on fire; can't you hear 'em calling out?' he shouted. I only replied by a feeble snore. 'Julie' could stand it no longer, but jumped out of bed, rang the bell violently, rousing the whole house, calling me a fool all the time, and asking me if I wanted to be burnt to death!

Another peculiar fancy of 'Julie's' was, that whenever he happened to get a small score, he thought that he should at once be left out of the Surrey Eleven. He was very confident that this would happen just before he played his magnificent innings of 111 for Surrey v. Cambridgeshire in 1862. Of course nothing was further from the committee's thoughts than leaving him out; but, as I said before, 'Julie' was of a very peculiar temperament, always being very elated when successful and terribly dejected after getting a small score.

Both 'Julie' and George Parr used to make a point of taking a certain amount of liquor before retiring to rest when they were in the thick of the cricket season. Once, it is said, they each agreed to lessen the quantity by half. They were both unsuccessful with the bat on the following day, but they nevertheless agreed to give their new *régime* another trial on the following night; but, alas! the result was the same as on the previous day – viz., small scores in both cases. 'George,' said 'Julie' to the famous leg-hitter as he came into the pavilion without having troubled the scorer, 'it is evident that we must take in our "usual quantity" to-night.' 'Right you are, my lad!' promptly replied

George; 'and we'll make up for what we went short of last night and night before as well!'

'Julie' was a very good shot and fond of the sport, but he had a sad experience on one occasion. When out shooting he happened to accidentally let off his gun in getting over a stile or through a hedge, and one of the keepers who was with the party was shot dead. Poor 'Julie' was in a terrible way, and I believe his mind never got over the shock till the day of his death.

Caesar was a native of Godalming, where I believe his family had long resided. There is a match on record where twelve Caesars played another eleven at the time when Julius was a young man. It is many years now since poor 'Julie' passed away, but his name still lives in his native country and in many a little out-of-the-way corner in various parts of England which he visited with the All-England Eleven. He had a brother Fred, a very fair player, a great big strong fellow, who for some years officiated as turnkey in one of the London jails.

The Lazy Tour of Two Idle Apprentices

WILKIE COLLINS AND CHARLES DICKENS

Wilkie Collins and Charles Dickens wrote alternate chapters of
The Lazy Tour of Two Idle Apprentices (1890) in the personas of
Thomas Idle (Collins) and Francis Godchild (Dickens).

⤜

WHILE THOMAS WAS lazy, he was a model of health. His first attempt at active exertion and his first suffering from severe illness are connected together by the intimate relations of cause and effect.

Shortly after leaving school, he accompanied a party of friends to a cricket-field, in his natural and appropriate character of spectator only. On the ground it was discovered that the players fell short of the required number, and facile Thomas was persuaded to assist in making up the complement. At a certain appointed time, he was roused from peaceful slumber in a dry ditch, and placed before three wickets with a bat in his hand. Opposite to him, behind three more wickets, stood one of his bosom friends, filling the situation (as he was informed) of bowler. No words can describe Mr. Idle's horror and amazement, when he saw this young man – on ordinary occasions, the meekest and mildest of human beings – suddenly contract his eyebrows, compress his lips, assume the aspect of an infuriated savage, run back a few steps, then run forward, and, without the slightest previous provocation, hurl a detestably hard ball with all his might straight at Thomas's legs. Stimulated to preternatural activity of body and sharpness of eye by the instinct of self-preservation, Mr. Idle contrived, by jumping deftly aside at the right moment, and by using his bat (ridiculously narrow as it was for the purpose) as a shield, to preserve his life and limbs from the dastardly attack that had been made on both, to leave the full force of the deadly missile to strike his wicket instead of his leg; and to end the innings, so far as his side was concerned, by being immediately bowled out.

Grateful for his escape, he was about to return to the dry ditch, when he was peremptorily stopped, and told that the other side was 'going in', and that he was expected to 'field'. His conception of the whole art and mystery of 'fielding' may be summed up in the three words of serious advice which he privately administered to himself on that trying occasion – avoid the ball. Fortified by this sound and salutary principle, he took his own course, impervious alike to ridicule and abuse. Whenever the ball came near him, he thought of his shins, and got out of the way immediately. 'Catch it!' 'Stop it!' 'Pitch it up!' were cries that passed by him like the idle wind that he regarded not. He ducked under it, he jumped over it, he whisked himself away from it on either side. Never once, through the whole innings did he and the ball come together on anything approaching to intimate terms.

The unnatural activity of body which was necessarily called forth for the accomplishment of this result threw Thomas Idle, for the first time in his life, into a perspiration. The perspiration, in consequence of his want of practice in the management of that particular result of bodily activity, was suddenly checked; the inevitable chill succeeded; and that, in its turn, was followed by a fever. For the first time since his birth, Mr. Idle found himself confined to his bed for many weeks together, wasted and worn by a long illness, of which his own disastrous muscular exertion had been the sole first cause.

Careful Arrangements

LORD HARRIS

Lord Harris played cricket for Kent and England and was a noted cricket administrator before becoming Governor of Bombay. 'Bob FitzGerald' is the same R. A. Fitzgerald of the W. G. Grace episodes. 'IZ.' is I Zingari, the long-established nomadic club. From *A Few Short Runs* (1921).

❧

OUR ROYAL FAMILY, though always great patrons of the game, have not yet excelled at it. Frederick, Prince of Wales, eldest son of George II, was really fond of the game – and indeed, as one report has it, met his death from the blow of a cricket-ball – but there is nothing to show that he played it well. The Prince Regent also constantly honoured great matches with his presence, and the crowds were consequently so great that the grounds had to be roped round. In the last century IZ. received a command to play at a royal residence, and His Royal Highness honoured IZ. by playing in the Eleven. All had gone most successfully, nothing untoward had occurred, and there only remained the innings of the local Eleven to be played. Bob FitzGerald summoned his merry men round him in anxious conclave. Was it possible that there might still be a catastrophe? Had they not managed everything admirably? Could an errant fly somehow find a loophole into the ointment? Alas! yes, there was one ghastly possibility. His Royal Highness might have a catch; and – oh, horror! – he might miss it, in the afternoon, just before tea, with half the County families looking on. Ghastly, ghastly possibility! It would be the worst of luck, but it might happen. What was to be done? The ready invention of emergency of the Captain was equal to the occasion: 'You, Billy, will stand quite close to His Royal Highness, and if a catch does go to him, you will rush in, and bump him enough to enable us, if he does miss it, to throw all the blame on you.' The gallant Zingaro – need I say he was a Kentish man? – undertook the horrid task. Of course, a catch did go to His Royal Highness – the Fates took care of that right enough. Billy did rush in, the catch was dropped, and there the delinquent stood, profuse with apologies, remonstrated with by His Royal Highness, and cussed volubly by all his comrades. 'What in Heaven's name did you want to snatch it for? His Royal Highness had got it all right! Sheer selfishness and conceit,' etc.

The other story is of a most genial and hospitable Irish Viceroy who was devoted to cricket, and could play a bit; and to prepare himself for the IZ. match he got over Shaw and Morley to bowl to him at the net. Gossip had it that he gave up putting a shilling on the wicket after about fifteen minutes' practice. The conundrum in His Excellency's case was how to secure as surely as possible his getting some runs. Again the IZ. Captain was full of resource. The bowler was not to bowl straight; His Excellency's partner at the wicket was squared to shout 'Run' the first ball His Excellency touched and come racing down the wicket; the fieldsman was to throw at his wicket hard and wide, and there was to be no one backing up. There could be no rehearsal, but the play went smoothly, and by these means His Excellency was secured a nice little score when lunch was announced, of which he would not partake: a glass of water and a biscuit sufficed. But IZ. could not afford to give away any more runs, and it was agreed that normal arrangements must be resumed. The fatal ball was delivered, the wicket fell, and His Excellency retired muttering 'Ah! lunch, lunch.'

16

'THE MEN IN WHITE COATS'

The Men in White Coats

TERESA McLEAN

Teresa McLean was the first woman to win a cricket Blue for both
Oxford and Cambridge. From the preface to *The Men in White Coats* (1987).

❧

I HAVE LOVED CRICKET since I was three years old. I used to sit on the
back doorstep in the sun, helping my older brother oil his bat before playing
family cricket on the lawn. Umpiring decisions in these games were made by
a parliamentary hierarchy in which my parents, when we could persuade them
to play, were the House of Lords and my brother, sister and I the Commons.
Umpires' decisions represented the survival of the fittest and, occasionally, the
triumph of authority.

My experience of umpiring since then has confirmed that impression,
with the balance in favour of authority but not so far in its favour that bullying,
arguing and battering by appeal are rendered futile. As I went to a school that
was starved of cricket, I saw few official, card-carrying umpires until I was
eighteen, except those who officiated at village matches, and at the one or two
matches I watched at my brother's school. These last provided me with my
first sight of serious umpires, dressed for the job and looking remote, unlike
our village umpires, who smiled and made faces as they fought out decisions
with the opposition.

Umpires soon became objects of fascination, and I watched Syd Buller
umpire Test matches almost as keenly as I watched Ted Dexter bat, Fred
Trueman bowl and John Murray keep wicket. One part of Syd Buller's charisma
for me came from the fact that as an umpire he was by definition mysterious.
Another part came from the trappings of his job – the long white coat with the
sleeves rolled up to reveal sunburnt arms – and another part of it came from
the inscrutable face topped by that central parting at which I never stopped
marvelling, every hair on either side of it lying short and flat, perfectly in place.

Though I only ever saw Syd Buller on television, I knew at the time that
I would never forget him. He stood out from the silent throng of his umpiring
contemporaries, splendid though they were, as the essence of English first-
class umpiring. I wasn't at all surprised, though horribly saddened, when I
heard that he had died only minutes after coming off the field for rain in the

County Championship match between Warwickshire and Nottinghamshire at Edgbaston in August 1970. I had always thought he would die in the middle of a game.

Buller notwithstanding, it would be wrong to pretend that umpires interested me as much as players. They fascinated me, as they still do today, but they were not, are not and never will be exciting. They are not there to be. A raised finger is not as enjoyable to watch as a cover drive, though it is usually more important. There would be something wrong if umpires were exciting. They are more like mute gods than film stars, and the more they imprint their personality on the game the more I feel uneasy about them.

My interest in cricket became really serious in the 'quiet umpires' era of the 1950s and 1960s, when Buller was the sovereign of unobtrusive authority. I did not get a glimpse of a 'character umpire' above village cricket level until I went to Oxford in 1969 when, having joined the University Women's Cricket Club just for fun, I was amazed to find myself chosen to play for them.

The standard of skill was abysmal and my knockabout games in the garden at home were enough to get me a fairly regular place in the team. More than that, being a potential female Botham with a talent for trouble, I was chosen to play in the Varsity match. Writing this now, I am ashamed to say that I cannot remember how the game turned out, but I rather think we won. I remember most things about it vividly, including the weather, the setting, the way I was out (run out) and the umpires.

We played in pouring rain on a pitch lent us by one of the men's colleges, miles down the Botley Road. It was more of a meadow than a cricket field, though it did have something approaching a pavilion – a grim little shed in which we sheltered when lightning stopped play. We did not have a set uniform and wore whites which ranged from jeans to shorts and, horror of horrors, divided skirts. There was nothing to distinguish Oxford from Cambridge, and team identity depended on us knowing each other.

I reckoned my forte was my unusual spin bowling, but my captain unwisely ignored this hidden talent and left me out of the bowling attack, so it was up to my batting to vindicate my selection. I went in at number seven. The storm was immediately overhead, with thunder cracking round the ground, and we had nearly got the total we were chasing. There was no point hanging around: I launched some uninhibited shots, made a quick little clutch of runs, then was run out when I slipped in the mud attempting a suicidal run.

The umpire, I remember, stood in the rain with his collar up, shook his head and said 'Out!' As I walked past him he added, 'Silly girl.' As far as I was concerned, coming from an umpire who looked authoritative, had the keys to the shed, was a man, and was standing in the Varsity match, that was 'character umpiring'. It made a deep impression on me.

Cricket then was even more sexist than it is today, difficult though that might be to imagine. We almost always played men's teams because there were hardly any women's teams. Once we played a prep school about fifteen miles outside Oxford and it was peculiarly humiliating to be given out by a small, spotty boy. Thank heavens there is genuine women's first-class cricket today, with women umpiring. Maybe one day I will be able to fulfil my ambition, though I know it is only a dream, to umpire a Test match.

[...] I went to ACU evening classes to learn to qualify as an umpire.

The classes were in a school gym miles out along one of the minor roads of West Oxford, which was where I lived; I had gone back there [after a spell at Cambridge] to teach. They were extremely well taught by an exact and dedicated man, the model fanatical umpire, but I had not expected thirty people to turn up week after week to listen to his talks, look at the ground plans he drew on his blackboard and the little magnetic feet he moved about on a magnetic sketch of a pitch to explain no-ball decisions.

At the end of an eight-week term came the exams, set each year by the Association of Cricket Umpires. There were two levels of examination, depending on the grade of game one wanted to umpire. The easier one would have qualified me to umpire local club and village matches, but I had big ideas and opted for the harder exam, which would qualify me to umpire any level of match, right up to Test match standard, subject to the usual requirements of experience and performance. I was the only woman who took the harder exam and one of only two women who took either.

I passed, the exam having an 80 per cent passmark, and the following year, when I married and moved back to Cambridge, I started to umpire for the East Anglian club circuit. My first game was ghastly. I was nervous, and was alternately showered with abuse and advice by the men over whom I was supposed to be asserting my authority. My authority anyway was minimal, regarded sceptically by the players and going from weak to moribund with every bad and hesitant decision I made. I gave one particularly unpleasant little man run out: he was out by a good four yards.

He stood staring at me and said, 'Are you seriously trying to give me out?' When I said I was, he retorted, 'Well, I'm not going.'

I looked at my watch and told him he had two minutes to get off the field and let the next man in: they were ticking away. Thank God, he went. I had no idea what I'd have done had he refused, and I decided umpiring was one of the most unpleasant jobs in the world. In future I would have as little to do with it as possible.

Cricket Extras

DICKIE DODDS

Dickie Dodds was an opening batsman who played for Essex from 1946 to 1959. From Hit Hard and Enjoy It *(1976).*

B EFORE THE FIRST World War, Worcestershire had a very promising young batsman called Frank Chester. During the subsequent hostilities he was wounded and lost his right arm – and thereby his capacity to follow the career that had begun with such high hopes. But Frank was a young man of character, and he turned to umpiring. Soon he became one of the best umpires in the country and, finally, was universally acclaimed as the best in the world.

It was easy to recognise Frank Chester on the field. His lean figure was always well and neatly dressed and topped by a trilby hat, and his dummy left hand was encased in a dark leather glove.

Frank stood in my first county game. I sensed his appraising eye on me, as it was on all new players. He was rather like a connoisseur of wine, savouring a new vintage. 'Who's this feller?' he would ask an old player. I am told he would always try and give encouragement to a beginner. At any rate, I seemed to pass his inspecting eye in that first match, and he said some kind words.

Perhaps because, in his playing days, he had made his highest score against Essex (178 not out, including four sixes off opening bowler J. W. H. T. Douglas), he always liked to stand in our home games – especially those at the sea. We enjoyed having him, and were forever trying to catch him out on the field. But you had to get up early to catch Frank. We only once succeeded – or thought we did!

The common or garden trick of coming out after an interval and trying to start to bowl from the same end as the one from which you bowled the last over before the interval never had a hope with Frank. However, one day we thought we had a winner. It was a hot afternoon at Westcliff. The match was in a moribund state. Ray Smith, who was always the moving spirit in these affairs, suggested that sometime in the middle of the afternoon he would run up to bowl and go right over the bowling crease to the batting crease, as though he was going to bowl from there. Frank would then call 'no ball', but Ray would not have released the ball – and at last the great man would have made a mistake. The moment came. The signal was given to let us all in on the fun. Ray ran straight past the wicket and he, and we, were all waiting for Frank's roar. Nothing happened. Ray finally just had to let the ball go. Had Frank nodded off, or had some sixth sense told him of our plot? Anyway, when Ray ran up to bowl his next ball, which was quite legitimate, we were all startled to hear a raucous 'No ball' come from Umpire Chester! Although afterwards we claimed we had him, he made a counter claim. At this distance in time, I think I would declare Frank the winner.

Smiles

FRANK CHESTER

Frank Chester was a Test umpire from 1924 to 1955, standing in a
then record number of forty-eight Tests. From *How's That!* (1956).
'Alec' is his fellow umpire Alec Skelding.

I BELIEVE IT WAS Alec who told me the story of the keen cricketing squire who had his 'own' umpire – his butler, in fact. All appeals against the master were flatly refused. After fourteen demands for lbw and a few more catches behind the wicket had been rejected the opposing side were becoming rather exasperated and the skipper instructed one of his bowlers to send down a slow high-flighted full toss.

With a glint in his eye the squire walked down the wicket, missed the ball completely and was yards out of his ground when the wicket-keeper gathered the ball. Even the squire smiled as the wicket-keeper turned to the butler-cum-umpire and demanded, 'What chance have I got now?'

Another village cricket story is of the batsman who arrived at the crease wearing only one pad – and that on his right leg. Assuming he was a left-hander, the field changed around. But no, he batted right-handed and three times in the first over was hit painfully on the unprotected leg. 'Why don't you change the pad to your left leg?' asked the wicket-keeper. 'That's no use now; I shall be batting at the other end in the next over,' came the reply.

In March 1950 I went to Rottingdean Cricket Club's annual dinner in Sussex and occupied a humble place in the 'speakers' batting order', which included Sir Noel Curtis-Bennett, Sir Leslie Bowker and Arthur Gilligan. Sir Noel told of visiting the back streets of a London district and finding a small boy, wet, weeping and thoroughly miserable. Sir Noel lifted him off the ground to console him, whereupon another small boy in a piping voice demanded: 'Hi, guv, what yer doing wiv 'im? Put 'im dahn – 'e's our wicket.'

The opening batsman arrived at the crease in a charity match and before giving him guard I turned to the bowler with the usual question, 'Over or around the wicket?' He looked somewhat surprised and went on rolling up his sleeves menacingly and vigorously exercising himself, so I repeated, 'Do you bowl over or around the wicket?'

It was then my turn to be surprised, for he gave me a pitying look and thundered, 'No – at the wicket, of course.'

One of my most frequent partners in 1924 was Bill Reeves, of Essex, whose cockney wit earned him a reputation as cricket's comedian.

At Swansea, against Hampshire, Glamorgan introduced a lanky medium-fast bowler obviously keen to do well and very, very green. After a few good overs he beat the bat and appealed for lbw. 'Not out,' decided Reeves, who at the end of the over whispered in the lad's ear: 'Look, son, when you appeal to an umpire in county cricket don't say "How's that". Say "How's that, sir". You'll stand a better chance.' The bowler nodded as though understanding why his previous appeal had been disallowed. A little later he rapped the pad again and roared, 'How's that?' adding respectfully, 'Sir.' Raising his index finger, Reeves said with a knowing wink, 'Ah, that's better.'

At Leicester bad light stopped play; the clouds were so low that it was almost dark and it should have been obvious to everyone why the players were trooping off the field. But a fussy little man ran up to Reeves and demanded, 'What have you come in for?' Placing his hand over his eyes in an exaggerated gesture and gazing up at the clouds, Reeves replied, 'We cannot stand the glare.' Far from being rebuffed, the little man thanked Bill politely and withdrew to his seat!

After the blank Test at Manchester in 1938 Jack Hobbs met Reeves leaving the Secretary's office, where he had been collecting his fees. 'Good heavens,' said Jack, 'surely you are not going to take money for being idle for the past four days; you haven't done a stroke.'

'I'm going to give the money to charity,' Bill replied.

'Charity?' repeated Jack in genuine surprise.

'Yes,' said Bill, striding away, '– to the Unknown Warrior's widow.'

Cecil Parkin was bowling at Reeves's end during a Battle of the Roses and appealed for lbw against Herbert Sutcliffe. At square-leg I could see the ball was far too high, but Parkin enquired, 'What was the matter with that?'

'Too high,' answered Bill.

In his next over Parkin hit Percy Holmes in the stomach and with considerable optimism again appealed. Reeves shook his head.

'Well, what was the matter with that one?' Parkin demanded.

'Too low,' came the solemn reply.

In another Lancashire v. Yorkshire match it was a near thing for Herbert Sutcliffe going for a quick run. 'Why didn't you give him out?' demanded a couple of the Lancashire players. 'Well,' said Bill sadly, 'he's got his old granddad here; come 150 miles to see him bat. You don't think I was going to upset the poor old man's day, do you?'

A young Lancs pro sat very disconsolately in the Pavilion after Reeves had given him leg before. At the luncheon interval Bill went up to him and said: 'Don't look like that; you weren't out really.'

'Why did you give me out then?' demanded the boy.

Bill replied: 'Well, the ground's a bit wet and I was thinking of your rheumatics. What would your poor old mother have said to me?'

Before a Surrey match Reeves said to me: 'Frank, do me a favour – go Alf Gover's end. The last match I had with him he was a nuisance; he bowled so many no-balls I had a sore throat.' I went Alf's end and Bill looked very happy when I called 'No Ball' a few times. The wind changed right round and it was decided to switch Alf to Reeves's end. When Bill saw him taking off his sweater he went down on one knee and pretended to pray.

In another game at The Oval both batsmen floundered half way down the pitch trying to steal a hurried single. They ran together to my end and then a couple of times up and down the wicket, still together, as the ball was overthrown. Reeves was almost on the ground laughing when the wicket was broken at his end with both batsmen out of the crease. 'Blowed if I know who's out; it will have to be the toss of a coin,' said Bill. He tossed up the coin and gave one of the men out, but I told him it was irregular and that he must give a considered decision. After a while we were able to work out who was the rightly-dismissed batsman.

Reeves was certainly the most refreshing character I met on a cricket ground; players and officials thought the world of him. When he arrived for a match he would go into the dressing-room and say: 'Good morning, you chaps. Just one word of advice – keep your pins out of the road. I'm in the mood.'

He was playing for Essex when Tommy Oates, of Nottinghamshire, became an umpire. During an M.C.C. match Oates was standing at Reeves's end, who was bowling. There was a snick to the wicket-keeper and Oates, from force of habit, shouted, excitedly, 'How's that?'

Without a second's hesitation Reeves lifted his finger in the approved manner and said, 'Out.' And the batsman walked, quite satisfied!

Several wicket-keepers find difficulty in overcoming the appealing habit when they have laid down their gauntlets. Jack Board, of Gloucestershire, in an Oval match during his first season as an umpire, roared at the top of his voice for a catch at the wicket and gave the batsman out at the same time!

Leslie Ames, the best wicket-keeping batsman of his generation, was batting at The Oval in a Test Match when he appealed as loudly as anyone against his batting partner for an obvious catch behind the wicket. 'What,' I chided, '– shouting against your own team?'

'Did I shout?' he asked in surprise, and he could hardly credit his subconscious action.

The Hampshire team just before and after the First World War were renowned for their cheerfulness. Jack Newman and George Brown were always having fun. They were at Lord's and by six o'clock Middlesex had piled up a huge total, so Lord Tennyson decided to put himself on. As his Lordship began to measure out a long run Brown, the wicket-keeper, watched with interest. After twelve paces had been counted Brown suddenly turned on his heel and walked towards the boundary. By the time Lord Tennyson was ready to bowl Brown had taken up his position a yard in front of the sightscreen at the Nursery end. Lord Tennyson's face was a study and the whole Hampshire team, even though leg-weary and dispirited after a hot day's leather-chasing, roared with laughter.

Brown was as tough as teak and very often deliberately played a fast bowler's bumper with his body. I have seen him breast the ball away as if he were clad in mail. He did not realize that his toughness diminished with age and towards the end of his career was facing the swift Gordon Hodgson from Lancashire at Portsmouth. Hodgson was staggered when he saw Brown twice do his breastplate act and commented, 'He's a tough 'un, isn't he?'

When Brown came to my end the next over he collapsed to the ground. Brandy revived him and rubbing his chest he said simply, 'Don't think I'll do it again.'

Jack Newman, a fine all-rounder who was most unlucky not to be selected for England, was a character beloved by all. His sole hobby was an innocent little flutter on the horses.

In 1925 Hampshire were at The Oval on the day of the Jubilee Race and I passed on to Jack a tip given me by two trainers – Amethystine, which won at 20 to 1. He came in to bat soon after the race result had been declared and as he passed me said, 'Amethystine's won all right.' The first ball he received from Peach I had to give him out lbw. I learned during the tea interval that he returned to the Pavilion saying, 'That ruddy fool Chester is so excited at Amethystine's win that he can't see straight.' It was a black day for Jack – out first ball and not backing a winning tip. Nor did I, for that matter!

Newman suffered from lapses of concentration. He batted extremely well at Northampton and when he took a single to complete his 50 there was a warm round of applause in which he himself joined.

I said, 'It's you they're clapping, Jack.' He awoke with a start. 'Good heavens, what am I thinking about?' he said, and belatedly raised his cap to the applauding crowd.

He was a dangerous bowler, varying his medium pace with off-spinners and occasionally slipping in an extra-fast one. At Old Trafford he was bowling from my end to Lancashire's Dick Tyldesley when he decided that Philip Mead was too deep at first slip. Jack called down the wicket, 'Come up, Phil, I'm not Larwood.' Mead obliged. Three balls later Jack let loose his faster one and it sped off the edge on to Mead's knee-cap, knocking him over. Mead passed not a few observations on bowlers in general and one in particular.

Two overs later Mead was again caught standing too deep and again Newman persuaded him to move closer to the bat. In due course the faster one was again unleashed. This time it flew off Tyldesley's bat on to Mead's temple and he was knocked clean out. When Mead regained consciousness Newman was standing over him offering profuse apologies. Mead's reply cannot be recorded!

Charlie Harris, the comedian of the Notts dressing-room, was a bowler before he established himself as Walter Keeton's opening partner, and when Notts were at their wits' end to dismiss Philip Mead he volunteered to turn his arm over. Phil was slowly yet surely nearing a double century and Harris, in that pseudo-serious way of his, warned me, 'As soon as I hit him I'm going to appeal.' Much to my surprise he did beat Philip's broad blade and strike his pad. Harris leapt with glee and bellowed an appeal, but he was so excited that his dentures shot out on to the wicket!

'What are you trying to do – bite me out?' cracked Mead.

I believe George Mobey, the Surrey wicket-keeper, had a similar experience at Derby, and mention of Surrey keepers reminds me of how Ted Brooks had his leg pulled after a visit to the House of Commons. The Lancashire and Surrey teams were shown over the House by an M.P. friend of Mr. Peter Eckersley, who was then the Lancashire skipper and a Member of Parliament. At the end of the tour Brooks, who was noted for his generosity and his ebullience, and who did not know that the guide was an M.P., offered him half a crown. When a team mate identified 'the guide' he almost collapsed. He was never allowed to forget the incident.

At Taunton in 1924 Jack Mercer was 12th man for Glamorgan and he told me he had received a good tip for the 2.30 – Lucentio, which duly won at 8 to 1; we both backed it. I was told the good news by George Hunt, one of the Somerset batsmen, when he arrived at the wicket during the afternoon. I had to give him out first ball. As he left for the Pavilion he called out to me, 'I only came in to tell you your horse had won – cheerio.'

When H. M. Garland-Wells was bowling for Surrey I was often so amused by his observations, his grimaces and his gesticulations that I had to hold up play to wipe the tears from my eyes. If he was not getting the best of luck he would cast his eyes and arms heavenwards and cry, 'Give me strength.'

I remember George Gunn, of Notts, being bowled for a 'duck' by Maurice Tate at Hove, and as he passed me on the way out he said: 'I think I'll go to the front and have a sunbathe while I'm waiting. Then I'll get a century in the second innings.' He did both.

Wilfred Rhodes used to bat with the toe of his left foot cocked much in the manner of Dr. W. G. Grace, judging from the photographs of the 'Old Man', and Harold Larwood, in a skittish mood after lunch, said to me as he prepared to bowl, 'I'm after Dusty's toe.' Of course, it was the last thing he meant to do, but the second ball was a full toss and landed bang on the cocked foot. As Rhodes was right in front of the wicket I had to give him out when Larwood appealed. Rhodes was too occupied with his immediate troubles to hear the appeal or to see my raised finger, for he took off his pad, his boot and finally his sock. He nursed his toe, finally pronounced himself fit and began to dress again. When he came to put on his pad I asked sympathetically, 'Can you walk?' Meditatively he replied, 'Aye.'

'Then walk slowly back to the Pavilion: I'm afraid you're out,' I said. He suffered the double blow with all the dignity he could summon.

There was a noted player, long since retired, whose command of length was far superior to his command of English, and his solecisms grew funnier as the seasons rolled by. With a sweep of his arm, indicating a built-up area near a ground, he said, 'I remember when all this land was dialect.' Hurting his knee when he was bowling he told his team mates, 'I believe I've slipped a cartridge.' He talked to me of sending down three full tosses 'in concussion'.

One of the funniest incidents of my career occurred many years ago when my colleague, rather an elderly gentleman, became embarrassed during mid-afternoon. The batsmen looked quite set, so he asked me if I could suggest an excuse for him to leave the field. I told him I would examine a bail, call him over, and after a consultation he would go off the field to change the bail. We went through the pantomime and he raced off the field with the bail. But a keen young member of the ground staff had been closely watching the proceedings; he met my colleague at the foot of the Pavilion steps with a new bail!

Harry Howell, who, if he had been an inch or two taller, would have been a devastating fast bowler, was beating the bat time and again only to shave the stumps with exasperating regularity. 'Hard luck, Harry,' I consoled as he walked back to his bowling mark, '– keep trying.'

'I'm trying,' he replied, 'but the blooming ball ain't.'

[. . .] A decision I was forced yet reluctant to give was against Bill Edrich in a Gentlemen v. Players match. The light was not too good and

Edrich was batting against Kenneth Farnes, who was bowling quicker than ever; he looked as if he was replying to the selectors who had dropped him from the Test side. One ball rose at great speed right on to Edrich's head and knocked him out. It went to that great enthusiast, J. W. A. Stephenson, in the slips. After taking some time to come round, Bill bravely indicated to Wally Hammond, the Gents skipper, that he was ready to resume. But Hammond said to Stephenson, 'He hit that.' They appealed to me and I had to give Edrich out as the ball had grazed his bat on the way to his head. It was a terrible crack and Edrich did not know what had happened. Fred Price, who had been sitting in the Pavilion to be night watchman, passed Edrich on the Pavilion steps, saw how white and drawn he looked, and said, 'I've got a wife; he's not going to kill me.'

I've nearly been maimed many times myself. At Hove, Jim Langridge was bowling his left-arm slows to F. R. Brown, then a member of the Surrey side. Jim liked the umpire to stand up close to the wicket and I said to him as I took my position, 'Don't bowl any half-volleys or he will murder us.' The second ball of the following over was a half-volley and Brown hit it straight back with all his great might. The ball struck my artificial arm, removing it from its socket, bounced on the ground once and then crashed against the sightscreen. There was a horrified silence around the ground as the spectators saw my arm dangling at my side. I left the field to readjust the socket.

'Here – have a brandy, old chap,' offered one white-faced member as I walked into the Pavilion. I accepted gladly!

It was fortunate for me that the ball did not strike my live arm; it would surely have been smashed. When I returned to the wicket I stood yards behind the stumps, much to the amusement of the crowd, and I took similar evasive action subsequently whenever I encountered the same batsman and bowler in opposition. There were few harder hitters in cricket than Brown, who still talks about the incident and mentioned it in a very kind letter he wrote me upon my retirement.

I feared my good arm had been broken in a Hastings Festival match when Lord Tennyson struck me with a powerful pull to the square-leg position. Happily, I was only severely bruised, but I did not fully appreciate his Lordship's remark, 'That would have been a four if you hadn't got in the way.'

Cricketers

SAMUEL REYNOLDS HOLE

Samuel Reynolds Hole was Dean of Rochester from 1887 to 1904 and a noted horticulturalist. From *The Memories of Dean Hole* (1893).

G EORGE PARR'S HITTING, especially to leg, was, I think, the most cheerful performance I ever saw with the bat. He went to play for his village at a country match, and there was a sort of panic among the little fishes in the presence of this leviathan. George ventured on an impossible run, and was manifestly out. But when the question 'How's that?' was put to the umpire, his courage failed. He hesitated, and, turning to the batsman, said: 'Now, Mestur Parr, you know a great deal more about these things than I do; what should you say?' 'I should say, "Not out",' was the reply. 'And so say I, Mestur Parr,' said the umpire. – 'Lads, get on with your gam.'

There are other quaint records of country umpires. My son was captain for a time of an eleven in a mining district, and refreshed me at intervals with his reminiscences. One worthy old fellow remarked, in returning thanks at a supper for the toast of the umpires, 'My opinion of an umpire is that he should be fair, and I don't hold with no foul dealings. What I always say is, Fairation with' (just a short pause) 'just a slight leaning towards your own side.' And I do not suppose that you would find an umpire without this little bias more quickly than Diogenes with his lantern could find a perfectly honest man.

In the same district it was solemnly decreed, at a general meeting of the club, that, though a certain umpire (I have his name, but must not reveal it) 'in ordinary fixtures gave general satisfaction, yet, *taking into consideration the peculiarities of other umpires, he must be regarded as a little too fair for such important competitions as the Derbyshire and Wake Cups'*.

And when one of these 'other umpires' exemplified his peculiarities by giving a man 'in', who certainly was so when the verdict was uttered, but not when the wicket went down, a voice came from a distant part of the field, 'Mestur Umpire, I don't want to have no unpleasantness with you; but if you come that little gam again, I shall just step in and pull out your mustassios by the rewts.'

Within my own experience and neighbourhood, another umpire, in speaking after a match to the united elevens, made his confession thus: 'Gentlemen, I think that the time has arrived in which I should offer you my hearty apologies for any prejudice which I may have shown in favour of local talent, and I confidently rely on your forgiveness, because I am sure that you must have noticed in the second innings I treated my own side with undue severity, in order to make an average.' He might have added that, when it was evident that his friends must win, he regulated his verdicts so that they should not win too easily.

One more delectable incident. I must alter the names of the dramatis personae, but that will be the only fiction. Mr. Stumps, an umpire, has had a quarrel with Mr. Batts, and on the morning of a match he addresses Mr. Bowles, *sotto voce*: 'Mr. Bowles, that there Batts is going to play again you to-day, and if ever you says to me consarning that ruffian, "How's that?" I shall lose no time in telling you, "*You can chuck her up, Mr. Bowles.*"'

But the 'out-and-I've-won-five-bob' umpire is now almost extinct, and the office of adjudication is entrusted to honest men, who love cricket too well to insult and spoil it.

Their long white coats are somewhat unsightly to us elderly gentlemen, who resent innovations; but their resemblance to the apparel of the kennel huntsman may reconcile them to hunting men.

The Golden Era

C. B. FRY

C. B. Fry played many sports at the highest level, representing England
at cricket and football, as well as holding the world long jump record.
This incident occurred during the second Test against the Australians
in June 1905. From *Life Worth Living* (1939).

THE SECOND MATCH, at Lord's, was drawn. The wicket was dead,
but not wet, when we won the toss. We scored 282 in our first innings.
A. C. MacLaren, Tyldesley and I made the runs. I was very much annoyed (of
course in private) because when I had made 73 and was well set for a century,
that obstinate umpire Jim Phillips gave me out caught at the wicket when
I hit the toe of my front boot at least a foot away from the ball. His heavy,
autocratic explanation was that he heard a click. I asked him – of course, after
the match – whether he was sure it was not the slamming of a door in the
pavilion. Jim and I were slight enemies, because years before he had no-balled
me for throwing. That was all right if he disliked my slightly bent arm action,
but it was no reason why he should have no-balled me for my other nine balls
of the over when I delivered slow round-arms and slow over-arms with an
absolutely rigid elbow.

This elaborate incident occurred in a match at Brighton between
Sussex and Oxford. Before the second innings I had my right elbow encased
in splints and bandages and took the field with my sleeve buttoned at the
wrist. But old Billy Murdoch, our captain, who had ostentatiously put me
on to bowl in the first innings at Jim Phillips' end, because he knew that Jim
had come down to Brighton to no-ball me, twisted his black moustache,
showed his white teeth, and refused to put me on. I was both astonished
and annoyed, but he refused further particulars. Jim Phillips was a famous
umpire. He was an Australian who came over, qualified for Middlesex and
was a second-rate elephantine slow-medium bowler. He was quite honest,
but was ambitious to achieve the reputation of a 'strong umpire'. His other
ambition was to qualify as a mining engineer, and he used to go about with
a Hall and Knight's Algebra in his pocket.

The Duties of an Umpire

WILLIAM SAPTE

William Sapte was a humorous writer of the nineteenth and early twentieth centuries. The following list is from his *Cricketer's Guyed* for 1886. R. Thoms is Bob Thoms, a famous umpire of the nineteenth century.

❦

(*For the first time explicitly laid down*)
'I cannot tell thee *all* I know.' – R. Thoms.

1. No umpire shall pay for his own drinks.
2. Every umpire shall be at liberty to call for such drinks as shall seem most desirable to him, and the game shall be stopped till he have them.
3. In future arm-chairs shall be provided for all umpires.
4. No umpire shall be expected to stand or sit for more than fifty runs at any one time.
5. The decisions of an umpire shall be given in favour of the side which employs him.
6. If the captain of the side which employs him is bowled, the umpire shall call 'Wide!' or 'No ball!'
7. If the said captain be caught, the umpire shall cry 'Bump-ball! Not out' – without being appealed to.
8. If the said captain be run out, or stumped, or hit his wicket, or be leg before, or handle the ball, the umpire shall, without being appealed to, declare the batsman 'not out'.
9. In short, he shall do all such and several things as may be within his power whereby he can benefit the side which employs him, and more especially the captain thereof;
10. *Unless* he consider himself treated with insufficient respect;
11. Or insufficiently well remunerated;
12. Or have backed the other side to win the match.
13. And it shall be lawful for an umpire to impede a bowler in the act of delivering the ball by shouting to him;
14. Or by tripping him up;
15. Or sprinkling sawdust in his face.

16. No umpire is called upon to explain or give any reason for any of his decisions.

17. Any umpire may order the game to be suspended, besides as per rule 2, when he desires to light his pipe;

18. Or read the paper;

19. Or converse with his fellow-umpire.

20. After the game, the ball, stumps, and bails shall become the property of the umpires, for their sole use and benefit.

21. It shall be lawful for an umpire to take charge of any money or valuable property entrusted to him by the players for that purpose;

22. But he shall on no account be compelled to return the same to their owners.

23. An umpire may object to any fieldsman, batsman, bowler or spectator, who in any way impugns or questions his decision; and such fieldsman, batsman, bowler, or spectator, shall be at once suspended. (*This is designed to counteract Law 3 of Cricket.*)

24. If any bowler throw the ball in lieu of bowling it, the umpire *may* call 'No ball!' But he may, if he prefer it, look the other way, or wink, or expectorate, or shrug his shoulders, or refer any objectors to the seventh law of cricket, as given on page 11 of the Guyed.

The Men in White Coats

HAROLD C. WOODS

From *Cricket in the Long Grass* (1995), a memoir of village cricket in Hertfordshire in the years before the Second World War. The names of places and people are fictitious.

SOON AFTER BECOMING the team's scorer Jim began to realise how very important was the role played by the Umpire, in the average village cricket match. Much more important than their counterparts in the first-class game; although, like them, they were usually ex-players suffering with a bit of arthritis or back trouble perhaps, which had caught up with them in later years.

To understand properly the extraordinary different problems he was faced with – compared to the Umpire in a test-match, it is necessary to visualise the isolation and consequent interwoven fabric of their lives. When virtually the only means of travel was on foot or by 'push-bike'; therefore, footballers and cricketers could play only for the Village or Parish in which they lived – where they went to school, grew up, married, and eventually expired. Our typical village umpire then, would probably be related to at least half the team either by blood or marriage and one or two more working colleagues during the week and might even be adding his voice to others in the Church choir on Sundays.

Because of all this it was most difficult for the poor chap to give a Home batsman out 'L.B.W.' when, only the previous day, the same man had given up his whole evening to help put up the umpire's new chicken shed! or, indeed, another possible victim of the upraised finger who came round during the week with two score of fine, upstanding brussel plants, for which he refuses to accept any remuneration.

Consequently, decisions were often dictated by *who* was involved and which team would benefit rather than by the boring technical laws printed in the back of the scorebook.

Rivalry was another factor in the arbitrator's decision making:– if Umpire 'A' bagged six victims in the afternoon – three L.B.W., two Caught Behind, and one Run-out, perhaps, on behalf of his fielding team – then his opposite number would be looking for at least six and, hopefully, seven when *his* team were bowling.

It may be argued that, in theory anyway, one biased official cancelled out the other but, as every cricketer knows, this does not work out in practice.

There were, of course, *some* Umpires who were strong willed enough to be honest and unbiased even though they might suffer for it socially and domestically afterwards. A batsman given out 'L.B.W.' by his own Umpire felt extremely hard done by and doubly damned.

One or two amiable and well liked adjudicators could be found on the circuit, chaps who could get away with anything, for or against, by sheer humour or wit: 'Old Harry' who 'Stood' for Cottam, had developed the art even further by shouting a loud 'Owzat?' himself when the ball hit the pad; his subsequent decision, however, still depended mostly on which side were batting.

Young Jim knew nothing of all this as yet, partly because he was not allowed into the local with the men after the match where the post-mortem arguments flourished. There would always be ample examples of dodgy decisions to be fought over and blame to be apportioned whilst who scored the runs and who took the wickets was of secondary interest.

So, it will be seen, that in many cases the 'Man in White' was considered more as a member of the team than as a trusted neutral. This conclusion is underlined by the fact that when the Captain found himself short of a player, prior to an away match, and no means or hopes of getting a replacement – he preferred to take the field with ten players with the Umpire retaining his official position – rather than to invite the gentleman (who was likely to be a handy player still) to become the eleventh man, thus leaving the umpiring open to all kinds of possible abuse. The thought of having *two* inhabitants of the Home village in charge of the match would have been quite untenable.

As one would expect, the one area of the game in which most village cricketers excelled, was their throwing: even Jack Hobbs, England's finest Cover Point of the day, would have envied the skills and power of these men who had been throwing stones at hares, rats, birds and anything else that ran, crawled, or flew around the countryside, since their schooldays. Many a rabbit ended up in the oven through foolishly running head-long into a fast moving stone – and many a pigeon and pheasant saw nothing of the cause of his sudden downfall from the apparent safety of his lofty roost in the dusk of a quiet evening.

Therefore, run-outs, and near run-outs were a regular problem for the Umpires. One such instance to illustrate the point involved 'Old Joe', the Shappley official himself, whose ambling journey to a Home match took him, by a slightly devious route, into the backdoor of the 'Dog And Duck' and, some fifteen minutes later, out the front door and eventually, to the cricket field.

On the day in question, it was very plain that the outcome of the match depended, to a large extent, on the early dismissal of the opposition's number 3 – a most feared batsman called 'Jake' – blessed with an exceptionally keen eye, backed up with huge shoulders and arms to match. Already he had bludgeoned twenty or more forceful runs and all seemed lost for the Home side when suddenly he misjudged a second run. Tom Green, fielding somewhere around the long-on area, swooped on the ball which, for once, had landed in one of the shorter cropped patches, and smashed the wicket down with a direct fifty-yard throw with the pugnacious 'Jake' yards short of his ground. The Shappley team rose as one man in a loud and triumphant appeal to the square-leg umpire; the peacefully grazing cows lifted their tails high in the air and stampeded blindly at the sudden, ecstatic roar from eleven throats on the field plus three more watching elderly enthusiasts who sat, as usual, on a dead fallen tree, as near as dammit square with the wicket in question. The rooks in the elms at long leg also took vociferous umbrage at this uncalled-for interruption to their normal Saturday afternoon domestic affairs.

On the field of play a stunned silence followed that single outburst – simply because there was no Square-Leg Umpire in sight to offer a response! Even as the players looked at each other in silent bewilderment Joe's ample figure came into view, carefully negotiating the stile that led back from the spinney to the field, still attempting to do up his buttons and no doubt wondering what all the 'Hoo-Hah' was about. He was quickly and loudly informed of the situation by a number of angry voices – chief amongst them, naturally enough, being that of Tom – whose mighty throw was responsible. Poor Joe knew not what to do for the best and could only repeat and over again – 'I '*ad* ter goo an 'ev a dror orf, I was bustin'.' The batsmen, meanwhile, were conferring with the Benton Umpire at the bowler's end and naturally insisted unanimously that 'If the Judge is absent there can be no sentence', claiming with confidence and vigour that the charge of 'Run-out' must be dismissed rather than the blatantly guilty batsman.

Eventually the match recommenced under a very heavy psychological cloud and minus the services of Tom Green who stamped angrily off – snatched his jacket and brown shoes from the holly bush, where they always hung during play, and set off for home, pausing only to turn and shout 'Doon't pick me when we play this lot ag'in – if ever we *dew*.'

Benton won the match easily enough and the Schoolmaster Captain of the home side tried hard to patch things up but, not being a natural 'drinking man' he was handicapped from the start, for many harsh and earthy Barfordshire words had been said by various members of his team. So the Benton team mounted their bikes and set off home – well pleased with the victory, which more than compensated for minor things like being sworn at or being accused of cheating because their hero had not 'Walked'.

Joe had quietly slipped away, after one more brief visit over the stile, to the spinney.

❦

Umpiring Curiosities

AN OLD CRICKETER

From *Curiosities of Cricket* (1897).

PARTICULARS OF OCCURRENCE (OCCASION/PLACE/WHERE RECORDED)

● Appeal by umpire to spectators to decide boundary hit
(Cricket, Feb. 25, 1893)
● 10 balls given in over (Blackheath Amateur v. Charlton/Sporting Life,
Sept. 9, 1848)
● 9 balls given in over (Coburg v. Ormond/Melbourne/Cricket,
April 30, 1891)
● Batsman given not out though bowled because umpire did not see ball
bowled (Norton v. Staffordshire/Norton/Cricket Field, June 18, 1892)
● Batsman given out for 'breach of etiquette' in making back-handed hit
(South Africa/Cricket Field, Jan. 5, 1895)
● Batsman given out hitting with one hand (Elstree School/Cricket Field,
May 13, 1893)
● Batsman given out leg before wicket by one umpire and caught by other
umpire (Ceylon, Cricket, Jan. 28, 1897)
● Batsman given out 'running round his ground' (being beyond his end of
crease) (Eng. Game of Cricket, by Box, p. 384)
● Batsman given out leg before wicket for knocking off bails with string of
hat (Captain Johnson) (Royal Artillery v. Mr. Fowler's XI/Woolwich/Scores
& Biog., v. xiv., p. 1057)
● Batsman given out for wooden leg falling off and fielder putting down
wicket with it (Walworth/Cricket Notes, by Bolland, p. 118)
● Batsman, though bowled and stumped, given 'not bowled out' by bowler's
umpire because he did not see ball bowled, and by batsman's umpire, 'not
stumped out' because first bowled (Bickley/Cricket Field, July 30, 1892)
● Block given as 'centre' and 'far stick' (Warley/Cricket, Aug. 20, 1891)
● Block given as 'a little east' and 'a little west' (Toronto/Cricket Field,
Dec. 31, 1892)

- Block given as 'a little more to the north' (Canada/Cricket, Aug. 20, 1891)
- Decision: 'I didn't see but I give him out' (Royston v. Littleborough/ Cricket, April 30, 1891)
- Decision ending match for 4 minutes' delay (Cranbrook v. Rolvenden/ Cranbrook/Scores and Biog., v. xii, p. 199)
- Decision over-ruled (Eng. v. M.C.C. & Metro Clubs' XV/Lord's/Scores and Biog. v. iv, p. 220)
- Decision over-ruled (England v. Nottinghamshire/Lord's/Scores and Biog., v. iv, p. 582)
- No ball called because delivered with both feet behind crease (Theory and Practice of Cricket, by Box, p. 117)
- Practice ball bowled called wide (Sussex/Cricket, Aug. 14, 1890)
- Short run called when only single attempted (Cricket Field, Feb. 25, 1893)
- Umpire ducked in pond for giving unsatisfactory decision (Bevenden v. Penshurst/Cricket Field, Feb. 25, 1893)
- Umpire fielded and returned ball (Threlfall Warrnambool v. Portland and Port Fairy/Warrnambool, Victoria/Cricket, June 4, 1891)
- 3 wides allowed for hit off ball called wide (Georgetown/Cricket, Jan. 27, 1887)

17

MORE HEROES

Players Past and Present

F. S. ASHLEY-COOPER

F. S. Ashley-Cooper was a cricket historian and statistician. From the anthology
The Light Side of Cricket (1898), edited by E. B. V. Christian.

❧

THE FIRST FULLY-RECORDED match is *Kent v. All England* in 1746.
After that we hear no more of cricket scores until the celebrated old
Hambledon Club became famous. The players of this club have been
immortalized by John Nyren in his work entitled 'Cricketers of My Time',
first published in 1833. From this book we learn that the most famous players
of the old club were John Small, Tom Walker, William Beldham, Lumpy, Tom
Sueter, and David Harris. Their names are household words to-day. These
men were the champions of the game

'When Cricket, glorious game, was young,
What time old Nyren played and sung.'

In the early years of the Hambledon Club, the wicket was one foot high and
two feet wide, the bat was curved at the end like a hockey-stick, and nearly
all the bowling was fast and all along the ground. What primitive times those
must have been when a ball twisting from the off to leg-stump was hailed
as an innovation! Lamborn,* the little farmer, was the first to introduce this
'teasing and deceitful kind of bowling'. 'The Kent and Surrey men could not
tell what to make of that cursed twist of his.' Tom Walker, 'the driest and most
rigid-limbed chap I ever saw', was the first man to try what Nyren terms the
throwing bowling, and he evidently met with success for it is recorded that
he headed a side against the redoubtable David Harris and beat him. 'We did
feel so ashamed of such baby bowling,' said Beldham. The Hambledon Club,
however, suppressed that kind of bowling, and Willes,** a famous Kent player,
had all the praise of inventing it some twenty years later. A famous member of

*Not Lambert, as stated in Nyren's work and several other publications.
**Willes is buried at Sutton Valance, in Kent, and the following appears on his tombstone:–
'He was a patron of all manly sports, and the first to introduce round-arm bowling in cricket.'

the Hambledon Club was Lumpy, whose real name was Edward Stevens. He was called Lumpy 'because he was so fat', or, according to another account, 'because he did once eat a whole apple-pie'. He was a Surrey man and in the service of Lord Tankerville. He was a fine bowler – fast and accurate. In his day the party leaving home pitched their own wickets and Lumpy would invariably choose the ground where his balls would shoot –

> 'For honest Lumpy did allow
> He ne'er could bowl but o'er a brow.'

Nothing pleased the old man so much as bowling down a wicket with a shooting ball. In the old days the bowler's name was not entered in the score-sheet unless the wicket was bowled down; for this reason Lumpy will probably be found credited with more wickets than David Harris, as the latter depended on the fieldsmen to make catches, whilst Lumpy would sacrifice everything in order to be able to bowl a wicket down. It is chiefly to Lumpy that we owe the introduction of the third stump. During a single-wicket match between Five of Hambledon and Five of England in the Artillery Ground, on the 22nd of May 1775, Small went in last man to get 14 runs, and obtained them. It was noticed that Lumpy three times bowled right through Small's wicket, and as this was considered very hard for the bowler, it was decided to add a third stump. Many people said at the time that the game would thereby be shortened, but Nyren rightly argued that the batsman, knowing the danger which would exist in missing a straight ball with three stumps instead of two behind him, would redouble his care and his innings be better played.

'The two principal bowlers in my early days,' wrote Nyren, 'were Thomas Brett and Richard Nyren of Hambledon; the *corps de reserve*, or change bowlers, were Barber and Hogsflesh.'

> 'Ah, where be Beldham now, and Brett,
> Barber and Hogsflesh, where be they?'

Brett was a 'steam-engine' bowler – very fast and very straight. His delivery was above suspicion – 'he was neither a thrower nor a jerker, but a legitimate downright *bowler*, delivering his ball fairly, high, and very quickly, quite as strongly as the jerkers, and with the force of a point blank shot'. He was described as 'the fastest bowler that was ever known' at a time when Osbaldeston and Brown, of Brighton, had been playing in matches for many years. Although the pace of Brett's bowling was so great, Nyren records that he has several times seen Tom Sueter 'stump out a man with Brett's tremendous bowling'.*

Noah Mann, another famous player, was able when bowling to give a curve to the ball the whole way, but the king of bowlers was David Harris. 'In bowling, he never stooped in the least of his delivery, but kept himself upright all the time.' His mode of delivering the ball was curious. 'He would bring it from under the arm by a twist,' says Nyren, 'and nearly as high as his arm-pit, and with this action *push* it, as it were, from him.' The ball, delivered high, naturally rose high – 'it was but a touch and up again' – grinding many a finger against the bat. Before this admirable bowler came upon the scene, batting was almost all hitting, defence being comparatively unknown – the bat and the wicket as well the style of bowling being adapted to a short life and a merry one. Length-bowling was introduced by David Harris, and by him first brought to perfection. It was this length-bowling which caused the alteration in the shape of the bat. About 1845, Lord Frederick Beauclerck [*sic*] and Mr William Ward both declared that Harris was, without exception, the best bowler they had ever seen, and also that he had done more to improve batting than any other bowler. And when those words were spoken Hillyer, Redgate, Clarke, Lillywhite, and Alfred Mynn were at their best, whilst Cobbett had been dead only a few years. We must also remember that neither Mr Ward nor Lord Frederick could ever have seen Harris at his *best* – he was at his best before their time. Taking it for granted that the bowlers of the forties were as good as those of the present day – they were certainly not inferior – is it not reasonable to suppose that David Harris was one of the very best bowlers that ever lived? Nyren, who saw many of the great matches up to 1837, said the same as Lord Frederick and Mr Ward, and he was a good judge of the game.

The earliest famous batsman was John Small of Petersfield. He was a great hand at the 'draw' and a fine judge of a short run. When at his best, a third stump was added to the wicket and the shape of the bat was changed, thus causing him to entirely alter his style of play, and great praise is due to him for maintaining his reputation after the alterations had been effected.

*In the match Gentlemen of England v. The Players, in 1849, Mr Ridding stumped Hillyer off one of Mr Fellows's terrific deliveries!

Once in a match between Hambledon and England he kept up his wicket for three whole days, and was even then not out! What his score was upon that occasion is not known. 'A pity his score is not preserved,' says the Rev. James Pycroft, 'we should like to compare it with Mr Ward's.'* Small was a celebrated cricket-ball maker, and over his doorway he placed a board on which was written:–

> 'Here lives John Small,
> Makes bats and balls,
> Pitches a wicket,
> Plays at cricket,
> With any man in England.'

The peculiarity of the balls made by Small was, that after heavy rain, when the ball had dried, it assumed its correct weight.

Rags to Riches

MIKE BREARLEY AND DUDLEY DOUST

From *The Ashes Retained* (1979). Doust, who was the author of this chapter, was an American sports journalist who lived in London and wrote about a wide range of sports. Derek Randall (Nottinghamshire and England) played in forty-seven Tests and was twenty-seven at the time of the 1979 Sydney Test, which England won by 93 runs.

O N T H E M O R N I N G of the third day of the fourth Test, Derek Randall woke after ten hours' sleep refreshed but uneasy. One thought had nagged deep in his mind throughout the night. Rags, you're going in to bat today, he thought, and you've got to get some runs. He swung his legs out of bed, gazed a moment at his dozing room-mate, Phil Edmonds, then got up and picked his way through a litter of clothes to the window.

The sun was already beating down. Sydney with the great Harbour Bridge and the glistening white fins of the Opera House lay below him. He

*Mr Ward scored 278 for M.C.C. v. Norfolk, at Lord's, in 1820.

was not impressed, his own idea of a fine view being one of green fields and a few trees and perhaps an English church spire in the distance. Still, the sky was blue and unblemished, much as it had been on the previous day, and this suggested a long, hot day for batting. The prospect lifted his spirits, and he broke into song. 'Oh, what a beautiful morning,' he hummed, '. . . I've got a beautiful feeling, everything's going my way.' He rubbed the palms of his hands together. 'Come on, Rags,' he said. 'Got to get some runs.'

Randall lives in a world of his own, peopled principally by himself, Rags. His team-mates call him 'Arkle', after the racehorse, for his speed about the field, but, to himself, Randall, now 27, has been Rags ever since his ragamuffin days as a schoolboy in Retford, Nottinghamshire. It was there, as a little boy, that he developed his skill in pulling a ball. His companions, bowling, would dig in short balls and Randall, the tiniest of them all, would smash away at the lifting balls. His unlikely hero was the tall and elegant Tom Graveney, whose picture hung on his bedroom wall. His dream was to play for the Ashes in Australia.

Now the Ashes were in danger. England had lost at Melbourne, where their comfortable two-game lead was whittled to one, and in this fourth game Australia had moved into a 96-run lead with three of their wickets still standing in their first innings. The thought of returning to Nottingham, to his wife and son, to his mother, with the Ashes gone, subdued Randall. Instead of moving about in his usual effervescent, bird-like manner, he consciously restrained himself. He dressed slowly.

The telephone rang. It was Barrington on his morning ring-round. '9.15 in reception,' he said. 'Don't be late.' Randall went down to the hotel coffee shop where he took his customary breakfast of fruit, poached eggs and bacon, haunted by memories of his innings two days earlier. He had got out second ball, caught for a duck at backward square leg off Hurst, *hooking*. Second ball and hooking. Randall recalled the lecture he had received from Insole that evening. The England manager had sought him out after stumps and, driving back to the hotel with him, had impressed two points upon Randall: if England were in trouble, as clearly they now were, it was his responsibility to stay in. It was his *responsibility* to have a long look at the bowlers and get the pace of the wicket before he started hooking. At Perth, Insole continued, Randall had been out fifth ball, senselessly mis-hooking Hogg. 'Another thing,' Insole later recalled telling Randall, 'you simply have *got* to learn to play your innings in segments. You have got to be there at lunch. You have got to be there at tea. You have got to be there at close.'

Randall had listened, half chastened. The bit about batting in segments was good advice, he agreed. But he was in two minds about restraining himself from hooking early in an innings. 'I've got to get a couple of good shots early on for my confidence,' he said. 'That's the way I play.' 'Well, in that case, and in these circumstances,' Insole had replied, 'maybe you had better give some serious thought to the way you play.' The lecture was over but, two mornings later, it was in Randall's mind.

[. . .] Boycott and Brearley went out to open England's second innings, Randall settling in a corner of the dressing room, uncharacteristically solemn. He sipped a cup of tea. Before he had finished it a roar went round the ground: Boycott had been trapped for nought, first ball, LBW – once again to Hogg. Silence fell over the dressing room, interrupted by curses. Randall rose to his feet, swivelled his hips, swung his arms round his waist, then strode across the dressing room. Suddenly he shook his fist at the ceiling. 'Come on, Rags,' he shouted. 'Come on, England!'

He made his way down the pavilion steps, hardly looking up when he passed Boycott, who as usual remarked 'Good luck.' Randall nodded gratefully, then passed through the picket gate on to the field. He does not immediately cut an imposing figure. He is small for a cricketer, standing 5 ft. 8 ½ in. tall and weighing 11 ½ stone. In contrast, his feet are enormous, size 11, and this lends a loping air to his entrance which soon becomes pure theatre. He windmills his bat full-circle round his side, then sweeps it forward in flowing cover drives. It is not just bravado: he feels this is his last chance to loosen up before receiving the dangerous first balls of an innings. It burns off nervousness, and enhances an image: here comes David to slay Goliath.

Thus began what was to be a tense, sweltering 582-minute battle between Randall and the Australians. His first minor skirmish was a personal one, with Yallop.

The Australian captain has no time for Randall, who he feels violates the spirit of the game. For example, Randall is cool towards the Australians: unlike Gower, Hendrick and especially Old and Botham, he does not join the Aussies for a dressing-room drink after a match. 'When in Rome,' Yallop will say, 'do as the Romans do.'

The Australian is irritated at Randall's constant fussing and jabbering at the crease. 'He's a clown – and that's putting it mildly. He sounds like an idiot, always talking to himself. A lot of people and players think his talk helps him concentrate in his batting. I disagree. I think if you can suggest a few questions for him to think about he will lose his concentration.' Accordingly Yallop was eager to fire off an opening psychological salvo. As Randall approached the middle Yallop beckoned to Graeme Wood and together they examined the pitch closely, picking at the wicket just short of a length. For almost a minute they conferred in hushed, conspiratorial tones then, their tactical mission accomplished, they resumed their places.

Randall saw what they were at and was not taken in. He knew that they were trying to suggest that the top surface of the wicket was breaking up for the spinners, but he could see plainly that it was still in fairly firm shape and wasn't worried. Nonetheless, he slowly paced down the wicket, he too now staring at the brown soil – but for a very different reason. Whatever Yallop might have thought, this was no counter-ploy: Randall's wicket-staring served a purpose. He had been in a darkened dressing room and he wanted his eyes to grow accustomed to the colour of the wicket – a tip learnt from Barrington during the 1976–77 tour of India. Yallop's antics allowed him precious extra time to acclimatize himself. Similarly, he turned to gaze down the wicket to the sight screen, so that his eyes might become used to the white glare of the screen.

Next he took guard. He scratched his right boot across the ground, loosening the hard-packed soil. Jabbing down his bat, he called to the umpire, Bailhache, 'Two legs, please, Robin.' By chance it came right, spot on, the face of his bat square to the line between middle and leg stumps. Bailhache signalled as much, and Randall was happy. A simple act had worked perfectly, first look and neat as a notch, and he found it remarkably comforting. Eagerly he knocked in his mark with the toe of his bat, deriving palpable pleasure from the feeling of it in the soil, then began talking to himself – softly at first but gathering in volume and venom according to the problems and pressures at hand. The monologue was maddening to the opposition, and it continued almost unabated for the nine hours and forty-two minutes that Randall spent at the crease. In part it would run:

'Come on, Rags. Get stuck in. Don't take any chances. Get forward, get *forward*. Get behind the ball. Take your time, slow and easy. You *idiot*, Rags. Come on, come *on*. Come on, England.'

If he makes a mistake or his concentration starts to flag, he will punch himself in the chest with his right fist. 'Wake up, Rags, concentrate. *Concentrate*, you idiot!' He especially pesters himself at the opening of an innings, an anxiety that dates back to the summer of 1974 when he 'made five ducks on the trot'.

[. . .] On the fourth day of the Test, the weather was even more humid – two drinks intervals, not one, were authorised per session for that day. When Randall got to the ground, the temperature had climbed over 100 degrees and he decided not to go into the nets. Unusually, he signed no autographs. The six changes of shirt, flannels and socks were again out waiting for him.

The Australians opened with Hogg, Hurst and then Dymock – whom Randall did not relish facing again – from the Paddington End. Hogg toiled from the Randwick End.

Higgs is a right-arm leg-spinner from Victoria, and, since England rarely face leg-spinners, he can be awkward. Yet he now bowled the odd full toss, and spun the ball too much. But he was also bowling into the rough outside the off stump, so Randall had to play him with caution. He glanced at the scoreboard – the overs ticked by, 55, 56, 57 – and he longed for the return of Hogg.

Higgs laboured on. He went round the wicket, bowled outside the leg stump, with a man at mid-wicket, a backward square leg on the fence, a short fine leg. He bowled around Randall's legs, trying to entice him to sweep. If he tries to hit it with any power, thought Higgs, he's going to be in trouble: I've got to get him to hit across a spinning ball. Randall fixed his mind on the task in hand: block and run for singles on the leg-side. Stay put at the crease. He thought of Barrington's cautionary aphorism: 'When it's going for you, book in for a bed and breakfast.'

At 11.50 England were 146, with Randall 73 and Gooch 10. It was then that an accident occurred in the stands which shattered Randall's concentration. Higgs was bowling at Gooch. Randall was at the non-striker's end when suddenly a cameraman toppled from his perch beyond the sight screen in the Bradman stand. The man, who had passed out from the heat, landed on his head and shoulders on a concrete passageway. Randall, genuinely upset by the accident, appealed for the game to be stopped while the man was carried out of the ground. Yallop protested, claiming that once again Randall was stalling for time. That Randall had indeed been shaken by the incident was attested to by the next seven balls, when he twice played and missed, groping at deliveries from the pace bowler Hurst.

The final ball of that over was a crucial one. Randall was flustered; Hurst knew it, and moved in for the kill. He had reached the conclusion, after three Tests, that unless he could get a ball to rise above face-level to Randall there was no point in bouncing him. The Englishman could shuffle across his crease and hook for four any bouncer that didn't get up. Yet there was Randall, still chattering to himself, shifting from one side to the other, a bundle of nerves. He decided to bounce him.

Hurst pounded in, and delivered the ball with that singular slingy action of his. But it didn't get up, and only reached Randall about waist-high. Rolling his wrists, he hit it with ease through square leg for four. Hurst stood, hands on hips, cursing. He had had Randall on the ropes and now, after just this one shot, the irksome little Englishman looked back on top, his taste for the fight renewed. The shot also took England to 150, and Randall to 77.

The new ball was due next over, the 65th, but Yallop persevered with the old, soon bringing on both spinners, Higgs and Border, to work a protracted spell in tandem for the first time in the innings. In the first over Higgs dismissed Gooch, well caught at silly mid-off by Wood, for 22. It was 12.32, England were 169 for three wickets, with Randall on 83.

Gower now came in, ill and with a high temperature. The England team recognised Gower as a virtuoso batsman, not to be tampered with, and, meeting him in the middle of the pitch, Randall did not this time urge caution. Yallop soon had his bowlers coming round the wicket to the left-hander, and constantly shifted his fieldsmen against him. At one stage, Randall even gave the Australian captain some help, correcting Yallop and motioning to a fieldsman still further along at fine leg. It was an act of pure mischief, and immediately the Australian captain complained to the umpire.

At lunch, England were 191, Randall 95 and Gower 18. Randall showered again, again changed his clothing and ate nothing. He drank 'stacks of tea'. He had been batting for a day, had received 314 balls and was both nervous and exhausted.

The afternoon began slowly, and at 2.06, just before the 85th over, Yallop finally took the new ball. When Hogg returned next over he had enjoyed a 160-minute, 28-over rest. He was fresh, or as fresh as one could hope in a cauldron of 105 degrees. Hogg's plan was plain. Randall was on 95, on the threshold of his century, but jittery. Hogg could hear him urging himself on:

'Come on, Rags. Keep forward. Don't throw it away.' Hogg reckoned the son-of-a-bitch was ripe for yet another bouncer.

The Australian came thundering in, past Gower. The first ball dug in short. Randall was across his crease like a cat. He was up on his toes, too; and hooked it square to the boundary. Randall was 99. Hitching up his box, he jabbed anxiously at the ground: the shot hadn't come sweetly off the bat and he nearly had got a top edge. Next ball, another bouncer. Randall middled this one, hitting it finer, and this, too, galloped untouched to the boundary. 103: he had reached his century. He had also, he learned later, earned himself a place in the record books for having scored the slowest century – 411 minutes – in the long history of the 324 Tests which at that time had been played between England and Australia.

The fans poured out. One man even brought his girlfriend to shake Randall's hand. Gower came down the wicket to congratulate his team-mate. Yallop came across. 'Seeing you've done so well, Derek,' he said, 'are you going to have a drink with us after the game?' Randall for once was at a loss for words. Then, 'Sure, I'll have a drink with you. But not until after we've won this Test match.' Perhaps for the first time the idea of victory seemed not wholly absurd.

County Cricket Introduces Me to Some Famous Players

A. A. LILLEY

A. A. (Dick) Lilley (Warwickshire and England) was the leading wicketkeeper
of his era and played thirty-five Tests for England. Lilley first played against
W. G. Grace in 1894, when Grace was forty-six. 'The Jam' was one of the nicknames
of England batsman K. S. Ranjitsinhji, who was the Jam of Nawanagar in
his native India. From *Twenty-Four Years of Cricket* (1912).

MY FIRST YEAR of county cricket necessarily brought me into personal
contact with many of the most famous cricketers of the time; but of
all the players I have ever met, either then or since, no one impressed me
to anything like the same extent as Dr. W. G. Grace, the greatest all-round
cricketer the world has ever seen. I was, of course, but young at the time, and
the imposing figure of this hero of cricket, with his great beard, seemed to
quite overawe me; and when he spoke to me, I must confess to a feeling of
considerable nervousness.

So long as I could remember, 'W. G.' had been the idol of the cricket
world. His name was on every boy's tongue, and, after hearing and reading
so much of him, when at last I was on the same cricket field, I could hardly
realise that I was actually playing against this eminent man. And as in later
years I came to know him better, so my personal regard for the individual,
and my unstinted admiration for the cricketer, correspondingly increased. His
knowledge and judgment were as comprehensive as his skill, and there was no
move upon the board with which he did not seem to be thoroughly familiar.
No subtlety by which a batsman might be legitimately dispossessed of his
wicket was unknown to the doctor, and all the finer points of the game were
as an open book to him.

But as a batsman pure and simple he occupied a position quite by
himself. And when studying his earlier records, one must remember that he
was opposed to some of the finest bowling that this country has produced,
and upon wickets widely different from the perfect ones of more recent years.
It is not easy for cricketers of the present decade to realise the difficulties
that batsmen of a generation ago had to overcome, and the skill that was

required to make a score of comparatively modest dimensions. Dr. Grace himself recalls that when he first played at Lord's the wicket was in a very unsatisfactory condition, and in 1864 the turf was so rough that Sussex actually refused to play there.

And throughout Dr. Grace's long innings England had a wealth of good bowling at command, distinctly superior to that of the last ten years. In the earlier portion of his cricketing career there were those famous bowlers Peate, Shaw, and Morley, and, if we may include the Australians of about the same time, Spofforth, Garrett, and Palmer. Then a little later came Emmett, Ulyett, Barnes, A. G. Steel, Lohmann, Watson, Attewell, Peel, Briggs, Beaumont, Richardson, Lockwood, etc., a bowling combination which certainly cannot be equalled to-day.

It does not need a bold spirit to prophesy that never again will W. G. Grace's record of 1895 be eclipsed. In that year the champion scored over a thousand runs during the month of May, when he was in his forty-seventh year, and had been playing first-class cricket for some thirty years! At that time I had been playing county cricket for eight seasons, and W. G. Grace was in the front rank of cricketers before I was born. Unfortunately, the remaining part of this year was wet, and batsmen's wickets were few and far between; but, judging by the cricket he played under adverse conditions, had the summer continued as it commenced, there is no reason to doubt that the doctor would have piled up sufficient runs during the season to stand as a record for all time.

It was during this particular May that Dr. Grace succeeded in registering his century of centuries, which resulted in the initiation of the movement for a national testimonial. The universal response bore indisputable testimony, if such were needed, to the position Dr. Grace occupied in the cricket world, and the result was a testimonial the like of which has never been approached. His number of centuries, however, did not end with the hundredth, for he added twenty-five more before finally retiring from first-class cricket.

Dr. Grace proved a valuable friend to me on many occasions, and I cannot speak too highly of his repeated kindnesses. The last occasion I played against him was at Shillinglee Park, Sussex, in 1909, when I was a member of the Jam's team, playing an eleven brought down by the doctor. He clean bowled me with one of his old round-arm spins, that never turned an inch. I played for the break that was not there, and so paid the penalty. As I passed him on my way back to the pavilion, he jocularly remarked, 'I thought you were a bit too old, Dick, to be got out like that.' I replied, 'Yes! and I am not the only one you have got out like it,' which was perfectly true, as in his time he had captured many wickets with similarly seductive balls.

I have had some happy times with W. G.: I have fished with him and shot with him, as well as played cricket with him, and have seen him play golf and bowls, and he can give a fine account of himself in all these departments of sport.

Although he made so many centuries in cricket, he only succeeded in making one such score against Warwickshire, and that so late as the season of 1902, when he was associated with London County, and scored 129 at the Crystal Palace.

So far as English cricket is concerned, it is difficult to estimate the debt it owes to the world's champion. For a whole generation his name was a household word, a constant force for all that was best in the game, and the one commanding figure that kept alive the smouldering ambitions of the young enthusiasts, many of whom, profiting by his example, have themselves occupied no mean positions in the annals of the game.

Patient Merit

C. L. R. JAMES

C. L. R. James (1901–89) was a distinguished Afro-Trinidadian historian
and writer. From *Beyond a Boundary* (1963), frequently cited as the best book on
cricket ever written. George John went on the 1923 tour of England;
Piggott never did play for the West Indies.

I HAVEN'T THE SLIGHTEST doubt that the clash of race, caste and class did not retard but stimulated West Indian cricket. I am equally certain that in those years social and political passions, denied normal outlets, expressed themselves so fiercely in cricket (and other games) precisely because they were games. Here began my personal calvary. The British tradition soaked deep into me was that when you entered the sporting arena you left behind you the sordid compromises of everyday existence. Yet for us to do that we would have had to divest ourselves of our skins. From the moment I had to decide which club I would join the contrast between the ideal and the real fascinated me and tore at my insides. Nor could the local population see it otherwise. The class and racial rivalries were too intense. They could be fought out without violence or much lost except pride and honour. Thus the cricket field was a stage on which selected individuals played representative roles which were charged with social significance. I propose now to place on record some of the characters and as much as I can reproduce (I remember everything) of the social conflict. I have been warned that some of these characters are unknown and therefore unlikely to interest non-West Indian readers. I cannot think so. Theirs is the history of cricket and of the West Indies, a history so far unrecorded as so much village cricket in England and of cricketers unknown to headlines have been recorded, and read with delight even in the West Indies.

George John, the great fast bowler, indeed knight-errant of fast bowling, had a squire. This squire was not short and fat and jovial. He was some six foot four inches tall and his name was Piggott. Where he came from, what he did in the week, I do not know and never asked. He came every Saturday to play and was a man of some idiosyncrasy: Piggott never or rarely wore a white shirt, but played usually in a shirt with coloured stripes without any collar attached. He did it purposely, for all his colleagues wore white shirts. His place in history is that he was John's wicketkeeper, and never was fast bowler better served. Piggott was one of the world's great wicketkeepers of the period between the wars. He always stood up to John, his hands one inch behind the stumps, and if you edged or drew your toe over the line you were through.

I wish some of our modern batsmen had had the experience of playing Lindwall or Miller with a wicketkeeper's hands an inch behind the wicket. Something startled where you thought you were safest. Your concentration on John was diluted. Everton Weekes says he pays no attention to short-legs. He plays as usual, keeping the ball down as usual, placing it as usual. Long may his method flourish! But, with Piggott so close behind, ordinary mortals felt as if they were being attacked from front and rear at the same time.

He had a peculiar trick that was characteristic of him. On the rare occasions that John bowled on the leg-side, Piggott jumped sideways with both feet and pushed his legs at the ball, hoping to bounce it on to the wicket and catch the batsman out of his crease. (He was also credited with being able to flick a bail if the ball was passing very close to the wicket and might miss. But I never saw him do it and never heard of any authentic instance. The legend, however, illustrates his uncanny skill.) He may not have been quite so good at slow bowling, but I am inclined to believe that it was the constant miracles he performed standing up to John which put his other keeping in the shade. He was no Evans. He didn't fall five feet to the right or hurl himself like a goalkeeper to the left and scoop up a leg-glance with the tip of his fingers. He had less need to, standing where he did. In his own way and in his own style he was unique. In addition Piggott was one of the few comic characters I have known in West Indies cricket. He walked with shoulders very much bent forward and with a kind of hop. When he was excited he gabbled rather than spoke. He was apt to get upset when things went wrong, usually a catch or sometimes two in an over missed in the slips off John. At the end of the over John would stamp off to his place in the slips glaring at the offender, while Piggott ambled up the pitch peering from side to side over his bent shoulders, gesticulating and muttering to himself.

He was without the slightest doubt the finest wicketkeeper we had ever seen, and to this day I have not seen or heard of any West Indian wicketkeeper who surpassed him. No one ever dared to say otherwise. The sight of him standing up to John and Francis in England in 1923 would have been one of the never-to-be-forgotten sights of modern cricket. Yet, to the astonishment of all Trinidadians, when the 1923 team was selected he was left out and Dewhurst taken instead. The only excuse current at the time was the following: 'You can't depend on a man like that. Who knows, when you are looking for him for some important match you will find him somewhere boozing.'

It was untrue. It was also stupid.

The real reason could be seen in a glance at the Trinidad contribution to the 1923 side. John and Small (Stingo), Constantine and Pascall (Shannon). Piggott would have meant three Stingo and two Shannon. All would have been absolutely black. Not only whites but the Queen's Park Club would have been left out altogether. Dewhurst was a fine wicketkeeper, and he was recognized as such and praised in England. But it was a guilty conscience that made so many people say to me: 'And, by the way, everywhere the team goes they comment on our stumper – they say he is very good.' I knew that as well as anybody else. I read more English papers than they.

Poor Piggott was a nobody. I felt the injustice deeply. So did others. He was a man you couldn't miss in a crowd and one day at the Queen's Park Oval during a big match I stood and talked with him. Dewhurst, now firmly established as the island and West Indian 'keeper, was doing his job excellently as he always did. But as the ordinary people came and went an astonishing number of them came up to tell Piggott, 'You should be out there, Piggie.'

'If you had his skin, Piggie, you would be behind today.' Most of them didn't know him except by sight. Piggott was very good-natured about it. What is most curious is that to this day I don't know whether this superb cricketer was a tailor, a casual labourer or a messenger. Socially he did not register.

The Demon Bowler

R. L. HODGSON

R. L. Hodgson wrote under the nom-de-plume 'A Country Vicar'.
From *Second Innings* (1933). The Berlin Congress took place in June and July 1878;
the Australia team had arrived in May, and Frederick Spofforth was twenty-four.

THEN THE AUSTRALIANS arrived, and my personal interest was engrossed in them. The Eastern Question and the Berlin Congress sank into insignificance with the presence, in our own country, of such formidable invaders. And a figure who loomed up in my childish imagination as altogether sinister and terrifying was F. R. Spofforth. The fact that he was known as 'the demon bowler' made me regard him as something diabolical – a kind of personification of Satan. Had I ever beheld him, in those far-away days, I should have certainly looked for the horns on his head! I quite thought he possessed these; and I rather fancied that, hidden away – decently concealed – was a tail! I had an intense awe and dread of Spofforth, and a boundless admiration for the four English teams – Notts, the Gentlemen, Yorkshire and Cambridge University – which, in spite of 'the demon bowler', defeated the Australians that year.

As a matter of fact, it would not have required much ingenuity to 'make up' Spofforth for the character of Mephistopheles. I met him in after years, and he had rather the type of countenance which one associates with the Spirit of Evil in *Faust*. A long face, somewhat sardonic; piercing eyes; a hooked nose; and his hair, parted in the middle, giving the impression of horns. He was also immensely tall – lean, sinewy, and loose-limbed – with long, thin arms; he would have looked the part of the stage-demon. Mr. Neville Cardus, in his delightful book, *Days in the Sun*, even appears to suggest that there *was* some secret, sinister power in Spofforth. He quotes one who spoke of his own experience: 'It was at the Oval. I were in right form and not afeared of him when I goes in to bat. He'd just taken a wicket, but I walks into th' middle jaunty like, flicking my bat, makin' rare cuts through th' slips as I went over th' grass . . . As I got near Mr. Spofforth he sort of fixed me. His look went right through me like a red-hot poker. But I walks on past him along th' wicket to th' batting end. And half-way down somethin' made me turn round and look at him over my shoulder. And there he was, still fixin' me with his eye.' It is tantalising that Mr. Cardus does not relate what happened next. The story ends there. Nor does Mr. Cardus tell us who the English cricketer was, but I fancy he must have been William Barnes.

I knew, eventually, many of the amateurs who played against the Australians in 1878 and the early 'eighties. Most of them have passed on to other fields; but, years after those famous contests, they used to talk of them. They were unanimous on one point – that F. R. Spofforth was the most deadly bowler they ever met on the cricket-field. None of them hinted at any hypnotism, or spoke of the power of his eye. The power of his arm and the cunning of his brain were the subjects upon which they waxed eloquent; and, above all, the varied nature of his attack.

It is a mistake to think that Spofforth was merely a very fast bowler. It is equally untrue to run to the other extreme and maintain he was never a really fast bowler. History relates that, as a boy of ten, he saw George Parr's team playing, in Australia, in 1863–64. One of the English side was George Tarrant, of Cambridge. The great pace of that professional fascinated young Spofforth; and he, then and there, determined to become as fast a bowler as possible. Ten years later, W. G. Grace's team visited Australia; and Spofforth watched Alfred Shaw and James Southerton. Those masters of length and spin convinced him that sheer force was not everything. He conceived a new ambition – to effect, in himself, a combination of the styles of Tarrant, Southerton and Shaw. In that he succeeded; and he became in consequence, the first great bowler to 'mix them', and accomplish that enviable feat without disclosing his intention.

Spofforth did not take an abnormally long run, but he ran up to the wicket very fast. At the moment of delivery he gave a terrifying bound, and the batsmen had a fearsome vision of a gigantic figure, with whirling arms, launching what appeared likely to be a veritable thunderbolt at him. It might be a very fast ball – possibly a devastating 'yorker'. It might be a medium-pace break-back. It might be a still slower ball. But, whatever came down, it was so well disguised that anyone was apt to be completely deceived. The difficulty was to know what was coming.

[. . .] 'The Demon' remained himself – peerless – on every type of wicket. He had an extraordinary facility for accommodating himself to the condition of the ground; he could bowl, equally well, at any pace. No game, in which he took part, was ever lost until it was actually won. Over and over again he carried his side to victory when the chances looked hopeless. I write the name of F. R. Spofforth as the greatest of all the great Australian bowlers; and possibly, the greatest bowler the world has ever seen.

It is a pity that so many of the matches played by the Australian teams of 1878 and 1880 were against odds: in a sense, that fact lowers the value of Spofforth's performances. But the figures, which include his doings in the Colonies and in 1878, some matches in America, at least show how he mowed the wickets down:

> 1878. 764 wickets at a cost of 6.08 each.
> 1880. 763 wickets at a cost of 5.49 each.

And it should never be forgotten that, in the famous match of 1878 v. M.C.C., he took ten for 20 and did the 'hat-trick'. Not only poor batsmen failed against him.

In what are regarded as 'Test matches', Spofforth bowled 4,185 balls, 1,731 runs were scored off them, and he captured 94 wickets – an average of 18.41. Of all the Australian bowlers who have played in these contests and taken as many as fifteen wickets, only two – C. T. B. Turner and J. J. Ferris – have better results.

'The Demon' was rather unlucky in the way of injuries. He was hurt in 1880, and was, in consequence, kept out of the first match between England and Australia on English soil. He was hurt again in 1884 and 1886; and curiously enough, both injuries occurred in exactly the same way, in the same fixture – v. Gentlemen of England – and the same batsman did the damage – Lord Harris. Spofforth had the habit of following each ball he bowled right up the wicket. By doing so he made many catches; but he also ran the risk of not putting his hand in exactly the right place for a hard return. That was what happened. On each occasion Lord Harris jumped out, drove a ball straight, and Spofforth's bowling hand was injured. The second injury was so severe that he always maintained he was never again the same bowler.

'Old Spoff' was a most popular fellow, a cheery companion, fond of a good story, and an excellent judge of the game. There was nothing demoniacal about him, except as a bowler. He died on June 4, 1926, aged seventy-two.

Kings of Cricket

RICHARD DAFT

Richard Daft was a well-known cricketer of the mid-nineteenth century who played for Nottinghamshire and the All England XI. His *Kings of Cricket* was published in 1893. 'Mr. Parr, senior' is Sam Parr (1780–1857); his son George captained Nottinghamshire and the All England XI, as well as the England team which went to North America in 1859, the first ever overseas tour.

GEORGE PARR WAS born at Radcliffe-on-Trent, on the 26th of May, 1826. His father was a gentleman farmer in that village, renting land under Earl Manvers, as his ancestors had done before him for several centuries. He resided in a large old-fashioned house, which is still standing, known as the 'Old Manor House'. This old gentleman was always a great sportsman, a fine rider across country, and an enthusiastic cricketer. In his latter days I knew him intimately. He had several sons, all of whom were good cricketers; one of the best being Sam, who was a few years older than George. Sam represented his county on many occasions, and also was at one time mostly included on the All England Eleven.

Mr. Parr, senior, at the time I knew him, had given up playing cricket, but he never tired of telling long stories of his bygone exploits in the field. He had been, by his own account, one of the hardest hitters the world ever saw, and this always much astonished his hearers when they came to look at him, for he was a very diminutive fellow.

One tale he never wearied of telling of a tremendous leg hit he once made in a match, always commencing with the sentence, 'The wind was in the west.' I should not like to say how far the ball went before it dropped. It went out of the range of vision, however, of all the fielders towards 'the east', and, according to Mr. Parr's account, nearly killed a farm labourer who was cutting a hedge several fields away from the cricket ground. The old fellow told the story so often that I believe he implicitly believed it himself at last.

Young George, in the matches in which he played for his native village when quite a boy, showed signs of his future greatness. In those days there was a great deal of rivalry between the village of Radcliffe and that of Bingham, about four miles away; and the cricket matches which yearly took place between their respective clubs were carried on in the keenest and not always in the most amicable manner.

Whenever the Radcliffe eleven were victorious on their own ground they never failed to have the church bells rung. On one occasion, however, when playing at Bingham, they suffered a severe defeat, and so elated at this were the other side that they determined to celebrate their victory in a manner worthy of the event. So they ordered a huge bowl of punch to be prepared at one of the inns in the place, in which the ball they had that day won from their opponents was set to float about, while the Bingham team and their supporters looked admiringly on.

All this was gall and wormwood to Sam Parr, who was racking his brains to devise some means of getting possession of the ball. At last he thought of one, and rushing into the room, panted out: 'Good heavens! Old —'s stackyard is all in flames!' Out rushed the winning eleven and their friends pell-mell, flying at the top of their speed to the place of the supposed conflagration, which was some half-mile away. On arriving there and finding everything as it should be, they immediately came to the conclusion that Sam had played them this trick in order to steal their ball, which on their return to the inn they found to be the case, for neither Sam nor the ball was to be seen or heard of.

When the return match came to be played at Radcliffe, one of the Bingham men, thinking to equalise things, walked off with one of the Radcliffe players' bats; but unfortunately for him, its owner hearing of this acquainted the local constable of the fact, and the unlucky Binghamite being taken red-handed, was run into the lock-up!

There resided at Radcliffe at this time a gentleman of means, who, though no player himself, always went about with the eleven when playing away. He was an immensely tall, gaunt-looking man, with very long legs, so long, indeed, that Sam Parr related an anecdote of himself and this gentleman once sharing a double-bedded room, the beds of which were so small that Mr. Blank – for so I will call him – was compelled to sleep with his feet and legs in the air.

In the early morning Sam was awoke by a cock crowing, which he declared had been roosting in the company of several more fowls on Mr. Blank's legs! This story I have no doubt Sam greatly exaggerated, though the fowls did, I believe, enter the room through the window, which had been left open.

Mr. Blank once accompanied a local eleven to Grantham, I think it was, to play a two-days' match, and at breakfast at the hotel, before the day's play began, he made a long speech to his own side, saying amongst other things that he hoped none of them would be tempted during the game to use any bad language, no matter what amount of provocation they might be subject to. 'And especially let what I say apply to you, Mr. Sam Parr,' he continued, 'for I know this is a little failing of yours.'

During the day, the Radcliffe eleven being in the field, one of them happened to drop a catch in the out-field and close to where Mr. Blank was standing amongst the spectators, and this misfortune had no sooner happened than he abused the unfortunate fielder in some of the most awful language imaginable.

Sam Parr, hearing of this soon afterwards, came up to Mr. Blank at lunch time, and tapping him on the shoulder, said:

'I thought, sir, someone gave us a little advice this morning about the use of bad language.'

'Mr. Parr,' he replied, 'you have me this time, and I will never lecture anyone on that subject again; for I find there *are* times when the use of strong language is excusable and necessary.'

The umpiring in some of these matches, I am told, was something extraordinary. In one match, one of the opposite party appealed for a catch at short slip, when Sam Parr was batting.

'Excuse me a moment, sir,' replied the Radcliffe umpire who was the one appealed to, 'did you play the ball, Mr. Parr?'

Sam, of course, promptly replied, 'Certainly not!'

'Not out!' said the umpire at once. 'I'm sure if Mr. Parr *had* played the ball he would have been the first to have said so.'

❧

Difficult Targets: W. R. Hammond

R. C. ROBERTSON-GLASGOW

After playing first-class cricket from 1920 to 1937, R. C. Robertson-Glasgow
became a cricket correspondent and author.
Wally Hammond (Gloucestershire and England) played eighty-five
Test matches from 1927 to 1947. From *Cricket Prints* (1943).

❧

W. R. HAMMOND IS the sort of cricketer that any schoolboy might
wish to be. Schoolboys are very good judges of most things and people.
They think and look straight on, unapprenticed to prejudice.

It might be interesting, and it would be unprofitable, to argue Hammond's
place as a batsman in the ranks of all the great, or to compare his ability with
that of famous contemporaries. It has been tried, and it ends in futility. To
me he is, quite simply, the greatest cricketer who began in the last twenty
years, and that, too, by a long distance. In the word 'cricketer' I count not only
batting, bowling, and fielding. In these combined arts there is not one, not
Bradman, not Constantine, who could stand a full and unbiased comparison
with Hammond as he showed himself in the decade from 1925 to 1935; when
he would make a hundred or two against Australia, then bowl down their
first three wickets, then make with ease a slip-catch which others would not
merely miss but would not even have rated as a miss. But I count also those
things which cannot be translated into words, far less into print, but belong
to the brain and the heart. I mean the effect on a match of his presence alone;
the influence on a bowler's feelings of the sight of Hammond taking guard at
about 11.50 a.m., when lunch seemed far and the boundary near.

Such abstractions belong as surely to a batsman's greatness as do his
technical ability and his power to make the numbers rattle on the board. It
is something to have seen Hammond walk out to the Australians from the
pavilion at Lord's; a ship in full sail. There is a pride in possessing such a
player. There was an anxiety for his success, not only from party reasons but
because his failure would be an affront to sense, a slap in the face to Nature.
Surely he would do it to-day. And none that saw it will forget his batting on a
June Saturday in 1938. He gave one chance in an innings of 240, and that split
a fieldsman's finger.

As a batsman he has it all; and with double the strength of most players; strength scientifically applied. In his prime his hitting, mostly straight and through the covers, was of a combined power and grace that I have never seen in any other man. I can't think that human agency could do more to a ball. To field to him at cover-point was a sort of ordeal by fire. You would take a ball, perhaps, with as much give as possible and in the middle of the hands, then wring them. I have heard the criticism that he is not a good hooker. I never noticed the deficiency when I bowled him a straight long-hop. It is nearer the truth to say that his method and strength enabled him to play straight, or nearly straight, many short balls which other batsmen find easier to hook.

I have seen him in trouble to leg-break bowling, but not often. Far oftener I have seen a leg-breaker preparing footwork for a dodge from violent death. I have known him lose his wicket through what looked like a sudden failure of concentration, generally to fast bowling. And I believe that from the first, when he was a free and sometimes abandoned hitter, he had to learn and hardly acquire concentration. It was not born in him. For his method, when he is allowed to play as he wishes, and his conversation, both show that he regards fun as the first reason for cricket. He got as far as acquiring the iron temperament of Test Matches for the necessary period. But he never wholly enjoyed that mood, and it never sat comfortably on him. You should see him in a Festival.

As you would expect in such a player, he has generosity and humour, especially in his judgments of other cricketers, given quietly and with a twinkling eye. I chanced to meet him soon after close of play, when he'd been cut over by a rising ball in the Old Trafford Test against West Indies in 1933. 'Well,' he said, 'we began it, you know; and now you can see just a bit of what it was like. Just the luck of the game.'

Hammond is not only a great cricketer.

❧

A Cricket Pro's Lot

FRED ROOT

Fred Root (Derbyshire, Worcestershire and England) was a fast bowler who played first-class cricket from 1910 to 1932. *A Cricket Pro's Lot* was published in 1937.

HAROLD LARWOOD, WHOSE name ever crops up when body-line is mentioned, is too good a sportsman to blame (if blame is fair) any one but himself for his adopting methods which came under criticism by people who should have known better. But I always think I was to some extent responsible. Larwood certainly acquired the seed which germinated so suddenly, and with such far-reaching results, in season 1926. In several matches that season, 'Lol', as we all affectionately call Larwood, bowled like a hero, only to see the batsmen refuse to play at ball after ball pitched just outside the off-stump. I have seen him shyly relaxing in a corner of the dressing-room at night, disconsolately wondering why his whole-hearted efforts have been rewarded with such figuratively poor analyses in return for magnificent fast bowling. Opposite to him has sat the wicket-keeper, tenderly caressing bruised arms and hands, and the humorous side of the whole thing has suddenly appealed to all three of us.

On one occasion, when Billie Woodfull had been more than usually careful not to play at anything with the slightest suspicion of a slip catch suggested, Bert Strudwick said to Larwood, "'Lol', after tea we will go on the middle on our own. It seems a waste of time for the other nine to leave the comfort of the dressing-room!' The point of this remark lies in the fact that for nearly an hour Larwood and Strudwick had been the only players to handle the ball when 'Lol' was bowling from the Nursery end.

In those days Larwood was a delightfully inexperienced youngster, direct from a Nottinghamshire colliery, having achieved his meteoric success by dint of sheer speed. The tricks of the game were unknown to him and, to his credit, he soon used his brains to overcome the guile of the best batsmen in the world. He realized that his method of bowling for slip catches was more or less a sheer waste of strength, when tried against cricketers who possessed the patience of a Job, coupled with infallible judgment as to where the ball pitched. He simply had to make batsmen play at him somehow, so, after much thought, he began to bowl at the leg-stump. This change of tactics made a changed field imperative, slips had to be moved over to the leg side, first one, then two, and, finally, four or five, until what has so erringly become known as the body-line field was formed. By sheer force of circumstance the tables were turned. Instead of Larwood's strength being wasted, it became capitalized. When a batsman missed a ball, it either bowled him out, or hit him, he sustaining bruises the wicket-keeper had previously suffered.

Although I said earlier that season 1926 was the year 'Lol' first conceived the idea, so great was his reluctance to bowl in that way that he went to great pains to control the ball before launching it at batsmen. In 1930, on the occasion of the Australians' tour in England, he stuck to the old ineffective off-theory. His analysis for the Tests that season read: 101 overs, 18 maidens, 292 runs, 4 wickets, average 73.00. No one called him a world danger then, nor did we have any of the bickerings and suggestions of unfair tactics which were to cause so much trouble later on.

There, in a nutshell, is the whole history of the alleged body-line, the cause of its coming into being and its effects. To those readers who have questioned Larwood's methods let me say that no fairer bowler ever played the great game than 'Lol' – and possibly no better bowler. Nothing upset him more than hitting a batsman. He would much rather the batsman punished him. To suggest that he deliberately placed his leg-side field to enable him the better to bowl at the batsman is a slander beyond forgiveness. He used his brains, he used his skill, he used his pace, never with the slightest suggestion of the bully, always with scrupulous fairness to all opponents, whether Australians or English; and the tragedy of his life was brought about by narrow-minded, ignorant critics and chicken-hearted, inept batsmen who not only ran away, 'ducked', and dodged, but squealed even when they had reached the safe security of the pavilion.

Fast bowlers have unintentionally hit batsmen ever since the game was played, and will continue to do so as long as cricket continues. It is all very well to subscribe to all the sentimental nonsense that has been written on the subject 'for the good of the game'. What would the game be without a fast bowler whose main attribute is power to make lethargic batsmen jump about a bit? I hope neither 'diplomatic' intervention nor anything else will be allowed to be the means of the good old leather ball being abandoned in favour of a soft tennis ball, or any other such nonsense.

Could Larwood have developed the in-swinger (he tried unsuccessfully), he would have been the best bowler ever, and finicky batsmen would indeed have had something to talk about.

18

WHAT TO DO
WHILE WATCHING CRICKET

Dawn of The Blob

HARRY PEARSON

Harry Pearson is a writer and journalist. From *Slipless in Settle* (2010), which won the Cricket Society/MCC Book of the Year Award.

❧

THERE WAS A decade of my life when I attended first class or indeed any other form of cricket every chance I got. The eighties were a troubling time in Britain. There was social upheaval, strikes, turmoil and Saint and Greavsie. Some of my friends resorted to heroin. I went to county matches.

I invariably travelled with a workmate who was universally known as The Blob. The Blob was inoffensive enough, but the thought persisted that one day the police would find something nasty under his floorboards and the newspaper reports would say, 'colleagues describe the accused as a quiet man who kept himself to himself'.

The Blob was single, with the narrow shoulders and bulging bottom of an emperor penguin. He smelled much like one too, the result of living off a diet of fish-paste sandwiches. Fish paste comes in a jar that is the olfactory equivalent of the Tardis – it looks tiny from the outside but it houses a pong the size of a galaxy. The Blob's sandwiches were made from bread with the springy texture of disposable nappies and the moisture content of wet wipes. A vein of fish paste ran through the middle of them like self-deprecation through a Waugh family gathering. Luckily The Blob was not a sharer.

The Blob used words like palpable and plethora, referred to Lord's as 'HQ' and of batsmen making hay while the sun shone. I did the same myself. It seemed more or less impossible to speak of county cricket without sounding like *Test Match Special*'s Peter Baxter. Fogey was the lingua franca of what The Blob and I invariably referred to as the Summer Game.

The Blob and I did not talk much during play, I should say. He was far too busy to converse. He was a compulsive scorer. The Blob wrote down the details of every batsman's innings with a sombre gravity – St Peter in man-made fibres.

One Monday, shortly after I had first started working with The Blob, I asked him if he had enjoyed his weekend. 'Veritably,' he replied. 'I scored the Leicestershire Sunday League match.'

'You went up to Grace Road?' I asked.

'Oh no, just off the tellygoggin.'

I pictured the scene: the curtains drawn to cut out the glare, the stale biscuity odour of bachelorhood filling the room, The Blob, his freshly sharpened pencils lined up neatly on the arm of his chair, a Thermos of weak tea between his feet, acknowledging the umpires' signals with an upraised hand. It was a measure of the uncertainty of the times that I found the vision extremely comforting.

Why did I go to cricket with The Blob? Well, frankly, who else would go to watch county cricket? Northamptonshire versus Derbyshire at Bletchley is not an event that attracts a hip crowd. It is the sporting equivalent of C&A; carp fishing without the excitement of firing a catapult loaded with live maggots every few hours. The only thing likely to set your pulse racing at county cricket is a bolt of static from the bloke behind you's bri-nylon blouson.

The tiny crowd that assembled was largely the same whether at Worcester, Basingstoke, or Tring. There was a smattering of elderly ladies in cream macs who would occasionally lay down the baby jacket or bobble hat they were knitting and call for Norman Cowans to pitch the ball up, or for Ray East, the 'Clown Prince of Cricket', to amuse us once again by walking like a chicken.

There was also Mr Pavilion. He was at every cricket ground I visited, with his binoculars and his cool box. Some people came to cricket to watch. Mr Pavilion came to talk. Though not actually to anybody.

Mr Pavilion wore a panama hat, terry-cotton shirt, shorts that terminated with turn-ups, fawn socks and sensible sandals. I imagine he and his forbearers had worn this garb since time immemorial or at least since shepherds first hurled balls of wool at one another on the Sussex Downs and Mr Pavilion's ancestors called out 'pitch it up, man' or 'use your feet to the spinners, sir' or whatever other phrase he had plucked at random from *The Golden Treasury of Cricket Wisdom for All Occasions* (abridged from the original Latin by Thos. Carlyle).

A day with Mr Pavilion always passed the same way. The captains appeared. 'A vital toss to win,' Mr Pavilion announced in the general direction of one of the matrons, a vital prop without whom too many of his thoughts would, like desert blooms, blossom and die unknown. 'I'd bat if I were skipper.'

The side which unwillingly followed this course having called wrongly was promptly reduced to eleven for four; a state of affairs which aroused in Mr Pavilion a grave distemper for which he sought physic in nostalgia. 'Hutton and Washbrook would have batted through till tea on this strip . . . Hammond would have torn this attack to shreds . . . Archie MacLaren would have posted his fifty by now.'

As Mr Pavilion railed on and on you noticed that he was retreating further and further back in time, praising cricketers who retired long before he was born. You realised that if he carried on at the rate he was going he would work his way back through Grace and Felix and Alfred Minn [*sic*] and, in a couple of minutes, would be proclaiming: 'Then in this time of shadow came the one they called the run-bringer, the flayer of long-hops; and his name was Beowulf, Prince of the Scyldings, and he'd have treated this Neil Foster fellow with the contempt he deserves, I can tell you.'

Lunchtime came and Mr Pavilion opened the cool box. From it came a quantity of food such as would have tested the seams of umpire David Shepherd's shirt front: chicken legs, potato salad, coleslaw, ham and pâté, hard-boiled eggs, a bottle of Chablis, bags of crisps, punnets of strawberries. It went on endlessly; while I listened to the crunch of crisp lettuce and the slurping of cherry tomatoes, a polythene glass of beer in one hand and a damp carpet tile that was once, allegedly, a sandwich in the other, peevishly damning the idiocy of man who brings smoked trout to a cricket match.

After lunch, fortified, Mr Pavilion hit a vein of form as thick as Rio Ferdinand's wage packet. 'Four all the way,' he crowed as the batsman mistimed a drive and sent it rolling gently towards mid-on. 'Elegantly done, sir!' as a tail-ender aimed a mighty hoik at a half-volley and sent it skimming over the slips. 'Textbook defensive stroke!' as a number eleven prodded forward and lost his middle stump. This latter event afforded Mr Pavilion the opportunity to make his joke: 'An excellent shot,' he guffawed, 'if only he'd hit the ball.' By mid-afternoon the jollity and the Chablis had taken its toll and Mr Pavilion would fall asleep, jerking awake every once in a while with the startled look of somebody emerging from an erotic dream involving their in-laws.

Geoff Millets was another recognisable face in the crowd. With his beige anorak, his taupe sunhat and his pale blue easy-fit trousers Mr Millets appeared indistinguishable from the rest of the crowd but his blandness masked a deadly turn as surely as does the spinner's flight. One minute you were sailing merrily along, the next you were stumped. We went to cricket to watch, Mr Pavilion to talk – Mr Millets went for a good argument.

Mr Millets was a master of his craft. Youngsters watching at home would have been well advised to study his action. As he approached the possible disputation Mr Millets's movements were quick and furtive, his head swayed from side to side as his finely tuned hearing sought an opening. Suddenly his left ear picked up a phrase, 'Knight has got to be . . .' His hawk-like eyes quickly identified the speaker and never left him as he gathered himself ready to deliver, '. . . the best one-day batsman in England.'

That was Mr Millets's cue. 'Cobblers!' he yelped with the strangulated ferocity of a wrist spinner appealing for a bat-pad catch he knows he has no chance of getting. His chosen victim should have shouldered arms and offered no response, but Mr Millets had pushed him on to the back foot and lured him into the corridor of uncertainty. 'Sorry?' he replied.

'With all due respect,' Mr Millets would say, finding his insidious length, 'you are talking a load of rubbish.' With that, he closed in for the kill. And a slow and painful death it was too. An argument with Mr Millets was so long and labyrinthine it makes the average meeting of the Yorkshire committee look like a drag race.

Despite the passing years Mr Millets never lost his focus. He had a resident's parking permit in The Zone and once in the groove he could not be distracted by anything, particularly cricket. Nor would he let his victim relax. A friend of mine missed the whole of Ian Botham's seventy-nine-ball hundred at Old Trafford thanks to an injudicious remark about covered wickets. Another can remember nothing of Shane Warne's first spell of bowling against England except for the vague smell of scampi fries and the phrase 'Actually, I think you'll find . . .' To a third, the very mention of Graham Gooch's three hundred against India causes him to slump forward, put his head in his hands and whimper, 'OK, OK, Doug Walters' record in this country was better than people give him credit for' over and over again until he is sedated by a large gin and the talking book of Henry Blofeld's memoirs.

People say that you didn't have to get involved, but the fact of the matter was that when your number came up you couldn't cheat Geoff Millets. You couldn't beat him in an argument either. He had all the facts at his fingertips and he used them to chip away at an adversary: 'In fact it was versus Uttar Pradesh', 'If you check your *Wisden* you'll discover it was 33.72', 'Yes, but D. H. Robins's XI v T. N. Pearce's XI wasn't first class'. There was no escape. The best you could do was accept what was happening, sit back and admire one of the game's true artists.

The matrons, Mr Pavilion, Geoff Millets, me and The Blob. A young man in stone-washed jeans and a Freddy Starr Ate My Hamster T-shirt whose social skills were that he could drink twelve pints and still do a passable imitation of a peacock completed the happy multitude.

As the eighties gave way to the nineties I drifted out of The Blob's orbit and, finally wrestling the monkey of county cricket off my back, burned my scorecards and moved on.

Five years ago I met another former workmate. I asked him what had become of The Blob. 'Got married,' the bloke said. 'Got married?' I asked. 'Are you sure?' The bloke nodded. 'Some girl he met at Arundel when Lavinia, Duchess of Norfolk's XI were playing the Australians. Oddly enough her name is Wicket. She's a scorer too. They've got a couple of kids.'

I can picture them now at The Parks or Chesterfield, all in a row, heads down in concentration, the silence broken only by the occasional murmured, 'He must have got the faintest of snicks to that, though it looked like a bye to me.'

Diary of a Cricket Lover

VERNON COLEMAN

Vernon Coleman is a former GP and author of over a hundred books.
This *Diary* appeared in 1984.

~&

FRIDAY 24TH AUGUST

I HAPPENED TO BE in Bournemouth today and, finding myself with an unexpected hour to spare, I gave a taxi driver enough to buy himself a small home on the French Riviera to take me to the Hampshire ground.

I have always liked watching cricket near the sea. I do not know whether it is because the air is so exceptionally bracing or because the sight and sound of so many sea gulls bring back happy memories of seaside holidays and days of lazy pleasure. I did live on the south coast, once, at Shoreham, just a couple of miles along from Brighton, but although I thoroughly enjoyed the experience I was, in the end, quite glad to leave. The problem was that when you live by the sea you take it all for granted. All the excitement of a day trip to the coast disappears when you just have to wander a couple of miles down the road to see the breakers and buy a stick of rock.

The Hampshire ground was pretty empty when I got there and I found myself sharing most of one stand with an extremely earnest-looking gentleman whose bald head was burnt to a dark brown colour by the sun. We were sitting some twenty or thirty yards apart, and to begin with I took no notice of him at all. He had a large notebook stretched out across his knees and seemed engrossed in it.

I had not been sitting there for more than fifteen minutes when I was awoken from my pleasant reverie by the sound of a sudden isolated burst of applause. I looked across and saw that the hairless spectator with whom I was sharing the stand had put down his pencil and was clapping enthusiastically. I thought little of it. I could not see any cause for such a dramatic expression of approval but I had been dozing a little and I was not sure if I had missed a well-struck shot or a keenly flighted delivery.

It happened again after another ten minutes. Once more I could think of no explanation for the applause. And no one else on the ground was clapping. And then again after another quarter of an hour or so. So it went on. Four or five times in the next hour my companion suddenly shattered the silence with a fiercely appreciative round of applause. Curiosity aroused, I kept a very close eye on the balding enthusiast. When, after another thirty minutes or so, it was time for me to leave I made my way over to where he was sitting, hoping to have a word with him and find out just why he was clapping and just what I and the other spectators on the ground had been missing.

As you have undoubtedly guessed by now (I had not guessed although I admit I should have done), the balding gentleman with the large notepad on his knees was an enthusiastic Amateur Statistician. He was applauding minor milestones in his club's history. The difference was, however (and this explains why the other spectators had missed these statistical milestones and failed to celebrate them with a little palmar oscillation), that the lone statistician was keeping track neither of the batsmen nor of the bowlers.

He told me that he had for many a year harboured an earnest wish to make his mark on cricket statistics but that the almanacs and cricket magazines all had their own resident experts. There was, he reasoned, no opportunity for a statistician who recorded all the usual statistics about wickets taken and runs scored.

And so he had decided to specialise in fielders and fielding. While he kept his records meticulously up to date, he told me that he kept records of every time a fielder stopped a ball, let a ball go through, caught a ball, dropped one and every other missed opportunity. With the aid of a complex system of handicapping which I did not entirely understand, he had worked out a way to measure the number of runs that each individual fielder had saved. He had averages only for his own home county but he could tell me which fielders had the best averages and which fielders were worth their places for the runs they had saved.

And the clapping that I had not been able to understand? Well, every time a fielder reached a small personal milestone (50 runs saved in an innings, 200 runs saved in a season or whatever) then he clapped.

I left Bournemouth confused and just a little wiser, and convinced that the statisticians will eventually take over the game completely. I was very impressed by my bald friend's dedication and singlemindedness. I wonder if the statistical gurus will ever follow his example. Heaven help us if they do. We will all have raw hands.

How I Built my Wisden Collection

DEREK BARNARD

Derek Barnard is chairman of the Cricket Society.
First published in *The Journal of the Cricket Society* in 2011.

❧

I WAS FIELDING IN the slips for Crowborough on a Wednesday afternoon friendly match in the summer of 1981. At second slip a friend said: 'Derek, do you collect *Wisden?*'

'Why do you ask?' I replied.

'Oh, because I bought a few advertised in the *Friday Ad* (our local free paper) last week,' he said.

These comments set me thinking, and on returning home that evening, I lined up my *Wisdens* on the kitchen table. I had a run from 1965 (the first year I bought a *Wisden*) to 1981. This was not a large run but it did cover Kent's 'glory' years from the late 1960s to the late 1970s. Then I thought about trying to trace the career of my boyhood hero Colin Cowdrey through the pages of *Wisden* and realised that I would need a run commencing with 1946. Only then would I be able to trace that illustrious career from Tonbridge to Test Match.

Obtaining the copies from 1946 to 1964 was not difficult as I was able to purchase these from general book dealers at modest prices, and within a couple of months I had a complete run from the end of the Second World War to 1981. Whenever I travelled to another town on school or family business I always made a point of visiting the second-hand bookshops, and in late 1982 I made contact with Christine and Robert Swift who ran a second-hand bookshop in Maidstone. I asked them to ring me whenever they had any *Wisdens* in the shop prior 1946.

Yes, you have guessed it, for within a few days Robert rang to say that they had a run of softbacks from 1920 to 1939. The asking price was £200 (today it would be £2000) and Robert would be quite willing to accept my collection of Gillingham Football Club programmes in part exchange. I had to acquire these as I would now possess all the cricket between the two wars with the exception of 1939. Parting with the Gillingham programmes was a wrench but cricket had become my number one sport. (By the way, I have been a Gills supporter for 57 years and saw my first game in 1953.) Some of us have our burdens to carry in life.

A couple of weeks later Robert acquired 1940 to 1945 in linen covers. Actually I believe he always had them but just kept them back so that I could have my appetite whetted again. Yes, another run appeared later in the year (1899 to 1914) and with the agreement of my wife Sheila and the bank manager I paid for them with a £250 loan. So by late 1982 I had a run from 1899 to 1982 with the exception of the war years 1915 to 1919 inclusive.

At about this time a friend suggested that a new Index to *Wisden* was needed and I approached MacDonald and James (owned by Robert Maxwell) to see if they were interested in my idea. They were, so I needed access to all the other *Wisdens*.

Martin Wood from Sevenoaks very kindly supplied 1916 and spread payment over three months, and the other war years were bought via the specialist dealers like John Mackenzie and John Eastwood. Facsimiles of the 1864 to 1878 issues were obtained from John Eastwood (these had belonged to comedian Tony Hancock's brother Roger), and reading copies of 1879 to 1898 from other collectors like Carl Openshaw who had spares. I did not mind the condition of the books – they just had to be readable. Over the years I have gradually replaced the softbacks with original hardbacks but this has now become a very expensive business. Recently an original hardback sold for £20,000 at auction.

Collectors of *Wisden* were dealt an excellent hand when the Willows Publishing Company decided to do reprints from 1879. They commenced this in 1991 and to date have reached 1930. These volumes are gradually increasing in value as all of them have been produced in a limited print run of usually 500 copies.

So today I possess a complete run thanks to the forbearance of my wife and the bank manager who was always willing to help. Friends have helped me by directing me to shops and sometimes even putting a deposit on a book until I could go and inspect it. No, I have not read every *Wisden* from cover to cover (I do intend to do so in the near future) but I think I know as much as anyone about the 'Cricketer's Bible'.

And the bargain buy? An 1874 original which I bought in a bookshop in Rye in 1984 for £4 and the lady apologised about the price!

Eliza Watches Cricket

R. L. HODGSON

R. L. Hodgson wrote under the nom-de-plume 'A Country Vicar'.
From *Second Innings* (1933).

❧

ANGELA HAS A relative, who lives in London. We always stay with her for the University Match, and on other occasions when we go up to see cricket.

[. . .] A charming hostess she is, but not a sportswoman. She is never quite sure, I fancy, in what months cricket is played. At least, she has been known to inquire when Angela and I were starting for Twickenham, on a Tuesday in December: 'Let me see! Is it cricket or football to-day?'

Sometimes – not often – Eliza accompanies us to Lord's. She is an enthusiastic cricketer, in theory. No one is keener that England should beat Australia! No one is more desirous for Cambridge to defeat Oxford! But, when it comes to watching the actual game, she is apt to make mistakes. There are points of detail, on a cricket-ground, which appear to her mysterious.

I realised this on the first occasion we took her with us. The match was M.C.C. v. Philadelphian Pilgrims, in August, 1921; and the score board announced: 'Last wicket fell at 230'. Eliza gazed at the sentence, looked at her watch, compared her time with the clock in the tower, and then spoke: 'Why do they say that?' she asked indignantly.

'Say what?' we responded.

'"Last wicket fell at two-thirty", when *it is not yet two o'clock!*'

[. . .] Eliza expressed her enjoyment of that visit to Lord's. She was delighted with the result of the match: she rejoiced that (to quote her own words) 'England had beaten America!' It was vain to point out that cricket is not America's game – that they play it but little except in Philadelphia – and that the visitors were simply a team of Philadelphian cricketers on holiday.

'Isn't Philadelphia in America, and are not Philadelphians Americans?' she asked fiercely.

One was forced to assent.

'And is not the M.C.C. English?'

There was but one possible answer.

'Very well, then! England *has* beaten America, and I'm glad of it! I don't like Americans, but I like cricket! I'll come again with you and watch it!'

She has done so. Once or twice a year, on an average, she renews her acquaintance with the game. But, even now, I doubt whether she realises fully how a match is conducted. She knows that two rival teams are in opposition; but, quite recently, she was in grave doubt as to whether the two batsmen were on the same side, or opponents. She asked the question!

As a matter of fact, for one who has never played and has no real knowledge of cricket, the various movements must be a little confusing. Why the 'over', and the consequent crossing to new positions in the field? Why this and that? So many doubtful points!

I think Eliza has almost abandoned the attempt to understand the whys and wherefores. Her interest in cricket has become, in the main, personal. She takes a liking for some individual player and, forthwith – so to speak – adopts him. Eliza is artistic and admires beauty, so the individual honoured is, usually, a young Apollo. But, strangely enough, he may be very small and plain: if he is also entirely unsuccessful that seems, in her eyes, to add to his charm – especially if he looks pathetic! She has a warm and kindly heart, and creatures in distress always arouse her sympathy.

Lord's Schools v. The Rest is a match she likes particularly: if we were always able to get to London for the first Monday in August, she would attend it annually. Oxford v. Cambridge she also finds attractive; and Eton v. Harrow, though for the crowd, rather than the cricket. She has not much use for County Championship games and the stern struggle for points. She prefers a rapidly-mounting score, quick changes and sustained excitement: she resembles Angela in that – it must be a family weakness. But Eliza possesses a very useful idiosyncrasy: whenever she is in the slightest degree bored she falls asleep!

It was when suddenly roused from slumber that she voiced what we consider her best saying, up-to-date. We – Angela, Eliza, and I – were watching a Middlesex fixture: at least, Angela and I were watching, and Eliza was dozing. 'Patsy' Hendren – Angela's favourite cricketer – had passed his century and was still undefeated when the last man joined him. He remained undefeated when the innings closed, and walked to the Pavilion amid thunderous applause.

The cheers awoke Eliza. 'Has something happened?' she inquired.

'"Patsy" has carried his bat!' Angela proclaimed with justifiable pride. 'Isn't it splendid?'

'Has he?' Eliza cried excitedly. *'Did the other man throw it down?'*

It was not she – though it might almost have been – who made the remark about the weathercock on the Grand Stand at Lord's.

'I see,' said this somewhat short-sighted lady, 'that they've put the figure of a man up there – a man with a beard. Was there not, once, a famous cricketer with a beard? I'm sure there was, and I remember his name. It was Dr. W. G. Grace. I suppose that's a statue of him. How very suitable!'

One day, Eliza may even eclipse that! Angela and I live in hope!

Name Dropping

FRANK KEATING

Frank Keating is the *Guardian's* former chief sports writer.
From *Long Days, Late Nights* (1984).

❧

I SPENT A DAY with Jackie Stewart, the former motor racing ace, at his sumptuous home above Lake Geneva. At lunch the subject of childhood heroes came up, and between pudding and coffee Jackie was away upstairs rummaging in his attic – to come down triumphantly with a battered, old autograph book.

It had been his most treasured possession – more so even than his first set of spanners – back in the 1950s when he was an apprentice garage mechanic in Dumbartonshire and had occasionally travelled with his elder brother, Jimmy, to the racetracks down south. There they all were . . . squiggles of Hawthorn, Ascari, Farina, Brooks, and – still Stewart's most coveted – Stirling Moss.

Are today's kids still at it? 'Sign here, please, Mister?' Or has the adventure, let alone the simple, wide-eyed romance, gone out of sport for a generation weaned on the inane, so-called intimacies of television after-match quotes, or meaningless newspaper confessions? If the 1930s were for cigarette cards, my 40s and 50s were for autograph collecting. What do they collect now? Anyway, I suppose one Henry Kelly is worth ten Henry Coopers.

The first autograph I 'collected' was Charlie Barnett's. He was Gloucestershire's opening bat – and once completed a corking century for England at Trent Bridge by rattling the first ball after lunch to the pickets for four. He hit as fiercely as he looked down on us local oiks. He owned wet-fish shops in Cirencester and Cheltenham and rode with the Beaufort and Berkeley foxhounds. He lived at Chalford, near Stroud, and one day a friend and I rode our bicycles up the winding Cotswold Hill and lay in wait with our brand new autograph books. He came neither in nor out, and we were far too scared to knock boldly on the front door. Then I had a brainwave. Charlie's daughter, Judy, was at the local convent school, in the same class as my sister. A modest bribe was negotiated and, lo and behold, a couple of days later, the book came back with Page One inscribed 'Best of luck, Francis – C. J. Barnett'.

It was cheating. But I was off. That was the early summer of 1947 and by the end of August's Cheltenham Festival I had the whole of the Gloucester team and quite a few of the 'visitors' too. Most valued of those was 'W. J. Edrich', and when, two years later, I nabbed the amiable, scatty sig. 'Denis Compton', on the same page, I headed it in my wayward, juvenile capitals 'THE MIDDLE SEX TWINS', making two words out of the London county in an unknowing, but interesting, Freudian slip.

My big coup of 1948 was to get the Australians. I simply sent my book to the Visitor's Dressing Room at Worcester at the end of April, marked 'For the attention of Mr Donald Bradman'. Back came a sheet of paper, on which all of them had written their names. It remains, perhaps, the finest side ever to tour. I breakfasted that morning in heaven.

Many years later the cricket historian, David Frith, warned me about second-hand signatures. He said he once knew a pre-war Aussie Test player who had been lumbered with a thousand autograph sheets on the boat coming over and to prove it had reeled-off for him a near-perfect Bradman, O'Reilly and Oldfield!

I suspected none of that in 1948. Wretchedly and alas, I have lost that old, beloved autograph book in the general jetsam of moving on, but I can still close my eyes and recall The Don's neat little, joined-together writing, 'D. G. Bradman'. If I keep them closed, I could still do you a passable forgery of the upright, well schooled 'W. A. Brown' or the cack-handed 'A. R. Morris' or his lefty apprentice, 'R. N. Harvey'. I drooled over them and I learned them almost by heart: 'C. McCool' was the most juvenile and unstylish of handwriting, and 'W. A. Johnston' and 'D. Ring' the most confusing couple of scrawls. You had to work those two out by a process of elimination. The two wicketkeepers, 'D. Tallon' and 'R. A. Saggers' were straightforward and standing up. 'R. A. Hamence' was schoolmasterly, well formed and correct.

Sid Barnes, cobber, and clobbering opening bat plus suicide-point fielder, was the only one to 'sign' his name with a rubber-stamp – 'S. G. Barnes' bashed out from an exciting, tearaway's, purply-coloured inkpad. The mesmerizing Miller signed just as the legend said he did – writing a very readable, sub-copperplate 'eith ille', and then adding the capitals, 'K' and 'M', with a gorgeous and flowering flourish.

That stuck-in sheet remained the highspot of my collection. I kept it going for another ten years or so. I had T. E. Bailey before he started writing 'Trevor' as his prefix, and likewise D. B. Close before he was 'Brian'. I got Tommy Lawton from soccer, and Dai Dower from boxing. I had a genuine Billy Wright, too – in person one evening when he opened a local soccer ground. I knew by then that the boaster's knack was to have approached them personally, not to write enclosing your book and the old s.a.e.

Once, at school, I stole from a friend's desk (just to own for a morning, and look, honest!) a piece of paper bearing the signature of a Cheshire dentist who that summer had played for England at cricket. It had been, temptingly, in an envelope marked 'Lancs CCC'.

This prep school was in the habit of having snap personal checks and searches whenever it happened to take the fancy of suspicious Benedictine monk teachers. Suddenly, that very morning, they announced a turnout of desks and pockets. Wherever we were, we had to freeze and wait for these ancient suss laws to be enacted. The stolen, valued, piece of paper was in my pocket. Briefly, I panicked. Then I did the only thing a hoodlum could do. Uneasy, but still unsuspected, I transferred the stolen piece of paper from pocket to hand; then I coughed and sneezed to create an innocent's disturbance as the fuzz approached; they were unaware that at the same time as I was snuffling, I was popping the guilty thing into my mouth. I am the only man I know to have actually eaten the signature of 'K. Cranston (Lancs & England)'.

I suppose I've become more cynical since, when Gloucestershire played a few county matches at Stroud, I daringly asked 'B. D. Wells' to add his much loved nickname to his autograph in my book – and he did, with a smile and a snappy line in inverted commas: *'Best regards, The Bomber'*.

Esther Rantzen might have made an important point when she once said, 'I don't know why these autograph-hunters don't just forge them: no-one would ever know.'

At Gloucester Wagon Works ground, Fred Trueman once lined up all us kids. The queue was as long as an M4 'tailback' in today's holiday season. Trueman asked each of us our name before planting that personalized, and hugely treasured, set of initials in our book – 'To Francis, from F. S. T.'. Yet, over a quarter of a century later, on the radio, Fred was sneering the other day at those faithful signature-sentries who have ever followed him. 'I dunno,' he said, 'men keep comin' up an' sayin' they want my autograph f'their nephew. I tell them blunt: if y'want me signature f'your nephew, then I'll get me own nephew t'sign the ruddy thing.'

Not the sort of thing we pleading, shaking, quaking autograph-hunters want to hear. Fred never toured India with England. Tony Lewis did, as captain in 1972. He was a marvellously civil, genteel, humorous and much-loved leader. In India you have to be; they worship cricket. Five hundred autographs a day is the norm even for a visiting net bowler. Lewis would sign his name into the night. One day, at Bangalore or Kanpur, or wherever, a man knocked on his door each hour of the day prior to the Test Match – 'My dear uncle, Lewis-sahib, please sign these sheets of paper for my big and beloved family!'

Tony would readily and dutifully sign each proffered piece 'A. R. Lewis'. By the second day of the Test, a gateman at last felt himself duty-bound to approach the England captain. Surely he had been too profligate with his invitations. Every sheet Tony had signed had been topped and tailed with the typewritten legend 'Please admit to Test Match. Signed, A. R. Lewis, Captain of England'.

The greats sign. I have seldom known Jack Nicklaus, Bjorn Borg, Pele or, if you plot the course to a quiet corner, Lester Piggott, refuse to sign an autograph. The most ready, and willing, and friendly signer of anyone I have observed over the years is the boxer, Muhammad Ali. He would go out of his way, even rip pages from spivvy autograph books to sign and give to kids in the queue who only had cigarette packets to offer.

Once, before some faraway fight, I asked him to sign a programme for my twelve-year-old nephew. 'Put "To Mark, Keep punching, Yrs Ali",' I asked, and the great man duly did, although he was going into the ring within minutes.

I sent it off proudly by airmail. When I got home, I asked to see the famous signature. Said Mark's father: 'I'm sorry you asked about that. I'm afraid he swopped it last week – for two Lou Macaris!'

19

TEA INTERVAL

A Two-Days' Innings

A. A. LILLY

A. A. (Dick) Lilley (Warwickshire and England) was the leading wicket-keeper of
his era and played thirty-five Tests for England. He is referring to the custom of
presenting the match ball to a player after a game because of a good performance.
Arthur Shrewsbury was a leading batsman for Nottinghamshire and England
between 1875 and 1902, and Johnny Briggs was an England teammate.
From *Twenty-Four Years of Cricket* (1912).

❧

IN THIS MATTER of presenting a ball to a player I am reminded of a story
Arthur Shrewsbury told me many years ago of an incident that happened to
him during an early tour in Australia. It appeared that in one of the matches
a certain Australian bowler happened to take his wicket, and was so proud of
the feat that he had the ball duly mounted and inscribed with the fact that
it was the ball with which he had bowled Arthur Shrewsbury without the
latter scoring off him. Some time later the same bowler was again opposed to
Shrewsbury, but this time did not repeat his former success. In fact, Shrewsbury
was particularly severe upon him, and continued so during the two days he
was at the wickets, when he was still unbeaten.

After the luncheon interval on the first day Shrewsbury said to Briggs, in
the hearing of this bowler, just before they were going on to the field, 'Johnny,
you might bring me a cup of tea out about four o'clock.' 'All right, Arthur,' says
Johnny, 'I'll be there' – nothing like giving plenty of confidence to the bowler!
The next morning before they went in Briggs said to Shrewsbury, still in the
hearing of this interested individual, 'Shall I bring you a cup of tea out this
afternoon, Arthur?' 'Thanks, Johnny, it will be very acceptable; it looks like
being a hot day.' Johnny Briggs took out that cup of tea!

At the conclusion of the innings Shrewsbury obtained possession of
the ball, and also had it mounted and inscribed with the bowler's name, and
the fact that it was the particular ball with which he had bowled at Arthur
Shrewsbury for two days without obtaining his wicket. The great batsman
presented him with this ball as a companion to the other.

❧

Tennyson's Captaincy at Leeds

ROBERT LYND

Robert Lynd was an Irish writer. This extract is from
The Sporting Life and Other Trifles (1922). The match is the third Test against
Australia at Headingley in 1921, perhaps best remembered for Tennyson
making 63 while batting with a badly damaged hand.

❧

THE FIELD AT Headingley is as round as that Round Table concerning
which the Hon. Lionel Tennyson's grandfather wrote a great deal of verse
that Englishmen no longer read. On the first day of the third Test Match it
scarcely looked like a field at all.

If you can imagine a long-disused billiard-table on which people have
been spilling tea and stout and cigarette ashes for a hundred years you will
get some notion of the ruin that had been wrought upon the grass by the
incessant sun. It had as many colours as Joseph's coat, and they were all the
wrong colours. It had been carefully valeted, no doubt, but none the less it was
frayed, faded, and in rags.

A Yorkshireman assured me that nothing worth calling a crowd was
present. Thirty-three thousand people have been known to pack themselves
into the ground, and on Saturday there were only twenty-one thousand.

I do not know where the other twelve thousand could have been fitted
in. The ground seemed to me to be overflowing with human beings right
up to the top of the walls, and the overhanging elder bushes. Large family
parties had collected on the balconies of the slated brick villas that overlook
the ground.

It was the first Test Match of the year at which thousands of the spectators
wore straw hats, and of these thousands hundreds wore handkerchiefs under
their hats to protect the backs of their necks from the evil eye of the sun.

Not that the heat was overwhelming; there was a current of coolness in
the air. What made the day almost intolerable, however, was a gramophone,
or rather a stentorphone, that bellowed advertisements at us during the waits.
It asked us in a voice louder than was ever used for selling coal in the streets,
'Have you read the —?' mentioning a paper of which you have perhaps never
even heard the name.

At length the crowd could endure it no longer, and groaned in impotent despair at each new mention of the paper. I foresee a time when all the rival papers will have stentorphones at cricket matches shouting raucously against each other like bookmakers. It is one way of destroying the peace of the cricket field, and bringing it nearer the ideal of a Bank Holiday on Hampstead Heath.

Seventy-One Not Out

WILLIAM CAFFYN

William Caffyn was a highly regarded cricketer of the mid-nineteenth century. This story, from his autobiography *Seventy-One Not Out* (1900), is from the 1854 season.

THERE IS A STORY told of one celebrated bowler who was generally engaged by local twenty-twos to oppose the All-England Eleven. The bowler, it appears, owed a debt of £12 or so, for which he was greatly pressed, and was at his wits' end to know how to pay it. He, however, at last made an arrangement with his creditor to have himself arrested on the —cricket-ground just prior to the commencement of a match. This arrangement was carried out, the bowler counterfeiting much surprise at the proceedings. The local cricketing authorities were in a great way at the prospect of being deprived of the services of their eminent bowler, and after a short consultation sent the hat round and quickly collected the required amount to set him at liberty – which was exactly what the bowler had anticipated would be done!

The Diary of Thomas Turner

THOMAS TURNER

Thomas Turner was a shopkeeper of East Hoathly, Sussex, whose diary (1754–65) contains occasional references to local cricket matches. This entry is from 1758.

❧

TUES. 20 JUNE. This is my birthday and the day on which I enter the thirtieth year of my age. How many ere they have arrived at this age have been cut off and taken out of this world, probably in the midst of their sins! Therefore as it hath pleased the Almighty Disposer of all events to give me my health and life, how careful should I be that I live not in vain, that as I daily increase in age, so may I also improve and increase in all virtue and godliness of life, for if we only look back and reflect upon the time that is past, we shall find him that lives to the greatest age will have room to say with holy psalmist that our days are passed as it were a tale that is told. Therefore my sincere wish is that I may ever endeavour to lay hold on the present minute, that when my exit shall be, I may evermore live a life of happiness and bliss . . . After dinner my brother came over, and I rode behind him to Eason's Green (where there was a cricket match a-playing between Framfield and Isfield) . . . Framfield beat their antagonists at one innings (though there were two played) . . .

❧

Cricket Memories

EDWARD RUTTER

Edward Rutter played cricket and served on MCC and Middlesex CCC
committees in the nineteenth century. His *Cricket Memories* appeared in 1925.
Julius Caesar (1830–78) played first-class cricket between 1849 and 1867.
V. E. Walker was one of seven cricket-playing brothers of the same era.

❧

V. E. WALKER HAD A good story, too, about Lockyer, the famous wicket-
keep, and Julius Caesar, an equally notable cricketer. They were playing
for the United XI v. a country XXII. It had begun to rain at the close of the
match, but the last two men of the XXII were offering a stubborn defence and
looked like playing out time. One of them hit a ball hard past Caesar to the
edge of the ground, which was a very small one, and through a coconut shy
set up for the amusement of spectators. Caesar, however, instead of pursuing
it, snatched up one of the nearest coconuts, threw it full pitch and accurately
to Lockyer, who whipped off the bails, put the coconut inside his shirt and
ran for the tent, followed by the field. The match was won! Everybody ran
for shelter, or for home, and if a few spectators saw Caesar's achievement
they were doubtless irresponsible folk who hurried off like the rest – the ball
probably found its haven in a ditch.

❧

Two Cricket Grounds

E. V. LUCAS

E. V. Lucas was a prolific writer and essayist on cricket.
From *London Revisited* (1926).

❧

ONE LITTLE PIECE of special Oval lore I can impart. Near Vauxhall Bridge Station there is a church, and this church has an open space, or unglazed window, in its spire. If the light through this window, as seen from the Pavilion is clear, there will be no rain; but if one can only just see through it, rain is likely.

❧

Hints to Young Players

WILLIAM SAPTE

William Sapte was a humorous writer of the nineteenth and early twentieth centuries. This list is from his *Cricketer's Guyed* for 1886.

❧

1. Always play with a full-size bat unless you can get a larger one. It will then be impossible for you, as you are probably about four feet high, to play with a straight bat.

2. Hit at everything that is slow: if you miss it, you *may* stop in; if you are unfortunate enough to strike it, you will be caught.

3. Run away from everything that is fast, but remember to drag your bat with you, or the ball may knock it and jar your fingers.

4. Start for a run whatever happens, unless, indeed, you have sent up a high catch. In that case wait and watch it.

5. Never try to throw until you have learnt to bowl. Then *gradually* introduce a bent arm and whatever else constitutes an unfair delivery, as it is sometimes called in fun. Do not, as a rule, throw more than three balls out of five.

6. Sacrifice everything to pace, as only professional bowlers really need know anything of pitch, spin, or length.

7. In fielding, stand with your legs wide apart; the ball is less likely to hit them.

8. Whenever you miss a catch, rub your finger on the palm of your hand vigorously. People will then think you are hurt, and will not blame you anything like so much as they might otherwise.

9. If ever you see anybody else miss a catch, applaud vigorously, and call out 'Butter fingers!' It is good form.

10. If ever you are captain of your side, go on to bowl first and don't take yourself off. Also go in first in both innings. These things show confidence in yourself.

11. Leave off when you are tired, especially if the other side hasn't had an innings.

❧

Hints to Old Players

WILLIAM SAPTE

This list is also from Sapte's *Cricketer's Guyed* for 1886.

1. Study carefully the revised laws of the game as given in the Guyed, and read up vols. 1–4 of Lillywhite's 'Scores and Biographies'.
2. Take the most prominent seat in the pavilion, and put your feet on the one in front of you.
3. Take care that your face be very red.
4. Talk very loudly.
5. Run down everybody who has played since 1860, especially Dr. W. G. Grace.
6. On no account be tempted to lay hands on a bat, lest you betray the fact that you have never done so before. Praise the bats of your own day.
7. On no account be tempted to bowl a ball. If you attempt round-hand, you will hurt yourself; if underhand, you will discover that you are too stout. Praise the balls of your own day.
8. Should the ball ever come near you, do not attempt to stop it with your hands, but point your stick at it.
9. Remember, should you ever be asked to field for a minute or two, there is more mathematical probability of your being struck in the stomach than on the hands. It is a question of superficial area.
10. If you hear that any boy is a promising cricketer, promise him a bat if he makes 200 without a chance. He is not likely to do it, and you will be deemed a liberal patron of the game.
11. Swear at the lunch and at the waiter.
12. Get on the committee of the club if you can.
13. Let them get you off if *they* can.

20

EXTRAS

A Cricket Match in 2000 A.D.

W. J. FORD

After a brief first-class career, W. J. Ford (1853–1904) became a schoolmaster.
From *A Cricketer on Cricket* (1900).

❧

I HAD RETURNED FROM watching a big match at Lord's, had dined with discretion, and was enjoying tobacco in an arm-chair, reading the while a somewhat tough book on the occult sciences of the East – Mahatmas, Tibetans, and the like – when falling into that semi-drowsy state, which arises partly from the unwonted concentration of thought which a difficult subject requires, partly from the enjoyment of the good things in life, I seemed to have acquired on a sudden a portion of these occult powers.

Cricket was mixed with esoteric Buddhism, cricketers with Mahatmas, and projecting my astral self some 100 years forward into time, I seemed to materialize at Lord's into my physical self, and to be standing in the pavilion, talking to the secretary.

He seemed, as is the way in dreams, to be more surprised at my unauthorized presence than at my knowledge of the past and my ignorance of the present, and he answered my questions with the kindly courtesy that is the inheritance of MCC secretaries.

The ground had an aspect of familiar unfamiliarity, the pavilion of 1890, moss-grown and ivy covered, was faced by a similar structure of similar size; while a gigantic series of stands surrounded the rest of the playing area, accommodating, I was told, some 30,000 people with ease.

'But are these huge places often filled?'

'Always when there is a big match, for people are well-to-do, and can easily earn in three days enough to keep them in comfort for the week; food, clothes, and other necessaries are now so cheap, owing to the improvements in machinery, etc.'

'And what is that curious tower with steel poles?'

'A wireless telegraph, which connects us direct with all the chief cricket grounds, and automatically registers the scores on those two huge screens; hence evening "cricket specials", such as you used to have, I believe, have no sale here. Nor have cards, for on those big scoring boards are recorded, as you see, the names of the players, the hits and scores of the batsmen, together with the bowling analysis up to the latest moment. I believe cards used to be sold in your time containing this information?'

'That is so, and the boy was always "sold out" before he got to me. Are there similar arrangements elsewhere?'

'Oh, dear me, yes; counties would refuse to play on a ground not properly equipped.'

'Has anything been done to put batsmen and bowlers on a level?'

'Not a great deal, as far as the alteration of the rules is concerned, for cricketers are (and I suppose, were) the most jealous and tenacious conservatives, but the new pitches quite prevent either abnormally high or abnormally low scoring, to say nothing of the new retirement system. I say "new", because they were only introduced about forty years ago, and so are new to you.'

'About the new pitches, then: what are they?'

'They are made of turf, but of a special composition, the ingredients of which are a trade secret, which has all the spring and elasticity of good turf, and yet allows the bowler to get on plenty of break, if he is skilful enough. By "plenty of break" I mean that a really clever bowler will make a good length-ball pitch on the off-stump, and hit, or even miss, the leg stump. This composition is unaffected by the sun or rain, and is laid down in slabs, like the slates of a billiard table, and with equal care. The facilities given to the bowler are thus largely increased, but the difficulties are not so great but that a good batsman may overcome them, while, better still, every match is played under exactly the same conditions, save the varying skill or luck of the players. It would never do to eliminate the personal equation, and even with these wickets the best man is not always the best man.'

'But suppose it rains. Surely the greasy ball handicaps the out side.'

'Not to any great extent; well look! They are just coming in to avoid the thunderstorm.'

I did look, and from under the stands shot a long cylinder, which unwound, as it went, a light waterproof fabric which covered the whole ground. The rain came down in torrents, but the water flowed off by proper conduits to a reserve tank, whence it was again drawn when the turf required watering.

'Then your groundsman's business,' said I, 'is to look after the fielding-ground rather than the wicket?'

'Exactly,' said the secretary; and I could do no more than murmur 'Tempora mutantur.' [Times are changing.]

I picked up a bat that had been laid on the table by one of the waiting batsmen, and tried it in the orthodox fashion, testing the spring of the handle, and wagging it to and fro as in back or forward play. 'I didn't know,' said my informant, 'that you had cricket in – I mean, where you come from.'

'Oh well, I haven't forgotten everything. You don't seem, however, to have made any change at all in the bats.'

'Look at that one closely,' he said smilingly; and I looked, and behold! It was not made of willow nor of any wood that I recognized. He answered my look of interrogation with, 'Aluminium-steel amalgam – lightness and strength combined. The bat is hollow; the face, you can feel, is flexible, elastic, what you will, and "gives" under pressure: hence it has all the driving power attributed to your wooden bats, of which we have a few in the writing room as curiosities, but we haven't been able to improve on their shape, any more than on the balls, which are identical to your own, but for a little improvement in materials and manufacture. As to the bats, you see the demand on English willow was too great for the supply, and for some reason or another foreign willow was never satisfactory.'

'Ah, I remember,' I answered, 'an American told me that very thing in 1897, Jubilee year, and said that all their bats were imported from England.'

'Well, willow trees – proper seasoned old willow trees gave out, so that after many experiments this amalgam was hit upon, and very well it works.'

'Does it drive well?'

'Yes, and not too well: at least no one has ever beaten your friend Thornton's record; you were a contemporary of his?'

'Yes.'

'And of Grace, then, of course? We have all heard of him and his feats, and if you ever meet him – er, anywhere – you might tell him that he still holds a good many records.'

At this moment the bell rang, the cylinders (driven by liquid air, I was told) rolled back, and play began.

I watched with much interest, but saw no very new features; there was bowling of all kinds, and batting of all styles; short slip missed a catch, as in the good old days, and mid-off dropped on his right knee to stop a hot drive. This seemed familiar, and I cudgelled my bewildered brains to all into the line of thought, when suddenly all came back to me and I said aloud, but half to myself: 'Stoddy!'

'No,' said my friend, 'Stoddart is the gentleman's name: I believe his grandfather used to play a little.'

Play a little! Shades of Middlesex, Gentlemen vs Players, Australia vs England! And I turned around to give a short recital of his feats, but fortunately refrained: fortunately for I remembered the cricket bore of 1900, with his interminable stories about the heroes he had seen in the days when I was trying to kick my toes through my long clothes, which stories always ended in uncomplimentary remarks on the game as then played and the exponents thereof.

I was pleased to note that practically no improvements had been made in the materials of the game: stumps, bails, pads, gloves and balls were only better in that the workmanship and material were of a higher class, but I noted that batsmen and bowlers wore special soles for the composition pitches, fitted on a sort of skeleton golosh, properly spiked, for fielding purposes. Full of interested inquisitiveness, I began to pump my friend the secretary further.

'You said something about a "retirement system": what is it?'

'Oh, it works well and simply; when a man has got 30 he retires and "stars a life", as at billiards; i.e., if he gets out before he has got 30 in the second innings, he has another life. Then when all four innings have been played the "stars" on either side, if there are any left, go in, with the not-out, of course, and play till one side or another is "dead". Under this system, which it is hard to explain in detail, supported by our special pitches, drawn matches are unknown, for the batsman has to "play himself in" perhaps three or four times in the same match; indeed 150 is a good average score for the side, and two days are quite enough for a match. Travelling again is so easy and quick that three matches a week are no great tax. Without this we could never get a proper county competition, now that nearly all counties are first-class. Ah, Rutlandshire are all out, and only one "star", that looks bad for the championship. Would you like to look at the pitch?'

There was nothing in the world that I desired so much, so we strolled out, I wondering at the absence of tall hats and black coats, but I learned that nothing of a 'black or subfusc hue' was now tolerated on cricket grounds, so that the dark background, the batsman's bugbear, was gone for ever. I looked at the new pitch with much interest; it had a distinct nap on it, to imitate turf;

it looked ideal, and it was set in the middle of the ground, one of the new laws being that from the centre of the pitch to the boundary the distance must not be less than 80 or more than 100 yards. 'This gives the sloggers a chance,' said my friend.

I noticed on the pitch that the wickets stood on a strip of a darker tint than the rest of the composition, and naturally asked the reason.

'That is to help the umpires in deciding l.b.w. The dark strip is 16 inches across, twice the breadth of the wicket; if the ball pitches on it and the batsman interposes his leg, he is out l.b.w., if the umpire thinks the ball would have hit the wickets. The umpire finds the difference in colour a great help, but always remembers the adage of your days, "when in doubt, not out". Of course with diminished scoring, the follow-on has quite disappeared, and our modern critics regard it as quite a clumsy contrivance.'

'Well, it was; and it cost many a deserving side a match, besides giving rise to heinous scandals or "incidents", as we called them.'

The secretary looked puzzled; this was ancient history to him with a vengeance.

'By the way,' said I, 'how does your new system work with regard to averages?'

'Averages!' he answered rather contemptuously, 'we have done away with them long ago. They did harm enough in your day, if the records in Somerset House can be trusted, as I presume they can. We play to win matches, not to make averages; and we have done away with maiden overs, or at least with the exhibition of them on the score-sheets. Our legislation has been guided by one main consideration – to give the bowler a chance, and the batsman a chance, together with a fair value for the batter's hits. You must have noticed that three-foot fence all round the ground. If the ball clears it the stroke counts six; but if the ball hits it, the stroke counts two plus the runs the batsman can run in addition; this principle keeps the batsman on the trot, and the fieldsman on the watch, to judge the angle of the rebound. I wonder you never thought of so simple a device.'

'Well, we'd plenty to do, and I think we did it pretty well, leaving you a capital foundation on which to put your superstructure. One question more: How do you deal with "chuckers"?'

'Do you mean men who throw, and don't bowl? We let them throw, and find them no more dangerous than bowlers, as far as getting wickets is concerned; but we handicap all bowlers including throwers, by making them bowl or throw not less than six yards from the wicket; if they bowl short of that line, it is a no-ball; if they hit the batsman as well, it's four no-balls. Consequently, fast bowlers have to be very careful of their length, and they are. Must be going? Well, good-bye; so glad to have met you; hope you will be up here again soon; I should like to chat about old times. Au revoir.'

And then I bethought me of bed.

The First Netting-Boundary Game

ANDREW WARD

Andrew Ward has written many books about sport.
This extract is from *Cricket's Strangest Matches* (1990).

❧

THE GAME BETWEEN MCC & Ground and Nottinghamshire, played at Lord's in the first week of May, 1900, was the first under the experimental netting-boundary rules and the last under the old follow-on rule (120 rather than 150 behind).

Netting, 2–3 ft high, was erected all the way around the Lord's boundary. If the ball reached the netting, two runs were added to all the batsmen ran. If the ball cleared the netting, only three runs were scored. The system was designed to reward gentle ground-strokes rather than slogs or powerful hits. The ageing Arthur Shrewsbury, pre-judging the idea (or perhaps realizing the extra running involved?) decided not to take part in the game.

Nottinghamshire, also missing Gunn and Attewell, batted first on a dry, firm wicket. Their total of 249 was considered good for so early in the season. The fielding team admitted to being tired at the end, as there was no such thing as a lazy stroll towards the boundary to collect the ball from a spectator after a four had been scored; everything had to be chased. The fielders were thankful that there weren't any exceptionally long partnerships.

It was a perverse reward system. Dench heaved one ball into the grandstand for three, whereas, on several other occasions, an edge through the slips sent the ball rolling up to the netting for six or seven runs. By the end of the day, when MCC were 111 for nine, there weren't many takers for the netting idea. It was also a nuisance for the incoming and outgoing batsmen, who had to step over the netting to walk on to the field. 'This MCC scheme of netting the boundaries has been tried and has failed,' reported *The Times* after that first day's play.

When play resumed on the second morning, MCC needed a further 19 runs to avoid the follow-on (whereas they would have been safe under the new law). They failed by five, so batted again, avoiding an innings defeat but setting Nottinghamshire a comfortable target of 60 runs. At 6.30, when 25 were still needed, it was decided to play out the game that evening.

Despite opposition from participants in this first match, the netting-boundary idea was given a fair trial before it was rejected. Later that month, Storer hit an undefeated 175 for Derbyshire against MCC & Ground, but that achievement was overshadowed by a bizarre event in the same innings. While scoring 43, Wood collected 10 of his runs in one hit from a ball by Burnup. Had the system been received more favourably, the game just wouldn't have been the same again.

NOTTINGHAMSHIRE

Mr A.O. Jones c Bromley-Martin (E) b Trott	47	c Trott b Hearne (J.T.)	4
Mr G.J. Groves c and b Young	0	not out	36
Mr W.B. Goodacre b Young	0	c Russell b Hearne (J.T.)	4
Dench lbw b Trott	29	not out	8
Carlin c and b Relf	23		
Mason c Russell b Relf	15		
Guttridge c Somerset b Trott	0		
J. Gunn not out	53		
Iremonger b Hearne (J.T.)	31		
Mr J.C. Snaith c Carpenter b Young	21		
T. Wass b Young	0		
Extras	2		8
Total	249		60–2

Bowling: *First Innings*; Young 20.2–7–48–4, Trott 34–11–111–3, Hearne (J.T.) 24–7–65–1, Relf 10–5–17–2, Hearne (A) 4–3–6–0.

M.C.C.

Mr C.W. Wright b Wass	0	c Snaith b Gunn	0
Mr G. Bromley-Martin b Wass	10	b Gunn	9
A. Hearne b Gunn	2	b Wass	3
Carpenter b Gunn	6	c Carlin b Gunn	15
A.E. Trott c Carlin b Gunn	7	st Carlin b Gunn	53
Mr E. Bromley-Martin b Wass	32	c and b Gunn	7
Relf b Gunn	3	not out	48
Mr A.F. Somerset not out	29	b Wass	23
Russell c Carlin b Wass	5	b Wass	15
J.T. Hearne c Groves b Gunn	6	b Wass	0
Young c Carlin b Gunn	17	run out	1
Extras	8		9
Total	125		183

Bowling: *First Innings*; Wass 23–5–43–4, Gunn 27–6–67–6, Dench 4–0–7–0.
Second Innings; Wass 19.3–0–84–4, Gunn 26–6–67–5, Dench 7–1–23–0.

The Street Called Fleet

C. B. FRY

*C. B. Fry played many sports at the highest level, representing England
at cricket and football, as well as holding the world long jump record. From* Life
Worth Living *(1939). Fry is referring to his publication* C. B. Fry's Magazine.

WHEN I WAS projecting the first number it occurred to me to get J. M.
Barrie to write an article on cricket. What I wanted was something
about cricket by someone who was sure to be original and certainly could
write. Barrie invited me to call at his bird's-nest of a house in Lancaster
Gate overlooking Kensington Gardens – or, rather, looking into Kensington
Gardens half-way up the railings. There I had interviewed this minute man
in his minute study. That is to say, he had interviewed me. He spent the best
part of an hour extracting from me in detail how the more prominent players
of the day made their runs or got their wickets. Especially he wanted to know
whether Bobby Abel really did play with a cross-bat and whether I thought
that Lockwood threw. I said 'No' to both these libels. On the precise object
of my visit all I got out of him was that I had far better ask his friend [E. V.]
Lucas. I noted his Scottish skill in avoiding a direct refusal.

From Shakespeare onwards successful poets, dramatists, and other artists
have been peculiarly interested in cricket. This trend of the first-class literary
mind is about the finest tribute to the merits of the game. What is it in cricket
that so fascinates novelists, poets, and dramatists? Myself, I believe that there
is a certain mystery in how a man becomes a famous batsman or bowler, which
is hidden even from the performers themselves, and has a curious appeal to
premier imaginations. Cricketers themselves have no imagination – at least,
no first-class cricketers. Otherwise they would be so nervous sitting in the
pavilion at Lord's that they would never make any runs or take any wickets.

I do not claim that all cricketers, even first-class cricketers, are running
examples of this interpretation. But unless it is correct, how comes it that one
never meets any man distinguished in literature and music, art, or the drama
who does not appear to be much more interested in cricket than in anything
else? For instance, I mention at random from my own acquaintance George
Meredith, who wanted to know whether I believed in the whip stroke or the

long swing; Andrew Lang, who wrote a better essay on cricket than he wrote on any other subject; Sir James Barrie, who did not mind a bit when my half-bred Scottish terrier Jane Brindle fixed him in the Achilles tendon; she was such a wonder fielder and knew at a glance where each stroke was going and could retrieve a cricket ball by scent from the middle of the cabbage patch over the wall. And the reason she bit Barrie's Achilles tendon was because he was standing too near to my Madame when she was bowling to me on the lawn. Then there is that beau Clifford Bax, who introduced his brother, Sir Arnold, to me as 'a very useful bowler', and who is prouder of having hit a six at Lord's than of *Socrates* or *The Rose without a Thorn*; John Galsworthy, John Drinkwater, Conan Doyle, A. E. W. Mason, Francis Thompson, Sir Hugh Walpole, Alec Waugh, A. J. Cummings, John Strachey, Ben Travers – to mention just a few of all colours of literary performance and cricketing promise. And there is every known actor under the aegis of Aubrey Smith, who does not count because he was a cricketer first. When I went to interview G. F. Watts about Physical Energy, he halved my precious hour in interviewing me about cricket. He had drawn a wonderful set of illustrations for the famous textbook *Felix on the Bat*, the originals of which are hung in the writing-room at Lord's; his picture of an Apollo-like young man doing the obsolete draw in a pair of dancing-pumps is superb.

Against the Current

C. L. R. JAMES

C. L. R. James (1901–89) was a distinguished Afro-Trinidadian historian
and writer. This extract is from *Beyond a Boundary* (1963), frequently cited as the best
single book on cricket ever written. He is writing about his schooldays
at the Queen's Royal College, Port of Spain.

❧

A ND I HAD been brought up in the public-school code.
  It came doctrinally from the masters, who for two generations, from the
foundation of the school, had been Oxford and Cambridge men. The striking
thing was that inside the classrooms the code had little success. Sneaking
was taboo, but we lied and cheated without any sense of shame. I know I did.
By common understanding the boys sitting for the valuable scholarships did
not cheat. Otherwise we submitted, or did not submit, to moral discipline,
according to upbringing and temperament.

But as soon as we stepped on to the cricket or football field, more
particularly the cricket field, all was changed. We were a motley crew. The
children of some white officials and white businessmen, middle-class blacks
and mulattos, Chinese boys, some of whose parents still spoke broken English,
Indian boys, some of whose parents could speak no English at all, and some
poor black boys who had won exhibitions or whose parents had starved and
toiled on plots of agricultural land and were spending their hard-earned
money on giving the eldest boy an education. Yet rapidly we learned to obey
the umpire's decision without question, however irrational it was. We learned
to play with the team, which meant subordinating your personal inclinations,
and even interests, to the good of the whole. We kept a stiff upper lip in that
we did not complain about ill-fortune. We did not denounce failures, but 'Well
tried' or 'Hard luck' came easily to our lips. We were generous to opponents
and congratulated them on victories, even when we knew they did not deserve
it. We lived in two worlds. Inside the classrooms the heterogeneous jumble of
Trinidad was battered and jostled and shaken down into some sort of order.
On the playing field we did what ought to be done. Every individual did
not observe every rule. But the majority of the boys did. The best and most-
respected boys were precisely the ones who always kept them. When a boy

broke them he knew what he had done and, with the cruelty and intolerance of youth, from all sides our denunciations poured in on him. Eton or Harrow had nothing on us.

Another source of this fierce, self-imposed discipline was the magazines and books that passed among us from hand to hand. *The Boy's Own Paper*, a magazine called *The Captain*, annuals of which I remember the name of only one: *Young England*, the Mike stories by P. G. Wodehouse and scores of similar books and magazines. These we understood, these we lived by, the principles they taught we absorbed through the pores and practised instinctively. The books we read in class meant little to most of us.

To all this I took as a young duck to water. The organizing of boys into elevens, the selection of teams, the keeping of scores, all that I had been doing at second-hand with Grace and Ranjitsinhji and Trumper I now practised in real life with real people. I read the boys' books and magazines, twice as many as any other boy. I knew what was done and what was not done. One day when I bowled three maiden overs in succession and a boy fresh from England said to me, 'James, you must take yourself off now, three maiden overs,' I was disturbed. I had not heard that one before; this boy was from England and so he probably knew.

Before very long I acquired a discipline for which the only name is Puritan. I never cheated, I never appealed for a decision unless I thought the batsman was out, I never argued with the umpire, I never jeered at a defeated opponent, I never gave to a friend a vote or a place which by any stretch of imagination could be seen as belonging to an enemy or to a stranger. My defeats and disappointments I took as stoically as I could. If I caught myself complaining or making excuses I pulled up. If afterwards I remembered doing it I took an inward decision to try not to do it again. From the eight years of school life this code became the moral framework of my existence. It has never left me. I learnt it as a boy, I have obeyed it as a man and now I can no longer laugh at it. I failed to live up to it at times, but when I did I knew and that is what matters. I had a clue and I cared, I couldn't care more. For many years I was a cricket correspondent in the West Indies, having to write about myself, my own club, my intimate friends and people who hated me. Mistakes in judgment I made often enough, but I was as righteous as the Angel Gabriel, and no one ever challenged my integrity.

❧

Indian Cricket through the Ages

BORIA MAJUMDAR

Boria Majumdar is an academic and cricket historian. From the introduction to
Indian Cricket through the Ages – A Reader (2005), of which he was editor.

INDIA DID NOT enter the World Cup 2003 as favourites, nor did it start
its Cup campaign with a bang. Rather, on the eve of the Cup, after having
had a very poor series against New Zealand, India was considered to be a dark
horse with an eroding reputation. Further, India's poor show in the first two
league matches led to widespread dejection, vandalism, and public wrath all
over the country. Security had to be tightened around the residences of some
of the cricketers as groups of frustrated cricket fans and angry mobs raided
their houses. The most startling expression of emotional public reaction was
the cremation of Indian cricket at Babughat in Kolkata. Saurav Ganguly, the
captain, was at the centre of this wrath and his portrait was among those burnt
to ashes. In fact, a fax was sent to one of the leading English newspapers in
Kolkata, which stated that a 'funeral procession of the Indian cricket team' was
scheduled to start at 2 p.m. the next day. The newspaper also conducted an
opinion poll on the issue, 'India as a nation is prone to over-the-top behaviour,
and public reaction to the cricket team's performance at the Cup proves it'.
The overall response of the readers to the poll points to a shared concern
of the public on the issue. Some of the opinions expressed are a key to an
understanding of the cultural implications of the event. To give an example,
one Sunil O. Varughese wrote:

> Does it mean that the Indian public should forget about cricket? I
> think not. After all, it will take only one good win for the fans to
> start hero-worshipping our cricketers again. Erratic or over-the-
> top behaviour, call it what you want. But that's what makes India's
> cricket-crazy public as popular as her players all over the world.

But once India started to recover from its initial hiccup and came closer to
making it to the Super Six stage of the Cup, the Indian public resorted to
their typical craziness about cricket in their everyday lives. In the market-

places, cricket stars began to occupy places of rare importance. Fruit vendors at different places around Kolkata adorned their stalls with posters of cricket players representing the nation in the World Cup. Holi, the festival of colour (18–19 March), was celebrated with renewed passion on the eve of India's possible march to the final. But this time, it was smeared with a new colour – blue. With the 'Men in Blue' achieving some amazing success in the Cup, blue, the colour of the Indian jersey, quite understandably, became the colour of people's hearts. Again, on the eve of the Cup final, metropolitan cities like Kolkata, Delhi, Mumbai, Chennai, Bangalore, and Hyderabad witnessed an increasing demand for hairstyles similar to the world's top cricketers – Tendulkar, Steve Waugh, Shoaib Akhtar, and Alan Donald. Interestingly, the enthusiasm for cricketing hairstyles was so popular that Sujit Bhagat, General Manager of Habib's Hair and Beauty Studio, a leading beauty parlour of Kolkata, planned a 'Hair Show' at their Ho Chi Minh Sarani premises, featuring hairstyles of cricketers only.

The Cup fever also affected the normal schedule of middle-class urban households. It created a severe problem for cricket-crazy children and teenagers since most of the annual school examinations as well as ICSE, CBSE, Madhyamik, and other secondary and senior secondary examinations were on during the same period. But for most teenagers, India's rare march to the Final was an experience to cherish and most tried to get on with the excitement by selectively viewing India's matches. Moreover, a large number of cricket-crazy Indians rescheduled their marriages and honeymoons to keep themselves free to watch India play.

It was widely reported in the media that cricket had cast its shadow on the markets too – be it the bazaars, government securities, corporate bonds or equity markets. Transactions in the bazaars and shops were hard hit on the evenings of India's matches as the inflow of customers reduced drastically. TV sets were installed in most shopping complexes with shop owners trying hard to satisfy both customers and themselves. Even the Bombay Stock Exchange (BSE) and the National Stock Exchange (NSE) Sensex fell, especially after India made it to the Super Six stage. On the day of India's Super Six clash with Sri Lanka on 10 March, Dalal Street in Mumbai wore a deserted look as dealers and brokers shifted their attention from trading terminals to TV sets. As a dealer at one foreign bank declared, 'There was virtually no work after 1.30 in the afternoon. We preferred to watch Sachin Tendulkar batting against Sri Lanka than the quotes on the screen. It was a nice break.' Thus, cricket was perceived as a partial opiate from the mechanical culture of daily life.

The politicians could not remain indifferent to India's progress in the Cup either. In fact, the Cup became an excuse to bunk routine work. Sometimes, it brought legislatures to a standstill. On the day of the India–Sri Lanka match, Trinamul Congress Member of Legislative Assembly (MLA) Saugata Roy urged the West Bengal Chief Minister Buddhadeb Bhattacharya to send a congratulatory message to Sachin Tendulkar and Virender Sehwag for their superb performances. On the same day, Deputy Prime Minister L. K. Advani demanded that he be given regular updates on the match during an all-party meeting in Delhi on Iraq. The West Bengal Budget was proposed on 20 March, the day of India's semifinal against Kenya. But as 'the MLAs of Bengal are practically not in the mood to listen to mundane speeches of the finance minister on the floor of the assembly', the Budget session had to be finished before the match started at 6 p.m. local time. In Bhubaneswar, members of the local legislative assembly demanded that there should be no power cuts during the World Cup final. Surya Narayan Patra, the energy minister, promised that the government would try to limit regulations on power supply for the day. Even the Indian Prime Minister Atal Behari Vajpayee, when urged by Rajiv Shukla, a Board of Control for Cricket in India (BCCI) official, to visit South Africa if India made it to the final, expressed a keen desire to remain present at the ground to support the team.

The instances mentioned above are but a very few to point to cricket's overwhelming presence in Indian public life. Due to the cricket fever, many unusual diversions took place in patterns of everyday life (repeated earlier this year). Doctors took breaks from their duties in hospitals, teachers skipped classes, thieves and robbers felt at ease as policemen left duties to watch TV, and attendance in offices dropped. Rahul Das raises a dissenting voice that deserves to be quoted in this context: 'The loss to the national exchequer would be phenomenal if we calculate the number of man hours lost to pink-white-blue collar staff watching cricket on TV.' Yet, most think that this can be excused on the count that cricket has become a marker of India's new assertive national identity, not to speak of the media hype and commercial boom. Here is a comment that sums up the brighter side of the picture:

India's mere presence in the final had fuelled hope, stirred the imagination, and turned the world's biggest, craziest cricket nation into an inferno of throbbing anticipation. The fans' poise and equanimity after the final, in contrast to the vandalism that had followed India's first-round loss to Australia, was a recognition by the grateful nation of their team's achievement. Ganguly's men had surpassed the expectations of a country that sets no limit on expectations.

India's cricketing culture reached a new high as religious rites and superstitious practices came to occupy pivotal places in mechanisms of desire, discipline, and good wishes that catered to India's success. The marked proliferation of belief in supernatural power, performance of religious rituals, the strict recourse to superstitions, and the use of astrology to ensure India's success in the Cup provide ample testimony to this trend. Leading newspapers magnified such news in detail to impress upon their readers the impact of such madness. On the eve of the Cup, Indian Captain Saurav Ganguly's brother, Snehashis Ganguly, attended a daylong *yagna* along with the local councillor and Mayor of Kolkata to boost the Indian team's chances in South Africa. A Christian priest, sadhus, maulavis, granthis, and cricket fans had also assembled to perform the *yagna*. Blowing of conches, burning of sacred fires, recitation of *mantras*, and chanting of prayers marked the occasion. Young women fasting on the occasion of Sivaratri on 1 March expressed deep satisfaction over India's victory against Pakistan while assembling for midnight prayer in temples across Bengal. In fact, it was reported that some of them had pledged large sums to Lord Siva to ensure India's victory. Ashok Nandi of Chittaranjan, in a letter to the editor of *Ananda Bazar Patrika*, requested Saurav Ganguly not to shave, in order to bring his fortune back on the right track. Cricket craze reached a peak in Cuttack where maulvis and brahmin priests conducted a joint mass prayer at the Syed Seminary School grounds for India's victory in the finals. The day before the grand finale, a cutout depicting Saurav Ganguly as Devi Durga and Sachin Tendulkar as her lion was displayed at Barasat, a Kolkata suburb.

There are instances galore to show how Indians – irrespective of caste, class, profession, or religion – started conforming to superstitious and religious beliefs to ensure India's success. Lalit Maken, then Delhi state minister, had a favourite chair on which he tried to stay put for the entire duration of every Indian match. The passion subsumed the partially blind Ritesh Kumar of Dumka, Jharkhand, who used to not only visit the temple before every match but also closed his medicine shop. Pandit Shyama Prasad Maharishi of Jodhpur, on the other hand, chanted *Om* in a marathon sitting at the Maru Ganga Temple for India's victory. In Mogalpura, Hyderabad, some Muslim youths organized a special thanksgiving after India won the match against Pakistan, and petrol station owner Shahnoor Tucy summed it all up in a banner: 'Allah-o-Akbar, Win India Win'.

It is not hard to understand these religious/superstitious propensities of Indians in view of their traditional susceptibility to spiritual overtones, which still exercises an overwhelming influence on their daily lives in an age of science and information technology. Yet, the kind of religiosity, supernaturalism, or superstition articulated during the Cup has a unique flavour of its own. Sharda Ugra explains the essence of this unique turn to the supernatural in India's public life:

> For a fortnight now, India has stood still. Held its breath, said its prayers, not moved off its chairs and *charpais* for fear of upsetting some cosmic order. An outer life is lived in a detached virtual reality where offices are attended, bills paid, food cooked, kids scolded, homework done. Mostly though it's an inner life where dreams are dreamt. A nation waits in hope and fear, anticipation and trepidation. For a fortnight now, another India has been on the move. Swift, decisive and bold, winning in Johannesburg and Durban, Cape Town and Harare, giving greater definition and surer shape to that curious, collective yearning of a billion people. The temperatures rise and the chattering gets more emotional and argumentative back home. The cricketers hang on to the boring brass tracks because not only are they the ones who have taken this team this far, they are also one of the few things that are for real in their otherwise unreal universe.

The cricket craze in India, even after the nation's defeat in the World Cup final, shows no signs of relenting. The common refrain in the media was 'Never mind Saurav: there's no shame in losing to the world's best team. You and your boys still did us proud.' Echoing this sentiment, Sandipan Deb wrote:

History is always written by the victorious. But that doesn't mean it's true. When you look back at World Cup 2003, remember Sachin Tendulkar lifting Shoaib Akhtar for a six over third man, remember Ashish Nehra bowling those incredible deliveries that no sane batsman can play, remember Mohammed Kaif running out Nick Knight so fast that no photographer on earth could take that picture, remember Saurav Ganguly snarling '*bhat!*' at Yuvraj Singh when he wanted a take a second run which wasn't there, and then going up to him and hugging him. Remember Javagal Srinath, the oldest fast bowler in the world, scaring the hell out of the batsmen. Remember, above all, Rahul Dravid, the man who played always only for his team, a true cricketer and a true man. And screw history as written by the victorious.

How to Get Out

W. E. W. COLLINS

W. E. W. Collins had a brief first-class career of seven matches in the late nineteenth century. From *Leaves from an Old Country Cricketer's Diary* (1908).

I WAS DISCUSSING WITH a friend one day the following question – What is the most annoying and most unlucky method of getting out? Curiously enough, after many pros and cons, we found ourselves in agreement, and concluded that we more especially resented being caught by a fieldsman who, from carelessness or ignorance or thirstiness, is obviously not standing in the right place. But what a lot of ground we had previously travelled over! I had been badly run out on one occasion by the only exciseman who ever asked me for my game licence; on another had called my partner and galloped down the pitch, to find that in addition to being deaf he had a fly in his eye. Per contra, I had with my own eyes seen my friend, when playing a very fine innings, knocked silly in the middle of the pitch by a heavy and blunder-headed partner who, being called for an easy run, lowered his blunder head and charged like a bull of Bashan *on the wrong side.*

'Queer thing,' remarked a caustic spectator, 'that in a park five miles round two men can't find room to pass each other.'

Both batsmen, I may add, were lying helpless in the middle of the pitch, and, the ball having been returned, one of them obviously had to go. It argued perhaps more worldly wisdom than chivalry on the part of the opposition that, after leisurely reviewing the situation, they elected to execute, not the primary offender, who had just come in, but the victim of the assault, who had been playing the cat and banjo with their bowling.

Both of us of course could allege that we had been given out unfairly time out of time by a partial and hostile umpire. As the older man I could claim a wider experience in that respect. For in village cricket thirty or forty years ago the umpire was commonly regarded as the most useful man on his side, and his path of duty lay in saying 'out' or 'not out', according as the appeal was made by friend or foe. We have it on high authority that school umpires were at that date actuated by much the same idea of fair-play. For has it not been recorded by Lord Cobham that in a certain house-match at Eton the rival captains were both 'chiselled out', and both umpires ducked on the conclusion of the game? If the punishment has gone out of vogue, he would be a bold man who asserted that in a match played against a public school, on the school ground, and with the school professional standing at one end, the umpiring is entirely beyond suspicion. By the way, the story of the most ingenious decision that I ever heard of was told to me by an old Etonian.

'Out,' suddenly shouted the umpire in a wet-bob match.

As there had been no appeal, the batsman was wholly justified in demanding a reason.

'What for?' he asked angrily.

'Two blocks, and I'm in next,' and the argument held good.

I fairly held my friend on the point that, though we had both been caught in our time off our own calves or pad-straps or an umpire's body, I had once been given 'out', caught first ball of a match, off the point of my funny-bone, and furthermore by means of the misadventure had been compelled to take a back seat for the rest of the day. Finally, however, as I said before, we both pitched upon the fieldsman standing out of his proper place as the most iniquitous and condemnable instrument of Providence.

In Kent, some fifteen years ago, a bowler just about to resume his over after the fall of a wicket noticed that a fieldsman was absent.

'Hulloa! Where is Frank M—?'

There was a general look in the direction where Frank M— ought to have been, but no sign of that individual.

'Only one ball to go,' muttered the umpire.

'Bowl away, then,' echoed an over-impatient captain; 'he'll be back before we have changed over.'

I was the unlucky recipient of that ball, an unmistakable half volley, which I hit high and hard straight for the scoring tent. And into the scoring tent it might have dropped if it had not been for what looked like the providential interposition of a stout party in boots and gaiters – the gamekeeper for choice – who was standing by the telegraph board with one hand in his pocket and a telegraph plate in the other. To drop the plate and catch the ball, without that preliminary agony of 'judging' which an outfield has to endure in the case of a skyer, seemed to the volunteer telegraphist matters of no moment. And then, having brought off the catch, he returned again to his temporary function, and quietly proceeded to alter the lower figures on the board from 6/38 to 7/0, at least as much to the astonishment of the field as of myself.

'Hulloa, old chap, you're out,' cheerfully remarked the bowler as he grasped the situation.

'Out? Why?'

'Caught, of course. Frank must have told the fellow to field for him.'

On my way to the tent I had my say with the gaitered scoundrel, but got wholly the worst of the argument. In cricket, as in moral philosophy, the 'fact is a first principle and starting-point', and when the fact happens to be that a batsman is out for 0, reasons are commonly superfluous.

'Surely Mr M— didn't tell you to stand there,' I suggested.

'I dunno as he said I was to stand nowheres in 'tickler. "Field a minute for me, my man," says he. And I were putting up the figures and all. Leastways I cotched you.'

First ball again, much after the same fashion, in a match at Woolwich. There the delinquent was a gallant but thirsty captain who, I believe, ought by right to have been somewhere in the slips, but happened to be in a sort of nondescript part of the field. The fall of a wicket after a long stand on a baking hot day had opened out to the gunner the prospect of a brief interval for refreshment, and, as most of the other fieldsmen were lying on their backs and gasping, his disappearance had passed unnoticed. A bowler, who had not the gumption to remark the absence of one of his fieldsmen, favoured me with a slow and stately half-volley, of a class that might have been hit to any given part of the field in front of the wicket. That which an old ally persists in describing as the 'drink-hovel' – it happened in this case to be a rather smart marquee – seemed to be as good a place to shoot at as any other, and my aim was only too accurate. For the gallant officer, having satisfied his thirst, was just stepping out of the tent to resume his proper place in the field when he was aware of a ball soaring through the air and manifesting every disposition to drop on to the end of his nose. Flight being precarious, obviously the next best thing to do was to catch the ball. He caught it accordingly, and was at least as much astonished as the striker when the performance was greeted with a round of applause. He had the grace to apologise for the act of cruel indiscretion afterwards, but the recording angel, who was vet twice over, – veteran and veterinary, – and whose language had been anything but angelic as the figures kept mounting on the board, quite recovered his temper and kept on chuckling for the rest of the day as he pointed to

c C., b B., . . . o

On a third occasion, in Shropshire, I was run out by a fiend in the shape of either a footman or a garden-boy fielding temporarily in the place of my host, his master. For some reason or other our hospitable entertainer for two most enjoyable days was over-much occupied in worldly business. Telegrams seemed to be flying to and fro, and there was generally either a footman or a garden-boy sheltering behind the short-leg umpire, as he waited till the end of the over to deliver or receive a dispatch. I had been in for some time, and had grown so much accustomed to the presence of an individual in workaday attire peeping out from behind the umpire that the fact of our host, whose position in the field was certainly nowhere near the umpire, having temporarily left the ground escaped my noticed. Presently my partner played a ball to short-leg. I called him, and was trotting leisurely down the pitch when the party behind the umpire emerged from his shelter and tossed the ball to the wicket-keeper, who whipped off the bails.

'How's that?'

Up went the umpire's hand, and I had to go.

'But the man wasn't fielding,' I expostulated.

'Oh yes, he is fielding for C—. You're run out all right.'

Personalities

COL. PHILIP TREVOR

Col. Philip Trevor managed the England team that toured Australia in 1907/08 and was also a cricket journalist. From *Cricket and Cricketers* (1921).

❧

IT HAS BEEN my duty (and I hope my pleasure) to watch first-class cricket played all day and every day since about 1897 (the war intervening), and ten or a dozen years ago I very seldom needed the score board or score card. One could tell a batsman's identity from his methods. Those methods were almost as indicative of individuality and personality as are finger-prints to the officials of Scotland Yard. Oftener than not to-day I have to glance at the score board and my score card. When a couple of batsmen are in whose physique is similar I cannot identify them merely from the strokes they make. There are, of course, exceptions to every rule. I remember saying more than twenty years ago that it was a practical impossibility to counterfeit 'W. G.' However, Major E. G. Wynyard, D.S.O., did it, and did it, too, in amazing conditions. I doubt if cricket history will ever give Wynyard the place he ought to hold as a batsman. Being a soldier, he could only play first-class cricket intermittently, and no one can get to the recognised top of first-class cricket without giving the whole of his time – and I might add his soul – to it. I suppose Wynyard had more scoring strokes at his command than any batsman who has ever lived, 'W. G.', 'Ranji.', and Victor Trumper excepted.

Consequently one day, when he suggested to me that I should take part in a little comedy which he proposed to enact, the plot and its execution (expounded by him) did not sound as impossible to me as it would have done to a man who had less reason to know Wynyard's capacity as a batsman than I had. Wynyard was an instructor at Sandhurst at the time, and he proposed to play for the visiting team against the cadets as W. G. Grace. The one and only Mr William Clarkson was to be called in to provide the big black beard and the padding necessary to produce the extra girth, and Wynyard himself was to provide the rather high-pitched voice, the jerky sentences, and the batting strokes. Knowing that I was not uninterested in the drama, and that I had wasted a considerable portion of my ill-spent life at amateur theatricals, he offered me a 'feeding part'. The 'Grand Old Man' was, we all know, a little impatient of correction, and well might he be, for where was the man who should dare to teach him batting? That role, however, was to be assigned to me. I was to go in first with Wynyard; he was to take the first ball, and I was to offer correction in the nature of suggestion. Then he was to reply. 'It is all admirable,' I said, but I thought the scene would bear extension, and I explained to Wynyard that, excellent as he was at collaring the bowling, my turn would have to come and I might at once get a straight ball. I protested that I could not allow the success of so delightful a comedy to be jeopardised. He then suggested my brother Leo as his partner, who, he said, was the best amateur actor in England. I put it to him that Leo was a worse batsman than I was, and I also laid stress on the point that the impersonator of 'W. G.' had got to do the acting as well as the batting. But never have I resigned any part that has been offered me with more reluctance. Well, a substitute who could bat was appointed, and I continue the story as it was told to me by an officer who was a member of the Sandhurst Instructional Staff at the time. A great big man with a great black beard duly made his appearance on the Sandhurst cricket ground, and cadets who did not care twopence about cricket forfeited their week-end leave to sit and watch the 'Grand Old Man'. The story also goes that a lovable old clergyman witnessing the start of the morning's play bicycled home in a great state of excitement to bring his family up to see what they had not seen before and might never see again. He hired a trap, which he could ill afford, and cramming eight of them into it he returned with them to wonderland. I hasten to add that means were subsequently found to recoup him for this outlay.

Well, Wynyard batted from noon till lunch time undefeated. My understudy also batted undefeated, for he was a good player. He did the necessary reproving, and got the retorts which his reproving merited. I do not know if any of the Cadet eleven had ever seen the real 'W. G.' bat, but my informer (the Sandhurst instructor) told me that the identity of the batsman was never suspected by one of them. The joke was continued at the luncheon interval, and the cream of it all was that the captain of the Sandhurst eleven, who sat next to the person whom he believed to be the 'Grand Old Man', was a Cadet in Wynyard's company! He had been coached by him at work and play many hours a day for many weeks. The bubble was never pricked; Wynyard burst it of his own accord. Such is the story. I can vouch for the first part of it. For the second, I have the volunteered statement of the officer of the

Sandhurst staff, who, when he made it to me, had not the least idea that the man who perpetrated it had, in the first place, suggested the comedy to me. I would have given worlds, I admit, to have seen that innings!

The Village Heath

ALEC WAUGH

Alec Waugh was a novelist and essayist, brother of Evelyn and uncle of Auberon. From *On Doing What One Likes* (1926).

IT WAS NOT a good side; although we always took our umpire with us we used to lose more than half our matches. But there was one match that we could always be sure of winning. We invariably beat 'The Toffs from London'. Twice a year they came down, rich in reputation. Cryptics they brought with them, and Cyphers and Authentics. They had even included once a county cricketer; and yet the result was from year to year the same. They came in the proud glory of their 'stripy coats'; they viewed with profound misgiving the rumpled nature of the outfield, the creased appearance of the pitch, the squint-eyed aspect of the umpire. They would win the toss; they would put us in to bat. We would compile some four-score runs; with extreme difficulty they would reply with forty-three.

There is a mysterious quality about village cricket, a hypnotic quality, an unknown quantity that discounts the balance of form and reputation. Village cricket stands low enough in the social scale. It stands below school cricket and below club cricket; no record of its activities appears in the sporting Press. *The Cricketer* does not publish the batting averages of All Muggleton nor the statistics of Dingley Dell. Occasionally, when a whole side is dismissed for 0, or when all ten batsmen are caught by the same fieldsman, a paragraph appears headed 'Curious Occurrence at Pidlington', in the same spirit that *The Poultry World* would report some feathered freak – 'Three-headed Cockerel at Maidstone'.

Village cricket is beneath the notice of the mighty. Yet on its own ground a village team is against any bowling and any batting in the world a toughish proposition. Your county cricketer who spends an afternoon with his local club expects to make a century; your first eleven batsman reaps a rich harvest in a house match; but county cricketer, club cricketer and school cricketer, they all make a dismal show upon the village heath. You do not expect the George Hebdens to reach double figures, and to have faith placed in one under such conditions is a doubtful compliment. Village cricket is not merely a lower class of cricket; the difference is not one of degree but of kind; it is a different game altogether, in which different tactics are employed, and different qualities are held in high esteem.

[. . .] Three years ago I spent a summer afternoon visiting with some friends the school at which their son was being educated. After lunch we naturally suggested that a couple of hours might be advantageously spent upon the cricket field. On the upper a senior match was in progress. But the small boy would not allow us to linger there. 'That's not my house,' he said. 'It would be frightful cheek for me to watch another house.' His nervousness finally carried us to the extremity of a long and sloping field, where a third league house game was pursuing an invertebrate existence. It was a melancholy spectacle. The bowlers could not bowl; the fieldsmen could not field, the batsmen could not connect their bats with the long hops and full pitches that were served up to them with rich profusion. When they did hit the ball they timed their strokes so ill that the ball either dribbled itself along the ground or ballooned itself into the air. No fieldsman, with the possible exception of a long stop, need have stood at a distance of more than twenty yards from the wicket. Slowly the innings trickled to a close. One thing alone puzzled me. The bowling was never changed. And even on this dismal side it seemed impossible that two better bowlers could not have been discovered. Finally I asked our guide his opinion. 'Well,' he said, 'Jones and Evans are nothing to write home about. But they don't bowl wides.'

That is my point. It is a different game. It is played under the same rules, with the same enthusiasm that are to be found at Lord's, at Richmond, and on Agar's Plough. But it is a cricket in which it is more important for a bowler not to deliver wides than it is for him to possess a spin and length and swerve; in which the batsman can be trusted to get himself out, but in which every extra is a valuable addition to the opponent's score. In club, in school, in county cricket the best batsman is the man who makes the most runs, the best bowler is he who most happily combines spin and length and swerve; the best wicket-keeper is he who catches most catches, and most speedily removes the bails. But in village cricket this is not necessarily so. Averages mean nothing. You will see what I mean if you will study the score book of any village side. Ten runs is a large score for any single batsman. It is rare for more than two people on one side to reach double figures. Extras on the other hand is consistently the highest scorer. Byes are usually the deciding factor. The village side does not quite realise this. But it is a fact.

The school pro. never tires of saying: 'Don't you be in too much of a hurry sir. You stick there, runs will come!' With equal appropriateness one might say to a village batsman: 'Don't you be in too much of a hurry, my lad, stick there, byes will come!' A man who can keep the ball out of his wicket for four overs, even if he has not run a run himself, will have done good service to his side. In that time he is pretty certain to have scored six byes.

The early batsmen are, of course, expected to make a few runs off their own bats. They have probably a certain idea of style. They have, in addition to the circular pull drive, a sort of half-cock defensive shot. And they have learned the technique of their craft.

The first batsman walks to the wickets. He takes guard. If his own umpire is opposite to him he takes 'one off'. If the opponent's umpire he takes 'one leg', and shifts away a little. At the wrong end it is as important for him to protect his pads as his wicket. Guard having been taken, the batsman's innings will, you may imagine, follow the course of all other innings. The batsman will either be dismissed early, or he will play himself in, to reap later in the day the rewards of patience. Wrong again; that he will never do; he may be dismissed early; but he will certainly not play himself in. There is no playing of oneself in on the village heath. The village batsman belongs to a different school of thought.

He is of the Cyreniac, of the 'let-us-drink-and-be-merry' school. He places no faith in an after life. He will not restrain his ardour in the belief that an hour later the opposing bowlers will be tired and his eye well in. Long before then will have come, he knows, that unplayable ball that will pitch a foot outside the wicket and will shoot with incredible speed into the base of the leg stump. He does not say to himself; 'if I can stick here runs will come'. He says: 'if I don't get runs blooming quick, I'll be meeting that unplayable ball before I know where I am', and so the bat is gripped at the extremity of the handle and swung violently from shoulder to shoulder at the least suggestion of a half volley. It is brief, but it is merry. The first five batsmen play just well enough to get themselves out. The last six do not. And it is the last six who manage to beat 'the Toffs from London'. They make no runs themselves, but they manage to stick there, and while they stick there byes mount up.

It is when all is said and done amazingly hard to get a man out who never takes the slightest risk, who covers up his wicket with an immovable bat (when he is opposite his own umpire he covers the middle and off stumps with his bat and the leg stump with his pads), and who never manages to touch a wide ball on the off. I am, indeed, not at all sure that these tactics of passive resistance are not more profitable to the side in the long run than the reckless aggression of the early stylists. There was one player in particular whose average was 1.3, but whose 'bye' average must have reached double figures. He does not know it, but he has reduced the practice to an art. He is old and stiff and heavy witted. He blocks straight balls; he never lifts his bat; it is extremely difficult to bowl him out. But he always tries to late cut the wide one on the off. He never succeeds. He is always a good half second late; his bat flashes in the air when the ball is halfway to the wicket-keeper's gloves. For the purpose for which it was intended the stroke is valueless, but it serves admirably another purpose. It unsights the wicket-keeper every time.

Instead of seeing the ball come to him through a hole in the bat, as it usually appears to the wicket-keeper, he sees it come to him in uninterrupted flight, and then just as he is preparing to take it a brown object is flashed between the ball and the background. It is as bad as a person walking across the screen behind the bowler's arm. You don't believe it. Well, have a try and see, or, perhaps, as a substitute field first slip with a wicket-keeper who moves across the wicket. He will unsight you every time. No one who has not had the misfortune to play against it can realise the value of that belated cut. I sometimes think that the village batsman should not only say to himself; 'Is that a ball that I can score off?' He should ask himself: 'Is that a ball I can safely leave alone in the hope that the wicket-keeper will fumble it?' Good tactics, I believe. And there is a stroke if anyone would dare to use it, that would win any village team a challenge cup; it should be played to the ball that passes between the leg stump and the pads. The batsman who could recognise this ball, who could play forward to it and contrive to miss it, would be worth international honours. There is no harder ball for the wicket-keeper to take; it would be four byes every time.

The art of bowling is equally subject to a complete reversal of existing standards. On the village heath a good bowler is not necessarily more dangerous than a poor one. 'We can understand', you may say, 'that a good batsman would be puzzled by the new conditions; that he could not, in a short space of time, adapt himself to the peculiar conformation of the pitch, the absence of screens, and the decision of a squint-eyed umpire. But bowling is different. If a bowler without length or swerve or spin can frustrate a good batsman, surely a decent bowler would be unplayable.' He isn't though. He bowls too well. As I have said before, village cricket is not in a different class from club cricket. It is a different game altogether. The principle of the thing is different. The tactics of the club or school or county bowler are aggressive. He has to get the batsman out. The tactics of the village bowler might be described as passively co-operative. He helps the batsman to get himself out.

Quite a good bowler came once to play against our village. He was an Authentic; he had played in the Oxford trials, his bowling average was on the right side of the twenties. The village rustics eyed him with reverential awe. The first batsmen walked to the wickets with trembling knees. They did not get their bats within six inches of a single ball of that first over. At the end of the innings his analysis ran:

O.	M.	R.	W.
20	15	11	6

On this performance he was, deservedly perhaps, congratulated by his side. But the figures of a bowler have not the same significance in village as in county cricket. I said nothing, but I gauged the number of the extras; forty-seven of them, and a good thirty of them must have been off that bowler.

This is what the star performer has done. He had bowled with plenty of swerve, and with the ground helping him an indecent amount of break. He had not, however, assisted the batsmen in the slightest degree in their amiable efforts to get themselves back to the pavilion. He had bowled much too well. He had not given them a ball they could hit. He had beaten the bat every time. Our rustics had never been so puzzled in their lives. They did their best. They felt for the balls on the off. They fumbled at the balls on their pads. They did everything within their power to give a catch to the wicket-keeper, to the slips, and to short leg. But they failed. They were not good enough. The swerve beat them. Five balls in every over found their way to the wicket-keeper. And all the time byes mounted up.

For the wicket-keeper, poor fellow, was in the same difficulty as the batsman: the bowling was too good for him. It is not easy at the best of times to take a ball that swings in the last yard of its flight from the leg stump on to the batsman's pads, and when that ball, in addition to swinging out of sight, decides to break and shoot simultaneously, the chances of boundary byes are four to one on. Moreover, his gloves were not of the best, and before the innings was half done his hands were very sore. He attempted to employ his pads as a substitute. It was not successful.

This would not, perhaps, have mattered had the star bowler been able to hit the wickets. But this he only managed to do every three overs. He would not trust the pitch. He spun the ball and he swung the ball, but he refused to appreciate the simple fact that on village turf there is no need for spin. The cracks manage that on their own account. Bowl a fastish ball on the middle stump and see what happens. It may shatter the leg stump. It may shatter the off stump. It may shatter the batsman's face. But there is one thing you may be quite certain it will not shatter. It will not shatter the middle stump.

In village cricket you must place yourself in the hands of fate; and if you spurn fate, if you do not rely sufficiently on the omnipotence of fate – if, that is to say, you try to do things on your own with finger spin and swerve – then fate will take its revenge as it did on the star bowler to the extent of forty-seven byes. Bowlers with an analysis of 3 for 0 have been taken off because they are too expensive behind the sticks. You cannot risk the byes in a village match. And this is the advice I would give to every young bowler who hopes to make a name for himself on the local green, at All Muggleton and Dingley Dell. 'Young man,' I would say to him, 'byes may not count against you in your analysis, but they mean invaluable runs to the other side. Avoid byes. If you can't hit the wicket, hit the bat.'

Byes are the beginning and the middle and the end of village cricket, and the wicket-keeper is certainly the most important man on the field. On his prowess depends the position of the best fieldsman in the side. It is always as well to put your best fieldsman where a catch is most likely to go. But if there is any doubt about the wicket-keeper, the best man must go long stop. And the qualities of a good wicket-keeper? I can best answer that by describing to you the tactics of one I have often watched. Were you to watch him perform for a quarter of an hour you might not be inclined to congratulate the selection committee. He stands well back to all manner of bowling. He never takes the ball with his gloves. He places his body in a line with the ball, presses his legs together, and bends his knees as the ball reaches him. As he makes his leap into position he turns quarter right so that should he fail to smother the ball he will deflect it in the direction of first slip. It is not elegant, but it is gallant. His shins are a peculiar sight at the end of a long innings. And it is useful. You will find at the end of Wisden elaborate statistics showing the percentage of captures by the wicket-keeper to the number of wickets that fell. It is not on that principle that the old Muggletonians appraise their stumper. He is not there to catch catches. Not for him the swift flick of the wrist as the right foot drags forward across the line. His job is to stop byes. His statistics if they were made out, should show the percentage of byes allowed to the number of balls that passed the bat.

[. . .] And so in all modesty, in all humility, I offer to the mighty wielders of the willow, to the men of whose prowess I read daily with appropriate reverence, this advice. To such great men I say: 'Sirs, take warning: when you next take a week-end in the country, and your host suggest that you should spend Saturday afternoon on the village green, be not tempted. Be you batsman, bowler or cover-point, here assuredly you will meet disaster. You will not make runs, you will not take wickets, you will chase after the balls that you have missed. Your many accomplishments will be of no value to you there. This village cricket is, believe me, altogether a different game. A word of warning, sirs, remain in the pavilion.'

❦

21

'THE LONG ROOM IN THE SKY'

Introduction to the
Wisden Book of Obituaries

BENNY GREEN (ED.)

Benny Green was a well-known jazz musician, broadcaster and writer. He edited
various *Wisden* anthologies. This introduction appeared in 1986.

༄

THERE ARE 8,614 of them. The population of a small country town,
except that they come from the four corners of the earth. A marauding
army, perhaps, were it not that among the ranks are to be found the occasional
lady and at least one resolute quadruped. They range from crowned heads
to vagrants, millionaires to beggars, reverend gentlemen to professional
politicians, Gentlemen and Players, geniuses and journeymen, dukes and
dustmen, those who died too young and those who perhaps lived just a little
too long, like that poor Mr Filliston, knocked down and killed by a motor
scooter at the age of 102. But then, who is to say when a man's time has come?
The club cricketer Charles Absolon took a hundred wickets in his 81st year,
while the Mackinnon of Mackinnon, generally believed to be immortal and
having apparently compromised his divine status by being seen entering a local
Kentish hospital in his 99th year, explained, 'I am going into hospital, but only
for the annual meeting, at which I shall preside.' None of these veterans could
be judged old compared to John Edward Taylor, whose wife died at the age
of 103, after 68 years of marriage, and who lived on as a gentle widower until
he was 105. There were pacifists and warriors, poets and peasants, professors
and creative artists, bishops and music hall comics, explorers and those who
were content, in the words of the Almanack, to die 'at their native place'.
Writers and farmers, actors and generals, miners and prospectors, schoolboys
and great-grandfathers, those who founded dynasties and those who finally
closed some dynasty's flickering account.

The cricketers of England and her dominions have come from every
walk of life, pursued every kind of path, embraced every sort of morality or
no morality at all, and experienced every kind of death. They passed away in
every imaginable way and one or two others besides. Being dedicated athletes
every one, several of them died in mid-stroke. They took their leave while

playing polo, squash, lawn tennis, golf, football, rowing, hunting, shooting, fishing, cycling, refereeing and umpiring. There is even one case recorded of death while bird-watching. Some of the very lucky ones died at the crease, like Andrew Ducat, or in the field, or even occasionally in the pavilion, like the gentleman to be found in these pages who 'died in his flannels in the Bristol pavilion'. At least one old cricketer would perhaps have wished to die at the ground but never quite mastered the timing; we read of A.W. Sheldon, who passed away while packing his bag for the Scarborough Festival. There have even been those who died in bed but clung to their cricketing credentials even unto the gates of Paradise. Among these was the umpire Harry Bagshot, who was laid to rest in accordance with his own carefully defined wishes, in his white coat, with six pebbles in one pocket and a cricket ball in the other, it evidently never having occurred to him that an excellent working definition of Heaven is a place where no umpiring is required. Bagshot had his colonial counterpart in the Australian who was placed in his coffin alongside a fragment of turf from the Melbourne ground.

Cricketers have died falling from windows, from horses, from express trains, and, in the case of Stanley McCabe, from cliffs. They have succumbed to earthquakes and have sometimes been incorporated in great public tragedies, like the players who went down in the *Titanic* and *Lusitania*. They have died through an unidentified virus, have been accidentally electrocuted, been bitten to death by insects, been found floating face down in the local canal, or, like A. W. Carr, died while shovelling snow, or even, like W. Whysall, from a fall in a dance hall. One cricketing K. C. dropped dead while walking to the Law Courts, and there was an intrepid Victorian called E. E. Bowen, who died in the act of mounting his bicycle during a tour of France. Some sad cricketers took poison, or cut their throats, or blew their brains out. It may be that the most bizarre fatality of all was the one suffered by Mr Eligon, who passed away through blood poisoning caused by a nail in his cricket boot. Another cricket-related death was that suffered by the father of the Australian batsman Peter Burge, who was struck down by a heart attack while listening to a radio commentary of a Test innings by his own son. This calls to mind the heroic case of J. W. H. T. Douglas, who was drowned, with his father, while attempting to save the old boy in a boating accident. And for sheer unexpectedness, there is the case, recorded in these pages, of the young Pakistani cricketer who died at the crease on being hit in the chest by a slow off-break.

Occasionally bloody violence has spattered the pages of the Almanack, as in the case of Captain R. K. Makant, who was 'murdered while on duty in Kurdistan'; the Rhodesian B. H. Williams, a victim of terrorist rockets; and the cricketing writer Jack Anderson, assassinated at his Jamaican home. From time to time the imminence of death to a cricketer has inspired gestures of sentimental affection. One Yorkshire cricketer in his last hours was awarded his Second XI cap, and there was the case of the dying Dulwich College boy appointed Head of School while lying in the coma preceding death. Most affecting of all these twelfth-hour melodramas remains the one involving the young Australian virtuoso Archie Jackson, who participated in a deathbed marriage ceremony with his childhood sweetheart. There have even been cricketing funerals brought about by cricketing funerals; Arthur H. Gregory of the great Australian cricketing dynasty, fell off a tram when returning from the burial of his cousin S. E. Gregory, and was returned to the cemetery much sooner than he or anyone else could reasonably have expected. For sheer pointlessness there is the death of Joseph Cummings, who found himself one day in the town of Pullman, Illinois, and was so overcome by the experience that he expired there from the intense heat. Nor is it generally remembered that at least one of the cricketing Graces breathed his last while participating in a match. There was even a cricketer once who died while ploughing, and another who was hanged for murder, although the Almanack decorously omitted to say so.

Extraordinary as the accumulated circumstances of the deaths of cricketers are, they might have been more extraordinary still had the editors of the Almanack not taken so long to think of the idea. When John Wisden published his first annual edition in 1864, he was so bemused by the beauty of his own invention that he had not the remotest idea what to put into it, a state of mind which caused him to fill the pages with irrelevancies so comic that to this day the researcher is vastly diverted, by tables showing the length of British canals, the dates of the principal battles of the Wars of the Roses, the date of foundation of the Antiquarian, Astronomical, Ethnological, Geological, Horticultural, Microscopical, Pharmaceutical and Philological Societies, and a brisk disquisition on the constitutional implications of the trial of Charles I. Not until 1892, a generation after the first appearance of the Almanack, did obituary notices first appear, and even then consisted of little more than a name, a country and a date. This means that cricketers were dying at regular intervals for 28 years after the publication of the first Almanack without so much as a mention in its pages. But once the editors realised what a rich source of fact and anecdote might be liberated by the elaboration of death notices, this section of the Almanack quickly flowered into one of the greater glories of English sporting prose. Gradually, as the editors themselves finally qualified for inclusion in the obituary columns, the style of writing changed; the mandarin approach of the late Victorians modulates into the orotundities of the Edwardians, and then, as sensibilities readjusted in the modern age, to the functional recitation of statistics of the last 60 years, an evolution which the reader cannot help feeling has seemed likely at times to inflict permanent damage on the readability of the finished article.

The Death of G. H. Hardy

C. P. SNOW

C. P. Snow (Lord Snow) was a novelist, physicist and government minister. This extract is from *Variety of Men* (1967). Snow is visiting the dying Hardy, a distinguished mathematician, in Cambridge in 1947.

MOSTLY, THOUGH – ABOUT fifty-five minutes in each hour I was with him – I had to talk cricket. It was his only solace. I had to pretend a devotion to the game which I no longer felt, which in fact had been lukewarm in the thirties except for the pleasure of his company. Now I had to study the cricket scores as intently as when I was a schoolboy. He couldn't read for himself, but he would have known if I was bluffing. Sometimes, for a few minutes, his old vivacity would light up. But if I couldn't think of another question or piece of news, he would lie there, in the kind of dark loneliness that comes to some people before they die.

Once or twice I tried to rouse him. Wouldn't it be worth while, even if it was a risk, to go and see one more cricket match together? I was now better off than I used to be, I said. I was prepared to stand him a taxi, his old familiar means of transport, to any cricket ground he liked to name. At that he brightened. He said that I might have a dead man on my hands. I replied that I was ready to cope. I thought that he might come: he knew, I knew, that his death could only be a matter of months: I wanted to see him have one afternoon of something like gaiety. The next time I visited him he shook his head in sadness and anger. No, he couldn't even try: there was no point in trying.

It was hard enough for me to have to talk cricket. It was harder for his sister, a charming, intelligent woman who had never married and who had spent much of her life looking after him. With a humorous skill not unlike his own old form, she collected every scrap of cricket news she could find, though she had never learned anything about the game.

Once or twice the sarcastic love of the human comedy came bursting out. Two or three weeks before his death, he heard from the Royal Society that he was to be given their highest honour, the Copley Medal. He gave his Mephistophelian grin, the first time I had seen it in full splendour in all those months. 'Now I know that I must be pretty near the end. When people hurry up to give you honorific things there is exactly one conclusion to be drawn.'

After I heard that, I think I visited him twice. The last time was four or five days before he died. There was an Indian Test team playing in Australia, and we talked about them.

It was in that same week that he told his sister: 'If I knew that I was going to die today, I think I should still want to hear the cricket scores.'

He managed something very similar. Each evening that week before she left him, she read a chapter from a history of Cambridge university cricket. One such chapter contained the last words he heard, for he died suddenly, in the early morning.

❦

Silence of the Heart

DAVID FRITH

David Frith is a leading cricket historian and writer who has won the Cricket Society/MCC Book of the Year Award three times. *Silence of the Heart* (2001) studies the consequences of obsession with cricket.

SOME BECOME DISENCHANTED with the game after long involvement at professional level with its backbiting and jealousies and uncertainties. Others continue to rely heavily upon it, though in later years it can provide only substitute satisfactions, as from coaching, umpiring, committee work, or media appointments.

Yet others depend upon it as a spectacle, an obsessional pursuit, a sublimation of their lives. When things go wrong, mental stability can collapse. Gordon Piper, a 23-year-old science graduate from Adelaide University, was found with his throat cut at his lodgings in Harpenden, Hertfordshire, in 1930. He managed to dictate his will to a fellow lodger while a doctor was summoned, and he gave as one of his reasons for his action Australia's recent loss against England in the Trent Bridge Test match (Bradman's first in England: the game was turned by substitute fielder Syd Copley's diving catch to dismiss McCabe). Piper, the grieving Australian patriot, died in St Albans Infirmary.

Almost 60 years later a Nottingham man took an overdose during a 1989 Ashes Test, also at Trent Bridge, where Mark Taylor and Geoff Marsh put on a record 329 for Australia's first wicket – the eventual total of 602 for 6 before Allan Border declared being sufficient for victory by an innings and 180 runs, Australia's greatest ever in England. The distraught man explained, after he had been revived, that he had committed his act because of 'the situation at the Test match'. (In passing, Allan Border, with honours and records galore to his name, compared retirement to death when the Australian Cricket Board decided he should take 'early retirement' in 1994.)

There can hardly be a more sorrowful case than that of Arthur Wills, a former sailor and prison warder, who threw himself onto a railway line near Portsmouth in April 1956. Only 35, he explained his plight in a letter for the coroner, a letter which survived the impact of the train:

I know, sir, that you will have in your mind that I took my life while the balance of my mind was disturbed. Maybe that is what you will think, but now I will tell you that two years ago, in July 1954, I was overtaken by a haemorrhage of the brain. I have tried to get fit, so as to play cricket again, but now I know I will never be fit enough to play that most enjoyable game again. If there is no cricket to live for, then I would rather be out of the world. It was all to me. I am convinced that I shall never play that finest and most glorious game again. I thank you for bearing with me so long.

His brother-in-law later said that cricket was Arthur's 'one passion in life' and that he was an outstanding bowler who 'was always improving his batting'. He played for clubs in South Africa and for the Royal Navy and several clubs around Portsmouth.

This poignant story prompted Imogen Grosberg to include in her privately published collection of verse, *Run Chase*, a poem entitled 'The Cricketer's Farewell'. It begins:

> I think I have played my last
> At England's greatest game
> And life, now all that has passed,
> Will never be the same.

Its tenth and final verse runs:

> Not that, for I cannot live
> Without our summer game;
> A coward, I ask 'Forgive'.
> My life runs out today.

While Asia seems to have an almost negligible suicide rate among cricketers, no such claim can be made for cricket *fans* in that part of the world, where degrees of spectator obsession and hysteria come close to matching those characteristic of South American football. After Australia had beaten India by one run at Brisbane in a World Cup match in 1992 – Steve Waugh's widish throw being gathered by substitute wicket-keeper David Boon, who managed to beat Raju to the finishing line – a young newly married man in Surat, western India, hanged himself 'in total despair and frustration'.

During the next World Cup staged on the subcontinent in 1996, India suffered again, this time when crowd disturbances at Eden Gardens, Calcutta, forced a stoppage to the semi-final. The match referee awarded the game to Sri Lanka. This was too much for countless Indian fans, one of whom hanged himself in the hill town of Jalpaiguri, while another, Ashoke Roy, 35, hanged himself in front of the television set in Debnagar.

Already millions of Pakistanis had become deeply depressed when India had knocked their team out in Bangalore at the quarter-final stage. Teenagers went on street rampages and the newspaper *Al-Akhbar* hardly helped pacify the population when its front-page headline screamed: 'A WAVE OF GRIEF HAS SWEPT THE COUNTRY – WE HAVE LOST OUR GLOBAL HONOUR'. One man living in the northwest district of Mardan shot his television set, then turned the gun on himself and was taken to hospital close to death.

Much as Sri Lankans everywhere hoped that Sanath Jayasuriya would take Brian Lara's world Test record as his score moved into the 300s against India in Colombo in August 1997, when he was caught for 340 his tears were nothing compared to the reaction of one wretched admirer. Ranasinghe Sarath, 33, went out and hanged himself in a well.

Hero-worship destroyed a young woman in September 1999 when Deepa Vasanthalaxmi, 18, who lived in Mysore, became so distressed at news that Sachin Tendulkar might have to retire because of a back problem that she poured paraffin over herself and set herself on fire. The pathetic note she left said: 'I love you, Sachin. I was sad about reports that you would never be able to play and hence I am taking this extreme step'. (Modes change: a man who recently hanged himself in Winchester after the break-up of his marriage left a suicide note on the screen of his mobile phone.)

Over-indulgence came at a price for two other young Sri Lankans in the late 1990s. One, in a village in the southern district of Kalutara, made his father angry by playing cricket with the local lads every hour available when, in his father's view, he should have been out looking for work. The scolding became so severe that the son killed himself by swallowing insecticide – as had another young man three months earlier in Galle after his mother had urged him in no uncertain terms to 'temper his devotion' to the game and seek employment: Wasantha Kumara, 20, left a request that his bat and ball be buried with him so that he might be a better cricketer in the next life.

And when the world cricket bribery scandals erupted in 2000 – the Cronje Affair (it was all too facile to assume, as some did, that the disgraced South African captain was now doomed to join the tragic legion) – it was recalled that one of India's leading bookmakers, Jeetu Bhai, hanged himself after South Africa's tour of India in 1992. He had lost huge sums; or, knowing what we now know, was a match-fixing scheme in ruins, or had there been intimidation?

Not that the Caribbean, for all its light heartedness, is entirely free of a fatal solemnity. After Australia had beaten West Indies on their own pitches in 1995 to win the Frank Worrell Trophy, one local confronted touring journalist Jim Tucker and told him he hated Australians because his friend had just committed suicide after Mark Taylor and his men had beaten his heroes.

Cricket in the Fiji Islands

PHILIP A. SNOW

Philip A. Snow played cricket for Leicestershire Second XI in 1936 and 1937.
Subsequently he was a colonial administrator in Fiji, for which country he played
five first-class matches. His memoir *Cricket in the Fiji Islands* was published in 1949.
Here, he is reporting on an account by Sir Basil Home Gordon Thomson KCB,
administrative officer in the mid-1880s, of customs in the Lau Archipelago.

❧

HE IS MUCH MORE expansive on the cricket in Lau and gives an
interesting account of the intermingling of high-drawn emotion and
cricket: 'In Lau I had a good example of the hold which formalism and
ceremony have upon the people. The island of Lakeba had sent a cricket
team to play Lomaloma. The match was about even, and there was a large
body of spectators from both islands to watch the second innings. Suddenly
a messenger arrived from the beach and approached the Lakeba captain who
was bowling. I was near enough to overhear the conversation. The messenger
had just landed from a fast-sailing cutter to bring the news of the sudden
death of the chief's brother, who was the uncle of the Lakeba captain and of
many of the native ladies assembled at the scoring-table. Play stopped: the
captain walked over to the group and gravely announced the news. "Will you
weep now or wait till the innings is over?" he asked. The women consulted
and said: "Go on with the match. We will do our weeping afterwards." So
back we went to play as if nothing had happened. When the last wicket had
fallen, and I had almost forgotten the incident, a piercing wail broke from the
scoring-table. It was taken up by all the Lakeba women. They were howling
with open mouths: tears were rolling down their cheeks: they tore their hair
and scratched their faces and breasts, and when the orgy of ceremonial grief
seemed to be dying down from exhaustion, a fresh shriek would set it all going
again. I looked at the faces of their mankind: they were quite unconcerned and
impassive, and so were those of the Lomaloma women. I met the mourners
later in the afternoon; they were laughing and talking as usual, and there
was nothing about them but unhealed scratches to remind me of their tragic
concession to ancient custom.'

❧

Fatalities on the Cricket Field

AN OLD CRICKETER

From *Curiosities of Cricket* (1897).

ACCIDENTS

PARTICULARS OF OCCURRENCE	NAME
Death of batsman from ball bowled	Dennison
"　　　"　　　"　　　"　　　"	W. Hyde
"　　　"　　　"　　　"　　　"	G. Summers
"　　from collision with umpire	T. Tomms
"　　from heart disease	Rev. J. W. Sharpe
"　　while running	W. Blonden
Death of bowler from ball hit	H. P. Lighton
"　　from over exertion	W. Beedham
"　　from rupture, through fall	J. Walker
Death of fielder from ball hit	Thos Field
"　　from being crushed between railway trucks when recovering ball	Tucker
"　　from collision with other fielder	A. Bennett
"　　"　　"　　"　　"	E. A. Stow
"　　from falling on stump when putting down wicket	Goddard
"　　from falling over cliff when following ball	Unknown
"　　from heart disease	W. Beresford
"　　from over exertion	Corderoy
"　　from snake bite	Unknown
Death of player from abscess caused by	
"　　blow from ball	Prince of Wales
"　　from ball thrown by wicket keeper	R. Prestwich
"　　from blow on head while attempting catch	W. Jupp

"	from blow on knee	T. Billam
"	from blow on nose	J. Males
"	from blow on side	H. Hounsome
"	from blow on thigh	R. Howarth
Death of spectator from ball hit		W. A. Barrett
"	"	"	"	C. T. Clayton
"	"	"	"	Isabella Cook
"	"	"	"	Jeal
"	"	"	"	H. Simpson
"	"	"	"	Miss Young
"	from blow on head with bat	Bishop
Death of umpire from ball hit		G. C. Cottrell
Death of wicket keeper from heart disease		Littlefield

22

THE LAST OVER

'Last Over, Gentlemen'

LORD HARRIS

Lord Harris played cricket for Kent and England and was a noted cricket administrator and later Governor of Bombay. From *A Few Short Runs* (1921).

❧

WITH WHAT DIFFERENT feelings do we hear, according to circumstances, the knell of another day's cricket.

Baked by heat, blinded by the evening sun, bowlers weary of bowling without success; wicket-keeper no longer eager to take each ball clean, but satisfied with stopping the majority with his legs; one half the field mad with the other half for missing chances, and the latter jealous of the former for their luck in keeping clear of mistakes: under such circumstances how we welcome the umpire's 'Last over, gentlemen.' He has, of course, given the most ridiculously bad decisions – indeed, how he can be regarded as either impartial or competent is inconceivable; but at last he proves himself a friend in need, and puts an end to our miseries.

Or, on the other hand, when everything is going our way, when our slogger is giving unaccepted chances in every direction, filling us with glee, and our opponents with gloom, and the tens jump up almost as fast as that stupid boy at the telegraph, who *will* put the figures upside down, can find and hand the right ones: how willingly would we, under these conditions, prolong the day's proceedings! Or when the other side have got the sun in their eyes, and we are holding extraordinary catches, and the bowlers can put the ball just where they like, and there is a 'spot' at each end: under such circumstances how we grudge the stumps being drawn: 'the umpires are suspiciously anxious to whip off the bails; their watches must be fast, and they ought to have set them by the town clock. At any rate, whether that is so or not, how ridiculous it is to "draw" so early on these fine summer evenings; there is nothing the matter with the light. These people never could have played our bowling, but of course they must find some excuse'; and so on, and so on. There is no occasion to make a long tale of it; it is an old story, and all know it by heart. And then having survived the purgatory of 'changing' in a hot and crowded dressing-room, found our boots, with only five spike marks in them, and rescued our hat from under the heaviest man on the side, the revival of hope commences.

We begin to get cool, we begin to get hungry, and the thought of a comfortable meal and a soothing smoke induces kinder feelings for the sinners to whom are attributable our misfortunes of the day.

'After all, that was a good pitched ball, and perhaps did get him "in two minds"; and certainly that catch did curl a bit in the air. Ah, well! they don't often make mistakes; let us be charitable, and say some kind word that will put things on the old friendly footing.

'Besides, there's to-morrow; the match isn't lost yet. The luck must turn some time or other, and perhaps the umpires will be more impartial.' And the poor umpires, so seldom right, so often abused – have they much to blame themselves for?

Very little generally. Eyes will get a little weary, thoughts will recur to the sick wife, or the debt that is due, and may cause a momentary want of attention, but the decisions, right or wrong, have been honestly given without fear or favour; so sleep the sleep of the just, good umpires, even though your feelings have been hurt by hard looks and indignant mutterings.

And after that 'last over' is bowled, and we have time to think over the day's doings, what lessons there are to be learnt?

Did we tell the strict truth when we came out and said that we did not feel the ball touch anything? Have we not rather a suspicion that there was a something, which certainly justified the appeal?

Was it altogether amiable to pass poor —— by each over after he had missed that catch, without some kind word which would have cheered him up and dispelled his hopelessness?

And why did we slog at that ball? Of course, it was very hard luck that that one ball in the whole day should have shot, as it certainly did, notwithstanding what the Captain says about 'half stump high'. Still, it was stupid, and may have lost the match.

Heart searchings such as these must come to every cricketer, and it is well they should. By them we note and record our mistakes; by them we shall know in future that we must always be keeping watch over our own weaknesses, as well as always looking out to seize every chance.

So in time with patience and experience it may happen that the days may come when 'last over' will be called, and we shall be able to think with just satisfaction that there has been a minimum of mistakes.

'Last over' is called at various stages in man's life, and eventually will be called for the last time.

At each stage and at the last, he will be fortunate who can point to but a few mistakes; at each stage and at the last, he will be happy who finds that his friends regard them leniently, and who can honestly say that, whether or not it has proved good enough, he has done his best to 'play the game'.

Hastings

DUDLEY CAREW

Dudley Carew was a journalist and film critic.
From *England Over: A Cricket Book* (1927).

ENJOYMENT IS A COMPLICATED and unstable emotion. It may hover ecstatically in one as one writes a good line of prose. It spreads itself comfortable and luxuriously in one after one has dined well and wisely. It stabs almost unbearably in one when, as a bad golfer, one has driven a long ball straight down the fairway. But all these enjoyments are precarious and evanescent. Life is not rolled far enough back, and enjoyment remains a white and fluttering figure before a sombre background. Enjoyment for me, at any rate, implies both security and repose. I like to be removed at times from contact with familiar situations and familiar faces. It is good occasionally to be a stranger in a comparatively strange land. Acquaintances are easy to make and acquaintances, because they make no urgent and serious demands on one, are sometimes more desirable than friends. To be put, then, in a strange town on a hot summer's day when a cricket match between two counties in whom one has little particular interest is going on, is, it seems to me, in certain moods, the height of human bliss. It is easy on such occasions to take one's own tormenting individuality off, fold it up, and lay it on one side. One is no longer an individual perplexed by one's own intimate problems, oppressed by a past, cowering before a future, one is simply a human being, free, for a little time, from the cage of one's own nature.

The Sussex and Nottinghamshire match, as it happened, was an ideal one. The weather was good, and lying back in one of the deck-chairs which the Hastings ground so thoughtfully provides, one let oneself be absorbed in the changing fortunes of the game. Enjoyment, no longer a shy and lovely guest, took command and painted her own background.

The Hastings ground, although it has a faintly shabby air about it, is friendly and small. If one sits on the pavilion side of the ground one is confronted by a towering cliff with houses built into it on which is perched the old castle. Once during the match a procession with banners and white surpliced choir-boys made its way along the winding path near the summit, and the chant of voices floated lazily over the cricket field. It seemed impossible, listening to those voices, watching the cricket, that there had ever been such a thing as war, that there could ever be such a thing again. The chanting of the boys and the sound of the ball hitting the bat was a strong invisible shield shutting away all the evil and brutality in the world. We were in a charmed circle, and the greatest tragedy that could happen would be that some one should be run out after making 99. There was no need to wrestle with the monstrous thoughts that breed in the darkness in which life wraps the soul, no need. One's next door neighbour, an elderly, mild-looking man, expected one to say nothing more startling or intellectual than 'That one swung a bit late.' Social custom demanded no more than that one should offer him a Gold Flake. Looking round the ground one knew that, for a little, one had escaped.

❧

Introduction to Kings of Cricket

ANDREW LANG

Andrew Lang is perhaps best known for his cricketing parody of
Ralph Waldo Emerson's poem 'Brahma'. This extract is from his introduction
to Richard Daft's *Kings of Cricket* (1893).

CRICKET IS AMONG the few institutions in England which Time has not spoiled, nay, has rather improved. The wickets are better, immeasurably better than of old. The bowling is better, the fielding is as good as ever; probably the wicket-keeping is improved, and the general temper of players and spectators leaves nothing to be desired. A fine day at the Oval makes us all akin, and a pleasant sight it is to see the vast assembly, every man with his eyes riveted on the wicket, every man able to appreciate the most delicate strokes in the game, and anxious to applaud friend or adversary. [. . .] An English cricketing crowd is as fair and as generous as any assembly of mortals may be. When the Australians defeat us, though we do not like it, we applaud them till these bronzed Colonists almost blush. It is not so in all countries, nor in all countries is there the ready acceptance of the umpire's verdict, without which cricket degenerates into a wrangle.

The Lure of Cricket

E. V. LUCAS

E. V. Lucas was a prolific writer and essayist on cricket.
From *English Leaves* (1933).

HOW TO EXPLAIN the fascination that cricket exerts? It is not simple. That it should attract the proficients is understandable, although they are liable to continual mischances and mortifications such as no other game presents; but the curious thing is that it attracts the incompetents as well; those who never make a run, and cannot bowl, and yet, doomed only to dreary waiting in the pavilion and to fatiguing fielding, turn up punctually on every occasion, hoping for the best, and even (such is the human heart's buoyancy) expecting it. There is no other game at which the confirmed duffer is so persistent and so undepressed. It is for the experts, victims of misfortune, that depression waits; it is they who chew the cud of bitterness.

The phrase about 'the glorious uncertainty of cricket' applies to the individual as much as to the fortunes of the struggle. For there is no second chance: the batsman who is out first ball must retire to the pavilion and brood on his ill-luck until it is time to field and forget it – when, as likely as not, he will miss a catch and enter purgatory again. The lawn-tennis player, no matter how badly he is playing, completes the set; the footballer, no matter how inept, kicks again; the polo player and the hockey player, though covered with shame, are assured of their full afternoon's sport. But it may easily be the best batsman's fate to have nothing to do but watch more fortunate batsmen receiving easier bowling than he did. This constant risk of making no runs would, you would think, deflect boys and men from the game. But no. The cricketing temperament, always slightly sardonic, accepts it. The uncertainty spells also glory.

There is also, still further to nourish this sardonic tendency, the weather. No game depends more upon friendly atmospheric conditions, and no game therefore is so frequently spoiled. One wonders sometimes if England may not have had a totally different climate when cricket was chosen as its national summer game; for one reads little of rain in the accounts of early matches. Were we to choose again should we again select cricket? The answer, I am sure, is yes, so undefeatable is our optimism; but surely there are more clouds than there used to be?

The conditions of the game are unique and fascinating. No other game lasts so long: Test matches are often played to a finish; first-class matches are spread over three days of changing fortunes which every ball may affect; the village match occupies four or five hours, equally packed with drama. If it is exciting to watch the ups and downs of these struggles, where the proverbial glorious uncertainty of the game is ever present, think what it must be to be one of the two-and-twenty participants. And under propitious skies how benign are the circumstances of the struggle! The sun shines, the turf is warm and scented. But perhaps, when all is said, the secret of the spell of cricket lies in the possibilities of every ball. The bat awaiting the ball is indeed an implement of destiny, but the ball which the bat awaits is more fateful. In its flight through the air, after it has left the bowler's hand and before it reaches the batsman, the spectator can live a lifetime.

The mechanics of cricket are, I imagine, now fixed. There will be no new strokes; no new varieties of bowling; all that the lawgivers of the M.C.C. will have to do in future is to deal with minor details and the politics and finance of the game: the control of Test teams, the county championship and so forth. But these are trifles. Let us do honour to the giants, let us go to see them when we ourselves are past playing and even when we are young and emulous; but gate-money cricket remains spectacular and apart. Cricket is not the county ground, although that may be the Heaven on which every boy's eyes are fixed; cricket is the backyard, the garden, the playground, the school-field, the club and college ground, and, above all, the village green.

'Oh,' wrote an old enthusiast to me during the period of strife at Adelaide early in this year (not of Grace) 1933; 'Oh, all this psychology! I like better the local match on a small ground where all the better balls were hit into the hayfield and lost. In despair a pudding was produced and a hefty butcher smote it so violently that he knocked the cover clean off it. The cover was caught by the wicket-keeper, but the core was missed by point. And the deuce and all arose. Was he out or not? I say he wasn't, putting the case before the cover. But never mind – that's cricket, and it's the reason why the game will always be loved in spite of journalists and prizes to readers. There's something about cricket that defeats snobs and conquers the press-gang. It's a lovely game, is now and ever will be.'

Should every county ground be closed and never another shilling of gate-money leave our pockets, cricket would still be in England's lifeblood, drawing its undismayable devotees from every section of the nation: the cricket that has such a hold on the young that they take their bats to bed with them, and on the old that they cannot see half a dozen urchins in the street, with only a lamp-post for stumps, without pausing for a minute or two to watch; the cricket that stirs up such a turmoil of hopes and fears in our breasts that to consult the barometer can be almost an anguish.

ACKNOWLEDGEMENTS AND INDEX

W E ARE GRATEFUL for permission to include complete articles and/or extracts from the following:

John Arlott: *Concerning Cricket: Studies of the Play and Players* (Longman Greens & Co., 1949), reprinted by permission of Tim Arlott for the Estate of John Arlott.

Derek Barnard: 'How I Built my Wisden Collection', *The Journal of the Cricket Society*, Vol. 25 No. 4, Spring 2011, reprinted by permission of the author.

Hugh Barty-King: *Quilt Winders and Pod Shavers: The History of Cricket Bat and Ball Manufacture* (McDonald & Janes, 1979), reprinted by permission of Jenny Barty-King.

Keith Booth: *Knowing the Score: The Past, Present and Future of Cricket Scoring* (Mainstream, 1998), reprinted by permission of Mainstream Publishing Co. (Edinburgh) Ltd.

Ian Botham: *Head On: The Autobiography* (Ebury Press, 2007), reprinted by permission of The Random House Group Ltd.

Mike Brearley: *The Art of Captaincy* (Hodder & Stoughton, 1985), reprinted by permission of the author.

Mike Brearley and Dudley Doust: *The Ashes Retained* (Hodder & Stoughton, 1979), copyright © Mike Brearley 1979, reprinted by permission of the publishers.

Vernon Coleman: *Diary of a Cricket Lover: Around the Counties* (Enigma, 1984), copyright © Vernon Coleman 1984, reprinted by permission of the author.

Dickie Dodds: *Hit Hard and Enjoy It* (The Cricketer Publishing, 1976), reprinted by permission of The Cricketer.

Frances Edmonds: *Another Bloody Tour: England in the West Indies* (Fontana, 1986), copyright © Frances Edmonds 1986, reprinted by permission of the author.

Graeme Fowler with Peter Ball: *Fox on the Run* (Viking Penguin, 1989), copyright © Graeme Fowler 1988, reprinted by permission of Penguin Books Ltd.

Angus Fraser: *My Tour Diaries* (Headline, 1999), copyright © Angus Fraser 1999, reprinted by permission of the publishers, Headline Publishing Group Ltd.

David Frith: *Silence of the Heart: Cricket Suicides* (Mainstream, 2001), reprinted by permission of Mainstream Publishing Co. (Edinburgh) Ltd.

C. B. Fry: *Life Worth Living: Some Phases of an Englishman* (Eyre & Spottiswoode, 1939/Pavilion, 1986), reprinted by permission of Peters Fraser & Dunlop (www.pfd.co.uk) on behalf of the Estate of C. B. Fry.

Benny Green (ed.): *The Wisden Book of Obituaries 1892–1985* (Macdonald & Co., 1986), reprinted by permission of Mrs T. Green.

Ramachandra Guha: *A Corner of a Foreign Field: The Indian History of a British Sport* (Picador, 2002), reprinted by permission of the author, c/o Rogers Coleridge & White, 20 Powis Mews, London W11 1JN.

Rachael Heyhoe-Flint: *Heyhoe!* (Pelham Books, 1978), reprinted by permission of the author.

Gerald Howat: *Village Cricket* (David & Charles, 1980), reprinted by permission of the publishers, F & W Media International.

Tony Hutton, Mick Bourne and Brian Senior: *Off the Beaten Track* (Cricket Heritage Publications, 2006), reprinted by permission of the authors.

Colin Imray: *Cricket in the Backblocks* (Book Guild, 1998), reprinted by permission of Book Guild Publishing.

C. L. R. James: *Beyond a Boundary* (Hutchinson, 1963), copyright © C. L. R. James 1963, reprinted by permission of the publishers, The Random House Group Ltd and Duke University Press (www.dukeupress.edu). All rights reserved.

Frank Keating: *Long Days, Late Nights* (Robson Books, 1984), reprinted by permission of the publishers, a member of the Anova Books Group.

Shaharyar M. Khan: *Cricket: A Bridge of Peace* (OUP, 2005), reprinted by permission of Oxford University Press, Pakistan.

C. P. Snow: *Variety of Men* (Penguin, 1967), copyright © C. P. Snow 1967, reprinted by permission of Curtis Brown Group Ltd, London, on behalf of the Estate of C. P. Snow.

Philip A. Snow: *Cricket in the Fiji Islands* (Whitcomb & Tombs, New Zealand, 1949), reprinted by permission of the author.

Marcus Trescothick with Peter Hayter: *Coming Back to Me: The Autobiography* (HarperSport, 2008), copyright © Marcus Trescothick 2008, reprinted by permission of HarperCollins Publishers Ltd.

Phil Tufnell with Peter Hayter: *What Now?* (Collins Willow, 1999), copyright © Phil Tufnell 2000, reprinted by permission of HarperCollins Publishers Ltd.

David Walker: 'It's a Great Day for Being a Boy', copyright © David Walker 2011, from *It's Not Lord's: A West Yorkshire Cricket Anthology* edited by David Walker (Shalliley Books, 2011), reprinted by permission of the author.

Andrew Ward: 'The First Netting-Boundary Game' from *Cricket's Strangest Matches: Extraordinary but True Stories from over a Century of Cricket* (Portico, 1990), reprinted by permission of the author.

Alec Waugh: *On Doing What One Likes* (The Cayne Press, 1926), reprinted by permission of Peters Fraser & Dunlop (www.pfd.co.uk) on behalf of the Estate of Alec Waugh.

Aᴌᴛʜᴏᴜɢʜ ᴡᴇ ʜᴀᴠᴇ tried to trace and contact copyright holders before publication, this has not been possible in all cases. If notified, the publisher will be pleased to correct any errors or omissions at the earliest opportunity.

Cᴏᴠᴇʀᴇᴅ ʙʏ ᴛʜᴇ ᴅɪsᴄʟᴀɪᴍᴇʀ

Derek Birley: *The Willow Wand: Some Cricket Myths Explored* (Queen Anne Press, 1979).

Neville Cardus: *Days in the Sun: A Cricketer's Book* (Rupert Hart-Davis, 1948).

Dudley Carew: *England Over: A Cricket Book* (Martin Secker, 1927).

A. W. Carr: *Cricket with the Lid Off* (Hutchinson, 1935).

Frank Chester: *How's That!* (Hutchinson, 1956).

J. N. Crawford: *The Practical Cricketer* (Health & Strength Ltd, 1909).

Jim Fairbrother & Reginald Moore: *Testing the Wicket: from Trent Bridge to Lord's* (Pelham Books, 1984).

Alan Gibson: *Growing Up With Cricket* (William Collins, 1985).

R. L. Hodgson: *Second Innings* (Hutchinson, 1933) and *Cricket Memories* (Methuen & Co., 1930).

P. C. G. Labouchere, T. A. J. Provis and Peter S. Hargreaves: *The Story of Continental Cricket* (Hutchinson, 1969).

Alan McGilvray: *The Game is not the Same* (David & Charles, 1986).

Jack Pollard: *Bumpers, Boseys and Brickbats* (K. G. Murray Publishing Co., Australia, 1971).

R. C. Robertson-Glasgow: 'Weights and Measures', originally from *Cricket Prints: Some Batsmen and Bowlers* (T. Werner Laurie, 1943), and 'The Gatekeeper', originally from *More Cricket Prints* (T. Werner Laurie, 1948).

Fred Root: *A Cricket Pro's Lot* (Edward Arnold, 1937).

A. A. Thomson: *Cricket Bouquet: Comedy and Characters in the Counties* (Museum Press, 1961).

Frank Tyson: *A Typhoon Called Tyson* (Simon & Schuster, 1961); no records at publishers.

Harold C. Woods: *Cricket in the Long Grass* (Cortney Publications, 1995).

R. E. S. Wyatt: *The Ins and Outs of Cricket* (G. Bell & Sons Ltd, 1936).

INDEX

A

Agnew, Jonathan 253, 270–1, 273, 274
All England cricket team 2, 3, 32–4, 77–9, 87,
    121–2, 170, 203, 318
Ames, L. E. G. 150, 301
Antigua (1994), Test match in 254
Appleby, A. 97, 246, 247, 248, 250
Archer, Ron 200, 201
Arlott, John 258–61
Ashes Tests 116, 135–6, 137, 165, 175, 411
    body-line 341–2
    at Headingley (1921) 365–6
    at Lord's (1953) 229
    at Lord's (1981) 104–8
    Melbourne (1954/55) 197–8
    the Oval (1882) 207–10
    overcrowding at Lord's (1921) 94–6
    radio commentary 261–7
    Sydney (1903) 217–18
    Sydney (1979) 321–7
Ashley-Cooper, F. S. 4, 318–21
Australia
    England team travel to 86–7
    gambling and cricket 167, 175–8
    New South Wales 175–6
    radio commentary 261–7
Australian cricket team 15, 47, 116, 117, 141–2, 150,
    171–3, 175, 195–6, 224–5, 333–5, 358–9
see also Ashes Tests; individual cricketers by
    name
autograph collecting 357–61
Aylward, James 3, 79

B

ball games, attraction of 226–7, 232–4
balls, cricket 67, 75, 80, 82–3, 131, 135, 232–4
Baloo, Palwankar 211–14
Barbados 115, 117
Barber, Bob 137
Barker, Tom 236–7
Barlow, R. G. 86–7
Barnard, Derek 353
Barnes, Sidney 141, 142, 359
Barnett, Charlie 358

Barrie, J. M. 382, 383
Barrington, K. F. 150
Barty-King, Hugh 82
bats, cricket 24–5, 66–7, 72–5, 76, 78, 80, 121
Bean, George 55
Beauclerk, Reverend Lord Frederick 167–70, 320
Beldham, William 318
Benaud, Richie 165–6, 198, 199
Benson & Hedges Championship 104, 188–94
betting 3, 14, 80, 81, 88, 146, 167, 168–70, 175–81,
    184
Birley, Derek 164–6
Blackham, Jack 116
Board, Jack 301
bodyline 341–2
Booth, Keith 149–50
Botham, Ian 132, 136, 150, 175, 188–94
Bourne, Mick 51–2
bowling 70, 78–9, 81, 110–11, 135–6, 212–14, 228,
    318, 319–20, 400–2
    introduction of round-arm 3, 121–2, 318
    see also individual cricketers by name
Box, Charles 15–16, 182–4
Boyce, Keith 149
Boycott, Geoffrey 273, 323
Bradman, Donald 165, 166, 171–3, 266
Bramall, Alfred 178
Bramall Lane cricket ground, Sheffield 42, 43,
    44–5
Brearley, Mike 136–7, 166, 321–7
Brett, Thomas 319–20
Briggs, Johnny 364
Brooks, Ted 303
Brown, George 301–2
Budd, E. H. 168, 169
Buller, Syd 294–5
Burnley CC 173–4

C

Caesar, Julius 33, 286–8, 368
Caffyn, William 33, 87–8, 286–8, 366
Cambridge University CC 123, 129–30, 204–6
Canada and cricket 90–1, 96–8
    W. G. Grace on tour 245–8

Cardus, Neville 42–9, 333–4
Carew, Dudley 52–4, 204–6, 422–3
Carr, A. W. 145, 280
Cartwright, Tom 189, 194
caste system, Hindu 211, 213–14
Central Lancashire Cricket League 171, 173, 174
centuries, fastest 149–50
Chester, Frank 138, 297–305
childhood memories
    Alan Gibson 29–31
    C. L. R. James 384–5
    Christopher Martin-Jenkins 228–9
    David Walker 37–9
    Marcus Trescothick 24–6
    Michael Simkins 27–9
    R. L. Hodgson 26
    Rachael Heyhoe Flint 34–6
    W. G. Grace 32–4
China and cricket 16
Churchward, W. B. 17
Clapp, Bob 192
Clarke, William 32, 237
Close, Brian 188, 189, 192–3, 194
clothing, cricket 18–19, 68–70, 88, 112, 145
coin tossing 114–17
Coleman, Vernon 62–3, 281–3, 351
Collins, W. E. W. 152–4, 391–4
Collins, Wilkie 288–9
commentators 258–67, 268–9, 270–7
Coote, Cyril 130
Cowdrey, Colin 137, 198
Crawford, J. N. (Jack) 2–4
Crawley, A. E. 226–7, 232–4
Cronje Affair 414
Crowe, Jeff 112

D

Daft, Richard 108–9, 235
Darling, Joe 116
Denmark, cricket in wartime 71–5
Denning, Byron 151
Dennison, William 121–2
Derby 138
Derbyshire CCC 143
Devon League 62–3
Dhoni, M.S. 117
Dickens, Charles 288–9
Din, Asif 135
Dodds, Dickie 128–30, 297–8
Doust, Dudley 321–7

E

Edgbaston cricket ground 35, 107
Edmond, Frances 251–3
Edmonds, Phil 251–2, 253, 321
Edrich, Bill 200, 304–5
Egar, Col 275–6
Egypt 10–11
Emburey, John 131, 133
England cricket team 86–7, 116, 131, 133–4, 137,
    195–6, 218, 334
    the ICC World Cup (2011) 270, 272, 273, 274
    on tour 1984/85 242–4, 251–3
    tour of Australia (1876/77) 175–8
    on tour of Canada and USA (1872) 245–8
    tour of India (1984) 242–4
    tour of New Zealand (1877) 99–101
    tour of South Africa (1995/96) 222–3
    Triangular tournament (1912) 141–2
    v. South Africa at Leeds 258–9
    v. West Indies at Old Trafford (1966) 27–9
    in the West Indies 115, 182
    women's team 35, 223–6
    see also Ashes Tests; individual cricketers
      by name
Essex CCC 30, 128–30, 151, 171, 173, 297
Evans, Godfrey 199, 200, 201

F

Fairbrother, Jim 104–8
fans, cricket 346–61, 386–8, 411–13
Farrands, Frank 245–6
fastest centuries 149–50
fatalities in cricket 416–17
Felix, Nicholas 68–70
Fenner's cricket ground, Cambridge 130
Ferguson, Bill 149
Ferslev, Frederik 71–5
fielding, improper 391–4
Fiji, cricket in 184–5, 283–6, 415
Fingleton, Jack 116
Fitzgerald, R. A. 96–8, 245, 246, 247–9, 250, 290
fixing, match 178–81, 184
food and drink 280–3
Ford, W. J. 114, 374–9
Foster, R. E. 215, 216–20
Fowler, Graeme 139–40, 242–4
France and cricket 4–7, 15
Fraser, Angus 131, 182, 222–3, 254–5
Freeman, George 245
Frindall, Bill 149, 156, 269
Frith, David 411–14
Fry, C. B. 141–2, 217, 308, 382–3

G

gambling *see* betting
Gandhi, Indira 243, 244
Garland-Wells, H. M. 303
gatekeepers 112–13
Gatting, Mike 131, 133–4, 242
Gentlemen v. Players match 216–17
Germany 15, 18, 19, 20, 71
Gibson, Alan 29–31, 89, 155–6
Giffen, George 207–10
Glamorgan CCC 151
Gleeson, Johnny 277
Gloucestershire CCC 188, 358
Gooch, Graham 133, 325, 326
Gover, Alf 300
Gower, David 133, 326, 327
Grace, W. G. 3, 43–4, 97, 116, 123, 208, 216, 328–30
    after dinner speeches 245, 246, 247, 248, 250
    childhood memories 32–4
    impersonation of 395–7
    tour of Canada and USA (1872) 245–50
    and university cricket 123
Green, Benny 406–9
Gregory, Syd 141
Greig, J. G. 212–13
groundsmen 50–1, 92, 104–8, 109–12, 130, 156–7, 255
Guha, Ramachandra 211–14
Gunn, George 303–4

H

Halstead CC 129
Hambledon Club 3, 78–9, 81, 202–4, 318–21
Hammond, Walter 165, 305, 339–40
Hampshire CCC 12, 144, 145, 182–4, 188–92, 301–3
Hardy, G. H. 409–10
Hargreaves, Peter 8–9, 71–5
Harris, Charlie 303
Harris, David 318, 319, 320
Harris, Lord 164, 248, 290–1, 335, 420–2
Harvey, Neil 198, 199
Hassett, Lindsay 116, 173
Hastings cricket ground 422–3
Hayward, Tom 143–4, 206, 217
Headingley cricket ground 365
Heyhoe Flint, Rachael 34–6, 223–6, 242
Hide, Jesse 54, 55, 56
Higgs, Jim 325, 326
Hill, Clem 195, 196
Hobbs, Jack 27, 130, 141, 142, 300
Hobbs, Robin 150
Hodgson, R. L. 26, 333–4, 355

Hogg, Rodney 323, 326–7
Hole, Graeme 199, 200
Hole, Samuel Reynolds 125, 199, 200, 236–7, 306–7
Holmes, Percy 155, 300
Hookes, David 149
Howat, Gerald 91–3
Howell, Harry 304
Howitt, William 237–9
Humphreys, Walter 54, 55, 56
Hunt, George 303
Hurst, Alan 325–6
Hutton, Len 116, 137, 198, 258
Hutton, Tony 51–2

I

I Zingari CC 290
ICC Cricket World Cup 117, 270–5, 386–91
ice, cricket on 54–7
impersonation of W. G. Grace 395–7
Imray, Colin 58–61
India 14, 360, 413, 414
    caste system 211, 213–14
    England tour of (1984/85) 242–4, 251–2, 253
    ICC World Cup (2003) 386–91
    ICC World Cup (2011) 117, 270
    M. E. Pavri 124
    Pakistan tour (1999) 178–9, 386
    Palwankar Baloo 211–14
    public love of cricket 386–91, 413
Insole, Douglas 322–3
Irish cricket team 270

J

Jackson, F. S. 116
James, C. L. R. 120, 330–2, 384–5
Jessop, Gilbert 149
John, George 331–2
John Player league 104, 149
Johnston, Bill 201
Johnston, Brian 268–9
Jones, Ernie 195, 196

K

Keating, Frank 357–61
Kent CCC 2, 12, 45, 77–8, 150, 182–4, 318
Khan, Shaharyar M. 178–81

L

Labouchere, P. C. G. 8–9, 71–5
Lancashire CCC 42, 44–5, 46, 47, 52, 108, 188,
    267, 300
Lancashire Cricket League 173
Lang, Andrew 424
Langridge, Jim 305
Lara, Brian 254–5
Larwood, Harold 280–1, 304, 341–3
Lazy Tour of Two Idle Apprentices (W. Collins
    and C. Dickens) 288–9
Leeds cricket ground 42, 46
Leer, George 202
Leicestershire CCC 42
Lewis, Tony 360
Lewis, W. J. 67
Lilley, A. A. 124, 195, 328–30, 364
Lillywhite, Fred 3, 176, 207, 236
Lindwall, Ray 200
Lloyd, Clive 267
Lloyd, David 188, 269
Lockyer, Thomas 368
Lord, Thomas 13, 169
Lord's Cricket Ground 3, 42–4, 52–3, 70, 87,
    94–6, 107, 121, 132, 230–1, 379–80
the groundsmen 50–1, 104–8, 109–12, 156–7
and Lord Frederick Beauclerk 167–70
Women's One Day International (1976) 223–6
Lucas, E. V. 54–7, 369, 425–7
Luff, Henry 82–3
Lynd, Robert 94–6, 365
Lynn, G. H. 54, 57

M

Maddocks, Len 200
Majumdar, Boria 386–91
Malaysia, cricket in 58–61
Malcolm, Devon 222
Mandela, Nelson 222–3
Mann, Noah 202–4, 320
Marks, Vic 117, 243, 244
Marylebone CC/MCC 3, 5, 50–1, 96–8, 170,
    379–81
    see also Lord's Cricket Ground
Martin-Jenkins, Christopher 228–9, 269
Massie, Hugh 208
Matlock CC 235
McGilvray, Alan 261–7, 275–7
McLean, Teresa 148–9, 294–7
Mead, Phil 144, 302–3
measuring gauges 80–1
Middlesex CCC 42, 53, 104, 131–4, 301–2

Milburn, Colin 29
Miller, Keith 172–3, 198, 199–200, 276–7, 359
Mitchell, Alison 272, 273
Mitford, Mary Russell 168, 237
Morley, Fred 87
Moses, Charles 261, 265
Mountfield, G. H. R. 90
Mountford, Adam 270–5
Murdoch, Billy 208–9, 308
Mynn, Alfred 236–7

N

Napoleon III, Emperor and Empress 5–7
NatWest Cup Championship 104, 267–9
netting-boundary experiment 379–80
New South Wales 175–6
New Zealand 35, 99–101, 244
Newman, Jack 144, 302–3
Noble, Monty 217, 262
Northamptonshire CCC 150
notchers 148, 149
Nottinghamshire CCC 46, 47–8, 145, 236–9,
    280–1, 379–80
Nyren, John 77–9, 81, 318, 319–20
Nyren, Richard 203–4, 319

O

Oates, Tommy 301
obituaries, Wisden book of 406
O'Brien, Kevin 270
Old Trafford cricket ground, Manchester 43, 46,
    47, 108
origins of cricket 2–4, 8–9, 10–11, 12–14, 15
Oslear, Don 106–7
Ottaway, Cuthbert 250
Oval cricket ground 3, 27, 42–3, 47, 52–4, 92, 107,
    141, 151, 369
Oxford University CC 123, 216, 295–6

P

Pakistan cricket team 178–81, 413
Palmer, Ken 106–7
Paris CC 6–7
Parker, Eric – *Playing Fields* 30–1
Parkin, Cecil 300
Parr, George 33, 287–8, 306–7, 336
Parr, Sam 33, 336, 337–8
Parsee CC 124
Pavri, Dr M. E. 124
Peach, Tim 271, 272, 302

Pearson, Harry 171, 346–50
Pepper, Cecil 171–2, 173–5
Peshawur (steam liner) 86–7
Peterbridge, Bill 151
Phillips, Harry 54, 56, 57
Phillips, James 82, 308
Piggott, C 331–3
Pilch, Fuller 236
Pocock, Pat 252
Pollard, Jack 116, 167
Pollock, Graeme 277
Pooley, Edward 177–8
Poona Club 212–13
Provis, T. A. J. 8–9, 71–5
Pullan, Toby 230–1
Pycroft, Reverend James 9, 49, 168, 321

R

race issues 211, 213–14, 330–1, 332–3
radio broadcasts 261–7, 270, 271, 272, 273–4, 275–7
Randall, Derek 321–7
Ranjitsinhji, K. S. 142, 195–7
rebel tour (South Africa) 131
Redgate, Sam 236–7
Reeves, Bill 299–301
reporters, newspaper 156–7
Rhodes, Wilfred 141, 142, 217, 218, 304
Richards, Barry 189
Richards, Viv 131, 150
Richardson, Vic 262, 266
Ringham, Mike 150
Roberts, Andy 190–1
Robertson-Glasgow, R. C. 66–7, 80–1, 112–13, 339–40
Rocca, Paul 171, 172, 173
Root, Fred 143–4, 341–2
Rose, W. M. 97, 246, 247, 248, 250
Rowan, Lou 275–6
royal families 2, 3, 5–7, 15–16, 290–1
Rutter, Edward 368

S

Samoa, cricket in 17–21
Sandham, Andy 205
Sangakkara, Kumar 117
Sapte, William 309–10, 370–1
school cricket 104, 384–5, 392, 398, 399
scoring 152–4, 155–6
Selby, Jack 176
Senior, Brian 51–2
Shappley village cricket 157–61

Sharp, Harry 150
Shaw, Alfred 99–100, 175–8
Sheffield Park cricket ground, Sussex 54–7
Shrewsbury, Arthur 364, 379
signals, cricketers' and umpires' 136–7, 275–7
Simkins, Michael 27–9, 267–9
Simmons, Jack 137
Slatter, William 50–1, 109–12, 156–7
Small, John 78–9, 318, 319, 320–1
Smith, Ray 129, 298
Snow, C. P. 409–10
Snow, Philip A. 184–5, 283–6, 415
Somerset CCC 76, 188–94
South Africa 131, 137, 218, 222–3, 258, 272, 273
Southerton, S. J. 123
Sparkes, John 168
spectators 346–52, 355–7, 366
Spofforth, Fred 208, 209–10, 333–6
Sri Lanka 117, 244, 413
Statham, Brian 199, 200, 201
Steel, A. G. 208, 209
Stephenson, Colonel 106, 107, 305
Stevens, Edward 'Lumpy' 78–9, 121, 203, 318–19
Strudwick, Bert 341
Stubberfield, Henry 54–5
suicides, cricket related 411–14
Surrey CCC 47, 107, 143, 204–6, 287
   early cricket 3, 4, 12, 78, 170
Sussex CCC 12, 42, 54, 121–2, 188, 197, 237–9
Sutcliffe, Herbert 155
Swann, Graeme 270, 271

T

Taunton cricket ground 188–9
Tennyson, Lord 301–2, 305, 365
Test Match Special 267–9, 270, 271, 272, 273, 274
Thomson, A. A. 214–19
travel
   arranging early matches 87, 90, 91–3
   England tour New Zealand (1877) 99–101
   MCC tour Canada (1872) 96–8, 245–8
   steam liner to Australia 86–7
Trent Bridge cricket ground, Nottingham 47–8, 108–9, 236, 281
Trescothick, Marcus 24–6, 76, 135–6
Trevor, Philip 395–7
Trinidad 384–5
Trueman, F. S. 165–6, 360
Tufnell, Phil 131–4
Turner, Glenn 149
Turner, Thomas 367
Tyson, Frank 197–201, 228

U

umpires 80, 106, 138, 164, 174, 255, 275–6, 294–5,
    296–315, 392
United States of America 14, 15, 96–7, 249–50
    W. G. Grace on tour (1872) 249–50

V

village cricket 37–9, 51–2, 62–3, 88, 91–3, 120,
    157–61, 310–13, 337, 367, 397–403

W

Waghorn, H. T. 12–14, 280
Walker, David 37–9
Walker, William 108–9
'walking' when out 164–6
Walsh, Courtney 254–5
Walter Lawrence Trophy 150
Ward, Andrew 379–81
Ward, William 77, 80, 320
Waugh, Alec 397–403
Webber, Roy 149, 156
West Gloucestershire cricket team 33–4
West Indies 131, 254–5, 272, 330–2, 414
wickets, condition of 88, 92, 108, 109–10, 114, 130,
    141, 255, 318, 329
willow for bats 72–3, 74, 75
winning the toss 114–17
Wisden Cricketers' Almanack 150, 353–4, 406–9
Wisden, John 82, 83, 408
women's cricket 34–6, 223–6, 242, 295
Wood, Harry 174
Woods, Harold C. 157–8, 174, 310–13
Woolley, Frank 141–2, 150
Worcestershire CCC 45–6, 132, 144, 214–16
World Cup, ICC 117, 270–5, 386–91
World War II, cricket during 71–5
Wright, Cecil 175
Wright, Douglas 260
Wrigley, Arthur 156
Wyatt, R. E. S. 115
Wynard, E. G. 395–7

Y

Yallop, Graham 323–4, 325, 326, 327
Yorkshire CCC 42, 44–5, 46–7, 151, 155